Practical Handbook of

DISTRIBUTION/ CUSTOMER SERVICE

First Edition

Practical Handbook of

DISTRIBUTION/ CUSTOMER SERVICE

Warren Blanding

WITHDRAWN

Published by THE TRAFFIC SERVICE CORPORATION
Washington ● New York ● Chicago ● Boston ● Atlanta ● Palo Alto

Library of Congress Catalog Card Number 85-50345

ISBN 0-87408-033-9

Printed in the United States of America

PREFACE

Even the most casual reader leafing through the pages of this book will quickly realize that it is not the thoughts of one individual set down on paper, but rather the synergism of many people. Herbert Goeler of American Cyanamid and Keith Slater of Johns-Manville, the latter now retired, are certainly the brightest stars in my particular customer service galaxy. They have been well-springs of information, thinkers and thought-starters, friends and fellow-believers, for almost two decades. Without the encouragement and inspiration they gave me, this book would be much shorter and far less relevant. In 1984, my firm presented Herb and Keith with our special "Patron Saint" Award; it doesn't say nearly enough for what they have meant to me personally and, through me, to the field of customer service management where I disseminate ideas and guidance as an editor and teacher.

Some years ago, the American Management Associations asked me to chair a series of seminars on Customer Service Management in the U.S. and Canada. Through this activity I met many wonderful people who in many cases taught me more than I taught them.

Later, Herb Davis of Herbert W. Davis and Company and I undertook a series of seminars for Penton Learning Systems which took us to some 45 colleges and universities throughout the U.S. and Canada. We found a rising tide of enthusiasm for this newest of management disciplines and gained an unparalleled resource in both the enthusiasm and depth of knowledge of the thousands of working managers we met through these seminars.

More recently, Herb Davis, Alex Metz of Hunt Personnel and I developed and have been conducting our "Advanced Customer Service" seminars, adding over the years several thousand more friends who have provided a wealth of information and—equally important—a wealth of enthusiasm and inspiration in my job of reporting the accomplishments of the field. Certainly this book belongs as much to all these friends as it does for me, for it is a chronicle of their achievements, not mine.

I had the good fortune to sit in on the formation of the International Customer Service Association in May of 1981, and in the three and a half years since then have seen it mature into a dynamic and truly professional organization of more than 1,000 members. Its members are not only open and sharing of their own ideas and management skills; they are good friends and great people.

This book started out as a seminar outline, and quickly grew into an unwieldy and highly disorganized mass of paper. Leslie Harps, Vice President of our company, undertook the crushing task of organizing and rationalizing this material at a time when she was already well occupied as an executive of this organization and as a "mover and shaker" in the Warehousing Education and Research Council. Where the book is easy to understand and apply, you can be sure it is her doing; where it is not, you will know that I failed to heed her suggestions. Suggestions, I might add, which she is fortunately never reluctant to express!

Beyond the myriad of "leads" and ideas and case histories that I can trace to these thousands of individual sources and resources, there is one other factor that has been instrumental in endowing this book with whatever utility and value it may possess. And that is the professional commitment, pride, interest and enthusiasm displayed by virtually everybody who works in the Customer Service field, managers and reps alike. During the past five years I have visited the customer service departments of companies of all types and sizes, and I have come away with the satisfaction of knowing that industry is in good shape with competent people performing its most critical job—Customer Service.

Warren Blanding
October, 1984

TABLE OF CONTENTS

ILLUSTRATIONS AND TABLES

To all my girls and little Albert, too . . . again

INTRODUCTION

The publication of the landmark study "Customer Service Meaning and Measurement" by the National Council of Physical Distribution Management in 1976 was a turning point in the evolution of American business. The study, conducted for the NCPDM by The Ohio State University, illuminated for the first time the unique nature of the customer service function in manufacturing and distributive enterprises. It revealed a rapidly-developing and increasingly sophisticated "nerve center" linking the diverse elements of the firm with the customer, and through the firm's distribution system meeting and satisfying customer needs in an increasingly competitive marketplace.

Just as physical distribution management itself was in many ways a product of the Computer Age, so customer service as a management discipline owed much of its dynamics to the same management sciences that first demonstrated the total systems nature of production planning, inventory management, warehousing, transportation and—customer service. For years, customer service had been typified as the "order department" or, worse, the "complaint department," a necessary part of the business but one that added cost but no value. By the time the NCPDM study was published in the mid-Seventies, that image was changing with the realization of many managements that it was no longer enough simply to *sell* customers the dazzling array of products that were pouring off production lines; but the costs of selling were becoming so great that attention must now be given to *keeping* those customers once they had been sold.

In many companies the distribution department had already established the logistics of that customer-keeping mission: efficient networks of distribution centers, effective inventory management systems and, in some cases, on-line order entry systems linking the system together. But the Arab oil embargo of the early Seventies had had a profound and—as some managers were realizing—irreversible effect on the way business would be conducted. First of all, the actual costs of selling—of traveling a salesperson—were increasing more rapidly than the inflation rate itself, then standing at about 14% annually. The cost of a single sales call on a customer had reached a new high of more than $100, and given that it required anywhere from four to 11 sales calls to actually make a sale, the business could ill-afford to service that customer inadequately once the sale had actually been made.

But here the second result of the Arab oil embargo was making itself felt. The fundamental cost relationships which had existed for years between transportation, warehousing and inventory had crumbled almost overnight. And there were widespread product shortages to complicate the picture, some of them associated with the embargo, others simply the result of poor forecasting and inadequate communications to the production planning and procurement arms of the business.

In this environment, many firms found themselves in the unique predicament of being unable to serve the customers they already had, let alone go after new ones. The product shortages that existed were compounded by information systems that by and large were totally inadequate to deal with the dual problems of resource allocation and the flood of communications between companies and their customers relating to those shortages. It was clear that the old tradition of *reactive* customer service— waiting for things to happen and then reacting to them—was no longer acceptable. That the customer service function had to be managed just as any other business discipline was managed: *proactively,* with the specific mission of creating strong ties with customers that would enable the company to grow with its customers; *interactively* with other departments so that the company could get the most advantage from its resources in carrying out that mission. To do this, the customer service department needed three things: 1. recognition by management that keeping and cultivating customers was indeed a major corporate goal; 2. a department with its own identity and a management mandate to achieve that goal; and 3. commitment of resources—particularly information systems and communications—adequate to operate the department as the nerve center that it was indeed becoming in any event.

Many of today's customer service departments have their origins in those adversities of the 1970s. And there is no question but that customer service management as a discipline in its own right has come a long ways. The International Customer Service Association, founded in 1981 with a handful of members, had grown to a membership of almost one thousand by the end of 1983. Surveys had shown significant increases in scope and responsibility of customer service departments, and commensurate increases in the salary levels of their managers and employees. Customer service courses are appearing at the community college level, and there is talk of developing a formal, college level curriculum in customer service.

The relationship between the customer service activity and physical distribution activities—traffic and transportation, warehousing, shipping and related functions—is perhaps one of the closest in the corporate family. Quite a few customer service departments do in fact report to a distribution executive, while others interface directly and almost constantly with one or more of the distribution entities in their companies. Like most family relationships, it isn't always perfect, often because different members have different goals. The distribution manager charged with cost optimization is likely to have different priorities from the customer service manager with 20,000 customers all of whom want their orders filled yesterday.

Yet it's not enough to say that different disciplines have different priorities within the corporate family, nor even to say that the different disciplines have to understand one another's different motives. The increasing emphasis on serving the customer as a *total corporate objective*—"the business of the business"—suggests that the most successful companies of the future will be those that best move as *a total entity to meet their customers' needs.* And this in turn will require abandonment and revision of many existing priorities and goals in favor of a broad corporate goal of customer service.

This trend does not mean that the customer service *department* will be the tail that wags the dog. Not in any way. But it does mean that the customer service *mission* will be the driving force behind almost everything the company does. Which is why this book is in no sense a book for customer service managers and for nobody else. It is for any manager or manager-to-be who has, or hopes to have, a direct responsibility for the bottom line. It is particularly for managers actively engaged in the customer service function itself: besides customer service managers themselves, it is for distribution managers, traffic and transportation managers, production planning and inventory managers—and distribution, sales and marketing executives to whom the customer service department may report.

For the bottom line of this book is the bottom line of the enterprises for which it was written. Customer service is treated as a strategic undertaking of the entire corporation with the direct goal of profit contribution plus corporate growth. It assumes the existence of a customer service department, but recognizes that it may not yet have the stature or degree of recognition needed to carry out all the programs and set all the policies recommended here. It recognizes that managers who have full or partial responsibility for the various customer service activities in some instances moved into their present jobs with little or no direct management experience.

Thus the emphasis of this book is on the practical: practical plans that can be made in today's environment; practical measures that can be taken today in the real-world corporate climate; practical results that can be obtained and taken *visibly* to the bottom line for all to see. There is very little theory in this book. The principles, procedures and case histories are drawn from the experience of real people in real companies solving real problems. During the dozen years he has been editor and publisher of *Customer Service Newsletter,* the author has served as a clearing house for customer service and distribution professionals' questions and answers, problems and solutions, tests, surveys, experiments, ideas, opinions, inspirations, triumphs and defeats, failures and successes . . . in short, all the real-world experiences that go into advancing the art.

This book is the composite experience of several thousands of these managers, translated into a format which is intended to be used on the job in existing, operating departments as well as in planning and organizing customer service departments-to-be. No attempt has been made to "genericize" the case histories reported here, i.e., to make them applicable to all companies under all circumstances. Every company is unique, and has unique circumstances and unique needs. What distinguishes the manager from the rank-and-file is the manager's ability to extract from the situations and experiences of others the particular grain or grains of meaning for his or her operations. And this book was written for managers, present and future.

Customer service as it is practiced in manufacturing and distributive industries is heavily involved with two dynamic technologies: data processing and communications. Each of these is clearly a subject for a book in itself, and indeed there are many books about both. For that reason, this book does not involve itself specifically with technology per se, but assumes the reader is familiar with its principal applications in customer service. Needless to say, staying abreast of the state of the art in information and communications systems is fundamental to good management—and particularly in management of a function that is so inextricably involved with, and so heavily dependent on, such systems. The manager reading this book will recognize that many of today's concerns with such specific functions as order entry, for example, will transfer elsewhere as computer-to-computer order entry, voice recognition systems and other direct entry methods become prevalent. Similarly, measures of productivity that are relevant in today's customer service department will have to be updated to the technology of the day, which will certainly be vastly different from the systems in place as this book goes to press.

Which raises a key point about customer service. A particularly significant trend of the recession years of the early Eighties has been the willngness of management to invest in machines for the customer service department—to invest in machines but not in people. This has some remarkable results. One department cited in this book doubled its order handling capacity without adding to its staff. Others have taken on greatly increased workloads through absorption of other divisions or centralization, often with an actual net reduction in total staff. They have been able to do this partly because of the technology available to them, but more importantly through innovative thinking.

For some of the most important breakthroughs in customer service have been achieved because a manager challenged long-standing beliefs of what would and what would not work. Historically, many promising customer service approaches have died in the planning stages because someone in power said "customers will never accept it." Today's customer service managers are increasingly likely to ask "who says so?" and proceed to prove that customers will indeed accept and adapt to change and innovation. The quick acceptance of automated banking and other interactive systems suggests that customers are indeed willing to accept change provided there are benefits for them as well as for the vendor. Manufacturing companies that have adopted an "honor system" on returns and exchanges have been pleasantly surprised to find, not only that customers did not abuse it, but also that it created a much more favorable climate for field salespeople to sell in. Companies that have adopted no-fault policies on claims and complaints have had a similar experience.

As these innovations continue, it's certain that the role of the individual will increase in importance in customer service—but as an individual, not as a doer of repetitive tasks. The repetitive tasks will be done increasingly by machines, and the individuals will be doing the important and challenging tasks that cannot be done by machines . . . including designing machines and systems and procedures that will do those repetitive tasks even better. The contrast to today will be considerable. For today, so much time and attention must be given to the actual mechanics of running the customer service department that very little time or attention can be given to underlying plans and above all the sensitive matter of writing policies and setting strategies.

Certainly in very little time it will become one of the manager's prime responsibilities, not only to write such policies and set such strategies, but also to assure their acceptance and implementation throughout the company. This book will provide many ideas and suggestions and insights toward that end, but the final result will depend, as it should, on the manager's ability to manage in a complex, changing world crying out to be managed through compassion, intelligence and integrity.

1

CUSTOMER SERVICE IS. . .

Filling Orders

Customer service is the ability to fill customer orders for products or services accurately and expeditiously, delivering them at the time and in the condition needed to meet customer requirements for marketing, manufacturing or other uses or applications—at a price that is competitive or consistent with customer expectations.

This definition stresses the point that customers' demands on us are neither randomized or unpredictable, although they may sometimes seem that way. Customers contract for our products or services in order to achieve certain goals of their own. If we don't provide the right product or service at the right time and in the right place—and at the right price—those goals will be defeated.

This same logic applies in both business and non-business situations, in industrial as well as professional and consumer applications.

For example, an automobile manufacturer requires certain parts to be delivered at a certain time so that assembly operations can proceed on schedule. This just-in-time delivery, known as "kanban," enables the auto manufacturer to achieve these specific goals: (1) A minimum investment in inventory, with savings that can be used to make the finished product price-competitive; and (2) avoidance of production line downtime, also involving significant savings that can translate into competitive price advantage. Conversely, should suppliers fail to meet the manufacturer's "kanban" customer service requirements, added costs would be incurred which the manufacturer would have to pass along to the consumer and in the end could well price the line out of the market.

Similarly, a consumer who ultimately buys one of those automobiles will have certain service requirements such as reasonable availability of parts and no-hassle in-warranty as well as out-of-warranty repairs. From the consumer's point of view, these are logical and legitimate customer service requirements which must be met if the car is to serve the customer's needs for work, commuting, traveling or general daily use.

The health care field provides many examples of the critical role of customer service in furthering customers' goals. A surgeon preparing to perform delicate surgery is the focal point of a hundred or more customer service "deliveries" of products out of the 20,000 normally inventoried by a major hospital, plus any of a wide array of services ranging from X-ray to blood chemistry. The proper equipment, of course, including life-support systems and surgical equipment; any implants or components to be used in the surgery itself, plus whatever supplies and medications may be required, all available, in sterile condition, at the time and place scheduled for surgery. And of course the hospital must provide an operating room properly equipped—and the patient properly prepped, as well as skilled support personnel in the OR and for post-operative care.

Although this may seem a rather complex, intricate example of customer service it is in fact an accurate reflection of the underlying logic of customer demands, and the delicate balance that has to be maintained in meeting those requirements. In short, customer service can and should be organized in a logical, systematic way in order to anticipate and meet customer needs and further customer goals.

Working with Customers

Customer service is the ability to work with customers and others to develop alternative solutions when the customer's need cannot be fully met.

This definition acknowledges that there are inevitably occasions when customer requirements cannot be met, either for economic reasons or simply because we did not sufficiently anticipate those requirements. Anyone who travels recognizes that weather and equipment problems sometimes prevent airlines from providing their scheduled service. It's not economically feasible to maintain standby equipment, and to do so would increase the cost of travel significantly. Nor is it possible to accurately predict the weather or the specific capacity requirements of any given day.

Similarly, manufacturers or distributors cannot economically maintain 100% inventories of all line items in order to be able to fill all orders on a day-to-day basis. Nor can they predict the specific orders with sufficient accuracy to cut back the right amount on slow movers and increase the right amount on the most popular items in inventory. Some stockouts—customer service failures—are bound to happen.

Given the inevitability of some customer service failures, it is an integral part of customer service to develop ways to minimize the impact of such failures on their customers. The airline, for example, will try to set up alternate routings. The manufacturer or distributor will recommend substitute products, or "borrow" from other customers in emergency situations. There are additional solutions by the hundreds, limited only by the creativity and dedication of the customer service personnel involved.

This aspect of customer service has a simple yet memorable name which everybody recognizes: problem-solving. It is one of the most important elements in the entire spectrum of customer service, and a reason both for having good customer service people on board and for supporting them with good systems and sound, customer-oriented policies.

Handling Complaints and Inquiries

Customer service is the ability to courteously and effectively handle complaints, inquiries and requests for information on products, services, applications and technical matters.

3

It's unfortunate—and misleading—that the customer service department has so often been equated with the "complaint department" when in fact complaint handling is usually a relatively minor part of the total customer service function. In fact, any time a customer service department is heavily involved in complaint handling it's usually a reflection of some serious problems with design or quality of services or products and in some cases failure to anticipate customer demands, giving rise to an excessive number of customer complaints. While it's only realistic to expect that there will be some complaints just as there will be some customer service failures, it is often more economic to remove the causes of complaints than to simply keep on handling them.

A good complaint handling system stresses the feedback or informational value of complaints, i.e., improvements that will make products or services more saleable, as much as it does the "psychology" of handling individual complaints. A good complaint handling system also contains the means for correcting or improving policies and procedures that lead to complaints. It's important to have good people in customer service, and it's useful to train them in dealing with the stressful situations that arise in complaint handling. But it's far more productive to discover and eliminate the causes of complaints, and train people across the whole spectrum of customer service activities.

In fact, concern with complaint handling per se has tended to overshadow other communications activities in the customer service department which take up a great deal more time than complaint handling, are often far more important and costly, and in many instances equally stressful to personnel. These are the communications involved in responding to inquiries of three principal types: (1) General inquiries about products or services, including availability and price; (2) product or service applications, including technical matters, and (3) status of orders entered for products or services that have not yet been filled.

Many companies overlook the potential for converting general inquiries and applications inquiries into actual sales at a time when the costs of field selling are so high as to preclude calling on smaller or marginal accounts which might otherwise be profitable. Training personnel and providing them with appropriate information system support is a minor investment in comparison to the untapped revenue potential that some companies have found runs into the millions.

The same companies are likely to underestimate the negative impact of not being able to respond appropriately to such inquiries. This can be measured in lost sales, loss of confidence in the supplier of the service or product and—particularly harmful—misapplication of the service or product and loss of accounts as a result.

An additional feature of inquiries in general is the stress they can exert on personnel who can't answer them, either through lack of training or insufficient information system support. Any underlying problem like product shortages or production delays is inherently stressful to people who have to keep saying "no" to customers. So it's important that the causes be corrected as quickly as possible or, when the situation is likely to continue or recur, that personnel be provided with scenarios, scripts or decision rules for dealing with such situations.

For example, one car rental company allows counter personnel to upgrade customer reservations without charge when there has been a long wait or similar problem. A manufacturer may absorb the freight on a late shipment, or a service organization provide extra services without charge. These "escape valves" recognize the importance of maintaining employee morale and motivation, particularly in the sensitive area of customer communications where the impact on the company itself can be so momentous.

Teamwork

Customer service is the organization's ability to generate genuine teamwork among all departments in the firm: Sales, Marketing, Manufacturing, Distribution, Shipping and

Warehousing, Customer Service, Quality Control, Production Planning and Control and others and to instill in every individual the constant awareness that customer service is everybody's *business, not just the responsibility of a single department.*

This definition emphasizes the importance of customer service as an organization-wide responsibility. It recognizes that in many companies the customer service department is held accountable for customer service failures that for the most part originate outside the department and beyond its control. Sales, for example, may make promises which Engineering or Production can't keep. Or Quality Control may be backed up and delay responding to a customer complaint which in turn is delaying further orders from that customer.

Needless to say, teamwork of the type envisioned here doesn't just happen because people want it to, any more than it just happens in a Superbowl championship football team. It's mandated by management, then translated into a system in which all participants have specific responsibilities to perform and standards to meet—responsibilities and standards designed to generate the desired levels of service at the least cost.

Companies which operate in this climate of mutual, interdepartmental accountability tend to have far higher levels of customer service than those where individual departments are driven primarily by cost-reduction goals without regard to their impact on other departments. For example, a production department driven solely by goals of minimizing unit production costs may manufacture large quantities of a particular item for which there is no immediate need while delaying production on other, shorter-run items that are completely out of stock and already causing repercussions among customers.

It goes without saying that the opposite of this, usually known as "giving away the store," can be equally harmful. Which is why it is so important that teamwork be translated into an organized system that reconciles conflicting interdepartmental goals and "optimizes" the firm's customer service in terms of both performance and cost.

And the first step is for management to make it clear to

every individual up and down the line that he or she has a personal commitment to the firm's customers and their needs.

Satisfying Customers

Customer service is customer-keeping, cultivating repeat business and stimulating increased purchasing by customers by serving them well and creating a climate of confidence, credibility and satisfaction.

This definition illuminates an area of customer service that many firms have overlooked in the past: the importance of customer service as an incentive to existing customers to continue buying, and to buy in larger volume. As one example, a firm with 24 distribution centers buys fork lift trucks from three different manufacturers, a different make for each of three pilot warehouses. At the end of a year, it makes a determination of which brand to standardize on for all 24 locations. The determination is based on a combination of performance, price and particularly service and parts support—customer service.

In a different type of situation, a company buying parity products from several different vendors may decide to nominate one vendor as a sole-source or principal vendor. Given that price and quality are already equal, the quality of the chosen firm's customer service is what swings the balance in its favor.

Customer-keeping can also take more subtle forms. Customer education and training, for example. A manufacturer of water-softening chemical finds that by training engineers and boiler operators in the proper use of its products they get better results from their equipment and continue buying the product—and recommending it to others. A camera and film manufacturer provides customers with free replacement film and tips for getting better pictures when their snapshots don't come out—because they know that when people learn to take better pictures they will take more pictures and buy more film as a result!

There is a negative side to the matter of customer-keeping, too. One firm found that purchases of additional equipment by an existing customer were held up because of dissatisfaction with the equipment already in place. The amount involved was about a million dollars. The dissatisfaction, it turned out, was the combined result of an obsolete operating manual and a new untrained employee charged with operating the equipment. The situation was cured and the purchases unfrozen by application of some basic customer services: providing updated manual pages plus basic training on equipment use for the new employee.

As this example illustrates, failure to take care of the customer *after* the sale has been made can have costly repercussions in lost opportunities for future—and often larger—sales. An additional point that is frequently overlooked is that after-sales service, i.e., customer service, protects a substantial investment: the high cost of selling a customer, which is often in excess of $1,000 for an industrial account. And it's an investment which *needs* protecting. Ask any company which has invested substantially in landing a new account, only to lose that customer after the initial purchase because of poor customer service or an indifferent attitude on the part of customer service personnel.

And it's worth mentioning here that if customer service personnel appear indifferent towards customers there is a very good likelihood that they are simply reflecting the attitude of their management, as they see it.

By contrast, managements which recognize the quality of customer service as the principal factor in customer-keeping and account growth often make special provisions for "greeting" new customers and familiarizing them with the vendor company's methods of doing business and policies on order acceptance, delivery, payment and the like. Some companies even go so far as to assign a specially-trained person to mother-hen such new accounts for a period of several months.

Growing with Customers

Customer service is helping customers grow—and growing with them.

Closely related to the customer-keeping function of customer service, this definition underscores the increasing realization by many managements of how dependent their own growth is on the growth of their customers—and how much of a vested interest they have in supporting and assisting in their customers' growth.

Helping customers grow can take many forms. The firm that sells to distributors or retailers, for example, will support those customers' sales effort via fast, accurate order fulfillment and—particularly—fast turnaround on reorders of seasonal merchandise. Or it may take the form of financial support—credit extension, consignment sales, field warehousing or similar arrangements. As mentioned above, it may take the form of helping the customer obtain maximum utilization from equipment and thus maximum return on investment. Or, it can simply be showing customers how to make the most economical purchases. In the high-volume grocery business, some manufacturers have provided substantial assistance to their customers in such matters as unit load preparation and handling, computer-to-computer ordering, sanitation and related matters.

Some firms provide specific assistance to their customers in such areas as traffic management, credit and collections, forecasting and inventory management. One manufacturer of fasteners provides customers with a complete two-bin inventory system plus equivalency lookup charts for competitive items. The result is that a broad spectrum of competitive products are forced out, while reorders for the manufacturer's products come through in a reasonable, timely fashion thanks to the in-place inventory management system. This in turn enables the manufacturer to plan workloads more effectively, to consolidate shipments and obtain distribution economies and—most importantly—to enable the customer to grow by having a ready supply of needed products to sell, thanks to the backup inventory management system.

Making Changes Successfully

Customer service is the company's ability to succeed when it introduces new products, lines or services, or decides to enter new markets . . . or when it introduces new policies or procedures which may be distasteful to customers.

This definition recognizes that customers who are satisfied with the service they are getting from a particular vendor are more likely to be receptive to "new and improved" products or services introduced by that vendor than they are to products and services offered by a vendor with whom they have had no customer service experience. This receptivity can be particularly important when the vendor is making significant change in policies and procedures that may affect some customers adversely: for example, changing from a delivered price basis to FOB shipping point, freight charges collect. Or tightening credit limits, increasing minimum order sizes, assessing special charges for rush orders, etc.

Customers who have been well served tend to be more understanding of the logic of such changes, and by and large are more willing to accept them. In addition, they are likely to be more tolerant of out-and-out customer service failures when they do occur. On the other side of the coin, customers who have not been served well see new products as well as changes in procedures in a different light: adding insult to injury. "If you haven't treated us right in the past," they reason, "why should we expect you to do any better in the future, regardless of what new products or procedures you come up with?"

Similarly, a company which decides to enter new markets can expect to be judged very critically on its ability to provide levels of customer service appropriate to those markets. An interesting example of this is the success of McDonald's and other fast food operations by providing levels of customer service that were by and large far superior to what was formerly available in the fast food field generally. In another example, a well-known manufacturer of graphic arts equipment came out with new, high-tech equipment superior to almost everything in the field. Yet the firm ultimately went into bankruptcy, and one of the reasons cited was the fact that the firm had virtually ignored the need for a systematic customer service activity—providing parts, service and technical assistance—to support the equipment once it had been purchased.

Balancing Customer Demands With Company Interests

Customer service is the ability to balance customer demands with company interests, to solve different and sensitive problems for customers in such a way as to earn their friendship and respect, and to retain them as customers even when it becomes necessary to say "no" to them in unequivocal terms.

As noted above, we can't give the store away just to make customers happy. Nobody knows this better than the customer service manager. But the manager also knows better than most how much the company can afford to invest in retaining a given customer as opposed to alienating that customer, losing his or her business and quite possibly the business of others as a result.

The emphasis here is on the real cost of losing a customer vs. the real value of keeping one who is already on board. A rule of thumb that is sometimes cited is that the cost of a lost customer is the equivalent of about five years' sales to that customer. In other words, a customer billing $100,000 a year and showing a 10% account growth rate would, as a lost account, represent a total loss of some $610,000. And although the numbers aren't as large, consumer goods manufacturers have found some startling numbers revealing the difference in purchases between customers who are satisfied with customer service versus those who find it only "acceptable."

This does not alter the fact that it is sometimes necessary to say "no" to customers for either economic or legal reasons. It is extremely important that such situations be precisely defined and that the customer service department have the full backing of management when it does say "no." Of course there will always be some exceptions where important customers are involved or there are extenuating circumstances. In such instances it should be made clear that the customer service department or the

John Q. Customer
Purchasing Agent
PDQ Company
111 Anywhere St.
Maintown, PA 00000

Dear Mr. Customer:

All of us here at ABC Company appreciate your decision to purchase our products, and we look forward to a lasting relationship.

When the need arises, our Customer Service Department and the representative assigned to your account are as near as your phone. Our lines are open from 8 a.m. to 5 p.m. EST.

Please call us whenever we can serve you. And if ever things are not handled to your satisfaction, please call me personally. We appreciate your business today, but we want it tomorrow, too.

Thanks again for being our customer.

Sincerely,

Frank President
Chief Operating Executive

FP:je

Figure 1-1. Example of a personalized letter sent to new customers of a manufacturing firm. The letters are signed by the company president, and are part of the increasing emphasis on customer retention—keeping customers.

individual employee is not being "reversed" or "sold out," but simply that upper management has elected to make an exception in a particular case, and at its own risk.

Representing the Company

Customer service is the ability to represent the company honorably and truthfully in all transactions, to protect its interests and public image and to earn the respect of its customers and community alike—the ability to maintain and advance the Free Enterprise System.

This definition needs very little by way of explanation, except to emphasize the fact that for many customers the customer service department *is* the company—and the quality of the contact plays a tremendously important role in shaping the firm's public image and in determining its position in the marketplace.

2

WHAT IS A CUSTOMER?

No definition of customer service can be considered complete without answering the question: "What is a customer?"

Ask this question in a typical company and you will get a variety of answers. On the positive side, they will range from "Someone who buys from us" all the way to "The person who signs our paychecks," "Our friend," "Our bread-and-butter," "The reason for our existence," and many others. But you will find negative perceptions, too: "A customer is someone with a problem for me to solve," "A customer is someone with a complaint" . . . even "A customer is someone who owes us money." Inevitably, there will be one or two people who will respond: "You shouldn't be asking me that question. I don't have anything to do with customers!"

The Best Definition

One of the best definitions we have heard of a customer is also one of the simplest: "A customer is anyone who can influence a sale." This definition permits a number of corollaries.

A customer is the end user of our service or product, but not necessarily the actual purchaser. In a commercial or industrial organization, most purchases are made by a buyer or purchasing agent, who is a customer in the sense of placing an order and approving a payment, but the "main" customer can be a design engineer, a production manager, almost anybody in the organization. It's often overlooked, for example, that maintenance personnel, warehouse workers and others can have a definite impact on purchases and repurchases of certain products and services that they use in their daily work. In consumer goods and services, the actual buyer is likely to be making the purchase on behalf of a spouse or for the entire family. They, too, can influence further purchases.

A customer is not always accessible. This is a very critical point. Companies spend large amounts for advertising, product literature and public relations directed towards customers, but it's often difficult or impossible to make person-to-person contact with the individual who is the key to a continuing, profitable relationship between the company and the customer. For example, the warehouse worker who complains about the fork lift truck because it takes too long to get parts. Or the janitor who doesn't want to use a certain kind of detergent because it's sometimes delivered in drums, which he likes, and sometimes in multiwall bags, which he doesn't. There's usually very little feedback from such end users to alert vendors to their dissatisfaction, which has a tendency to build until a "trigger" incident causes their firms to switch suppliers almost without warning. This problem of inaccessibility means that a vendor's customer service often has to speak for itself, has to be in tune with the expectations of end users. The problem is finding out, first of all, who these end users actually are, then what their service expectations are, and after that developing service that will in fact meet those expectations within reasonable levels. This is not nearly so easy as it sounds, but it underlines the importance of two major facets of customer service which are often overlooked: (1) the responsibility for performing sound customer research with respect solely to customer service needs and perceptions; and (2) the responsibility for developing standards and measures of performance which will assure that those needs are being met.

Attitudes Influence Sales

Intermediate customers can strongly influence attitudes and purchasing decisions of end users. Consider this actual case. An office manager called the stationer to order a supply of a certain type of ballpoint pen. The individual on the stationer's order desk replied: "I'm sorry, but we don't stock that particular brand. We've found it's not a very good pen." The office manager had found the particular pen quite satisfactory and said so. In fact, she said, she liked it better than any brand she'd tried so far. "Oh, it's not the pen itself," the stationer's rep acknowledged, "it's just that the company gives us so much trouble on deliveries—they're always late, half the time they don't have what we ordered, it takes them forever to issue credits and so forth and so on. It just isn't worth the hassle of dealing with them!" The important point of this vignette is that the stationer's rep initially claimed that the poor quality of the pen was the reason for not stocking it when in actual fact quality had nothing to do with it. This practice is often found at the retail level, and understandably so; after all, the sales clerk is more highly motivated to sell a product that's available than one that isn't, or where the supplier has created problems of various kinds. Here again, it is important to establish service standards and measures that minimize "negative passa-long" of this type.

All persons in the distribution chain are customers, including truckdrivers, delivery personnel, receiving clerks and others. Here again, the end user's perception of a service or product may be largely determined by others. For example, a receiving clerk who fails to notify the end user that a shipment he or she was waiting for has in fact arrived. Or the truckdriver who has a running feud with the warehouse foreman and is always made to wait until last for pickups, delivery personnel who misdeliver, and so forth. The blame for the resulting service failures will usually be placed on the vendor, seldom on intermediate handlers who may be responsible. This underlines the importance of establishing measures of customer service that reflect service *throughout* the distribution chain . . . and bearing in mind how important it is to cultivate and maintain good relationships with all elements in that chain: a constant reminder that the customer is indeed anybody who can influence a sale.

The customer can be anybody in the vendor company itself. This very important fact is often overlooked, yet it's true that anybody in the vendor company can indeed influence a sale—and every department is in one way or another a "customer" of every other department.

A customer can be somebody who neither buys nor uses our products or services. Members of the general public, public officials, legislators and regulators have the potential for exerting significant influence on a company's sales and profits. Public interest groups, trade unions and others have amply demonstrated how great this influence can be. This is not to suggest that companies should be fearful of every move they make, but they should certainly be aware that their public image—the attitudes that are developed through contacts with the public— should always be a concern in the training of everybody who has any type of contact with the general public as well as with regular customers.

Hidden Factors Influence Customers

A customer may deal with several divisions of a large company—and base his/her attitudes on the "lowest common denominator" in terms of customer service. The story is told of an executive in a major aircraft manufacturing firm who was considering a particular supplier's jet engines for a new design. Unbeknownst to the salesperson, this same buyer had been experiencing a great deal of trouble obtaining service on the family's new dishwasher which had been manufactured by another division of the same parent firm as the jet engine manufacturer. Did it influence the ultimate buying decision? How could it *not* influence at least the buyer's attitude to the extent of setting extremely rigid standards of performance covering the most minute details and in general being a really tough, unreasonable and demanding customer to deal with?

Different customers have different customer service requirements, even though the products or services involved may not be identical. It's often overlooked in planning customer service that there can be significant differences between customer requirements both by class of customer and even within the same category. In health care manufacturing, for example, a hospital will typically have service requirements that differ significantly from those of a wholesale drug firm. In the tire business, an OEM (Original Equipment Manufacturer) customer will have vastly different requirements from a dealer or distributor. Within the same category, one retail chain may require deliveries to half a dozen distribution centers while its competitor requires drop shipment to several thousand locations. There are also differences based on volume of purchases, region of the country and of course importance or influence of customers. A General Motors executive once observed that his organization's very best customer service in terms of filling parts orders was to be found in West Palm Beach, Florida, because of the high number of Cadillacs to be found there . . . and the influence of the people who owned those Cadillacs. Here again, the customer service manager has the responsibility to identify differing requirements where they exist, and then design the service accordingly.

"Hidden" customers who misuse or misapply products or services frequently blame the vendor and take their business elsewhere. This is one of the end results of failing to recognize the broad spectrum of individual customers whom the vendor may not be aware of or have any direct contact with. The most common examples are in retail business where self service is the order of the day, and floor sales personnel are often unavailable—or unable—to provide customers with product information. But it happens almost as frequently with machinery and equipment and industrial supplies. A manufacturer of automated storage and retrieval equipment observed that when a breakdown occurred at a customer location, onsite personnel often attempted to make repairs themselves before calling for help—and this often aggravated the problem, delayed repairs and saw the manufacturer

being blamed for problems that the customers themselves had actually caused. On the other hand, some part of the responsibility may be the vendor's for simply not being aware of the environments, attitudes, skill levels and the like at the points where the firm's services or products are being used.

Some customers are more articulate than others, and this has a strong bearing on who does and who does not continue doing business with a vendor when there's been a negative experience. Customers who complain do so for two reasons: (1) They know *how* to complain; and (2) They expect to get results. Customers who don't complain often don't know how to go about complaining, and they very often feel that it wouldn't do any good anyway. This dichotomy is reflected in their purchasing habits: customers who complain tend to continue buying the same brands of products or services; those who have a problem but don't complain tend to switch to other brands. There is also a high correlation between educational level and income, on the one hand, and the frequency with which complaints are articulated or registered, on the other. The more upscale the individual, the more likely he/she is to complain and to do so effectively. The less education and the lower in economic scale, the less likely the individual is to articulate a complaint, or to feel that it will do any good.

The Well-Informed Customer

Deregulation has reshaped the customer. There is an entirely new breed of customers for newly deregulated firms. These customers realize that where in the past they pretty much had to take what vendors offered, today the shoe is on the other foot. Not only do they have a much wider range of options available to them, but also they no longer have to go to their vendors—their vendors have to come to them. Some vendors have not fully realized the marketing significance and a semi-dictatorial, take-it-or-leave-it attitude towards customers persists in the way they perform customer service. It's enough to say that by so doing they are leaving the door open for customer-oriented competitors.

Customers know very little about your products or services, or the levels of customer service they are receiving. It's a truism that customers typically know far less about our business than we credit them with knowing. In many instances they are unaware of the full range of products or services that we have available, while in others they know almost nothing about the way we do business. It's impossible to estimate how much business firms lose each year by failing to inform customers of savings in volume purchases, substitutable items for those out of stock, complementary products to those being ordered, unrelated products made by the same firm, special services and the like. This underscores the importance of incorporating in the customer service plan a program for insuring that customers are in fact well-informed, and that persons servicing their accounts maintain this level of knowledgeability. It may come as a disappointment to some managers to learn that most customers are not particularly aware of good customer service—they are much more likely to notice poor service and complain about it than to commend you for good service. But this very fact points up the importance of continuing communications with customers and timely reminders that they are in fact getting good service or, if not, that they will be shortly. It can be very costly to lose customers to competitors who compete on price alone, simply because the customer has never been made aware of the tradeoff between price and service. One potential—and extremely damaging—outcome of this type of situation is the customer who switches to the new source to buy high-margin items which are always available from that source, but continues to come back to you for the low-margin items which the new source doesn't stock.

Non-commercial Customers

The definition of a customer given here also requires inclusion of a category of individuals who receive services but are not customers in the usual commercial sense. These would include the following:

- *Students at a school or college.* Many of the transactions between them and the institution are comparable to those in a business setting: enrolling, signing up for specific courses or activities, paying for services, etc. Many college administrators now recognize that their problems in resource allocation are similar to those in business, and that the queuing problems encountered can be handled far more efficiently through application of current management science techniques used regularly in customer service operations.

• *Patients and inmates at hospitals and other institutions.* Whether there voluntarily or not, such individuals are essentially customers of the system, and it is usually far more efficient and less costly to plan for them as if they were in fact paying customers. Inefficiencies in the customer service-type administration of institutions is invariably passed on in one form or another, either to the inmates themselves, to support groups, or to the taxpayers.

• *Members of professional groups, non-profit organizations and similar bodies.* Here again, the transactions between an organization and its members are quite similar to those performed between a business and its customers. There are of course some organizations which are businesses in virtually every sense except for their designation as not for profit and their exemption from certain taxes.

• *Members of the public serviced by government bodies.* Departments that issue licenses, passports, patents and copyrights are in the customer service business as fully as a profit-oriented firm. The performance of inspections, levying of taxes, carriage of mail and the whole spectrum of services involved in law enforcement, welfare, various kinds of regulation, etc.—all these have customers for their services and in some instances products such as maps, books and the like from the Government Printing Office. Customer service costs are underwritten in some instances by direct user charges as in the case of license fees or highway tolls, while others—generally for public services—are widely distributed through the tax base.

Customers Are Human Beings

Particularly in companies which sell to other companies, the attitude sometimes develops that "the customer" is a faceless, monolithic entity that is something less than human. It is extremely important to impress on personnel that every single member of the customer organization is driven by identical motives to their own: a wish to succeed in their jobs, a wish for security for their families and themselves, a desire for recognition, safety and self-preservation. Customers who are excessively demanding or unusually irate when problems arise are usually that way because they perceive that these goals of theirs are being threatened: they will be held accountable within their own firm for the problem, their job or promotional opportunities will be compromised, they will lose status, their security will be threatened . . . or whatever. Because of this, personnel should be made aware that the simple fact that a problem has been caused by the customer himself or herself doesn't in any way diminish its importance or severity. If anything, this even increases the necessity of helping the customer solve the problem and maintain his or her job and status within the customer company.

Two True Stories About Customers

1. *The customer service rep who blew his stack.* This rep worked in the retail division of a conglomerate whose other divisions were mainly industrial. One day a customer phoned, explaining that he was calling on behalf of his wife who had experienced a very unsettling confrontation with a clerk who had refused to accept merchandise for exchange. The caller had no way of knowing it, but the customer service rep had already serviced a number of similar calls, and was near the breaking point. As it turned out, the customer's call was the straw that broke the camel's back.

"Sir," said the customer service rep after listening to the caller's tale of woe, "your wife strikes me as being an exceedingly stupid woman!"

There was a long pause, and then the caller said quietly: "Do you know who you're talking to?"

The rep knew he was in trouble already. "No, I don't know," he said with exaggerated politeness. "Whom am I talking to?"

"My name is _____," the caller said, "and I am the president of _____ Corporation. Last year, my company spent $3 million with your company's Industrial Division, $2 million with your company's Products Division, and $900,000 with your company's Special Services Division. Now what do you think of *that*?"

Now it was the customer service rep's turn to be silent for a few moments. After a long pause he asked in a small voice: "Do you know who *I* am?"

"No," said the caller. "Who are you?"

"Thank heavens," said the customer service rep, and hung up the telephone.

2. *The customer service manager who forgot.* The distribution manager of a well-known consumer products firm went on a tour of inspection to the firm's distribution centers. At one center he interviewed the onsite customer service manager . . .

"How are things going?" the distribution manager asked.

"Pretty good," the customer service manager replied, "except that we're having a problem with the customers."

"A problem with the customers?" The distribution manager thought this seemed a little unusual.

"Yes," replied the customer service manager. "They just can't get it through their heads that we have to run a warehouse here!"

This true anecdote illustrates the all-too-common attitude that develops among customer service people and others when the pressures of the job become too great and they begin to see customers as an interference with doing their jobs. And it explains why an integral part of the customer service manager's job is maintaining constant awareness in the customer service department and throughout the firm of two fundamental characteristics of customers which are central to the firm's survival . . . and to their own jobs, *everybody's* jobs:

1. Customers are the lifeblood of the business, the concern and responsibility of everybody in the business—without exception.

2. "Troublesome," dissatisfied and complaining customers represent a miniscule fraction of a firm's total customers; the vast majority are *satisfied* customers who demonstrate their satisfaction, not by calling up or writing letters, but by continuing to do business with the firm—speaking the language of reorders.

3

THE CUSTOMER SERVICE MISSION

Many of today's customer service departments had their origins as mainly clerical functions at a time when customer service as we know it today was handled by field sales personnel. As this practice became increasingly uneconomic, more and more customer service responsibilities were brought inside and tacked on to the ongoing clerical activities. And thus was born the customer service department. There are still some companies that do not have recognized customer service departments, and others where the customer service function as such is less than five years old. And many of those that do exist reflect their haphazard growth in poor status in the company, inefficient operations and impaired effectiveness in achieving their mission.

Which gives rise to the question: What *is* the customer service department's mission, and how can it best be achieved?

And that's the major part of the problem for most customer service departments. Their mission hasn't been defined beyond the stage of drawing up an organization chart and writing a few job descriptions. This simply isn't enough. Without a formal statement of departmental goals and the means whereby they will be achieved, customer service departments can't begin to make the tremendous contribution to corporate growth and profits they are capable of.

The Statement of Mission: What It Is

The statement of mission is basically a statement of corporate policy in regard to the customer service activity. It is usually drawn up by the customer service manager but is responsive to views and reservations of other departments as well as top management. In a larger company, the statement may be drawn up by a specialist in systems and procedures, with input from the customer service manager and others. Generally speaking, the statement of mission is written to reflect a broad management philosophy and is accompanied by a more down-to-earth statement defining more specifically how the department is expected to fulfill its mission.

The statement of mission has several very important functions. First of all, for many companies, it's the first articulation, the first formal statement of what the customer service department is expected to contribute to the corporation's overall goals. Secondly, it becomes the basis or reference point for developing policies and procedures which will make it possible to achieve those goals. Third, the statement of mission provides guidelines for the cooperative behavior of the different departments involved in any given customer service situation. Finally, and perhaps most important, the statement of mission provides a sense of identity and continuity and pride to the department and its members where little such awareness has existed in the past.

From the manager's point of view, the actual development and writing of the statement of mission is almost as important as what's done with it after it's been written and approved. In the process of working up the statement, the manager is—often for the first time—defining his or her goal as a professional manager identified with corporate goals rather than just day-to-day operations. Gaining concurrence from others in the process of developing the statement creates a vastly improved status for the department and reaffirms the validity of its mission.

Naturally, the relevance of a statement of mission is not confined to the customer service department; every department in the firm can benefit from preparation of such a statement.

However, it should be remembered that the need is often far more pressing in a customer service department which has grown more or less haphazardly and thus is little understood or appreciated in the firm.

Figure 1 illustrates a typical statement of mission for a customer service department in a firm that either manufactures products or provides services other than field service on equipment. It is accompanied by a detailed statement of implementation which can serve as the basis for developing specific statements of policy and written procedures for day-to-day use in departmental operations.

Figure 2 is a comparable statement of mission developed specifically for companies in high-technology and similar companies where the primary emphasis is on field support of the firm's equipment sited at customer locations.

These statements are necessarily somewhat general in nature, but readers are encouraged to use them as models to be modified and adapted to suit the unique needs of the individual company.

Implementing the Mission: Six Types of Environments

Obviously, there is no "best way" to set up the customer service activity that will apply to all companies or organizations in all situations. Each company or organization is unique and has its own strengths and weaknesses which must be taken into account along with special competitive situations. There are also differences in the way different firms do business and the marketing channels they employ. And institutions, government agencies or organizations performing member services reflect further differences.

For purposes of this book, six basic types of business or organization are assumed, each with differing customer service requirements and practices—each with its unique customer service environment.

1. *Firms that sell and ship from inventory.* While these will be preponderantly manufacturing firms and distributorships, wholesalers, steel service centers, etc., the category will also

---

Statement of Mission—Customer Service Department

The mission of the Customer Service Department is to:
- Establish, maintain and improve the firm's position in the marketplace; provide a measurable competitive edge.
- Develop specific strategies for customer retention.
- Develop specific strategies to stimulate account growth as the result of high levels of customer satisfaction with the customer service provided.
- Strengthen the firm's public image through the excellence of its service, and specifically through the professionalism of customer service personnel in their contacts with customers, prospective customers and the general public.
- Develop contingency plans for emergency situations including production problems, strikes, weather and other problems which could adversely affect customer service and the company's relationships with its customers.
- Increase the firm's share of market *and* its profits.

The Customer Service Department will perform this mission through effective sales support appropriate to its products or services by providing resources—personnel, skills, systems and communications—and participation in forward planning and other cooperative activity with management and inter-departmentally: before the sale, at the time of sale and in ongoing relationships with customers after the sale.

Implementation of Mission

The Customer Service Department will perform this mission through the development of an appropriate organization, policies and procedures of such quality as to meet customer requirements with reasonable cost constraints.

The structure of the Customer Service Department will relate to its specific functions in respect to customer orders for products or services: order acceptance, review and editing; order entry; dealing with exceptions including credit matters, backorders, custom work, special pricing where appropriate; activities related to order fulfillment; handling of inquiries and complaints; authorizing of returns and exchanges; and performance of other activities related to overall servicing of customer accounts.

---

include mail order firms selling to consumers and/or industrial customers. The products involved tend to fall into two broad categories: durables and non-durables or consumables.

The Customer Service Department will work with other departments in the firm including Sales, Scheduling, Technical Service, Credit, Quality Control, Traffic, Shipping and Warehousing and others as appropriate. It will do so in an atmosphere in which all departments recognize that no one department will be the "tail that wags the dog," but that *all* customer needs must be carefully evaluated in terms of the company's well-being and long-range growth and profit goals as well as its image in the marketplace.

The Department will conduct formal customer research and then develop service standards that will meet customer needs within the firm's cost constraints. On the same basis it will develop policies and decision rules for such matters as complaints, returns and exchanges that will make for the highest levels of customer satisfaction while protecting and contributing to the firm's economic interests and profit goals.

As appropriate, customer service personnel will participate in special sales support activities including attendance at trade shows, customer visitation in the company of field sales personnel, and inside selling activities as designated, such as order upgrading, recommending substitutions and order solicitation from designated smaller, remote or marginal accounts. Customer service personnel will be kept abreast of all promotions, new product introductions and other marketing activities with a bearing on their ability to serve customers and represent the company in the most effective way.

The Customer Service Department will stay abreast of state-of-the-art developments in communications technology, information systems, data retrieval, as related to the performance of its mission, and will make recommendations as appropriate for improvement or replacement of existing systems.

Similarly, the Customer Service Department will stay abreast of state-of-the-art developments in management of the Customer Service function through participation in professional activities. Management of the department will periodically furnish recommendations to corporate management and other departments incorporating ideas and procedures that will improve overall performance and profit contribution of the Customer Service activity.

The Customer Service Department will provide training and career pathing, plus a good working environment, in order to attract and maintain personnel of the high caliber necessary to perform this mission and satisfy the firm's overall profit and market share growth.

Figure 3-1.

31

Manufacturers in this category tend to be high-volume, broad-line operations. Customer service is heavily involved with information systems. In a typical operation, order processing will generate the order assembly data, i.e., picking documents, shipping labels, bills of lading, invoices and other paperwork. In the process, the computer will update inventory records and financial data, signal reorder points and measure aspects of performance like line fill. In some applications, the computer will measure orders against forecasts and adjust production schedules upwards or downwards as necessary. An increasing number of firms in this category are trending toward computer-to-computer ordering, either directly from customer to vendor, or through a third party system. As a further refinement in such situations, the host or vendor computer may create direct input media for an automated order assembly system without human intervention.

Statement of Mission—Field Service Department

The mission of the Field Service Department is to:
- Establish, maintain and improve the firm's position in the marketplace.
- Strengthen its public image.
- Enlarge its share of market through customer retention and account growth.
- Increase its profits.

The Field Service Department will perform this mission through effective engineering and technical support, professionally rendered, for the firm's products, equipment and systems: prior to installation, at the time of installation, and in on-going use at the customer site.

Implementation of Mission

The Field Service Department will perform this mission by providing resources—personnel, skills, parts, state-of-the-art technology—and management communications as necessary to meet customers' requirements within cost constraints.

Field Service personnel will support the sales effort overall as well as in specific instances by accompanying sales personnel on calls where their presence may be a major factor in closing sales or, in some instances, preventing competitive in-roads.

Companies in this category tend to have fairly high levels of product availability and relatively short lead times. While wholesalers and distributors have traditionally acted as stockpoints or inventory-holders between manufacturers and end users, in recent years they have been cutting their own inventory levels sharply and in effect forcing inventory back on manufacturers. They do this simply by shortening their lead times and requiring faster delivery from their manufacturers. Kanban or just-in-time delivery is an example of this, and the more generic a manufacturer's products, the more that manufacturer's customer service has to be responsive to these customer pressures because of the risk that customers will simply switch sources of supply.

Customer service is often a relatively mature management discipline in such companies. It is often supported by state-of-the-art information and communications systems permitting quick response to inquiries on product availability and order

---

Field Service personnel will also be alert for relevant market intelligence about customer attitudes, performance of equipment—including potential hazards and design problems—and competitive activity. They will provide feedback, documented whenever possible, on sources of dissatisfaction to customers, as well as on potential opportunities for additional sales and sales renewals and extensions of service contracts to new and existing customers.

Field Service personnel will recognize that their mission is to "repair the customer" as well as the equipment, and to produce a high level of satisfaction with equipment and performance. To this end, they will insure specifically that customers' manuals are up to date and customer personnel are specifically trained in optimum operation and maintenance of equipment. They will be particularly alert for such factors as personnel turnover and failure to update manuals, both of which can adversely affect equipment performance and with it customer satisfaction.

As appropriate, Field Service personnel will advise customers of new equipment, upgrades, retrofits, parts kits and service contract features that will provide benefits for customers as well as the company.

Field Service personnel will implement the mission of the Department by comporting themselves professionally at all times, bearing in mind that for the majority of the firm's customers they *are* the company.

Figure 3-2.

---

status; some systems include sophisticated substitutability programs (see page 417) to capture sales that would otherwise be lost. A few companies have entirely paperless systems, and others will soon. There's a trend toward interactive systems which will "prompt" the customer service representative taking an order to upgrade, suggest tie-ins or perform other marketing functions. In some companies, the customer service department is directly involved in forecasting. An increasing number participate regularly in marketing planning. Some have inventory management responsibilities, and a few have responsibility for purchase of resale items, i.e., parts and components which are simply purchased and resold to customers without any intermediate finishing or processing.

The mail order firms that have been included in this category have somewhat different customer service characteristics. The majority of such firms sell directly to consumers and are required to comply with certain regulations of the Federal Trade Commission covering order fulfillment, refunds and the like. For the majority, the average order is likely to average in the neighborhood of $50, and this automatically imposes a requirement for a high level of automation, few exceptions, and limited human intervention except for actually taking orders.

2. *Firms that manufacture and ship to order.* This category of firm ranges from companies which manufacture essentially stock items but do so only to order all the way to firms which design, engineer and manufacture completely custom products. One of the country's largest manufacturers of storm windows, for example, manufactures virtually 100% to order, even though the majority of orders are for standard items. Plastic film used in converting and packaging is quite often a custom item, and of course converting, packaging and printing exemplify a completely customized manufacturing item. An intermediate range of products in this category would be a basic product available with different options as ordered by customers. A firm manufacturing dental furniture and equipment, for example, has a basic "mainframe" system of controls and instrumentation, but every unit that is assembled contains different options of mate-

rials, color, control configuration, etc., specified by the end user dentist.

Customer service in businesses of this type usually involves longer lead times resulting from planning and engineering requirements as well as actual production scheduling. Where customer service personnel in Category 1 or stocking companies tend to be highly trained in operating the "system"—communications and information databases—to serve customers, in the custom design and manufacturing sector customer service personnel are likely to have special technical skills and often are directly involved in specification, estimating and pricing, and technical and engineering matters. In the printing industry, customer service personnel often have full responsibility for a job from the time it is received until it has been delivered to and accepted by the customer. In some printing firms, in fact, salespeople call on non-customers only. Once an account has been sold, it is handled entirely by an assigned customer service representative. Other types of firms in this category appear to be trending in the same direction.

Companies in this category tend to have fewer orders, but a great deal more detail in each order. Thus order entry may be a largely manual operation for economic reasons, or if computerized the system is more likely to be oriented towards generating bills of materials, manufacturing plans and pricing. Two types of products—elevators and metal buildings—exemplify this approach. Both are made from standard components but are highly customized to meet customer requirements, architectural and engineering constraints, and local building codes. The computer can be used to develop appropriate plans, specification and pricing in much less time—and with greater accuracy and lower cost—than if each order had to be worked up manually. This also enables firms in the respective businesses to reduce actual selling cost and cover more territory; salespeople do not have to have the engineering skills formerly required to write up orders for customers and develop estimates.

It's quite likely that firms in this category will be in several businesses: they will be manufacturing some stock items and some custom items, they may provide complete "turnkey" installations in some instances, and they are very likely to provide extensive field service, including parts support, on equipment installations. In the case of high-ticket capital equipment, the matter of parts support is usually one of the most important customer service activities. It's also a major problem area in companies where the production and purchasing departments are preoccupied with manufacturing and shipping complete units rather than providing the parts needed to support units already in the field. At least one company has dealt with this problem—quite critical when capital equipment costing $500,000 and more is involved—by setting up a completely separate customer service division, physically housing it some miles away from the manufacturing plant, and giving it its own complete machine shop in which to manufacture any parts that are not immediately forthcoming from the firm's manufacturing or purchasing activities. While this may seem an expensive solution to a recurring problem, it is in fact a relatively modest investment to make in terms of what's at stake: the potential loss of markets in the billions of dollars.

Field service is often an important customer service activity in companies in this category. Sometimes field service and inside customer service report to the same manager, but more often than not they are distinct activities, each with its own manager. Customer service tends to be centralized, while field service is necessarily a dispersed activity because field engineers have to be where their customers are. Even so, more and more companies with large field service staffs are moving towards central dispatch systems to maximize the utilization of these expensive field personnel. And although field service is a separate subject in itself, many of the principles and procedures discussed here will apply equally to field service management and operations.

3. *Firms that provide post-installation and repair.* This is a very large category of mostly smaller firms providing a so-called "third party" service repairing and maintaining equipment or products manufactured by others. There are a few large third-party organizations, mostly in electronics and high-technology

industries. Some manufacturing companies have separate divisions or companies which are solely in the repair business, for example, General Electric and RCA. The most common examples of a third-party service would be in auto repair; from the local "alley mechanic" all the way to large corporations like Midas International, their basic premise is quite similar: to deliver a combination of skills and parts or components in an environment where machine downtime is expensive and annoying to the customer.

Some of the firms in this business came into being via a process of "skimming," i.e., selecting a specialty which they could perform better, faster and more cheaply than, for example, a full-service dealer. The automotive muffler, transmission and brake service businesses are all examples of business that has been spun off in this way. Even well-established service organizations like General Electric's service division sometimes find they are losing significant business to local independents. Customer service shortcomings on the part of the original dealer are often cited as a primary factor in such switches, and many independent third-party organizations as well as national franchises do in fact make customer service a basic tenet of the business, whereas figures have been cited to show that poor service from dealers is the main reason consumers have very little brand loyalty and only one in four buys the same brand of automobile or appliance on their next purchase.

Customer service in this category of businesses, whether they operate in the industrial or consumer fields, tends to be quite different from customer service in large manufacturing or distributor organizations. A great deal of emphasis is placed on developing an image and supporting systems that strike a balance between the back-alley image of some independents and the impersonality and lack of responsiveness associated with some manufacturers. In the high-tech and electronic fields, of course, customer service quality has to be high enough to compete effectively with the well-implanted belief that manufacturers know more about their products, can get parts faster and in general are better motivated to provide better service.

4. *Service businesses.* This is an extremely broad category of businesses, including banks, insurance businesses, public warehousing, transportation companies, computer service centers, communications, credit and collection, hotels, entertainment, advertising, management consulting services and many others. Health care, legal services and other professional activities would fall into this category. Some governmental and institutional services would be included, while others might more properly be classified as retail businesses.

The variety of businesses in this category is so great that it's impossible to generalize about customer service except to say that in many of the businesses listed it's a relatively neglected area. A very common perception in service businesses is that poor service is the fault of "the kind of people we have to hire." This is not only offensive, but it's also wrong. Most customer service problems arise from *management* shortcomings: failure to provide adequate training, compensation and a suitable working environment; failure to support the customer service activity with appropriate policies, systems and procedures; and failure to appreciate that in the final analysis customer service is a management responsibility.

It is true that contact people in service businesses do often tend to have an extremely negative attitude towards customers. Some of this is a direct result of the stresses associated with the job arising from lack of support systems, decision rules and policies mentioned above; some, as mentioned earlier, is simply a reflection of management attitudes.

On the other hand, the service area has also produced some of the most outstanding examples of efficient and effective customer service. The airline and car-rental industries, for example, have invested heavily in both training and support systems, and maintain extremely high levels of customer service, both in the delivery of the service itself and in the satisfaction of customers served. On the industrial side, some transportation and public warehousing organizations have made remarkable turnarounds both before and since deregulation. Carrier support of the Transportation Data Coordinating Committee (TDCC)—with equal measures of support from shippers and financial organizations—has been a major factor in development of computerized tariffs and computer-to-computer transactions. Some railroads—traditionally the last bastion of difficulty to deal with—have done an excellent job in making their systems easier to deal with in terms of ordering equipment, tracing, invoicing, adjustments and the like.

This category of business would also include service businesses which are predicated on high levels of customer service—and charge accordingly. For example, the one-hour photo-finishing firms which are found in major metropolitan areas. The service costs nearly double conventional processing costs, yet there's a ready market for it. Other examples would include new emergency medical services operating independently of hospitals, comparable veterinary services for pets, various courier services and temporary employment services.

Also included would be various types of professional and non-professional franchise businesses like legal services, optometric centers, tax services and similar businesses which essentially make it easier for the customer to do business, generally but not always at a lower price than conventional channels. The price-service mix is aimed at a specific market segment, an important point because it illustrates management's understanding that customer service is indeed an essential part of the total marketing mix.

5. *Retail businesses.* These include some of the best as well as some of the worst examples of customer service as a concept, as a strategy, and in actual operations. Although it is categorized as a mail order firm, the great L. L. Bean organization in Freeport, Maine, is legendary in its attention to customer service: its retail store, for example, is open 24 hours a day, 365 days a year, and the attention the company lavishes on customers—in person, by mail or by phone—is the subject of endless tales, most of them true. Besides an extremely liberal and customer-oriented returns and exchanges policy that is a model for the industry, Bean has been able to impart a high sense of customer commitment to its employees. So much so that when an irate customer

called one day to complain that he hadn't received his catalog, the customer service rep obligingly read the entire catalog to him over the telephone . . . and then wrote an order in excess of $1,500.

What is not as well known about Bean and similar organizations is that they support their customer service commitment with order processing and order assembly/inventory management/warehouse management/shipping systems that are indisputably outstanding. This would seem to establish beyond reasonable doubt the premise that the commitment also requires a commitment to investment and a willingness to push back the frontiers of technology in this whole sector of customer support.

By contrast, there are many more retail businesses which have installed sophisticated information systems for processing sales transactions—but primarily for the store's benefit in terms of inventory management, turnover and other indicators. Although the food industry has adopted optical scanning with generally positive results (after some false starts due mainly to inadequate marketing of the concept), department stores and similar organizations have generally increased the amount of data entry that must be performed by sales clerks. The result is that customers wait longer and sales clerks are less available for assistance to customers on the floor. Although it hardly seems a solution, some chains have apparently "solved" this problem by reducing the number of floor sales personnel and using cashier stations to promote self-service. Although in some instances the cashiers double as sales clerks and vice versa, informal observation seems to indicate that their overbearing concern is with data entry and making the system work, rather than with customers. A recent visit to one such store established that the sales clerk/cashier: (1) did not know the actual length in inches of a "medium" inseam (and did not volunteer to measure it); (2) did not know whether the size of a belt referred to the length of the belt or the waistline it was intended to fit; and (3) did not know how to handle a return without an accompanying sales slip.

While it's unfair to generalize from isolated examples of this type, it's a basic premise of any business to *sell by helping customers buy.* Anything that makes it more difficult or unpleasant for customers to buy can't help but reduce the volume of their purchases. A customer who waits in a long line at a cashier's stand in a department store will be disinclined to make impulse purchases in other departments of that same store and thus have to go through the long waiting process all over again. A customer who can't get information or assistance on a purchase will be reluctant to make the purchase. A customer who's treated rudely (or ignored altogether) is likely to consciously take reprisal by going elsewhere. Whatever the outcome, inattention to specific customer service needs defeats that basic objective of selling by helping customers buy.

These principles apply throughout business, of course, and retail businesses have certain unique characteristics that complicate the job of providing customer service. In some stores, for example, sales clerks have to contend with security problems—shoplifting and holdups—and other incidents that seldom concern inside customer service personnel working in offices. Additionally, retail customers in many instances are less knowledgeable in actually making purchases and are likely to demand levels of service that simply aren't practical to give. As one example, the consumer movement in general has created higher levels of awareness of service and product shortfalls. What it has failed to do, however, is to educate consumers in the added costs that would often have to be passed along to consumers just to provide those increased service levels.

Rulings by the Federal Trade Commission on availability of advertised products have largely overlooked this cost factor. One such ruling required certain retailers to maintain 100% on-hand inventory availability for advertised items. This ruling ignored one of the most elementary rules of customer service: the higher the level of customer service in terms of inventory availability, the greater the cost. To maintain 100% inventory of an advertised item, given that this would require overestimating stock needs, would actually *increase* the price consumers would pay for this item.

Retail businesses and sellers of consumer products and

services in general can learn from this example, however. And the lesson is quite clear: it's less expensive to keep the government out of business by providing good customer service *before* the fact than to have to render it after.

6. *Trade and professional organizations, member service organizations.* There are literally thousands of such organizations, ranging from the 175-member Pickle Packers Association to the 237,000-member American Medical Association. They perform a range of member services, many of which parallel conventional business transactions. Customer service requirements tend to be similar to those in the magazine publishing business and the insurance industry; entering new memberships, handling membership renewals, expirations, changes of address and similar activities lend themselves well to automation: larger organizations may segment their membership lists in various ways in order to provide informational services of different kinds to suit different interests.

Associations often sell specific products and services to their members on a fee basis: books, clothing and membership paraphernalia, insurance, consulting services, research and informational services, seminars, meetings and educational services. A non-profit organization like American Management Associations is actually in a number of businesses and on the whole its business operations would be indistinguishable from those of publishing and commercial training and consulting organizations in the business sector. Even some exotic-seeming organizations like the Jockey Club perform rather conventional and "machinable" functions like researching, authenticating registration of thoroughbred racehorses, registering names, etc. Political and charitable or fund-raising organizations may not provide member services as such, but many of their transactions fit within conventional customer service techniques. And of course customer retention is *extremely* important!

Distinctions in Requirements

In addition to these basic categories, there can be distinctions in customer service requirements of a firm selling durables vs. those of a firm selling non-durables. The health care field has specific requirements imposed by the Food and Drug Administration relating to sanitation, non-returnable items, controlled substances, product recalls and the like. Similar requirements exist in the grocery products field. Differences may exist within an individual company as to customer service requirements: in the publishing industry, a college bookstore is likely to demand considerably higher levels of service than a public library. Again, in the health care industry certain life-saving products may require close to 100% customer service levels, while other, more generic items may only warrant 92% or 95% service levels.

In this connection it should be mentioned that changes within a customer industry will almost automatically change that industry's customer service requirements from its vendors. The health care industry has made a dramatic transition to disposables. This has affected its own ordering and materials management procedures which in turn has had a significant impact on what it requires from suppliers. Any customer service manager, regardless of industry, who has an opportunity to visit the materials management operations of Henry Ford Hospital in Detroit or Walter Reed Army Medical Center in Washington and similar institutions should do so. It's an excellent lesson in a unique form of customer service—customer service to patients—and in state-of-the-art materials management in a customer sector which, in turn, imposes unique requirements on the vendor sector.

And all businesses have a comparable requirement to structure their customer service organization around a combination of product and service characteristics and the needs of the business's customers, whoever and wherever they may be.

4

THE CUSTOMER SERVICE DEPARTMENT: ORGANIZATION AND RESPONSIBILITIES

The typical customer service department in 1983 consisted of 15 persons in a centralized department in a manufacturing firm with annual sales of over $27 million. Figure 1 shows the actual distribution by department size, and it's important to note that a significant 28.4% of all departments actually have 25 or more employees. Although the size of the department naturally varies with the size of the company, there can also be significant differences by industry group. One study showed food and grocery product manufacturers with an average of 7 persons in the department; chemicals, plastics and glass manufacturers with an average of 28 persons and book publishers also with an average of 28 persons. The tabulation did not include the extremely large customer service departments of 100 or more persons found in public utilities and similar organizations.

Principal Functions

The principal functions of these customer service departments fell into eight major categories, as follows:

Functions	Departments Performing
Complaint Handling	96%
Inquiries, Order Status	94%
Inquiries, Product Availability	91%
Returns and Adjustments	89%
Order Fulfillment	86%
Order Entry	86%
Customer Files	86%
Inquiries, Product Application	86%

Other functions reported by customer service departments but not tabulated by percentages include warranty administration, price list maintenance, inventory planning and managing,

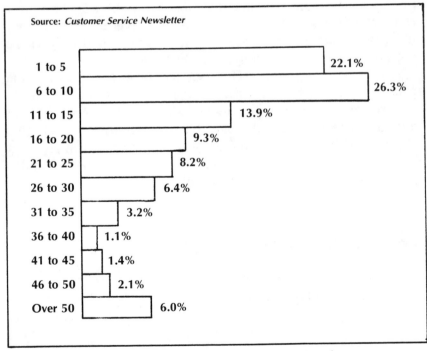

Figure 4-1. Number of employees in customer service department.

forecasting, technical applications, training of customer personnel, export, production scheduling, warehousing, shipping, customer research, customer service standards, credit and collection, freight claims, and others.

An increasing number of customer service departments are engaged in some version of inside selling, ranging from simple order upgrading to actual telephone sales or telemarketing. Some examples are shown in Table 1. One factor in the trend towards telemarketing is a diminution in order-taking by customer service personnel as computer-to-computer and direct customer entry techniques increase, plus large increases in field selling costs forcing more economic methods of selling to smaller, marginal customers.

Customer Service Job Summaries

Although there is considerable variation in actual job descriptions and from company to company, the following listing summarizes the principal job functions in primarily manufacturing firms. Note that these are summaries only, and do not list the full range of functions performed in each job category.

• *Customer Service Manager.* Has overall administrative and operational responsibility for the customer service department, including planning budgets, hiring and training of personnel, setting standards, monitoring performance, introducing more efficient procedures, writing and/or updating customer service manuals, and maintenance of customer files. Is responsible for customer relations and relations within the departments; keeps abreast of and advises management of new technology and new management techniques applicable to the department. Implements policies, and recommends changes as appropriate. Maintains liaison with other departments such as marketing, sales, credit, accounting, traffic and distribution, production, quality control. Has functional responsibility for receipt of orders, order processing, billing, returns, adjustments, product and other status inquiries.

● *Assistant Manager of Customer Service or Customer Service Supervisor.* Has functional responsibility, under the Customer Service Manager, for one or more areas of customer service, for example, order processing, and the customer. Serves as operating head of warranty administration. On behalf of the Customer Service Manager, performs actual liaison with sales, credit, inventory control, warehousing, shipping, traffic, data processing , and the customer. Serves as operating head of the department in the absence of the Customer Service Manager. Occasionally delegated to perform special functions: customer research, preparation of the customer service manual, customer visits, etc.

● *Order Processing/Manager/Supervisor* (Rank equivalent to Asst. Manager of Customer Service or Customer Service Supervisor). Responsible for receipt of orders, order editing and

---

Inside Selling—Reactive

1. Order upgrades—
    a. By economic lot or shipping quantity
    b. By price or quality
    c. By special incentive, e.g., assured supply

2. Substitution
    a. Similar product or service
    b. Dissimilar product or service

3. New product or service introductions

4. Tie-ins
    a. Integral products or services
    b. Non-integral products or services

Table 4-1. Examples of inside selling/telemarketing applications increasingly engaged in by customer service departments. Reactive inside selling

review, credit check, order entry, manual or computerized systems, maintenance of records associated with order processing system: order status, inventory levels, backorders, order fulfillment ratio, etc. Responsible for training, motivation and supervision of order entry clerks and support personnel. Controls access to customer records and computer databanks, and maintains security as necessary. Supervises entry of new data, changes, product descriptions, weights, price information, etc. Responsible for order processing supplies, maintenance of equipment service contracts, etc.

   • *Senior Customer Service Representative or Assistant Customer Service Supervisor.* Often functions as a team leader or account executive or working supervisor. Primary contact for customer, responsible for taking orders, handling routine inquiries and complaints, claims or credits and refunds below a certain

---

Inside Selling—Proactive

1. Initiating calls to customers
   a. As time permits
   b. On a rotating basis
   c. On a per-rep quota basis
   d. By appointment

2. Initiating calls to small or inactive accounts

3. Initiating calls to non-customers

4. Initiating calls to remote or inaccessible customers

5. Special situations
   a. Seconds, irregulars
   b. Overruns
   c. Refused shipments

---

refers to calls made by customers; proactive inside selling refers to calls initiated by the customer service department.

dollar limit. Is expected to have extensive knowledge of account requirements and special situations, ability to cut red tape and get results for customers. Handles exceptions, substitutions, allocations and other special problems. Often possesses specialized technical knowledge about firm's products and their applications.

• *Customer Service Representative.* Receives and processes all incoming orders and prepares appropriate forms for pick lists, invoice generation, etc; gives customers product availability and delivery information; initiates credit checks when necessary; advises supervision of unusual situations. The primary contact for customers for inquiries, complaints, product information and returns.

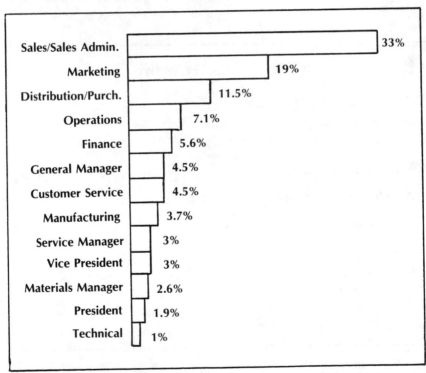

Figure 4-2. Customer service department reporting relationships.

● *Order Entry Clerk.* Responsible for auditing and batching order entry documentation for computer output or, with on-line systems, enters orders on CRT terminal; maintains entry reports.

● *Customer Service Clerk.* Performs routine filing, clerical, typing and similar functions.

● *Secretary.* Performs standard secretarial duties for the department head or for the entire department.

● *Switchboard/reception.* Screens and routes inbound calls as well as acts as information and message center.

● *Customer Service Specialist.* Expedites orders, processes out-of-the-ordinary orders and emergencies, handles special requirement accounts.

● *Traffic Coordinator.* Arranges transportation, freight rate negotiation, freight claims and tracing.

● *Billing Coordinator.* Coordinates order processing and billing cycles; also issues credit memos.

● *Office Equipment Operator.* Responsible for microfilming, mailroom, document control, data base maintenance, word processing, etc.

Positioning the Customer Service Department In the Firm

Where should the customer service department report in the corporate organization? This is one of the questions asked most frequently by customer service managers, and Figure 2 shows reporting relationships of a sample of departments in 1983. More than half of these departments report to a sales or marketing function, and a significant percentage report to distribution, operations or materials management functions.

Of course there is always the question of whether where customer service does report is where it *should* report. The answer is that it should report where it can function most effectively in the particular company. Customer service managers who report to a sales or marketing function seem generally satisfied with the relationship, except that they sometimes observe that they are overly subordinated to field sales personnel who place excessive service demands on them. Managers who report in a distribution or materials management organization feel that they benefit from having warehousing, transportation and distribution under the same roof, but that their ability to serve customers is sometimes constrained by a certain amount of inflexibility and cost-consciousness on the part of distribution management.

For example, one customer service manager in a volatile, high-tech industry complained that warehouse management continually placed roadblocks in the way of change orders when orders had already been placed on the warehouse. While the customer service manager recognized the problem they created, he pointed out that change orders were a characteristic of the industry and that sound management would indicate finding some way to accommodate them. Again, a traffic department's insistence on consolidating all small orders can seriously hamper effective customer service even though it may generate significant savings.

The other side of this particular coin is that in a reporting relationship to sales or marketing, the customer service department may be required to give unrealistically high levels of service—in effect giving away the store for no useful purpose. In fact there are some levels of customer service that are *too* good. Consider the case of a company where it's required that every order is picked and shipped as received. This appears to be a sound policy, but in the particular company some customers may place 20 or more orders in a single day. Shipping these separately provides no benefit to the customer, and in fact represents a considerable inconvenience and adds an entirely unnecessary transportation cost. Yet the sales manager will not back down from the policy of process-and-ship.

As a generalization, customer service appears to report to distribution mainly in companies where there's a high component of transportation, warehousing and inventory management. This group would include grocery products manufacturers and bulk chemical producers, among others, but the relationship is by no means restricted to these two groups.

While customer service managers reporting in sales-marketing or distribution organizations seem generally satisfied with the arrangement, two specific relationships that are generally *not* satisfactory occur in departments that report to finance or to manufacturing. A customer service department reporting to finance tends to be perceived as an opportunity for cost reduction, a "necessary evil" type of expense which has to be incurred but should be held in check as much as possible. On the other hand, the financial sector of the business is very heavily involved with computers and information systems and in this particular reporting relationship some customer service departments have been able to acquire top-notch systems which make them much more effective in spite of the constraints they work under.

From all indications, a reporting relationship to manufacturing is probably the least satisfactory of all those listed. The reason is that manufacturing personnel tend to be production oriented and in fact are rewarded or penalized in terms of capacity utilization or production economies. As mentioned earlier, production economy, or capacity utilization as it is sometimes called, requires relatively long and unbroken production runs. Good customer service typically requires a much higher degree of flexibility: changeovers, short runs, some customization—all "enemies" of production economy. And when customer service reports to production it is most often subordinated to the traditional production philosophy.

It should be clear, even so, that it is not the responsibility of production management to change its philosophies to suit the needs of customer service. The real responsibility lies with management, which tolerates a rewards-and-penalties system in which different departments are forced to compete and are in effect penalized for cooperating. In this event, the customer service manager must convince management of the need to displace the present rewards system for one in which the criterion is to corporate goals rather than to "efficiency" of the individual department. This concerns the customer service manager because there is frequent confusion between customer service department *efficiency* —basically a measure of productivity— and customer service *effectiveness,* which is the measure of the department's contribution to corporate goals of growth and profit.

This raises the question of whether customer service should in fact report to top management. There are in fact some companies with a vice president of customer service who is at that level, and perhaps an additional 10-12% where the director or manager of customer service reports to a vice president or general manager. When the department itself is headed by a vice president, customer service clearly has good status in the company and has good representation in management planning and decision-making. In fact the existence of such a title most likely reflects a conscious corporate decision to make customer service a key strategy in the company's operations.

Reporting relationships of directors and managers of customer service to the top management level appear to be satisfactory but some managers have indicated a preference to report elsewhere than to the president, mainly on the grounds that they don't really get much attention at that level. On the other hand, there's a certain amount of prestige value in the relationship which can be quite important to a department which has had an image problem in the past.

Figures 3 through 6 depict some of the more prevalent types of reporting relationships, while figure 7 shows a typical customer service department organization chart. It should be emphasized that there are infinite variations on these formats, and the charts shown here are not intended to represent any particular "ideal" type of organization.

Centralized vs. Decentralized Departments

Centralization-decentralization is an issue which involves many factors over and above customer service operations. This

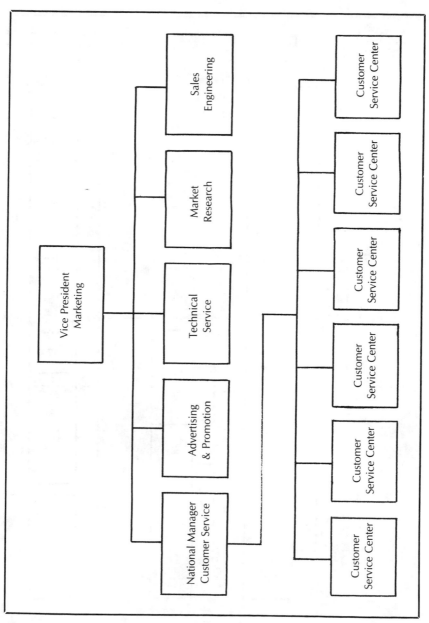

Figure 4-3. Centralized customer service department with line responsibilities.

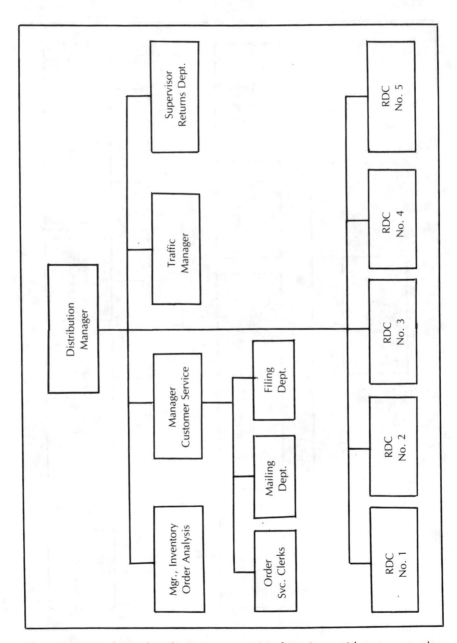

Figure 4-4. Decentralized customer service function, with corporate department performing staff functions.

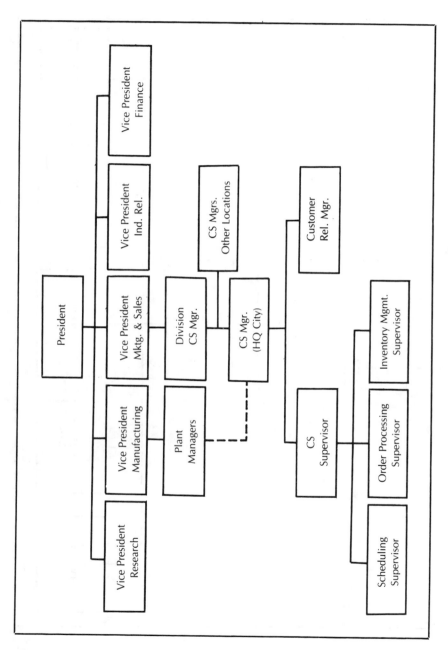

Figure 4-5. Customer service function reporting to sales.

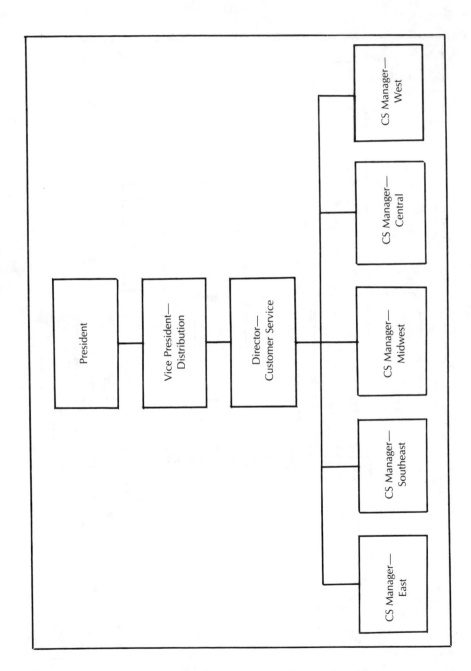

Figure 4-6. Customer service function reporting to distribution.

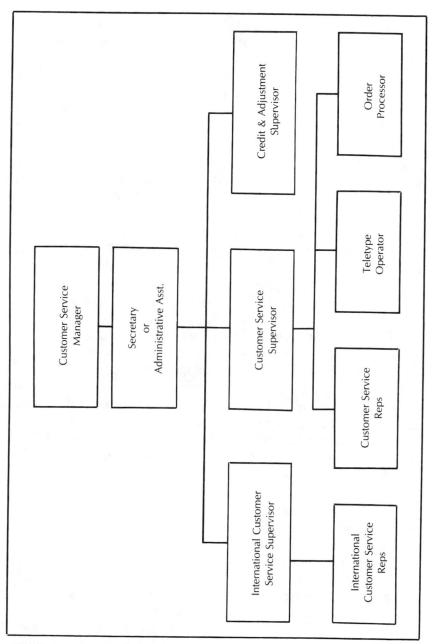

Figure 4-7. A typical customer service department.

Productivity. Centralization often enables greater efficiency, productivity and capacity utilization. Many economies can only be realized when there is a high concentration of activity at one location. These are called "economies of scale." When customer service is centralized, the volume of mail, telephone calls, outbound orders, invoices, credits—everything associated with customer service transactions—becomes concentrated at the central location. It becomes economic to install more advanced information systems, automatic call distributor telephones, a micrographics installation, a word processing center, and higher levels of automation generally. With four, six or more locations, it simply would not be economic to invest in hardware of this order for each location. In addition, with more people at the one location it's more practical to use job engineering and other management science techniques. Workload balancing is often practical, and communications today are such that it's possible to deal almost instantly with customers anywhere in the world.

Higher skills. Because more work can be done by fewer people at a centralized customer service department, it's usually possible to pay higher salaries and attract more highly skilled personnel. It's often possible to hire specialists in particular fields, which wouldn't be practical on a decentralized or local basis except where there is unusually high volume.

Quality control and testing. If customer service also involves quality tests, small instrument repair, adjustments, calibration and similar processes requiring sophisticated equipment, a central location is more economical in terms of both equipment investment and specialized bench personnel, although part of this may be offset by the added costs of transporting products to and from customer locations.

Inventory productivity. With a central location, inventories that are in short supply can be concentrated at the central point in order to serve more customers with a smaller overall inventory. This is practical with items that are relatively low in weight and high in dollar value, so that transportation costs do not become a major factor. In fact, if the items are sufficiently high in value, centralized inventories plus air freight may be a feasible customer service strategy in times of product shortages. Some companies do in fact employ this type of distribution on a permanent basis because of the combined factors of inventory cost and urgency of customer requirements. Many computer and high-tech components fall in this category, as well as a number of health care products.

The personal touch. Advocates of decentralized customer service operations argue strongly that centralizing the customer service function when it's historically been at field locations will destroy the "personal touch" that's an important element of customer service. While this is sometimes true, companies deal with it by transferring key people in from the field to the central location where they continue dealing with the same customers as before. There are sometimes regional considerations, where it's felt that Southerners prefer talking to Southerners, New Yorkers to New Yorkers, and so forth. Centralized customer service operations deal with this situation (where it's felt to be relevant) simply by hiring Southerners to handle their Southern accounts, New Yorkers to handle their New York accounts, and others as necessary.

Inspections, field service and repairs. Generally speaking, decentralized locations are more suitable where frequent visits are made to customer locations to inspect, repair and maintain heavy equipment or equipment that cannot be taken out of service for lengthy periods. In some cases, firms will maintain field engineers at branch locations with senior engineers at the central location, mainly for consultation by phone but available to fly out to assist in highly complex situations. But even with a decentralized field service force, an increasing number of companies are turning to centralized dispatching as the key to improved utilization of their costly field service personnel.

Presence in the marketplace. It's a fact that many customers prefer doing business with a firm that has a local branch or warehouse. They find it reassuring that the firm is there, because it suggests fast response to their needs and good customer service. In actual fact, however, the branch may not give any better service than a more remote location; after all, the more branches a firm has at which it inventories goods, the more difficult it becomes to maintain adequate inventory levels at all branches. Some companies overcome this problem by processing orders at a central location and then filling them from the nearest branch that has the items the customer ordered. Which of course is not necessarily the branch that is physically nearest to the customer. In any event, the fact that a warehouse or branch is at a certain location does not mean its staff has to include customer service personnel. Most computer networks today are set up so that orders processed centrally can be transmitted immediately to branches or warehouses and shipped as soon as, if not sooner than, they could have been shipped had customers placed the order directly with the local branch. The central processor can also be programmed to transmit only orders that can actually be filled at a given location, passing the unfillables on to other locations where stocks are adequate.

Trend towards centralization. In mid-1983, about 80% of customer service departments were centralized, and 20% were decentralized. The majority of decentralized operations were in companies with two to five locations, although a sizable segment—20% of all decentralized operations—were in companies with nine or more locations. Also, it should be pointed out that some companies with regional distribution centers have full-fledged customer service staffs at each location that are to all intents and purposes "centralized" for the region served by the distribution center. This is particularly true if the distribution center is in effect a corporate warehouse handling products of some or all of the parent corporation's divisions. Such corporations may not even have a customer service department as such at the corporate headquarters, but rather a staff function serving as consultant to the various regional operations.

A final word on the subject of customer service organizations. Preoccupation with organization charts is no substitute for the manager's skill in dealing with the practical constraints and opportunities of his or her situation, nor for learning how to get results by working with other departments and providing high quality leadership for members of the customer service group.

5

WHAT'S EXPECTED OF THE CUSTOMER SERVICE DEPARTMENT

What may well be one of the most troublesome and neglected areas of customer service is determining what's expected of the customer service department by the various entities in the company and by customers themselves—and then deciding which expectations can actually be met and which have to be readjusted to conform with reality.

For example, consider this conversation between the president of a well-known firm and his customer service manager:

President: "Starting next week, I want you to adopt a policy of shipping every order the same day it's received."

Customer Service Manager: "A ship-same-day policy? I think that may present some problems."

President: "I don't care if it does. I'm sick and damned tired of customers calling me direct when their shipments are late."

Customer Service Manager: "But that isn't the problem. The problem is that we don't have the merchandise to ship. It's an inventory problem, not an order processing or shipping problem."

President: "Don't bother me with details. Just get the damned orders out and get the customers off my back!"

This exchange (which really took place) demonstrates the problems that can arise when more is expected of the customer service department than it can ever hope to deliver. In this particular case, the company had a serious inventory problem resulting from a combination of forecasting error and limited manufacturing capacity, compounded by raw materials procurement problems. The sales department, meanwhile, was selling product without regard to present levels of availability. To bring the situation under control, two alternatives were available: (1) coordinate the sales effort with existing stocks, which would require placing some customers on allocation and reducing actual sales of some lines; or (2) making a multi-million dollar investment in added production capacity and inventory. Management was not prepared to take either of these steps and therefore saddled the customer service department with an assignment that was impossible to perform.

Consider by contrast the situation in a midwestern chemical manufacturing firm, where a different type of conversation was taking place between the president and the customer service manager:

President: "Al, we've decided to change from selling on a delivered price basis to shipping FOB, freight charges collect."

Customer Service Manager: "That's going to be a tough one to sell to customers."

President: "I know it is. That's why I'm telling you now. What do you think you'll need by way of time and input from us to make the change?"

Customer Service Manager: "Let me ask you this first. Are you absolutely sure you want to make this change?"

President: "Yes. So much so that the Board of Directors is involved. When we prepay the freight and then sell on a delivered price basis we're giving customers interest-free loans for 30, 60 or 90 days. For the amount of the freight, that is. And we figure that something like $25 million is constantly tied up like this, not earning a penny for us. No, we're committed. No doubt about it."

Customer Service Manager: "I'd want to talk to some of my people before giving you a detailed answer to your question, but offhand I'd say about a year to make the change, including time to work up some literature and scripts for our people, time to train them, and time to work up some scenarios for customers who are going to want to talk directly to you. I'd say we'd want to get the public relations people involved pretty early, too, and set up some kind of budget for direct mail. We might even want to invest in a little customer research just to make sure we've covered all the angles."

President: "I think we're on the right track. How about giving it all to me in writing by the first of the week?"

This conversation, too, really took place. The changeover was planned, scripted and implemented within the one-year time-frame. A great deal of attention was given to making the program palatable to customers, and the customer service department played a central role. The projected savings were realized, and the customer service department became the heroes of the company. A lot of doors and opportunities were opened for the customer service department as a result. And it all came about because management's expectations, although high, were not unrealistic—and because the customer service manager was willing to make the extra effort required to meet those expectations.

A somewhat different type of situation arises when management decides to apply "organizational" solutions to customer service problems. "We're going to hire a crackerjack customer service manager and get this situation straightened out once and for all!" This type of statement is not at all uncommon, and it often forebodes trouble. It usually signifies unrealistic expectations; management has not yet recognized the need to make its *own* commitment before expecting miracles of others.

Even so, it should be acknowledged that some customer service managers aggravate the problem of unrealistic expectations by *reacting* rather than *proacting,* i.e., waiting until such situations arise rather than anticipating them and starting right away to correct them before they get out of hand.

The customer service manager should also be aware of the prevalance of unrealistic expectations in other departments. There are two aspects to this. In the first, field sales personnel expect customer service personnel to deliver on commitments they have already made to customers without verifying that they can in fact be met; sometimes the matter involves other departments over which customer service has no control. The second aspect is where departments inside the company expect customer service to be a buffer between them and demanding customers, the get-'em-off-my-back syndrome; unlike salespeople who expect customer service people to *meet* customer demands, these inside people expect customer service people to persuade customers to *reduce* their demands. Both positions are equally unrealistic.

Perhaps the best way to deal with the problem of unrealistic expectations is in the course of drawing up the customer service department statement of mission as described in chapter 3. It's a logical time to be talking to management as well as other departments in a friendly environment, i.e., one where no specific problem exists between the departments.

What Customers Expect

Although the specifics of customer expectation are best determined by objective customer research of the type outlined in chapter 10, certain standards of performance represent virtually universal requirements from the customer's point of view.

● *Availability of the product or service.* Having the product or service readily available is seen by most customers as the number one requirement of a vendor's customer service. In the case of custom products or services, the expectation would be for a reasonable lead time, while for stock products or services current expectations are generally quite high and may even involve same-day response.

● *Price.* Although pricing itself is not a customer service responsibility in most companies, customers typically perceive it as one aspect of the entire cluster of customer service activities. Apart from expecting that prices be reasonable (and in some cases negotiable), customers have high levels of expectation that price quotations will be readily available, accurate and binding on the vendor. There is a trend towards expecting that price estimates for custom orders can be quickly computed and given to the customer. Some companies have developed computer programs that enable working up estimates on complex jobs while the customer is still on the phone.

• *Accuracy.* This would include accuracy in information provided customers on product applications, order status and delivery dates; accuracy in order processing, order assembly and actual delivery; and accuracy in invoicing and other documentation.

• *Timeliness.* There's considerable misunderstanding on this subject, most of it arising from the common assumption that all customers want the fastest service they can get. They don't. In fact, what customers *really* want is *consistency* and *timeliness*. Consistency refers to the time interval between placement of an order for product or service and the actual delivery of that product or service. Timeliness refers to meshing with the customer's needs; the customer may need information or product or service in order to complete specific projects on specific schedules. There are some occasions when customers do genuinely need fast service or a fast response, but there will also be many instances where they will willingly accept extended lead times in exchange for a higher percentage of line item fill or complete orders.

• *Quality—product or service.* It's accepted that product and service quality can vary with price and situation. The "deluxe model" is expected to be superior to the standard and economy versions . . . and to cost more. The same is true of services; first class on an airline is much more expensive than coach or economy, and is expected to warrant the difference in quality of service. Whatever the case, when quality of the product or service fails to meet customer expectations, the main customer contact is likely to be with the seller's customer service department . . . which in turn is expected to bring the problem to a quick resolution.

• *Quality—delivery of product or service.* Absence of loss or damage to products shipped is a basic customer expectation. The customer expects the product to be properly packaged and protected, including proper blocking, bracing and unitizing in common carrier equipment. And even though vendors may sell on an FOB shipping point basis with the customer responsible for filing claims with carriers, smaller customers in particular will want help from the vendor's traffic department in filing and collecting such claims. In the case of delivery of a service rather than a product, customers expect no impairment of the service resulting from the way it is delivered.

• *Convenience of delivery.* This refers to both suitability of the mode of transportation and delivering carrier, in the case of products, and the method in which services are made available to customers. For example, shipping products in bulk carrier equipment suitable for unloading at the customer's bulk storage facility; or, in another situation, assuring that the delivering carrier is equipped with a power tailgate for delivery of equipment to a customer site where there is no loading dock. The convenience involved in delivery of a service could relate to avoidance of long waits in line at banks or government agencies, the arrival of a field engineer to maintain equipment at a time when it is not needed for other uses, or such features of travel as advanced seat selection, express service in car rental, etc.

• *Reasonable customer service policies and procedures.* Customers respect the need for orderly procedures in sales administration, but unreasonable or excessive "rules and regulations" on returns, credits and adjustments are often perceived as unilateral on the vendor's part and indicative of a lack of good faith as well. Many companies have addressed this particular problem by allowing no-fault or automatic adjustment below a certain dollar level. As a matter of economics it is usually less expensive to take the customer's word for it on smaller claims, simply because, honest or not, the cost of investigating the claim usually exceeds the cost of paying it off regardless. The time factor is particularly important; a company which takes a long time to process claims for small amounts is often perceived as deliberately delaying payment in order to get "free" use of the customer's money for an extended period.

• *Courtesy.* There are two aspects of courtesy which are especially sensitive: (1) the more conventional "language" of courtesy, i.e., the manner in which customer service personnel and others actually address customers; and (2) the "demonstrated" courtesy of follow-through, of notifying customers in advance of delays or other problems and other actions which translate concern for the customer into tangible acts on the customer's behalf.

- *Attitude.* Closely related to courtesy, but also involved in the individual rep's attitude towards his/her company, its products or services, co-workers, and overall identification with customer needs and service-mindedness. And of course attitude towards self in terms of pride in quality of service, and willingness to accept responsibility for one's actions. It has been said that the ten most important words in customer service language are: "Please call on me. I am here to serve you."

- *Accountability.* From the customer point of view one of the fundaments of a sound business relationship is the accountability of the vendor—and particularly individual vendor personnel—for commitments made to the customer on price, product, service, applications, terms of sale or whatever. And of course accountability when there are customer service failures. In this perspective, accountability means acceptance of responsibility without buck-passing or attempts to evade responsibility altogether . . . and in particular taking immediate action to mitigate the damage or rectify the problems that have been created by the customer service failure.

- *Responsiveness to customer needs.* Whether it be in the design of a product, the hours a customer service department is available to customers, the length of time a caller is placed on hold, the understanding of customer requirements for packaging or marking, the provision of understandable instructions for installation and maintenance of equipment, parts support, professionally qualified customer service personnel, or whatever—customers feel that it is incumbent on their vendors to understand both their general and their special needs and to design their customer service accordingly. In this connection, surprisingly few customer service departments (or their companies) conduct serious customer service research to determine what these needs are. One major transportation company acknowledged that it was unwilling to ask its customers for suggestions on improving its service on the grounds that customers might interpret this as a commitment to actually make such improvements!

The Customer Service Manager's Expectations

Certain basic capabilities in the department or in the company are so fundamental that the customer service manager should take it that they either exist or, if not, will be quickly brought into being. He or she should, in short, expect these capabilities to characterize the department's posture of overall responsiveness to customer needs.

• *A coherent, companywide policy on customer service.* Not a broad, generalized statement about glittering goals of customer service, social responsibility or the like, but rather a highly specific statement of standards of performance, departmental obligations and commitments to specific inventory levels, production schedules and delivery times. Specific standards and how to set them are discussed in chapter 10.

• *Ability to answer inquiries on order status quickly and accurately.* Many companies see this as one of their highest priorities, and some go further and specify the ability to notify customers immediately when it appears that there may be even the slightest deviation from a promised delivery date.

• *Ability to trace and expedite.* Closely related is the ability to trace orders which are already in the transportation/ distribution network but presumably lost or delayed at some unknown location, and when necessary to expedite orders which are in-house but have fallen behind schedule or are needed by customers sooner than was originally anticipated.

• *Knowledge of product.* Sales people and customer service representatives alike are expected to have a sufficiently broad knowledge of the product line and individual products to be able to answer customers' general questions, and to assist in the correct choice of the most suitable products for given applications. In some situations (for example, ethical pharmaceuticals, complex machinery), a separate staff of specialists or engineers may be maintained to advise customers on product properties and applications, while regular customer service personnel concentrate mainly on order fulfillment and associated activities.

• *Knowledge of pricing.* An absolute must in any volatile market situation where prices change frequently and customers' buying decisions may be predicated on up-to-date, accurate information.

• *Knowledge of packaging units (or formatting, configuration).* "How many facecloths to a carton?" "How many cartons to a truckload?" "How many lessons is the course divided into?" "How many lessons (records, books) in the set?" These questions, including questions about weight and dimensions, are frequently asked, and should be readily answerable.

• *Written service policies.* Not to be confused with the overall companywide policy on customer service described above, these are specific service policies for guidance of customer service personnel in day-to-day activities. For example: how the company deals with complaints, claims, requests for emergency service, etc.

• *Effective organization.* This could refer equally to the organization of the customer service department and the organization of the company as a whole. Within the department, overall efficiency will be largely determined by the manner in which the workload is distributed and performed via the internal structure of the department, plus of course the skill with which the activity is managed. It goes without saying that, given the customer service department's built-in need for cooperative action by other departments, the manner in which the company is organized overall will have the determining effect on how well the customer service department achieves its various missions across the board.

• *A sound logistical plan.* The correlation of inventory management, warehousing and order assembly, and distribution methods with customer service is a major step in carrying out the customer service mission. If the company operates its own truck fleet, for example, it may wish to coordinate customer deliveries with purchases and vice versa in order to achieve good equipment utilization. It may find opportunities to make sales in certain areas based on equipment capacity that's available—a situation which benefits the vendor as well as the customer. The logistical plan may involve developing unit load programs, consolidations, "free shipping" days and other approaches which level the workload in the warehouse and at the same time maximize transportation efficiency. There may be a need to set policies which limit unscheduled customer pickups to the extent that they interrupt the workflow in the warehouse, or procedures for selling off refused shipments at destination rather than pay return transportation costs. There are numerous logistical interfaces of these types, many of which will be discussed later.

● *Trained personnel.* In many companies, the job of customer service representative is an entry level position close to the bottom of the employment scale in both status and pay. With more and more emphasis being placed on the importance of customer service, few companies can afford to have amateurs handling critical customer contacts. Many are already upgrading the position itself in order to attract persons of greater qualifications, and at the same time developing appropriate training programs in order to maximize their productivity and justify the additional cost of higher-rated personnel.

● *Effective information systems.* While it is generally recognized that effective information systems are fundamental to today's business operations, particularly in respect to order entry, inventory management and financial records, what is not so well understood is how important such systems are to the morale and performance of customer service personnel. Systems that break down frequently, or do not provide complete or accurate information on product availability or order status, create strong negative pressures from customers and an equally strong sense of frustration on the part of the customer service reps involved. In a busy department, even a few seconds' lag in obtaining data via a CRT can create annoyance and build up to a strong sense of frustration.

• *Understanding of the importance of maintaining high levels of morale and motivation and an appropriate working environment.* In a job which is characterized by many "negatives"—the individual rep tends to hear only the problems—it is extremely important that the psychological needs of those on the firing line be taken into account. Career pathing, participative management and improvement of the physical work environment are among the measures to investigate.

6

THE CUSTOMER SERVICE CYCLE

Customer service has often been labeled a "reactive" function in the company. An inquiry is received, an order is placed for products or services, a complaint registered—and customer service reacts. It's a randomized world, and customer service people themselves see their job as mainly concerned with putting out fires.

This is not the way customer service should be performed, and in well managed companies it is not the way it *is* performed. Customer service can be systematized the way any business activity can be systematized. The infeed of inquiries, orders, complaints and other communications to the customer service department can be tracked and measured and therefore predicted. Repetitive characteristics of customer service transactions can be identified and rationalized by means of decision rules. The system can be measured, monitored, evaluated and optimized.

In short, customer service lends itself to management principles and management science techniques that are readily available. And managers who claim that they are too busy putting out fires should reexamine their priorities and make use of these management tools in their own situations.

A good place to start is with the customer service cycle. This should not be confused with the order cycle, which is only part of the total customer service cycle and is essentially a linked series of transactions highly susceptible to mechanization or automation. The customer service cycle is a *management* function, and it has six main components.

1. *Planning.* The planning function begins with forecasting: forecasting of sales by regions, markets and periods. Whether or not the manager has an official responsibility for forecasting, he or she should do so as a matter of course. Beyond sales, the manager should also forecast and plan in terms of any technological developments that will be available in communications and data processing.

Planning will also consider what the competition has done and will be likely to do in terms of customer service, and whether countermeasures should be planned at this time. Realistically, the planning stage must also consider how top management thinking will evolve in the months ahead, and what opportunities or problems will be presented to the customer service manager as a result.

The final element of planning is of course resource allocation and budgeting. Here again, not all customer service managers have been directly involved in this activity. But it is clear that they should be. The earlier stages of forecasting and assessing the future provide a basis for estimating workforce needs, communications and data processing capacities, and of course the stock levels or service depth estimated to meet customer requirements. Many managers report that they are expected to handle a considerably increased volume of business with little if any addition to staff. This means generally that such growth will be accommodated through technology—hardware—investment, and the manager must certainly be prepared to go this route if necessary.

2. *Operations.* This stage of the customer service cycle concerns itself with the specifics of organization (see chapter 3), and procedures for each of the functions to be performed, including (as applicable) order processing and fulfillment, claims, complaints, adjustments, inquiries, inside selling and telemarketing, and other activities. In some firms, customer service personnel may have specific assignments related to warehousing and shipping, purchase of resale parts, credit and collections and related activities. Decisions will be made at this point on whether to assign customer service reps by territory, account, industry or

other basis (see chapter 9) for a detailed discussion of this subject).

The operations stage also involves codifying the policies that will be applied in day-to-day operations, along with decision rules to aid in interpreting and applying those policies. The subject of automatic refunds will probably be considered here, as will constraints—designations of what *cannot* be done, either for corporate or legal reasons.

The final element of the operations phase is the communications and information systems supporting the customer service activity. If order processing is performed in the department, this automatically imposes certain requirements; if it is performed elsewhere, other options will be available. The rapidity with which change is being introduced, however, suggests that the manager should avoid getting locked into a system which will not accommodate the new technology as it comes along.

3. *Control.* This is a basic management function, requiring the establishment of standards of customer service response, quality and performance, and accountability and responsibility for customer service failures. An important point here is the setting of internal standards as well as external, i.e., standards for interdepartmental response within the firm as well as conventional standards for response in customer transactions of various types. (The subject of standards is covered in detail in chapter 10.) Accountability is closely related to internal standards, because a preponderance of customer service failures can be traced to happenings outside the customer service department where responsibility tends to "fall between the chairs" and the same events recur because the cause isn't corrected.

4. *Monitoring.* This is simply the method of establishing feedback to determine the levels of performance of the department and other departments against the standards that have been established. Much of this process can be handled as a byproduct of order processing via conventional exceptions reports. Most systems are capable of measuring line item fill, complete order fill, dollar fill, backorders and similar exceptions on a periodic basis. Many carriers provide performance reports

on individual shipments, and of course proof of delivery can be obtained as well. Inclusion of reply cards with shipments to customers is another useful feedback method for determining customer satisfaction and order cycle times.

Other methods of monitoring include tracking of customer service failures (see chapter 7 for a discussion of this subject), and particularly following up on all orders that have been lost or cancelled to determine the reasons why.

An important aspect of monitoring is direct qualitative observation of performance of customer service representatives in their telephone contacts with customers (see chapter 20).

5. *Measurement.* This element of the customer service cycle has two major dimensions: (1) measurement of customer service *efficiency,* in terms of departmental productivity or output in orders processed, complaints handled, pounds shipped, etc.; and

---

What Are Some of the Things We Can Measure in Customer Service?

1. Total order cycle time: order inception to delivery
2. Discrete elements of the order cycle: order processing, order assembly, delivery to customer, etc.
3. Movement of orders by batch
4. Variable costs: labor, communications, transportation
5. Personal productivity
6. Qualitative performance, e.g., telephone skills, problem solving, accuracy
7. Exceptions by source or cause
8. Throughput
9. Errors and credits
10. Loss and damage
11. Line item fill, complete order fill, dollar fill
12. Inquiry response, complaint resolution
13. Customer profitability

Figure 6-1. Typical areas of customer service that lend themselves to measurement.

(2) measurement of customer service *effectiveness* in meeting customer goals. Both measures are important to the manager, but they should be recognized as entirely distinct.

Quantitative measures of productivity would include number of orders processed per hour, day or week; number of complaints handled, inquiries responded to, letters written, etc. For straight data entry, performance is usually measured in keystrokes. In order taking by telephone, the measure may be the number of orders and lines, along with a negative measure of errors per 100 orders. In an inside selling or telemarketing environment, the measure may cover the ratio of completed calls to attempts, the ratio of sales to completed calls, the ratio of dollars to sales, etc.

Quantitative measures of customer service effectiveness would include, as mentioned, line items filled vs. line items ordered, complaints-to-orders ratios, complete order fill, customer delivery dates met, and actual performance against customer service standards that have been established.

An important part of the measurement element of the customer service cycle is assessing customer perceptions of the quality of customer service. This is typically done via conventional market research techniques, which are discussed in the customer service context in chapter 11.

6. *Analysis.* The first five elements of the customer service cycle have now provided the manager with virtually all the tools for managing the department. It is now time to ask a series of questions including: How well are we doing? What are we not doing that we should be doing? What are we doing that we should not be doing? What improvements should we make, what changes in procedure? What opportunities are presented that we should capitalize on? Overall, what should we do?

7

IDENTIFYING
CUSTOMER SERVICE FAILURES

Success in customer service means having the right product or service at the right place at the right time, in the right condition and at the right price. It also means that the customer service department has met its company marketing and profit goals. Failure in customer service is the absence of one or more of these conditions, but the actual severity of the failure has to be taken into account in planning. And it's sometimes overlooked.

Transportation Failures

For example, one customer who receives a shipment a day late may consider this an extreme customer service failure. The shipment consists of industrial air conditioning equipment, and the contractor has work crews on hand—riggers, plumbers and electricians—plus their equipment, waiting to make the installation, timed to mesh in with work to be performed in sequence by other trades. The cost of the day-late shipment in standby pay for crews and equipment runs quickly into the thousands. Similar, but even more costly, is the case where a kanban or "just in time" shipment is received half a day late and an entire production line or even a plant has to be shut down. These are indeed customer service failures!

By contrast, in another situation a customer's order was shipped not half a day late, not a whole day late, but *fourteen days* late—two full weeks—and not a peep was heard out of the customer. The reason? The order was only for routine stock replenishment and the customer always allowed a sufficient cushion of safety stock. But was it a failure? Today's manager would say it definitely was!

Another type of customer service failure may occur when a customer's instructions are not followed but no apparent harm results to the customer's operations. For example, the customer specifies shipment to be made by carrier "A" and the vendor uses carrier "B" but otherwise meets all delivery conditions specified by the customer. Is *this* a customer service failure? It most likely is, for either of two reasons: (1) the customer specified carrier "A" in order to create inbound-outbound load balance for the particular carrier; or (2) any unexplained digression from instructions, regardless of consequences, suggests inattention to the customer's needs.

The Under-Informed Customer

Then there are situations where the customer does not know all the facts, or makes a mistake in ordering that isn't corrected by the vendor. In the first type of situation, the customer complains that dry chemicals ordered in drums were actually shipped in multiwall bags, which added to handling costs at the manufacturing line. The customer isn't aware that no drums were available at the shipping point and the customer service rep OK'd the shipment in bags on the premise that having the chemical in the wrong package would be preferable to having no chemical at all. This would probably not change the customer's perception, even so. "Well, you could have told me!" is the most likely response, or "Well, why *didn't* you have drums?"

The second type of situation occurs when the customer makes a mistake in ordering that isn't corrected by the customer service representative. This could include specifying the wrong product, wrong ship-to-address, wrong quantity, wrong wanted dates, etc. The vendor is presumed to have some knowledge of customer needs (that's what salespeople sell) and failure to catch what customers consider obvious errors on purchase orders is a customer service failure whatever the law might say. The truth is that the law might come down on the buyer's side on the premise that sellers generally hold themselves out to be knowledgeable about their products and about customer requirements, and should be able to readily detect major errors or variation from past practice on the customer's part.

The problem is more complicated, however, when there is onsite equipment at customer locations and the operators try to fix it themselves before calling the vendor's service department. One manufacturer of automated storage and retrieval equipment used in warehouses says this is a common problem. The equipment operators take considerable pride in their knowledge of its workings and thus attempt to fix it themselves. When they don't succeed and decide to call the service department, considerable time has elapsed and the service people are under great pressure to get the equipment up and running immediately. Many times, the attempts at do-it-yourself repair have only created further damage and expense. Although the *severity* of the problem is due to the customer's failure to call immediately for service—and the do-it-yourself attempt may technically violate the warranty—the fact is that the customer service *failure* is likely to be perceived as the vendor's responsibility. The customer will sometimes say that the equipment shouldn't have failed in the first place, or that a call wasn't placed to the service department right away because they are so slow in responding, or it was after hours, or whatever. The underlying failure, however, is a communications problem in "educating" customers to do the right thing, so to speak.

Criteria for Judging Customer Service Failures

The examples cited illustrate the complexity of deciding what is and what is not a customer service failure, and the following criteria are suggested for judging whether or not a customer service failure actually has taken place.

• *Impact on the customer in measurable terms.* These are the situations where the customer is actually damaged, suffers significant financial loss or is seriously disadvantaged. When it's the clear result of error by the vendor, the customer often seeks some form of compensation, or may simply refuse to honor the vendor's invoice. There are also situations where the customer makes or contributes to the problem, but blames the vendor. Liability cases that arise out of this situation and get to court are often won by the customer on the premise that the vendor is expected to have superior knowledge.

• *Perception of the customer, no apparent harm otherwise.* In this type of situation, the customer asserts that there has been a customer service failure although there's been no apparent harm done. For example, not using the specified carrier, delivering in two shipments instead of one, shipping 10 packages of 24 instead of 20 packages of 12, and similar events. This category might also include situations where the customer claims service discrimination even though all terms of the order were met.

• *Shortfall of performance against standards.* Perhaps the most reliable of all indicators, assuming that performance standards have been developed that realistically meet customer requirements. In some instances, standards will not be met but customers will not complain. If this happens frequently, it may be that standards have been set higher than necessary and the company is spending more than it needs to in this area. By the same token, an excessive number of emergency-type orders may suggest that standards have not been set high enough to begin with.

• *Impact of failures on the vendor's profit-and-loss statement.* This will generally be reflected in one of two ways: actual reimbursement to the customer or extra expense involved in rectifying a customer service failure, on the one hand, or loss of valuable accounts with growth potential, on the other. In the first type of situation, the customer may not even be aware of the problem: a customer service rep's oversight, coupled with failure to supervise adequately, results in failure to load and ship heavy machinery moving by rail to shipside, and the vendor has to ship by air at staggering cost or risk loss of the entire overseas account. Of course if a case goes to court and the vendor loses, the effect on the P&L statement is measured in the amount of the award. The loss of an account may be somewhat more difficult to quantify, but one rule of thumb is simply to multiply the current year's revenues by five to determine the real loss.

• *"Near misses" or potential customer service failures that go unreported.* Very often these are related to chronic system deficiencies that don't get attention until after a serious failure has occurred. The most common is the absence of sufficient constraints or checkpoints to detect errors in order entry, either by order entry personnel or by customers in their original specifications. A customer orders 10,000 units of a custom manufactured item when only 1,000 are intended, and the order is confirmed in writing and entered as given. Neither do the various people handling the order catch the mistake, nor does the customer on receiving the written confirmation. Ten thousand units are custom manufactured to the customer's specifications and shipped to the customer. The customer refuses to accept the shipment even when confronted with the fact that the order was properly filled as given, saying only "You should have known I never order more than 1,000!"

The manufacturer now faces a tough decision of whether to sue the customer for the $120,000 at stake, or to simply "eat" the loss in order to retain the customer. In an attempt to get at the cause of the problem and eliminate recurrences, the manager talks to all the customer service personnel. The keypunch clerk says: "Gosh, I catch about half a dozen like that every week—you can't expect me to catch them *all!*" The clerk had never been instructed to report near-misses, and was not aware that a simple subroutine in the computer would avoid such problems altogether. Of course this is a management problem as well as a customer service failure, but the consequences on the firm's relationship with customers and on its own profit and loss are

Customer Service Failures

1. Customer's order for product or service is lost, misshipped, misrouted or delayed.
2. Products or services ordered by customer are not available.
3. Shipment or service person arrives late—or not at all.
4. Customer's special instructions were not followed.
5. Shipment is incomplete or service person lacks parts, tools, etc.
6. Shipment contains damage, infestation, etc.
7. Means of delivery incompatible with receiving facilities.
8. Unit load, packaging or labeling instructions not followed.
9. Errors of substitution or count on orders.
10. Errors on invoices.
11. Backorders not filled; orders lost.
12. Inquiries not answered promptly, courteously, correctly, completely, and sometimes not responded to at all.
13. Problems concerned with returned goods policies.
14. Failure to meet warranty terms and conditions.
15. Failure to issue credits or revised invoices promptly.
16. Failure to catch and correct obvious error by customer.
17. Misquotation of price by customer service rep.
18. Excessive delay or red tape in responding to complaints.
19. Failure to comply with legal requirements.
20. Placing customers on credit hold without justification.
21. Failure to respond in genuine emergency situations.
22. Failure of packaging at destination from high-stacking, humidity, etc.
23. Favoritism on the part of vendors toward certain customers.
24. Machine or product failure resulting in personal injury or product damage.
25. Failure to maintain regular communications with customers.
26. Failure to notify customers of price changes, discontinued items, etc.
27. Miscellaneous field service failures.
28. Matters of courtesy, attitude, general customer relations.

Figure 7-1. Some typical customer service failures.

potentially so severe that the presence of unreported near-misses or error potentials should be categorized as a major failure in serving customers—because they are constantly at risk—as well as a serious error in itself.

Figure 1, some typical customer service failures, is by no means complete, and it includes some situations—an out-of-stock condition, for example—which some managers might not consider failures, but which in the customer's view may be extremely serious.

It should also be pointed out that the customer service department is not necessarily committed to avoiding *all* customer service failures. In the first place, it's generally impossible to be 100% perfect in all respects at all times. More importantly, it's generally too expensive. The fact that customers consider an out-of-stock condition a customer service failure does not mean that the department should aim for 100% product availability in every product line. In actual practice, and for sound economic reasons, product availability may range from as high as 99% for some lines to as low as 30% for others. A company manufacturing auto aftermarket parts, for example, may set a 90% availability goal for non-critical parts like hubcaps, molding and trim, etc., and 97% for critical parts like starter assemblies, carburetor parts and the like.

Factors in Developing Failure Preventive Measures

The same general philosophy will apply to other types of customer service failures. Three major factors will determine how much attention is given to developing preventive measures:

1. *The actual dollars involved in a customer service failure or potential failure.* This is a good index of how much time and effort should be invested in avoiding such failures and/or mitigating their consequences once they occur.

2. *The size of the account—the importance of the customer.* Some companies categorize accounts by dollar volume and growth potential, so that it's automatically known by all con-

cerned where extra care has to be given in order to avoid *all* customer service failures if possible.

3. *The social or public implications of a failure.* These are generally associated with consumer products: pharmaceuticals, food, health and beauty aids, toys, etc. A standard practice in many firms in this category is to supplement rigid lot control procedures with an in-place recall program so that if a failure does occur involving public safety or health the actual severity of the problem can be mitigated by a swift, effective recall program and appropriate public communications on the subject. The McNeill Laboratories handling of the Tylenol recall in 1982 is a superb example of a well-managed recall program under extremely adverse conditions. The quick manner in which the product recaptured both public confidence and share of market attest to the value of the substantial investment made by McNeill in supporting both the logistics and the public relations aspects of the recall.

Decision Rules and Contingency Planning

Clearly the majority of customer service failures will be far less spectacular than the Tylenol case, but this does not diminish the importance of laying out the whole problem of customer service failures *before the fact* and developing appropriate controls and contingency plans. Decision rules are an important part of this preparation: recognizing, for example, that when a certain type of situation exists certain specified actions are to be taken immediately.

For example, a company supplying the power transmission industry receives an emergency order for anti-vibration components immediately following an ice storm. The item ordered is not available in stock; but there are 200 units that have been packed for shipment to another customer on a routine, non-emergency order. Without hesitation, the customer service rep instructs the warehouse to "rob" the routine order of the necessary number of units—or take the entire order if necessary—and ship immediately to the utility in the emergency situation. The rep does this because he/she has a decision rule covering exactly that type of situation, and approval of both management and other customers was obtained long before.

Another example concerns a manufacturer of telephone equipment. As the customer service manager puts it: "The customer service rep knows automatically that if a hospital switchboard goes down and can't be fixed or replaced locally, that rep has the authority to charter the company plane and fly the switchboard there."

There are of course customer service failures that can occur due to computer-down situations—perhaps the most pervasive—weather, illness, strikes, etc., and these are an integral part of contingency planning. It's implicit that in the more severe situations management and other departments have to participate in such planning.

Steps to Contingency Planning

Contingency planning as a management function is a subject for a book in itself. To summarize its application to customer service, the procedures are not unlike PERT (Performance Evaluation and Review Technique) and CPM (Critical Path Method) approaches. There are three major steps:

1. *Define the principal customer service failure contingencies.* These will usually be "worst-case" situations resulting from a strike, explosion or other catastrophic occurrence, plus the more conventional computer breakdown. As mentioned, these can be rated by dollars, account size, or social or public consequences. A brainstorming session may help in identifying such situations, asking "what if" questions about a variety of situations. The brainstorming may bring to light situations that normally aren't considered: "What if we were to accidentally put Sears Roebuck on credit hold?" "What if we were to make a mistake and ship birth control pills to a nunnery?" (Both events actually occurred, and the consequences were severe enough that

Departmental Planning

1. Communications to employees re strike situation and contingency plan.
2. Production plans, available inventory, alternate shipping points, etc.
3. Company policies on referring customers to other sources, including competitors.
4. Procedures for order processing and release, if different.
5. Procedures for order assembly, small parts, samples, etc.
6. Procedures for emergency orders vs. stock replenishment (e.g., customer line-down situations, health care life-threatening situations).
7. Policies on allocation, levels of service.
8. Decision rules for various contingencies.
9. Security arrangements for employees.

Customer Communications

1. Advance notification of possibility of a strike.
2. Periodic reports on status and progress of negotiations.
3. Potential impact of strike on overall operations.
4. Potential impact of strike on lead times and ability to deliver.
5. Suggestions for inventory buildup prior to strike.
6. Potential restrictions on order sizes.
7. Recommended substitutions; alternative sources if approved.
8. Possible changes in method of shipment or shipping location.
9. Possible restrictions on pickups by customers in their own equipment.

Communications to Vendors

1. Arrangements for inbound deliveries of resale goods, parts, samples, etc.
2. Possible need to ship to different company location.
3. Possible need to ship to different customer location.
4. Possible need to use alternative mode of transportation.

Transportation

1. Insuring that drivers will cross picket lines.
2. Providing carriers specific instructions for access.
3. Security arrangements as needed.
4. Personnel for loading and unloading.
5. Possible restrictions on use of company fleet.
6. Standby or alternate carriers.

Figure 7-2. Contingency planning for a possible strike situation might include these actions tied to milestones or specific trigger points.

1. Type of Contingency

Major computer failure affecting order processing, inventory adjustments, warehouse releases and similar customer service activities.

2. Trigger Point

User or operator notifies the customer service manager as soon as it becomes evident that substantial downtime may be involved before system is operative again.

3. Action to be Taken

1. Order Entry and Inventory Management meet to assess problem.

2. Determine short term and/or long term downtime (short term is system up same day).

3. In all cases:
   a. Alert shipping department.
   b. Rush orders must be entered immediately: order entry refers to inventory management; database backup report used to determine inventory with manual assignment; inventory management calls warehouse and/or enters order by Telex or TWX; warehouse cuts bill of lading.

4. Implement overrides to eliminate potential duplication when system comes back up.

5. Downtime for short period:
   a. Retrieve orders.
   b. Review for customer pickups and emergency orders.
   c. Manually process customer pickups and emergency orders.

6. Downtime for long period:
   a. Retrieve orders and process on manual system, including preparation of shipping documents.
   b. Phone orders to remote warehouse.

7. Continue to enter orders into front end processing system.

8. Check into borrowing equipment.

Figure 7-3. Condensed outline of a contingency plan outline covering major computer failure.

the managers involved decided to take measures to avoid recurrences!)

2. *Identify symptoms of potential failures—"trigger points."* This is largely self-explanatory. When a labor contract has only several months to run and there is talk of a strike, this may be the trigger point for starting to put a contingency plan into effect. Or, when a product has been backordered for 60 days and the condition appears likely to persist, this may be defined as the trigger point for a contingency plan for allocating available supplies among customers in an equitable fashion. For potential errors in placing important customers on credit hold, the trigger point could be the receipt of the information—account delinquency or whatever—that usually triggers the credit hold. Except that in the case of an "A" customer, the credit hold would be automatically reviewed by sales management before going into effect. The important point in identifying the symptom or trigger point is that it work as an "early warning system," i.e., allow sufficient lead time to take countermeasures or remedial action to avoid or minimize the effect of the failure.

3. *Set "milestones" defining what action to take and when to take it.* When there is a potential strike situation, for example, a decision must be made at which point in or prior to the negotiations to notify customers of the possibility of the strike. This is a milestone in the contingency plan which says, in effect, "At such-and-such a point, we will have taken such-and-such an action." Further milestones would define the point at which to urge customers to build inventories, to make arrangements for alternate shipping points, new ordering procedures, allocation programs, etc. Figure 2 includes a list of certain actions that would be taken in the face of a possible strike, and these would be tied to specific points or milestones in the unfolding of events associated with the possible strike.

8

CUSTOMER SERVICE AS PROFIT CENTER

What may well be the most important step the customer service manager can take in organizing the customer service department and planning its activities is the moment he or she decides: "I am going to make this department into a moneymaker, and I am going to make every member of this department—and eventually the whole company—as customer-oriented and *profit-conscious* as I am!"

It's a tall order, but an important step. It's a commitment the manager must make if customer service is to succeed in its mission. Historically, very few customer service departments have ever been treated as profit centers. This is equally true of the distribution departments of which they often form a part.

The typical customer service department has been a "reactive" entity with no role in marketing until after a sale has actually been made. Like distribution, customer service was triggered by the sale and was treated strictly as a "cost adding" function and nothing else. Customer service standards and policies were often set by individuals with no knowledge of logistical costs of meeting those standards and carrying out those policies. Very often, these costs have been far higher than necessary because of failure to include distribution and customer service personnel in overall standard and policy development.

The "Magic Moneymaker Formula"

The "magic moneymaker formula" is nothing more than the realization that customer service begins before the sale. A major railroad—the Missouri Pacific—developed a series of booklets instructing customers and potential customers how to make the best use of its services. The booklet covered procedures for ordering equipment, interpreting freight bills, tying into the railroad's computer system, outsize shipments, shipment location and tracing, and other procedures. This type of "pre-education" increases the probability that the customer will make better use of the service and get more satisfaction from it, thus coming back for repeat business in the future. A favorable side effect is the fact that field sales people can do more selling and less "educating" in their contacts with customers, and in general a reduction in telephone inquiries will give the company's customer service personnel more time to devote to the more complex situations requiring individual attention.

In another example, a company made a study of its freight movements nationwide and determined that if 90% of the customers—and of course the firm's sales department—could be persuaded to participate, a consolidation program would save substantial sums of money without degrading customer service in any respect. When the program was finally put through, the director of distribution was able to record a year-end cost saving of over one million dollars, the equivalent of the profit on $20 million in sales. Additionally, the program imposed certain order deadlines and lead times on customers, which in turn enabled planning and balancing the warehouse and shipping department workload for maximum productivity.

The first step in applying the "magic formula" is to get the customer service department involved in the planning process, as discussed earlier: to identify potential profit contributions of this and other types which can be realized, in many instances, mainly by changing the posture of the customer service department from "reactive" to "proactive." Gaining the acceptance and cooperation of other departments may require some preliminary public relations activity; appropriate strategies are discussed in Chapter 16 under "Gaining Acceptance for Proposals."

How High Selling Costs Favor the Customer Service Department

Field selling costs are increasing every year, and thus management is placing great pressure on field sales forces to become more productive in terms of sales calls made and total sales volume obtained.

The American Management Associations reports that actual selling costs are five times customer service costs on a per-customer basis. A major reason for this, of course, is that most customer service functions are performed at a central (or regional) location by hourly or non-exempt personnel in the medium-to-low classifications, whereas field sales people generate high expenses and are typically among the most highly paid individuals in the firm. However, this disparity can be turned to good advantage.

Clearly, one of the best ways to make field salespeople more productive is to relieve them of clerical-type duties associated with taking orders, responding to inquiries and handling routine complaints or claims. Given appropriate support systems (information and communications systems, for example) the customer service department can take over these functions and perform them more efficiently (and in some cases better) than the salesperson in the field who usually has to involve the customer service department in such matters when they do come to him or her. Relieving the sales force of such chores releases time which can be used more productively in direct, face-to-face selling—either to make more calls, or to spend more time on existing accounts in order to generate greater volume. It's also true that a salesperson who is greeted with a complaint when making a call isn't going to accomplish much in the way of selling on that particular call, whereas if the customer had been able to communicate the complaint to the customer service department when the problem arose, it might well have been resolved by the time the salesperson called. Certainly the climate would be more conducive to selling!

Currently, industrial selling costs are calculated at $200 per sales call, with 4.3 calls typically required to close a sale—or a cost of close to $900 per actual sales transaction. Given costs of this order, few companies can afford to concentrate solely on "getting" customers, i.e., making sales. More than ever before, they must place comparable emphasis on "keeping" customers through effective customer service.

Some Profitable Customer-Keeping Strategies

• *Development of customer buying profiles.* Although this may already be performed by the sales or marketing department, the customer service department profile will differ in some important respects. In addition to the conventional ship-to, bill-to and other data carried on purchase orders, the profile will show data on previous orders, as to size, items ordered, special pricing, usual ship-to points and other data. The computer may be programmed to flag significant deviations from past ordering practice and avoid potential costly mistakes. The profile will also include some information about customer personnel to contact, alternative persons, and may even include a few "prompts" about customer personnel's personal interests in case some personal conversation is in order. (It should be noted that personal conversation is completely acceptable if it contributes to the sale or helps overcome a difficult situation.) A key element of the program concerns logistics: customer preferences in palletizing, shrink wrap, banding, etc.; loading facilities at customer sites, width of alleys, preferred carriers, receiving hours, etc.

Besides helping avoid errors and speeding up the actual order transaction, these profiles have another extremely important benefit; they give customer service reps time for telemarketing or sales-related activities like order upgrading. For example, a major air express firm profiles logistical data about its customers in order to dispatch the appropriate equipment, be there at the right time, and ask for the right people. Having this information already available gives the agent time to ask questions like this: "Would you like our driver to stop by every day at a certain time and save yourself the trouble of phoning?" or "Did you know we have a special palletload rate between X and Y?" In some industries, the customer profile will include such data as "Will accept substitutions (partial shipment, backorders, etc.) up to 'X' percent of order," or specific instructions to contact the customer in designated situations.

• *Development of substitutability programs.* Particularly important where commodity- or generic-type items are involved which can be readily procured from other sources. Substitutability programs can range from relatively simple substitutions (size, color, price range) to complex substitutions of components meeting similar military or other specifications, substitution of plastic for metal, etc. Substitutability programs are critical in industries like electronics where buyers will automatically switch sources if a wanted item is not available and no substitute is offered. For a more detailed discussion of this subject, see chapter 21.

• *Assignment of reps (or teams of reps) by account.* This builds a personal relationship and sense of belonging on the customer's part, while reps develop a better understanding of customer needs and service expectations. One customer service manager reported that assignment of reps by accounts where they had previously been on a "random" basis actually had a measurable effect in reduction of customer abuses of the system in the forms of groundless claims for non-delivery, excessive order status inquiries—that matter of confidence again!—and other problems.

• *Development of special routines or procedures for new accounts.* Making the new customer feel welcome, and acquainting him or her with internal procedures, returns policies, lead and cutoff times, pool shipping arrangements, terms of sale, invoicing, etc.—all of these are vital parts of customer-keeping. It's particularly important to remember that the new customer is not familiar with your policies and procedures, and failure of reps to recognize him or her as a new customer is apt to create a difficult climate of alienation at the very outset of the relationship, and an image of indifference that may be difficult to overcome.

• *Development of special procedures for key accounts.* Accounts can be classified as "a," "b," "c," "d," etc., so that customer service reps know immediately what special services are or are not permitted. For example: "a" accounts are allowed prepaid air freight shipments and purchases below minimum order size without penalty or extra charge; "a" and "b" accounts are permitted returns on verbal authorization by the rep; "c" accounts require written approval from regional sales manager, etc. Other decision rules may be established as necessary for special handling of orders, complaints, requests to expedite, etc.

• *Development of systems to keep customers informed of price changes, potential work stoppages, specials.* Establish your concern and interest in customers and they will repay you with loyalty.

• *Establishment of automatic refund policies for claims or complaints below a certain dollar level.* The vast majority of small claims are legitimate, and in any event it is usually cheaper to allow them without investigation than it is to investigate and run the risk of alienating a large number of customers with legitimate complaints. It also takes a considerable amount of pressure off your customer service reps when they are permitted to make such adjustments.

• *Set standards that are relevant.* This means relevant to customers' needs, of course, but it also means relevant to your firm's own profit objectives and the needs of the marketplace. Remember the old saying, "In the land of the blind, the man with one eye is king." If the competition is offering two-week service, for example, you can offer 8- or 10-day service and "be king." To offer two- or three-day service would be too much; in fact it might make customers suspicious that you're making them pay for the extra service in some hidden way, like cheapening the product. Remember, too, that there may be regional differences in the service levels customers demand. In the wholesale drug business, for example, the standard for Los Angeles is same-day delivery of orders, while elsewhere in the country it may range from next-day delivery to once-a-week delivery. Clearly, a company could go broke if it imposed the Los Angeles standard nationwide! Also, the higher your levels of customer service, the more your customers will get in the habit of taking advantage of them—buying hand-to-mouth, for example—and in effect causing you to carry their inventory for them. As one customer service manager put it, "We were so good to our customers they were practically buying off the tailgate of our truck!"

• *Make your system reliable.* Contrary to common belief, most of your customers are far more concerned with reliable service than they are with fast service as such. One major firm successfully persuaded its customers to accept longer lead times in exchange for a higher degree of complete orders and fewer stockouts or backorders. With a few added days' time they could level their customer service and warehouse workload, cut costs significantly, and, where necessary, ship to customers from alternate locations—and still come out ahead.

• *Make your people credible.* Support them with good information systems, train and motivate them to really care about helping customers, create good working conditions for them and make sure that *the system supports them*— that the promises they make are kept (this also implies that you prevent them from making promises that *can't* be kept). Do not require your people to lie, and do not permit them, in talking with customers, to blame other departments or outside suppliers or, of course, the computer. Credibility is the heart of profit-contributing customer service: customers who trust you tend to buy more from you and less from others, and you're in an excellent position to become their No. 1 or even sole source supplier. Also, when customers know you square with them and deliver on your promises they're much more willing to go along with you when you do have emergencies and service failures. As an example, some companies have found that improving their internal order-status reporting systems has a directly measurable result. A company that improved its "early warning" system and was able to report potential delays and production problems to customers earlier than in the past measured a 25% decline in order status calls from customers, including a high volume of calls which had been unnecessary but were occasioned by the customers' lack of confidence in the system. This decline in inbound calls makes reps more productive and in effect is a direct contribution to the bottom line. (It's worth observing that when reps can move from routine and repetitive activities to non-routine activities that only they can perform, then there's an automatic improvement in productivity.)

• *Make it understood that courtesy is as much a part of the job as getting to work on time.* It's surprising how many companies ignore this point by rewarding surly reps who are always on time, and ignoring those who are occasionally late but otherwise are superior in both customer relations and account management. In impressing employees with the importance of courtesy, set standards for all who come in contact with customers *and* with others inside the firm. This is an important point. Even though personnel may be able to distinguish between outside and inside calls, there is no justification for answering an inside call

---

26 Ways You Can Make Customer Service Go Straight to the Bottom Line

1. Consolidate orders and freight.	14. Publish customer service policies.
2. Balance inbound phone calls.	15. Build departmental credibility.
3. Reduce call length 1 second.	16. Cut unwanted acknowledgments.
4. Reduce/eliminate busy signals.	17. Increase order handling capacity.
5. Upgrade orders, cross-sell.	18. Qualify inquiries and leads.
6. Computerize specs and pricing.	19. Convert inquiries to sales.
7. Rationalize large/small orders.	20. Develop complaint strategy.
8. Develop substitution programs.	21. Monitor blanket purchase orders.
9. Telemarket marginal accounts.	22. Identify key error sources.
10. Streamline returns system.	23. Automate data retrieval.
11. Improve order fill rate.	24. Coordinate CS and logistics.
12. Telemarket seconds.	25. Publish "contact" directory.
13. Telemarket refused shipments.	26. Enforce economic standards.

Figure 8-1

with a grunt or "yeah" or other display of discourtesy. It is essential to monitor actual performance on the phone as well as in personal contacts. Retrain where indicated, but if people cannot or will not improve, then terminate them the same way you would terminate any employee for substandard performance of whatever type.

• *Write decision rules for the most common exceptions, complaints or problem situations.* This is simply to enable your customer service reps to respond in a uniform way to similar situations, and also to be spared the necessity of "reinventing the wheel" or requiring you to re-decide an issue you've already decided in the past. Your people, your department and yourself all become more productive when you can minimize the amount of repetitive decision-making you have to engage in.

• *Use form letters, cards and checklists where appropriate.* This is often part of the decision-rule process, assuring a response that is consistent with policy and has uniform language. It also saves money, and forms and form letters need not be sloppy or unattractive. But respond fast; otherwise the impersonal nature of a form reply may be offensive. And don't try to stretch form letters to situations where a personal reply—by letter or phone—is called for.

9

PRODUCTIVITY AND CAPACITY UTILIZATION

Productivity is a relatively new word to distribution managers and customer service managers alike. The landmark National Council of Physical Distribution Management study* on productivity, issued in 1978, and updated in 1983, reflects the importance this subject is achieving in management circles. The work of consultant Herbert W. Davis in establishing a cost database** by industry group now makes it possible for a company to measure its distribution and customer service costs against comparable averages for its industry group. These measures include costs per hundredweight, costs per order, costs as a percentage of sales and a number of other useful ratios.

Conflict with Service

But concern with productivity can also lead managers into direct conflict with customer service standards. In one company (and probably others), the customer service manager was found

---

* *Measuring and Improving Productivity in Physical Distribution,* National Council of Physical Distribution Management, Chicago, IL

** For information, contact Herbert W. Davis and Company, 111 Charlotte Place, Englewood Cliffs, NJ 07632. (201) 871-1760.

to be "stockpiling" orders for a week and longer in order to "balance the workload" and avoid the loss in productivity that would result from working overtime or hiring additional personnel. Additionally, the manager was concerned with the possibility of future lulls in orders which would also reflect a decrease in productivity.

Distribution managers are well aware of these conflicts. The customer service department may want to ship every order the day it's received. The shipping department may want to hold all orders except genuine emergencies for consolidation. The end result may be a compromise in which consolidations are scheduled for certain days and customers are urged to place their orders in time to meet the deadlines established for consolidations. But this type of conflict underlines the importance of not confusing measures of efficiency or productivity with measures of customer service effectiveness. Customer service effectiveness is measured in terms of the extent to which the department has accomplished its mission and met its customer service standards within the budget established. Productivity is a measure of the units of work produced against the labor required to produce them without any reference to customer service as such.

It should also be observed that productivity measures do not need to be restricted to personnel. They can be applied to anything representing an out-of-pocket cost or investment on the part of the company. In the case history described on page 94, the Missouri Pacific Railroad made a substantial investment in advertising space and educational booklets for its customers; the return on that investment can be measured in a number of different ways, including reduction in inquiries and the associated costs, fewer complaints, fewer customer-caused failures and so forth. This is a measure of the productivity of the investment vs. a comparable investment in people to do the educational job.

Many managements insist that customer service is an "intangible," or, as one financial vice president put it, "We know customer service is important but you can't quantify it." This is just not so. The value of customer service improvements can be quantified, and increases in actual productivity can be quantified.

As one example, a firm which takes routine orders from field salespeople only via recorder will immediately increase productivity of its customer service reps by freeing them up to solve problems and handle other higher-level jobs. One firm discovered to its surprise that its new on-line system was actually less productive than its old off-line system because order-takers had to spend more time on the phone and thus tied up more lines for longer, and were unavailable for other, non-order calls. The point is that there are well-established management science and market research techniques which can be used to measure customer service effectiveness, efficiency, productivity and return on investment just as they can be—and are being—applied to physical distribution, inventory investment, and the overall operations of the company. The customer service manager should make it his or her special business to learn about these measures and make sure that management is aware of them. And will see that they're applied.

Definitions

Productivity is a measure of output against input. A typical measure of productivity might be: "Five orders processed per hour," or an output of five orders vs. an input of one hour's labor. All other things being equal, i.e., size and difficulty of orders, a rep processing six orders an hour would be 20% more productive than a rep processing five orders per hour. Productivity may also be measured in terms of money input vs. results output: "$12 per hundredweight" inventory, warehousing and delivery costs.

Capacity utilization is a measure of productivity which can be applied to people, machines and buildings. Few people work at 100% capacity, simply because that would mean being productive a full 100% of the time while on the job. In most inside occupations people are actually engaged in measurable work 70% to 80% of the time. In field service, that percentage may drop as low as 50%. Similar measures apply to machines and buildings. A truck trailer with 40,000 lbs. capacity that is loaded to 30,000 lbs. is operating at 75% of capacity. The reason that truckers sometimes split up extremely light and bulky shipments is that they try to use their full *weight* capacity as well as their *cube* capacity on any given trip. Most warehouses operate, on the average, at about 70% of capacity because it may not be possible to restock a given slot or bay until it is entirely emptied of its current stock, which is being drawn out a palletload at a time. In the customer service department, capacity utilization refers to the (largely theoretical) output the department might achieve if it could operate on a mainly planned, uninterrupted basis rather than in its typical fashion of having to react to more or less randomized, and frequently emergency or crisis-type, demands on it.

Workload planning is the means employed to maximize capacity utilization of personnel and equipment. In general, workload planning implies arranging the flow of work so that employees won't be overloaded one minute, idle the next, and having to work overtime the next because of last-minute orders. Workload planning also implies changing working procedures and sometimes policies. A firm that extends lead times may be doing so in order to accumulate more small orders and ship them at a lower cost and often with faster delivery. Another firm may assemble small orders in the morning and large ones in the afternoon, using the same people but two different systems of order assembly for greater efficiency. A department may schedule its outbound calls for slack periods during the day in order to get better utilization of telephone equipment and not have lines tied up during the busy part of the day when customers are trying to call orders in. Organizing the department into account teams may be another approach to workload planning. While workload planning may involve specific improvements in procedure its main concern is with the distribution of work itself.

Overcoming the Crisis Atmosphere

A common complaint among customer service managers is that they are so busy putting out fires that they never have time to plan and organize an effective customer service operation. This is seen as a major roadblock to customer service productivity *and* effectiveness, and it certainly is. But this doesn't mean that the problem is insurmountable. As discussed in chapter 5 dealing with the customer service cycle, the reactive nature of many customer service departments combined with the (apparently) randomized nature of demands on the department are major elements in the "crisis atmosphere."

But the fact is that many of these randomized demands are not random at all but recurring events which can be identified by time and frequency of occurrence, as well as by type and reason or accountability. It's no secret in most companies that the bulk of telephone calls comes between 10 a.m. and 3 p.m., or that orders from the field tend to bunch in the last 15 days of the month as salespeople strive to get orders written and shipped so they will get their commissions earlier. And of course it's relatively easy to record these events with considerable precision, thus enabling the development of an organized approach to categorizing problems and developing meaningful priorities.

Figure 1 reproduces a form which was developed by the customer service department of a chemical company to help the manager apply just such an organized approach. It is a format for capturing information about the types, frequency and sources of that particular company's most common "fires" or customer service crises. Since the chart applies to a particular company, it is recommended that readers adapt it for use in their own situations.

The chart enables the manager to tally the principal customer service problems that the department has to deal with, showing both the frequency and the accountability for each type of problem. Using the chart over a period of time, the manager is able to get a good idea of what is happening, how often it is happening, and where the principal problems are originating. After six months or so in use, the chart will make it quickly evident that most so-called "exceptions" are not exceptions at all, but repetitive occurrences which can be tabulated and quantified, and most important of all, tracked down to their particular source.

Exceptions	Loc. A	Loc. B
A. Marketing		
1. Administrative error		
2. Price availability delay		
3. OSHA date not available		
4. Oversold maximum or forecast		
5. Allotment delay		
6. Unreasonable sales request		
7. Import material not available		
8. Credit approval delay		
9. Altered production schedule		
10. (Other) _____		
Total _____		
B. Customer Service		
1. Administrative error		
2. Order transmission delay		
3. Tank cars not available		
4. Truck carrier failed to pick up		
5. Commercial warehouse error		
6. Customer pickup not ready (comm. whse.)		
7. Lot assignment problem		
8. Carrier performance at destination		
9. Customer failed to pick up		
10. Shipping classification not available		
11. Hazardous info not available		
12. (Other) _____		
Total _____		

The Importance of Accountability

An important feature of the chart illustrated in figure 1 is the manner in which accountability can be established. The manager should prioritize the major problems that have been identified

	Loc. A	Loc. B

C. Shipping Point

1. Administrative error
2. Tank truck not available
3. Tank truck delivery late (over 4 hrs.)
4. Tank truck (hot shipment) late (over 2 hrs.)
5. Tank car not loaded on time
6. Tank car not ready for loading
7. Tank car not on spot
8. Railroad scheduling problems
9. Product not re-packaged in time to ship
10. Material not drummed
11. Drumming conflict delay
12. Delay—receipt of inventory
13. Customer pickup not ready/loaded in time
14. Couldn't locate packaged goods inventory
15. Matls. handling/loading eqpt. inoperable
16. Work load too heavy to handle
17 (Other) _____

Total _____

D. Manufacturing

1. Material not available from production
   A. Process equipment malfunction
   B. Process quality problems
   C. On-site scheduling conflict
2. Material not available from research
3. Material not available from foreign vendor
4. Material not approved in time by Q.A.
5. (Other) _____

Total _____

Figure 9-1

through use of the chart, in terms of frequency, cost impacts, damage to customer relations and other relevant criteria. The point is not to establish blame as such, but to demonstrate that many of the problems can in fact be avoided via simple changes in procedures.

For example, if shipments are being held up due to a lack of packaging materials, improved coordination of usage between the shipping and purchasing departments may help avoid the problem. Or perhaps the shipping department could be put in charge of its own packaging purchases, just as some customer service departments are placed directly in charge of purchases of replacement parts which are purchased from outside vendors and sold directly to customers. The cost of increasing packaging inventories by small increments would be very little in terms of the cost penalties of late shipments, emergency shipments and overall loss of customer confidence.

One company encountered a situation where several hundred thousands of dollars of fabric shipments were delayed over a week because the supply of "cotton content" labels required by law—each label less than half an inch in diameter and costing less than a penny—was completely exhausted, and shipments had to be delayed until more labels could be procured. The incremental cost of an added thousand of the labels included in the original order would have been about $7.50. Determining accountability for the shortage enabled improving the system of ordering so that it would be unlikely to ever happen again.

A manufacturer of farm equipment was handling an excessive number of emergency shipments for "machine down" situations and at the same time was hearing a growing number of complaints from farmers about the poor quality of its equipment. By analyzing the emergency shipments in the manner described earlier, the customer service manager discovered that dealers did not have reliable parts usage and therefore did not know which parts to stock, and in what depth. Once the source of the problem was identified, a relatively inexpensive inventory management package was made available and in short order emergency shipments—and the crisis atmosphere accompanying them—were cut in half. Equally important, customers who had been blaming the equipment rather than the parts system had their confidence restored and the firm's image improved significantly.

Pareto's Law in Customer Service

In analyzing any business operation it quickly becomes evident that 20% of the customers provide 80% of the revenue, or 10% of your customers generate 90% of your problems, and so forth. This enables you to concentrate your customer service improvement efforts where they will do the most good. The 80-20 version of the ratio, which is the most common, is called Pareto's Law after the Italian economist who first postulated it.

Pareto's Law is a useful reminder that your solutions to customer service problems don't have to apply 100% across the board, nor do your policies have to be acceptable to 100% of your customers. If you can develop solutions and policies that will work for the 80% of your customers who give you only 20% of your business, you will find plenty of time left over to deal one-on-one with the important 20% who give you 80%.

Identifying Corporate Policies That Defeat Customer Service Productivity

These are of two main types: (1) policies that restrict investment in the customer service function itself—for training, competitive salaries, state-of-the-art communications and information systems, improvements to the working environment; and (2) policies that defeat customer service logistics. Changing the first type of policy is a slow, long-term process that is discussed later in this book. The second type of policy is often more difficult to deal with because it is often intertwined with virtually everything the company does.

Most companies operate on a system of rewards and penalties in which department heads are rewarded for reaching certain levels of productivity, and penalized when they don't. The problem is that the goals of one department are often in direct conflict with the goals of another; and customer service is usually the loser, both as a department and as a company mission. The conflict between shipping and customer service described at the opening of this chapter is the direct result of such a reward-and-penalty system: customer service is rewarded for meeting certain standards, and shipping is rewarded for holding transportation costs down. If customer service achieves its reward levels, then shipping can't; if shipping does, then customer service can't.

A common area of conflict is between customer service and production. Production is rewarded for achieving minimum unit costs, but in achieving them it needs to mount long production runs which in turn make it impossible to provide fast turnaround on customer orders for items that are already on backorder. Production schedulers are typically rewarded on the basis of their "hit" rate—and penalized if they make changes once a schedule has been set. When customer service seeks to change schedules in response to customer requests, production schedulers tend to resist such changes because they know they'll be penalized if they do. The warehouse similarly resists change orders on work that's already in the stream because they're measured strictly on tons per man hour or some similar numeric yardstick. As mentioned previously, traffic and shipping personnel are rewarded for holding transportation costs down, and this often means accumulating orders until there is sufficient weight to earn volume rates. This of course frequently conflicts with customer service goals to ship all orders within a particular time frame like 24 or 48 hours. Some traffic departments have approached the problem by charging back the cost of all emergency or non-consolidation shipments to the department making the request, but this only transfers the cost rather than resolving the underlying conflict.

These are examples of the types of conflicts that arise when management establishes reward-and-penalty policies that tend to subordinate customer service goals to productivity standards of departments other than customer service itself. Because these conflicts exist, the number of exceptions or customer service problems requiring attention tends to increase, and this in turn defeats customer service department productivity.

There is another class of management policies which can be

equally detrimental to customer service productivity. The most common, mentioned earlier, is the policy of paying salespeople's commissions at month end. In most companies, the result of this policy—as opposed to one with different cutoffs for different groups of salespeople, spaced evenly throughout the period—is that some 80% of the orders tend to hit the customer service department after the 15th of the month. This imbalance is compounded by another policy which says that commissions shall be paid only after shipment has been actually made. So, in addition to being loaded down with orders, the customer service department is also loaded down with phone calls from salespeople trying to insure that their orders will go out on time and their commissions included in the check for this month instead of next.

The practice of some companies of launching major promotional campaigns without consulting or advising the customer service department can also wreak havoc with productivity there. While it's essential to be flexible in customer service, productivity is gained through planning—and ad campaigns or promotions that generate a lot of new sales have to be anticipated just like any seasonal or other surge of business. The customer service manager who is not now being advised of promotions and campaigns should make it a point to find out about them well in advance and to be included in the planning sessions. It's not unusual for a firm's marketing department to launch a major promotion for a product that's already in short supply, or to set up a complex promotional "deal" without advising customer service of the details so that reps can be properly instructed and supplied with scripts or scenarios if necessary.

Similarly, if customer service standards for order processing and release are set independently of the customer service department (as they sometimes are) they may very well decrease the department's productivity without necessarily improving customer service. Lead times which are promised and then can't be met simply generate more phone calls and inquiries to answer, and more expedites and emergency shipments to take care of.

The true story related in chapter 5 of a company president who decided to set a ship-same-day policy to placate irate customers who were complaining directly to him illustrates the problem of unreferenced decisions generally. One company's management decided to institute, on very short notice, a strict new credit policy at the very same time the marketing department was mounting a major promotional effort. The results of both hit the customer service department simultaneously, and the combined impact on productivity was aggravated by the effects of the extreme stress on customer service reps who had to deal with both situations simultaneously. Given time and resources, the customer service department is an excellent channel for introducing new policies to customers—even unpleasant policies. And the more the department can plan and systematize and automate its routine tasks at good levels of productivity, the more time it has to devote to the tasks that *can't* be routinized or automated but require the experience and excellent people-to-people skills and relationships that develop between the department and the company's customers.

Pinpointing Bottlenecks in Order Fulfillment

Although many stages of the customer order cycle are handled by the computer either on-line or off-line, a useful measure of productivity is to track orders over a period of time to determine how long it takes them to move through the various stages of receiving an order and getting it to the customer, including all the associated informational and financial transactions.

From a planning point of view it's more meaningful to measure time from the *origination* of the order rather than from the time it is actually received at the order entry point. This is particularly true when orders are mailed, less important when orders are received by phone, telex or direct computer-to-computer. However, some allowance should be made for slippage between the time the end user writes a requisition (when this is the case) and a formal purchase order is issued. In some organizations, particularly public bodies, this may take as long as several months. One company which receives a high proportion of its orders by mail builds in a standard inbound transit time for all such orders, based on point of mailing. The standard time allowance for orders from the Pacific Coast states will be "X" days, Mountain states, "Y" days, North Central "Z" days and so forth. Then, actual measurements are taken from the time of receipt when the order is actually logged in.

The next step is to log each order in and out for each step as it is performed, and to be sure to include the waiting time between one element and another in the measurement. For example, the warehouse order assembly measurement would begin from the time the order is actually received at the warehouse and terminate only when the completed order is delivered to the next stage; to measure from the time the actual order assembly starts being physically perfomed would understate the actual time lapse by so much as to make the numbers meaningless.

Finally, it is just as important to measure what happens *after* order processing and assembly: how long it takes for the order to be picked up and delivered to the customer, plus any post-delivery transactions including returns and adjustments, payment of the invoice, etc. Readers may not wish to measure in this great detail, but at the very least they should measure the total order cycle from the time the order is received until it actually leaves the shipping dock. For a better appreciation of how customers perceive service, however, the total cycle should be studied including delivery and post-delivery transactions of the type mentioned.

Figure 2 is a form for capturing this type of data covering 32 discrete elements of the total order cycle. Readers should of course adapt it to their individual situations and include only the relevant order cycle elements and time frames. At the end of the sampling period, any particular bottlenecks or delays in the order cycle should be immediately evident. For example, if there is an unusually large number tallied in the "2-3 days" column for the order cycle element "order editing," this suggests immediately a bottleneck at this point which may in turn be traceable to a need for more educating of field salespeople in how to format orders. One company pinpointed a bottleneck in just this way; by going

Order Cycle Element or Activity	0-4 Hours	4-8 Hours	8-12 Hours	1-2 Days	2-3 Days	3+ Days
End user requisition						
Formal purchase order issued						
Order transmitted to vendor						
Order received, sorted, logged						
Sales management review						
Credit check, approval						
Holding for cause, query						
Order editing						
Production Plan (non-stock)						
Traffic/routing/pickup plan						
Order set preparation/invoice						
Exceptions reports-backorders						
Warehouse order assembly						
Change orders						
Unitization, staging for shpt.						
Pickup/shipment/transit						
Customer receiving						
Exceptions, claims reported						
End user receives order						
Returns authorized						
Adjustments, credits issued						
End user approves invoice						
Accounts payable issues check						
Check is mailed to vendor						
Check received, posted, banked						
Customer deductions researched						
Customer contacted as necessary						
Customer records updated						
Inventory adjustments made						
Collection efforts as necessary						
Transaction completed						
Performance data entered						

Figure 9-2. Form for pinpointing bottlenecks in order processing can also be used to pinpoint duplications of activities between departments. Steps listed are for illustrative purposes, as order cycle elements will vary from company to company, and the form should be modified accordingly for individual company use.

back to its field personnel and instructing them in formatting, it virtually eliminated the bottleneck by eliminating the need to correct and reformat, and made a substantial contribution to increased productivity in the department.

Another company which uses this approach selects every 10th order for tracking, and a machinable card accompanies each such shipment to each stage and the appropriate data is entered. At the shipping stage, the card accompanies the shipment as a postcard, which the customer fills out and returns showing time of receipt and condition of shipment. By using this approach, the customer service manager can get at the underlying cause of any late deliveries simply by going back to the record which shows the complete history for that order including any unusual delays that occurred along the way. By reviewing the overall statistics as updated by receipt of the delivery cards, the manager can quickly get a reading on overall service performance and at the same time identify important trends and trouble spots in time to take remedial action. The final stage of this measurement, i.e., the postcard reply from customers, will be considered in greater detail in chapter 11.

What about departments that are not directly involved in order processing? How relevant is this type of analysis? First of all, the type of analysis illustrated by the form shown in figure 2 is also an excellent way to identify duplication of activities between departments. Additionally, bottlenecks in order processing, wherever they occur, can readily back up into other elements of the customer service system, simply by generating complaints and inquiries that otherwise would not have to be researched and resolved.

Small Investments in Productivity That Bring Big Returns

It isn't always necessary to think in complex industrial engineering terms in order to be able to increase departmental productivity measurably. Several brief case histories illustrate this point, and others appear elsewhere in the text.

As selling costs go up, smaller customers get fewer and fewer visits from salespeople; given the average order size, it's just not worth it—not at $200-plus per sales visit. Yet customers who don't get called on tend to drift away, and one company discovered that it had lost about 1,000 smaller customers this way—customers who would be profitable provided the heavy field selling costs could be avoided. So they instituted an informal system of workload balancing within the customer service department whereby designated reps would make calls to smaller, inactive accounts during slack periods of the day. The average cost per call was under $10, and within very little time the customer service department had recovered a majority of the "lost" accounts and had written several million dollars of business.

A well-known health care products firm increased order processing capacity in its customer service department by 100% without adding a single person to the staff, and did so with a relatively modest investment in hardware. The department receives all orders by phone from field salespersons, and the first thing the company did was to specify the hours that salesmen for different divisions and product lines could call in their orders. This balanced the workload in some respects, and the rest was accomplished by installing recording equipment to take the orders. The only time a salesperson would talk directly to a customer service rep would be when all the recording devices were tied up. Naturally, the reps would be available for inquiries, exceptions and other special situations. What happened, of course, was that by having the recording machines as a buffer, reps could work more productively with fewer interruptions and could maintain a steady flow of orders from the machines rather than having to deal with the intermittent, feast-or-famine nature of most patterns of order receipt. Another point, too, is that salespeople talking to a recording machine don't waste time talking about the weather, company gossip, etc.!

Another company with a basically captive customer group—

in this case brokers—found that mailed-in orders were being delayed in the mail room because of the lengthy sortation process where a great deal of mail had to be actually opened to determine its internal routing. This meant that on some days orders didn't reach the customer service department until noontime, at which time it became a crisis situation, trying to get as many orders out as possible in the few hours remaining. The firm did two things:

The High Cost of Rush Orders

Here are the findings of an engineering study of warehouse productivity conducted by a U.S. Government agency. It is a study of the elapsed time vs. the total time required to perform a given job in the warehouse—e.g., assembling an order—which would normally be done by one person, but in an emergency may be divided among several people simply to get it done sooner in order to meet a shipping or customer pickup deadline.

Crew Size (Persons)	Elapsed Time	Time Savings	Total Man-Hours	Added Cost
1	2 hours	—	2 hours	—
2	1 hr 25 min	29%	2 hr 50 min	+ 42%
3	1 hr 27 min	28%	4 hr 21 min	+118%
4	1 hr 25 min	29%	5 hr 40 min	+183%

This is a good demonstration of the high cost of rush orders when you have to add extra people. It also illustrates how the cost of handling orders (as one example) can escalate with the number of people who actually handle such orders. This is also true of letters and documentation in general. If one person can answer a letter by himself or herself, the cost is "X" dollars; involve a second person and the cost is likely to become "X" plus 42%.

Other costs of rush orders that are not reflected in the chart would include:
1. Work left undone by Persons 2, 3, and 4 when they're pulled off their regular jobs.
2. A higher error rate.
3. General domino effect.

(1) converted to a lockbox system for payments, which cut down the actual volume of mail significantly; (2) for orders, provided its customers with large mailing envelopes printed a fluorescent orange. This isolated payments from the regular mailstream and made all orders immediately visible in the mail. This enabled the mail room to pull such orders out and get them to the customer service department at the beginning of the business day rather than the middle. A Canadian firm uses a variation of this, providing its customers with fluorescent orange pressure sensitive mailing labels carrying its address. Another approach is to use a dedicated P.O. box number, to which customers mail all orders.

Rewriting Internal Policies In Order to Improve Productivity

Any policy which cuts down the number of handlings or reviews is likely to cut costs and improve productivity. The main thing to consider is the element of risk that may be involved in eliminating steps or handlings that are for purposes of checking accuracy, policy, legality and other points. Some suggestions of policy changes that might be made follow.

Automatic refunds. Referred to earlier, this policy says basically that all claims or requests for credit by customers below a certain dollar amount will be automatically refunded without question or investigation. The customer service rep receiving the claim or request for credit is authorized to do so automatically— and in fact is required to honor all claims without question provided they are below the authorized dollar limit. Naturally, if a rep feels a particular claim is questionable, he or she will report this fact to the supervisor or manager for further scrutiny. The economics of automatic refunds are easy to demonstrate. If there are 100 claims for $20 each and all are refunded, it will cost the company $2,000. If they are all investigated and 20% are disallowed, it will cost at least $1,000 to investigate and another $1,600 to pay those which were not disallowed. That is $2,600, $600 more than if all claims had been paid without investigating.

There is also the matter of the 80 customers whose claims were deemed valid and who may have been alienated by the fact that their claims were questioned and they had to go through red tape and delays in order to get their money.

Responsibility for errors. In a version of the automatic refund policy, a well known firm which handles hundreds of phone orders daily for printed stationery and similar materials in short runs is able to record remarkably fast turnaround time with an extremely low incidence of errors. What's also unusual is that the firm automatically assumes responsibility for *all* errors without investigating, and quickly redoes work or replaces materials at no expense to customers. The philosophy behind this unusually generous policy is that some 95% of the firm's business is repeat business from the same customers and there are hundreds of orders weekly from many of those same customers; given this, it's more efficient to keep the order flow moving smoothly than to delay reruns while trying to determine accountability. The average order is relatively small in dollar volume and the company reasons correctly that their policy will save them money in the long run and create good will which can be measured in account growth. In the company itself, the policy is a dramatically effective incentive, not only to accuracy in taking orders and completing them, but also to making absolutely sure that the customer is providing the correct information. Customer service reps are rated by the number of orders taken along with the errors charged against those orders, regardless of actual accountability, and it's a measure of the effectiveness of the system that the reps who record the highest rate of order entry also have the lowest error rate.

Setting and enforcing standard lead times. Recognizing that there will always be exceptions and emergencies, standard lead times should not be overridden by salespeople and others except under prescribed circumstances and through specific channels. Exceptions should be handled by the manager himself or herself on a judgmental basis considering customer priority, size of account and other factors. Establishing a rule that says customer service reps are not permitted to make exceptions, and defining the general conditions under which they will be made by the department head, will usually reduce unnecessary pressures on the department and at the same time contribute to increased productivity on the part of reps. One customer service manager went to considerable lengths to portray on slides—photos and diagrams—what happened in the customer service department when a field salesperson called in a last minute order for same-day shipment. She showed this to field salespeople at the firm's various branches. Almost none of them realized how much detail had to be handled on an exceptions basis for such orders as they were walked through various departments, and the time it consumed to do so. Many said that had they known the amount of extra work such orders were causing they would have run them through on conventional lead times, requesting same day service only in the case of genuine emergencies. And in fact the number of such orders did drop significantly after she made her presentation.

Courtesy and helpfulness. "It's hard to be productive when you're always being interrupted." This observation—which is quite true—was made by a customer service representative who had forgotten to mention that most of the "interruptions" were calls from customers who did not see themselves as interrupting at all, but rather exercising their right as customers to place orders, make inquiries or register complaints. And discourtesy tends to inhibit productivity by fostering an adversary climate rather than a cooperative one; antagonistic customers will demand more and will be more likely to haggle over small amounts or trivial details—actually creating more interruptions—while customers who feel they've been well treated will generally be less demanding and more likely to accept minor delays or deviations from orders without protest. Also important in this respect is the individual rep's willingness to help the customer to the extent possible before referring the customer to a supervisor or to the manager. Reps who are unwilling to accept the responsibilities that have been assigned to them but instead refer customers or decisions to others are contributing to departmental inefficiency and are often a major element in the fires that managers have to spend so much time extinguishing. What's more, customers tend to become antagonistic when problems can't be solved at the point of contact, and this can start the cycle all over again. Courtesy and attention to the needs of customers are an investment in the future relationship, and every rep should be reminded that *attitude towards customers* is a major factor in the department's success, spelled out in the old familiar saying: "Take care of your customers . . . and they will take care of you."

Workload Alternatives

The method by which the customer service department is organized and work assigned to customer service representatives will have a distinct impact on the overall productivity of the department. In many instances it will also strongly influence morale and motivational factors within the department and thus affect overall productivity and quality of work on the part of the individuals affected. Again, when it comes to assigning work in the department there is no "best way." The nature of the business, the firm's services or products, trade customers and other factors will all enter into determining which is best suited. Several alternatives are discussed here, and it is implicit that in very large customer service organizations such as exist in major mail order operations, credit card companies, airlines and similar organizations, it is possible to develop computer software that will balance the workload, including scheduling of part-time personnel for heavy periods, assign work, and measure the productivity of individual workers. The same basic techniques are applicable to many business operations, including warehousing, production scheduling, maintenance and the like, but are beyond the scope of this book which assumes the majority of customer service departments represented among its readers to have fewer than 50 persons.

Next available rep. Under this system, orders are taken, inquiries handled and other services performed by the next customer service representative who is available. This is basically the system used by the airlines, rent-a-car companies, mail (and phone) order firms and similar businesses where the service or product is relatively uniform and the major portion of the work is done by the computer. Indeed, under this arrangement, peak-hour, late-night or overflow calls can actually be handled by recording devices which interrogate the customer in a certain sequence. The customer's responses are taken off the tape later and entered into the computer much as the rep would do taking the information live. The next-available-rep system is also used in industrial applications where there are large numbers of customers with relatively uniform requirements and ordering in relatively small lots: palletloads, perhaps, but more likely cases. In businesses of this kind, it is more important to have a trained order-taker available than it is to have somebody who is a technical expert, or knows the account well, but is not necessarily available when the particular call comes in. The advantage of the next-available-rep system is a high degree of productivity, and the ability to handle surges by taking on part-time people or, as mentioned, using recording devices. The disadvantage is that the method is relatively impersonal and where knowledge of accounts, special industry practices or technical applications are involved, reps tend to be limited to the information that's available to them in the computer. To offset the impersonality problem, it may be desirable to give high levels of training in courtesy (again, the airlines and rent-a-car businesses do very well in this respect) and then to monitor actual performance to assure that it remains up to standard. In this system, too, there is apt to be a considerable element of stress. In one company, a rep may handle as many as 150 calls a day, a good proportion of them complaints. This "down" situation needs offsetting incentives in the way of pay, working conditions, job rotation and other arrangements.

Assignment by region or territory. Under this arrangement, one or more reps are assigned to handle all the accounts within a designated region or sales territory. If two or more reps are involved, they will handle the individual accounts more or less interchangeably—when a call comes in, it will be responded to by the next available rep assigned to that region or territory. This system is in general an improvement over the next-available-rep system because it gives individual reps a chance to become more familiar with customers, and also transportation and delivery conditions in their territory. It may be difficult to set up initially with equal distribution of accounts among reps, but your existing sales territories may be suitable for this purpose. Assignment by territory is one of the more prevalent methods of workload distribution; sometimes the reps are actually out in the regions, but as often as not they are all at a central location.

Assignment by account. Another popular option used by many firms, assignment by account is one version of assignment by territory, but other criteria may be used as well: type or size of business, annual volume of purchases, whether an OEM (Original Equipment Market) customer, distributor or end user. Again, some difficulty setting up initially, but an arrangement that is especially popular with customers.

Assignment by industry or business type. A variation of assignment by account, but one implying that reps assigned to a particular industry or business group have special expertise in that industry or business and can provide technical or applications assistance as well as routine order fulfillment support, expediting and the like.

Assignment by product line. Also a popular arrangement, although there may be some inconveniences for customers who buy a wide variety of products from the firm and may have to deal with several different customer service reps. Assignment by product line is often found in commodities and chemicals industries, where reps require special expertise in high-volume transportation, sanitation requirements, hazardous materials regulations, loading and unloading requirements and other specialized subjects. Another factor in the chemicals and commodities industries is that, with products and prices virtually identical among competitors, customer service is one of the few areas where an individual firm can develop competitive advantage via technical expertise and knowledge of applications within a given industry.

Assignment by team. This may involve one or more of the

types of arrangements outlined above. Where reps are assigned by account, for example, each rep on the team will be the No. 1 rep for designated accounts, but will also be the No. 2 or No. 3 rep on other accounts. That way, if a certain rep is tied up when his or her customer calls, there is always a backup rep who has above-average knowledge of the account's requirements and general ordering patterns. Where accounts are assigned on a product line basis, the team approach may also be used. In fact, a product line team may also involve assignment by account within the overall product line assignment, adding the valuable personal dimension to the relationship.

Job rotation. In this approach, the assignment system re-mains essentially the same, but the individuals are rotated from one job slot to another. This enables offsetting particularly stressful assignments with less pressureful tasks. It also makes for fairer distribution of the workload in general. The problem is that it's easier to describe this approach than it is to actually implement it. When people get good at a particular job it's very easy to rationalize keeping them on that particular job "just a little bit longer" . . . a year or two.

Job segmentation. A more workable version of job rotation, in this approach the individual performs the same job every day, but instead of performing the same general "mix" of work all day long, does one particular type of thing in the morning, and something different in the afternoon. A rep may handle phone calls—orders, complaints, inquiries—during the morning, and spend the afternoon researching the inquiries and complaints, but without having to take phone calls. One firm found this approach very helpful with customer reps who handled a number of complex technical questions every day but complained about the constant interruptions of phone calls all day long which made it difficult to research the questions properly and hampered their productivity to the point of extreme frustration. Simply by segmenting assignments so that half the reps handled phone calls in one half of the day and research in the other half, and vice versa, the pressure was removed and the reps became sig-nificantly more productive overall.

Inside selling and other special one-day assignments. One firm has found that it has been able to balance the workload, improve morale and generate added sales by scheduling reps to spend one day per week each contacting smaller, marginal and inactive accounts and solicit business. Reps who did not wish to were not required to participate, but the majority did. The approach was an excellent morale builder, produced significant sales—and didn't cost the department a penny except for the actual phone calls. And productivity soared!

10

SETTING STANDARDS
AND MEASURING PERFORMANCE

A standard is anything that can be used as a basis of comparison. It can be Greenwich Mean Time, the length of British King Henry I's arm (said to be the basis for the modern 36-inch yard), the Air Quality Index, tons per man hour . . . in fact anything usable as a point of reference or measurement. In business, a standard is generally a formal statement of the required level of quality or composition of a product as in purity or viscosity, or the expected performance and productivity of machines. MTBF—mean time between failures—is a standard for the "uptime" of computers and similar equipment. In the warehouse, there are literally thousands of standards covering virtually every operation performed: time required to lift and position a palletload on the first, second, third and fourth levels respectively; time required to dismount from a fork lift truck; time required to position a dockbridge; and so forth. There are as many standards for manufacturing operations, and also for many of the routines that would be involved in customer service operations. A keystroking standard would be an example, as would a mail-opening or file retrieval standard.

Quality vs. Productivity Standards

The customer service manager is concerned with two kinds of standards: those that relate to the actual *quality* of the service performed by the department in respect to customers, which would include quality of individual work as well as the department's output as a whole; and those which relate to individual and departmental *productivity* in providing that service. It bears repeating that the two should never be confused. A department providing the highest levels of service can score relatively low in productivity, while a highly productive department can be rendering a low level of customer service. The customer service manager's challenge is to set standards which will find the ideal standards between these two extremes which will maximize profits *and* customer satisfaction.

Another important distinction between quality standards and productivity standards in customer service is the question of who decides what the standards should be. The development of quality standards, i.e., those relating to actual customer service performance, is one of the most important responsibilities of the customer service manager. It's a job that should not be entrusted to anyone else, except for such research and tabulation as may be necessary beforehand. Quality standards may have to be approved at a higher level, and they certainly should not be arrived at by the customer service manager independently of distribution, production and sales—but the customer service manager must be the prime mover if the standards are to have any relevance to the customer service mission. And the setting of standards should be spelled out in the statement of mission as well as in the manager's job description, so that there won't be any doubt or question about it.

Productivity standards, on the other hand, are best handled by industrial engineers trained in observation and measurement of the steps and motions involved in performing tasks, as well as in the design of the jobs themselves. Naturally the manager should be involved in the process in order to keep it on target. Additionally, it should be understood at the outset that the purpose is not to "engineer" the whole customer service operation, but rather to streamline repetitive tasks that can be performed more efficiently without compromising the quality of the individual's performance or the service levels the department provides.

Some Different Kinds of Standards

Engineered standards are based on many samplings and observations over a period of time. They represent practical performance goals in various tasks, based on what most people can be expected to accomplish over a period of time and under different conditions. Engineered standards are quite common in warehouse operations and in other applications with a high labor content. Engineered standards can also be applied to production activities: so many units per hour; no more than "X" quality rejections per 500 units manufactured, etc. They are sometimes applied as well to office operations and paperwork handling and flow. A standard for typing a 250-word letter with .001 errors per 100 words can be established by observation; similarly, standards for data entry and related tasks are not uncommon. Generally, however, engineered standards' principal relevance to actual customer service performance is in warehousing and distribution activities—and of course is one of the reasons you can quote standard lead times on customer orders, as well as average delivery time by region or postal or other zone. In office and warehouse alike, engineered standards often involve actually improving the specific procedure in order to make the worker more efficient: providing the typist with a copyholder advanced by foot pedal; giving the truck unloader a pallet jack so that there's no delay waiting for a fork lift operator to remove pallets that the unloader has stacked.

Throughput standards or system standards are particularly important in measuring customer service performance. They are also frequently misunderstood because of the segmented nature of many business operations. The "bottleneck" chart appearing in chapter 8 illustrates this point; there are many discrete operations involved in getting an order through the system and completing all the associated records transactions, but it's the total cycle from beginning to end that is the true measure of customer service. The bottleneck chart is a means of locating the weak link or links that defeat system productivity. The customer service department may show excellent productivity in pro-

Some Standards and Measures

STANDARD	HOW TO STATE IT	REMARKS
Order generation and transmittal	"Inbound orders from area X arrive in Y days. (For each area)"	If possible, build in factor to represent customer's internal order generating time from requisition to purchase order.
Processable orders received	"X percent of orders processable upon receipt."	Variances may reflect inadequate product sheets, catalog descriptions, price lists.
Internal order cycle: Mail opening and delivery	"Mail to be delivered (or picked up) at P.O. box at _____ intervals."	A dedicated P.O. box (for orders only) will bypass mail room bottlenecks. But time pick-up to post office distribution schedules.
Order confirmation	"X percent of orders confirmed within Y hours."	Set corollary standard for orders not confirmed timely; followup on legal matters.
Exceptions	"Customers (or other departments) contacted about exceptions of all types within X hours."	Include discrepancies on orders, information not supplied; restricted articles, stockouts, delays, etc.
Credit check/reports	"Credit report on existing customers within X hours, on new accounts Y hours (days)."	Excessive divergence from standard would suggest prescreening accounts before selling.
Sales review, edit, etc.	(Time standards as appropriate)	Include elements unique to the company.
Order processing	"X percent of orders processed within Y hours." (Time, accuracy standards as appropriate)	Set corollary standard for completion of orders not processed timely.
Subroutines: bill of lading, invoices, etc.		Terms of sale (FOB plant, delivered, delivery proof required) may be a major factor.
Plant/warehouse order filling	"X percent of orders to be assembled (produced) within Y working hours (days)."	Include packing, stencilling, strapping, etc., along with order assembly elements.
Staging and shipping	"X percent of shipments to be picked up/shipped within Y hours of availability."	An element often overlooked.
Transit	"X percent of orders delivered within Y days of shipment."	Should allow for differences in location, mode, length of haul.

Figure 10-1

Order status, inquiries by customer	"Inquiries on order status to be answered within X hours."	Also: tracing and expediting.
Product availability **Line item fill** **Dollar fill**	"X percent of line items ordered to be available on presentation of orders." "X percent of dollars ordered to be filled on presentation of orders."	Can be misleading. A measure of inventory investment strategy and its effectiveness.
Complete order fill	"X percent of orders to be shipped complete."	One of the more reliable indices of customer satisfaction.
Orders accepted as shipped	"X percent of orders accepted as shipped."	Can reflect acceptance of substitutions, minor errors, or intentional over-shipping.
Errors and credits	(By dollars, orders, or as percentage of invoices or invoice dollars.)	Also classifiable by source.
Complaints	"X percent of complaints to be resolved in Y days, balance within Z days (weeks)."	Should include provision for regular review of all unresolved complaints.
Customers' target dates met	"X percent of orders to meet customer due dates after acceptance."	Another reliable index of customer satisfaction.
Phone response	"X percent of calls answered on second ring."	Other standards: maximum busy signals per hour, maximum wait by customer, etc.
Courtesy, effectiveness	(Attitude towards customer, ability to handle the situation.)	Rated by monitoring or after-the-fact questionnaires to customers.
Accuracy	"No more than X percent errors in responding to customer inquiries."	Error rate will reflect adequacy of information system.
Timeliness	"X percent of inquiries to be handled while customer is on the phone."	Provision should be made for followup on inquiries referred to other departments.
Callbacks	"All callbacks to be made at the promised time, whether or not there is anything new to report."	Very important from the customer's point of view.

Other: above minimum order, damage-free delivery, conformance to marking-labeling-packaging requirements, full palletloads, personnel performance standards, security and other standards as appropriate.

cessing orders and getting them through to the distribution center, and the distribution center in turn may show exceptional productivity in assembling those orders and staging for shipment. However, if they sit on the loading dock—or in a carrier terminal—for a day or a weekend, the determinant of throughput is that particular delay, not the efficiency displayed by the customer service department and the warehouse. Thus throughput standards must take into account all linked operations involved in a particular transaction. This is a vital point in setting system standards, as illustrated in the box below.

Measuring Customer Service Department Throughput

Operation A = 50 transactions per man-hour
Operation B = 5 transactions per man-hour
Operation C = 6 transactions per man-hour
Operation D = 80 transactions per man-hour
Operation E = 20 transactions per man-hour
Operation F = 15 transactions per man-hour
Operation G = 40 transactions per man-hour

The actual throughput rate is 1.849 transactions per man-hour.* Note that this is less than half the slowest rate of all operations, and must be taken into account in setting throughput standards for operations that are linked. This type of analysis is also useful in determining staffing requirements and work assignments, for example, assigning more time-consuming tasks to several people and perhaps two or three of the less time-consuming tasks to one individual.

---

* This is determined by calculating the time required to perform one operation at each rate—.0200 hours for Transaction A, .2000 for Transaction B, .1666 for Transaction C, and so forth—and adding all these time elements together to a total of .5407 hours required to perform one complete set of linked operations; this is the equivalent of slightly more than half an hour (32.44) and translates into an effective rate of 1.849 transactions per man hour.

Assigned or imputed standards are the most common kind in customer service operations. While they may be based in part on engineered data and observations, in most instances they're based on experience, judgment and "gut feeling." For example, a standard may be set that says 90% of orders should be shipped within 48 hours of their receipt. The manager knows from experience that this is a reasonable time because most orders do in fact go out in 48 hours. Setting a standard and measuring performance against it will now give the manager a numerical yardstick, and may even lead to tightening the standard if it proves too easy to achieve. Response standards on field service may similarly be assigned: "On all field service calls, a tech rep will be at the customer's site in four hours or less." Or, an assigned standard may be stated as a negative: "No caller will be placed on 'hold' for longer than one minute."

At some juncture, assigned standards may run into situations requiring engineering: the ban against placing customers on hold more than a minute may end up with reps calling customers back when they can no longer hold them on the line—and this may tie up additional telephone time requiring queueing studies to determine whether additional personnel and/or telephone lines are needed. The same could be true of the 48-hour standard for shipping orders; company equipment may be going out only half-full because of the policy, and the situation may have to be restudied in greater depth. Standards for order fill, errors and the like may also be assigned, although they, too, may cause some economic "negatives."

Economic standards. Assigned or imputed standards may also be economic standards, as suggested previously. The company sets a standard at a level which it feels it can practically meet—a level of customer service it can provide without giving away the store, so to speak. Line item fill standards and delivery standards are among the most common economic standards. As one example, an economic analysis may determine that in order to maintain 90% product availability (line item fill) in its stores, a retail chain must maintain a safety stock of 1200 cases of product at its distribution center. Management wants to improve product availability, and judges that an improvement from 90% to 96% would be good. But when it examines the economics, it discovers that it will have to actually *double* inventories of all "A" items that it holds in inventory. This would require a substantial capital investment . . . and added warehouse space as well. It takes another look, and finds that an improvement from 90% to 93% is far more practical, because any more would cost so much that prices would have to be increased and loss of customers would result.

The "ship-same-day" policies that have been discussed previously can be prohibitively expensive unless pricing accurately reflects the total cost of meeting such a standard.

In the long run, many standards end up as economic standards—a compromise between what the company might like to do, and what it can practically afford to do and maintain its market position. Since it is also possible to determine the impact of improved customer service on sales, some standards that may seem too high may in fact be the best way to go after new business. Convenience stores are an example of this type of business strategy. A Massachusetts firm that sells computer parts and components charges from 10% to 20% more than the manufacturers, but fills orders in less than half the time; there are many other examples throughout industry.

Although it's a good strategy for capturing premium business, or for showing a profit on previously unprofitable business, high prices for high service standards should not be used if the firm cannot actually meet those standards. Some managers have used this strategy in an attempt to discourage excessive emergency orders. But it often doesn't work that way. Customers now feel that by paying more they can get the service they couldn't get before. If the vendor still can't provide the service, as is often the case, the customer service manager sometimes faces the problem of dealing with even *more* emergency orders than before the attempt was made to price the emergency service out of the market. One firm discovered that customers were paying the emergency premium to get orders out faster . . . and then making it up by shipping by surface carriers rather than air freight!

Policy standards are often established to reflect management's genuine desire to serve customers in a particular way, and to impress customers and employees alike with the firm's orientation and commitment. These are generally more specific than "service with a smile," although in the fast food business, airline ticketing and similar activities, making eye contact and smiling may represent an actual standard of performance for contact employees. In industry, a policy standard could be reflected in a statement to the effect of "All complaints will be responded to in 48 hours or less." "All refunds to be made within five working days of receipt of merchandise" could be another. The "ship-same-day" standard referred to earlier can be considered a policy standard when it's used in advertising and promotion. As a practical matter, most customer service standards do in fact represent management policy. And that is as it should be. The problem arises when management sets such standards but does not provide the customer service department with the means or resources to meet them. Here again, it's part of the customer service manager's job to initiate development of standards that meet both economic and policy goals. The manager who waits until such standards are imposed from above is very likely to be in trouble soon, and this is just as true for standards that are too low for the market as it is for standards that are higher than the company can afford.

Qualitative standards cover the whole range of customer service. They range from judgment calls to actual numerical analysis of performance. Supervisors will periodically rate customer service reps on the quality of their telephone work in terms of courtesy, empathy, ability to withstand stress and irate customers, conflict resolution and problem solving. At the other end of the spectrum, the manager will analyze percentages for line item fill, complete order fill and dollar fill, as well as on-time shipment, transit time, acceptance rate of orders as shipped, and other standards where performance can be measured numerically. "I ranked Joyce and Bill as 'superior' in their telephone work, but I ranked Frank as 'needs more training.'" This is an observation based on qualitative standards without using numbers, although a 10-point rating scale might have been used in place of the language. "We filled 95% of orders complete and shipped 91% within 48 hours" describes a numerical interpretation of a qualitative standard.

Another very common qualitative standard which is typically measured numerically is percentage of error. In warehouse order assembly, for example, the standard may be for an error rate of no more than one half of one percent, with a policy of downgrading or dismissing employees who consistently fail to meet the standard. Some qualitative standards may be misleading, depending on the language employed. "Percentage of on time shipments" and "Met promise dates" are two examples. If the phrase "on-time" means the order was shipped when the customer wanted it shipped, then the standard actually does measure customer service. But if it means, "We shipped the order when we said we would," then it reflects the actual performance but not necessarily the satisfaction of the customer. The same is true of "Met promise dates"; if this is not what the customer asked for but rather what the vendor said it could provide, that's basically all it measures: the ability of the company to do what it said it would do. The danger of this kind of standard is that it's very easy to get a good report card simply by making the standard easier to meet, without reference to customer expectations.

Researched standards represent the most desirable type of standards because they are based on formal research into what customers need and want and take into account what the competition is offering in the way of customer service . . . and because they will have been researched to the extent that the manager knows how much additional business can be generated by raising and meeting standards, and the point at which the cost of doing so is no longer justified by the return. This subject is discussed at greater length later in this book.

The Steps in Setting Standards

☐ *Draw on experience.* Even though it may never have defined customer service standards as such, any company that has been in business any length of time is already meeting certain industry standards just as it is offering competitive products or services at competitive prices. Many firms operate quite successfully without formal standards because they know their markets and their customers well, and because their managements have a commitment to customer service that is understood and carried out throughout the company.

There is certainly no substitute for experience in this respect, but there are also limits to experience and some risks in relying solely on instinct or a feel for the marketplace. There is the risk of giving more customer service than is needed, or too much of one aspect and not enough of another—or too much to some classes of customers and not enough to others, or the wrong kinds in the wrong markets. There is also the risk of being influenced by the "squeaky wheels," often smaller, hand-to-mouth customers, when the firm should be paying more attention to its larger and more important customers. Or, customer service standards ought to distinguish between requirements of OEM companies buying for the assembly line and distributors buying for stock.

A distinction should be made between the actual experience of the customer service manager and members of the department in dealing with customers, on the one hand, and those of sales personnel and management, on the other. Customer service people have a sense of what's important to customers and what isn't because they live with it every day. Sales personnel and management tend to base their opinions on complaints that reach them—the exceptions—rather than the day-to-day feedback from customers experienced in the customer service department.

☐ *List the most important customer service elements.* Circulate questionnaires to customer service personnel and others in the company asking a single question:

Question: What are the three most important aspects of customer service in this company?

Answer: 1. _____
                2. _____
                3. _____

                      Signed _____

Although there will be some overlapping, there will also be a surprising variety of answers, including some which will be quite perceptive and thought-provoking. The manager should compile these questionnaires into a single list, eliminating duplications, and then add any that appear to be important from experience but did not appear on the questionnaires. The final list then becomes the basis for the next step.

☐ *Conduct research.* The primary research in connection with setting standards is conducted to determine what's important to customers . . . and *how* important. Some of the principal elements that are likely to surface include, in approximate order of (descending) importance:

1. Order cycle time
2. Transportation
3. Order status information
4. Order size (minimums)
5. Technical information
6. Handling of returns
7. Response to emergencies
8. Training customer personnel
9. Time or jobsite deliveries
10. Meet special customer needs

These will naturally vary from one market to another, and any research that's conducted at this stage should be sufficiently open-ended to uncover special customer service needs that may not have occurred to anybody in the company. One quick way of doing so is via a very brief questionnaire to customers asking these three questions:

1. What do you like *most* about our service?
2. What do you like *least* about our service?
3. What *changes or improvements* would you suggest?

This questionnaire will often turn up some surprises. Although it's a common belief that order cycle is almost universally the most important element of customer service from the customer's point of view, one company found out that putting the packing slip in the same place in each carton was more important to customers than the order cycle itself. Even when order cycle is important, there's likely to be confusion between what customers really want and what sales, for example, may say they want.

One company surveyed its sales force and determined that customers absolutely required a one-week delivery cycle, which could only be accomplished by opening additional regional distribution centers. When it surveyed customers themselves, it learned that a four-week lead time was perfectly satisfactory. The salespeople's response was governed, quite naturally, by the fact that their commissions would be paid only after shipment had been made, while customers were accustomed to—and quite willing to live with—lead times of four to six weeks. An investment of a few hundred dollars in research saved an unnecessary investment ranging in the millions . . . and also meant that more resources were available for customer service in areas that did in fact need upgrading.

The specific techniques for conducting customer research and developing rankings for different standards are explained in detail in chapter 11.

☐ *Review legal, trade and public standards.* These would include mail order rules; regulations for availability of inventory to support advertising; Food and Drug Administration standards on lot control, recall, returns and exchanges; industry standards for overruns and underruns; trade conventions on substitutions, overflow truckloads and carloads; and the various standards applying to consumer product service and consumer credit. These should of course be included as standards as appropriate to the individual company. Where the firm actually exceeds such standards, it may be useful for marketing purposes to impress this point on customers and prospective customers.

☐ *Identify competitive standards.* There are various ways to find out what customer service standards are being offered by the competition. The best way to find out is to combine observation with formal research. Some customers regularly tabulate performance by vendor within a category of product or service and use this as an incentive for better performance by low-scoring vendors. Otherwise, perceptions of competitive performance and/or standards by a company's sales force is apt to be biased.

The question of whether to beat competitive standards, or simply meet them, is a policy or marketing strategy decision. There may be benefits in offering better service; there may not.

Improving customer service beyond competitive levels does not always attract additional business. In highly competitive industries, customer service standards tend to be remarkably alike. Competition forces the competitive firms to have highly efficient distribution systems providing the highest levels of customer service consistent with costs that permit competitive pricing: in short, low-cost but efficient distribution and customer service. At this point, improving customer service will increase distribution costs and, ultimately, raise the prices paid by customers. In effect, by improving service to beat the competition, a firm will price itself out of the market. On the other hand, if it decides to cut prices below the competition, it will invariably have to cut service to do so—to levels that have already proven to be below what customers want and need.

This is not always the case, of course, and it is a perfectly legitimate strategy in some markets to discount prices and reduce service, and in others to increase service and raise prices accordingly. What's important is determining how a particular market will respond to a particular strategy. This is a particularly cogent reason for upgrading the customer service function in the company and including its manager in all discussions and planning of marketing strategy.

In making comparisons with the competition, the manager should make sure that customers are actually aware of competitive differences, and that the same elements of customer service are in fact being compared. A Richmond, Virginia firm sought to break into the Atlanta market by offering second-morning delivery on all orders received by 3 p.m. weekdays. Customers responded that they were already getting second-morning delivery from their present vendor, also in Richmond, and in some instances next-morning delivery. The Richmond firm undertook some independent research and found that its competitor was actually providing second-morning delivery in Atlanta on two out of every ten shipments. In the majority of cases, these customers were getting fifth- and sixth-morning delivery.

From the point of view of setting standards, these findings convinced the company that there was little point of trying to come in competitively with significantly better standards. If the service customers were getting was good enough that Atlanta customers thought it was better than it actually was, there seemed to be little potential for a marketing strategy based on improved customer service.

Another aspect of this is misdefinition of service on the customer's part. A firm that sells and services equipment hears complaints that its response time on service calls is eight hours, while the competition consistently responds in four. What the customers don't mention is that the competition's equipment breaks down much more frequently, and has to be called three times as frequently for service. This is a more subtle version of the apples-vs.-oranges comparison.

☐ *Set differential standards as appropriate.* In many lines of business, there are sharp differences between different classes of customers. For example, a producer of kaolin clay sells large volumes of the product to the paper industry where it is used in the finish of fine enameled papers. The same company also sells large volumes of kaolin clay in another form to an entirely different market: as kitty litter sold to consumers through retail stores. Differences like these are reflected in differences in customer service requirements. Papermaking is a continuous process type of industry with extremely heavy capital investment; late delivery of a carload of kaolin could shut down a plant at a cost of hundreds of thousands of dollars. Late delivery of a comparable shipment of kitty litter would result in some lost sales and extra odoriferousness at cat lovers' homes, but not much more.

Most manufacturing companies recognize differing customer service requirements between such customer groups as:

Group A	Group B
Businesses	Consumers
Original equipment mfrs. (OEM)	Distributors/wholesalers
Domestic customers	Export customers
Institutions	Wholesalers

Group A	Group B
Wholesalers	Retail chains
Private sector	Government
Hospitals, clinics	Drug wholesalers/retail chains
Large customers	Small customers
Licensed (controlled substances, explosives, etc.)	Not licensed

Companies may also classify their customers within a different category, for example a chemical company may see a need for differential standards between customers in the paint, detergent, health care, plastics and food processing industries.

There are some industries where there is little opportunity for setting differential standards. In the printing industry and custom manufacturing in general, most customers have the same degree of need for on-time delivery and accuracy in filling the order. About the only distinction that can be made is between large customers and small customers, or in some cases customers where there is a penalty associated with delay, as in some contract and government work, and customers where there is no penalty. It's one of the less pleasant jobs in the customer service department to have to delay a smaller customer's job to take care of a large and important customer's "emergency," knowing that the small customer is going to be hurt and that the large customer's emergency isn't so much an emergency as it is just plain poor planning. Yet it's part of the customer service manager's job to deal with such situations, and part of the challenge is to learn how to break the bad news to the smaller customer and still retain the account.

Another basis for differential standards is of course the nature of the order itself. An order for Christmas ornaments placed in January would normally have less urgency than the identical order placed in October. An order received by mail would usually indicate lower service expectations on the customer's part than one placed by phone. An order for a single part would usually be considered a higher priority than a stock order for many parts. An order for operating or running gear—a throttle valve shaft or wheel bearing—would be seen as more urgent than an order for molding or trim. Additionally, there are many cases where the customer will indicate the level of service required, and the reason why, at the time of placing an order.

The fact that there can be so many different categories of customers and situations does not mean there has to be a complex hierarchy of differential standards. Not in the least. Many companies have two main types of standards: standards for emergency shipments, and standards for non-emergency shipments. An emergency shipment is a shipment to meet a specific need like a machine-down situation, or a situation involving health or safety. Emergency shipments usually go out the same day, and the customer pays for premium transportation, and occasionally a surcharge for the same-day shipment. Non-emergency shipments may have a lead time of as much as a week and may be sold on a delivered price basis with certain minimum order sizes specified.

The chances are good that in any given company much of the job of classifying customers by category of business, size or other criteria, and some decisions on whether or not differential customer service standards are in order will be self-evident. Others will require research of the type discussed above.

Setting differential standards does not mean setting *discriminatory* standards, however. It is generally accepted that larger and more important customers tend to get better service and that certain types of urgent situations and emergencies permit overrides of priorities that might be considered discriminatory under normal circumstances. But if there is any question at all as to whether a proposed differential customer service standard might be discriminatory, the manager should clear it with the firm's legal department.

□ *Develop inventory standards.* Product availability is one of the cornerstones of good customer service, and yet it is often overlooked as an opportunity to set differential standards that can save the company substantial amounts without seriously affecting service. Here is an example of differential inventory availability standards based on considerations of demand, value, sensitivity and impact of stockouts on customers:

Inventory Category	Availability Standard
"A" items- Fast moving, wide demand, profitable and/or situational need (health and similar)	98%
"B" items- Moderately fast moving, essential but lower margins and less urgency overall	92%
"C" items- Slow movers, non-essential, mainly decorative and ornamental type items	88%
"D" items- "Accommodation" items which customers will wait for over long periods of time.	70%

Depending on the number of lines in each category, this particular inventory mix (which is used for purposes of illustration only) might have an average availability standard of 94 to 95%. This does not mean that a customer would have a 95% chance of finding any particular item in stock, because depending on the inventory category, that chance might be as low as 70% and as high as 98%. Moreover, if an order contains more than 10 lines and includes items in all four categories, "A" through "D," there is a less than 50% chance that a complete order can be shipped. These probabilities are illustrated in figure 5. The inventory analysis should determine whether there are enough orders embracing all four categories that the high proportion of incomplete orders would present any problems from either a cost or customer relations standpoint.

Setting Standards for Departmental Productivity

When it comes to setting standards and measuring productivity within the department, one of the manager's first concerns will be to make sure that whatever standards are employed will be fair to all concerned, and will take into account differences in difficulty of work assignments given to different people and other factors which would affect conventional measures of productivity. The manager may also want to consider whether it might be preferable to bypass standards for individual performance altogether and concentrate on standards for performance by the entire group. There are advantages and disadvantages on both sides; standards and measures of group performance require less record-keeping, but it's implicit that there's somewhat less of an incentive in a system that rates the group rather than the individual.

For convenience's sake, standards of productivity in the department should be confined to major tasks. No attempt should be made to set standards for everything individuals do, or to account for all their time. The biggest gains in productivity are usually to be made where the most work is performed, and too much "studying" of personnel can be a strong demotivator in itself. It's recommended, however, that the firm's industrial engineering department be involved in any standards with the customer service manager participating fully to make sure the standards being developed are relevant, and that employees do not find the approach intimidating.

The following description of a method for establishing standards of individual performance and then measuring against them was developed with the assistance of Jeffrey A. DeVries, Manager of Sales Administration, Becton Dickinson Co. It appeared originally in *Customer Service Newsletter* in response to a reader's question.

1. *Decide which tasks are going to be measured.* Remember, the more tasks you measure, the more time must be devoted to measuring, and this in itself can be counterproductive.

2. *Describe each task.* Write down a specific description of the physical activity, including travel to files, search, keyboarding or whatever.

3. *Break each task down into discrete segments.* These are generally relatively small movements: reach, grasp, pick up, set aside, remove sheet, etc.

4. *Look up the TMUs for each segment.* These are time

standards that have already been established for the segments making up each task. A TMU—Time Measurement Unit—is a decimal measure generally used in engineered measurement in preference to minutes and seconds; one TMU is equal to .00001 hour, or .0006 minute/.036 second. Stated differently, there are 100,000 TMU in an hour. This allows for relatively fine measures of all the movements and activities, segment by segment, comprising a given task.

5. *Add up the TMUs for each task.* This will give you a "standard time" for each task you elect to measure. Here are some examples of what you might come up with:

Task	TMU
Manually file order document	639
Retrieve document from file	585
Open mail by machine (per piece)	21
Open mail by hand (#10 envelope, per piece)	102
Open mail by hand (large, per piece)	251

You will probably want to store this data in the computer where it will be easier to work with, but your calculations can be done manually without too much trouble.

6. *Calculate allowances.* If you're concerned that your people are being treated like machines, don't worry: your industrial engineers will see to it that appropriate allowances are made for personal rest, fatigue, normal delays and of course tasks which are productive but not currently being measured.

7. *Record number of tasks performed by each person.* Usually, the individual keeps this record; some telephone systems will generate the data as a byproduct of order-taking or complaint or inquiry handling. A five-day workweek is the usual period measured, or two five-day workweeks. Note that the individual records only the number of tasks performed, and only those being measured at the time, *not* the time required to perform them. You may expect some resistance here, and it's important to prepare your personnel beforehand, so they won't see the measurement as a threat.

8. *Enter data and perform extensions for each individual.*

This is simply a matter of multiplying the number of tasks by the appropriate TMU for each task. For example, if the person processed 55 orders and the standard has been established as 7242 TMU per order, the net standard for processing 55 orders would be 55 x 7242 = 398,310 TMU. In similar fashion, all measured tasks are extended and totalled, giving a total TMU or standard for the number of tasks that individual performed.

9. *Compare actual time expended on measured tasks.* So far we have calculated how much time it *should have* taken the individual to perform the tasks actually performed. The next step is to measure how much time it *actually* took, and this is simply a matter of comparing the actual records and using the standard allowances that have been calculated. Let's assume that you get numbers like this:

Total TMU for all measured tasks
    performed .... 2,956,000 TMU
Converted to hours .... 29.56 hours
Actual time spent on measured tasks .... 36.0 hours
Less 15% allowance .... 30.6 hours
Productivity: 29.56 ÷ 30.6 = 96.6%

This tells you that the person is for all intents and purposes producing right on target. It says that the job could have been performed by 96.6% of one person, and the variance of 3.4 percentage points may be due as much to your measuring system as to the employee. However, if the employee were to show up at 86.6% or below, you might have reason to be concerned that you're not getting a fair day's work for a fair day's pay.

10. *Measure group productivity in similar fashion.* Here is where you may really find cause for concern! Add up and convert the TMU as above, but for *all* workers, and again compare the standards with the actual. Here is a simplified version of what you might find for a nine-person crew:

Total TMU converted to standard hours .. 189.560 hours
Actual time spent on measured tasks .... 296.0 hours
Less 15% allowance .... 251.6 hours
Productivity: 189.56 ÷ 251.6 = 75.34%

Take this a step further, and it can be interpreted as follows:

the same number of tasks could have been performed by 25% fewer people, or a crew of seven rather than nine. Of course you will recognize that this is not necessarily so, depending on how the work is divided, where the people are physically located and so forth—but it may get you to take a closer look at the workflow in your department and the familiar questions of who does what and why.

11. *Use incentives.* One of the drawbacks of a measurement program of this type is that if you don't provide some sort of incentives to people to meet and exceed standards then they are likely to feel resentful. And they could even sabotage your program. Even a modest incentive program will do wonders to take the sting out of being measured in this way.

12. *Consider measuring group productivity only.* This is one way to avoid the "Big Brother" feeling that individual measurement sometimes engenders. Set the system up to measure the relative productivity of the group or department as a whole and develop incentives accordingly.

The Missing Link: Internal Standards

In organizing their customer service function, many companies overlook the central point that a customer service department is principally a communications center relaying instructions, inquiries and responses to other entities—a sort of clearing house dealing with customers and the company's own departments alike. This means that in fulfilling its mission the customer service department must depend on cooperation and feedback from many other departments in the company— cooperation and feedback that is not always consistently forthcoming. As an example, the customer service department receives a customer inquiry on location of a carload shipment. The customer service rep calls the appropriate person in the traffic department and gets an immediate answer, which can be relayed immediately to the customer. That's fine, but when a similar situation arises the following day, the traffic department person responds: "I'll check it out as soon as I can, but I've got a whole pile of claims here I have to deal with first."

There are numerous variations on this. The problem is not with the person in the traffic department, who is prioritizing in the way he/she judges best, but rather with a system which sets no guidelines or standards for such interdepartmental communications. Often there is no spelled-out responsibility for such departments to respond to the customer service department, or to take requested action within a designated time frame. This "gray area" sometimes results in excessive delays in processing credits, issuing refunds, accepting returns, responding to quality control complaints and providing technical or applications information.

This absence of standards often results in some type of customer service failure or complaint which has to be dealt with by the customer service department. For example, in one company the purchasing department buys parts both for the production department and for the customer service department, but it typically holds the customer service department requisition until it has received one from the production department. When there's a delay in issuing the purchase order or actually procuring the parts, the production department begins "robbing" parts from the customer service department. Unfortunately, the customer service department's requisition was held up so long that it, too, is out of parts and now must deal with the problem of customers with machine-down situations who are calling for parts that are just not in stock. This is a relatively commonplace type of situation, but one that could be largely avoided by developing lead time standards on requisitions which would be binding on all the parties concerned.

In another company, the credit department is at headquarters, the customer service department at the main manufacturing location. There is a requirement in the company that all orders received at the customer service department must be re-teletyped to the credit department before they can be filled and released. There is, however, no corresponding standard setting forth the time within which the credit department must give its approval, and many orders are needlessly delayed because the credit department may have different priorities at any given time. Clearly such standards are needed, because without them the customer service department is subjected to tremendous pressures from customers, and an added burden is placed on the warehouse and shipping departments when the clearance finally comes through and orders must be rushed out at the last minute.

Understandably, internal standards have to be mandated by management. And they have to support the firm's external standards for service to customers. A policy which states that all customer complaints below a certain dollar level are to be resolved within 30 days must be supported by an internal policy setting forth the standards of response required inside the company, i.e., from the departments involved, in order to meet those external customer service standards. In setting such internal standards, it is essential that management also institute a pro-

Some Useful Ratios	
Stock Availability	_____%
On-time Shipment	_____%
Late Deliveries	_____%
Early Deliveries	_____%
Errors-to-Orders	_____%
Processing	_____%
Billing	_____%
Assembly	_____%
Shipping	_____%
Other (specify)	_____%
Above Minimum Order	_____%
Accepted as Shipped	_____%
Complaints/Orders Ratio	_____%
Non-CS Complaints	_____%
CS Complaints	_____%
Other	_____%

Figure 10-2

cedure for reporting exceptions—i.e., responses that have not been made within the designated time frames. This procedure will simply move complaints up to the next level of supervision or management any time the standard has not been met. Figure 4 shows a type of memorandum which management might circulate

---

Setting Standards for Inquiry and Complaint Response

Correspondence   **Days**

Letters, high priority . . . . _____

Resolution of complaint by correspondent . . . . _____

Resolution of complaint by supervisor . . . . _____

Letters, routine or acknowledgement only . . . . _____

(All letters unanswered after _____ days to be referred to next level of supervision)

Telephone   **Percent**

Telephone answered within 4 rings . . . . _____

Resolving complaint on first call . . . . _____

Answering inquiry on first call . . . . _____

Maximum interval before callback . . . . _____
  (days, minutes, etc.)

(All callbacks not completed within _____ days to be referred to next level of supervision)

Adjustments   **Days**

Maximum interval, automatic refund (meets criteria) . . _____

Maximum interval, automatic replacement (meets
  criteria) . . . . _____

Maximum interval, adjusted invoice . . . . _____

Maximum interval, posting credit to customer's
  account . . . . _____

Maximum interval, policy or judgemental refund . . . . . _____

Maximum interval, policy or judgemental
  replacement . . . . _____

Maximum interval, declination of requested
  adjustment . . . . _____

Interdepartmental Matters   **Days**

Forwarding complaints to other department . . . . _____

Response by other department to customer . . . . _____

Report by other department on action taken . . . . _____

Figure 10-3

Interoffice Memorandum

To __All Customer-Contact Personnel__   Date _____

From __President's Office__

Subject __Corporate Complaint Handling Policy__

1. It is the policy of this company to facilitate the placing of complaints by customers dissatisfied with our products and services, and by others who may feel they have legitimate grievances against us. Names, addresses and telephone numbers of individuals with appropriate complaint-handling responsibility are to be made available to such persons, and no attempts will be made to obstruct in any way their efforts to communicate their complaints.

2. It is our policy to respond as quickly as possible to all complaints. Time standards have been established for handling complaints at different levels of severity or cost. Complaints that are not handled within the designated time-frame will be reported on designated exceptions reports to the Division Manager on a weekly basis.

3. All customer complaints are to be treated as bona fide. No assumptions are to be made about complaints or complainers until there has been an opportunity to investigate. Complaints are not to be downgraded in any way on the basis of the manner or attitude of the complainer.

4. It is our policy to make good will settlements in specific situations. Complaints below a designated dollar amount will be resolved automatically in the customer's favor on the grounds that it is less expensive and less damaging to customer relations to do so than to attempt to investigate each case on its merits. Other good will adjustments are to be made by designated managers only as indicated in procedures manuals.

5. The customer's "right of appeal" is to be honored. Customers who do not agree with the disposition of their complaint must be made aware that it may be presented at the next higher level of authority in the company until such time as it has reached the highest applicable level of authority.

6. It is our policy to resolve complaints equitably. Criteria will be established for resolving complaints fairly and with due protection to the rights of both parties.

7. All complaint resolutions as well as handling and investigations shall be consistent with company standards and the company code of ethics.

8. Standards for handling complaints, including permissible time frames for resolution of complaints, will apply equally to all personnel, including heads of other departments to whom complaints may occasionally be referred.

Figure 10-4. Management memo regarding complaint handling. Note references to reporting of unresolved claims in paragraph 2, and accountability of other departments mentioned in paragraph 8.

in regard to the standards for complaint handling shown in figure 3.

The standards themselves can be relatively straightforward: "All inquiries from the customer service department about status of an order in process shall be answered within one working day;" "Quality control tests requested by customer service on behalf of a customer shall be conducted and the results reported within ten working days;" "Special pricing requests to be handled within one working day;" "Equipment returned for rebuilding or repair to be completed and shipped back to the customer within 30 days." If a particular department finds it cannot meet a particular standard because of work overload, then it is that particular manager's responsibility to either improve the situation with better procedures or more people, or else to request that management change internal standards *and* the external customer service standards that depend on them.

In an ideal world it would be easy to establish internal standards as described here. In the real world that most customer service managers must live in, it's often more practical to develop informal understandings with the various department heads involved with the hope that one day, down the line, they too may see the desirability of such standards. In this connection, it should not be necessary to add that the customer service manager's interpersonal skills should be used just as widely *inside* the company as with its customers. And, as with customers, one of the most prominent of these skills is the ability to get the other person to accept an idea that may be inherently unpalatable to him or her. As one customer service manager put it, "The customer service manager's real skill is in being able to tell someone to go to hell—and have them look forward to taking the trip!"

Measuring Performance Against Standards

Most of the customer service standards discussed in this chapter will adapt readily to some sort of computer tabulation, and many can be generated as a byproduct of other customer service department activities. Some records may be kept by individual employees but this may in itself interfere with productivity and has the potential for creating an entirely different set of problems. Reliability of data is an absolute must, and it should be recorded in sufficient depth and over sufficient periods of time that it won't be distorted by seasonal surges or other isolated phenomena.

Once data has been recorded and tabulated, the manager must be careful not to concentrate on finding "good" scores to the exclusion of symptoms of serious underlying problems. Reference was made earlier to having an average line item fill rate of 95% with a complete order fill rate of only 30%. Even a 99% line item fill rate can mislead, if the 1% of unshipped goods happens to be a critical item. A firm manufacturing steel shelving can accomplish 99% line item fill and ship its merchandise, but with little benefit for the customer. The missing 1% happens to be fasteners for that very shelving—which will remain useless until the fasteners are received. Some years ago, a congressional investigation was threatened because of a shortage of lids or tops for a popular home canning jar. The jars were available by the trainload, but as for the lids to complete the home canning process, none were to be had. The manufacturer's exceptionally high line fill rate was totally negated by its 1% backorder rate.

The more standards are used, the more reliable the findings —provided that they are not "soft" standards like "on time shipment" or "met agreed shipment date" that are subject to misinterpretation and can be manipulated in any event. But when readings against standards tend to be consistent and reinforce one another, the overall findings should be considered reliable.

It may seem desirable at this juncture to start using a single number to describe the department's total performance. To be able to say "Our service level is 95%" is easier than saying "Our line item fill rate is 98%, our on-time shipment rate is 94%, our dollar fill rate is 96%, our complete order fill rate is 93%, etc., etc." It's also more meaningful to the person to whom it's being said. But it tends to distort the purpose of standards, which is primarily to measure performance scientifically rather than sim-

Probability of a Complete Order				
Number of Lines In Order	**Line Item Fill Rate**			
	90%	**92%**	**94%**	**95%**
1	.900	.920	.940	.950
2	.810	.846	.884	.903
3	.729	.779	.831	.857
4	.656	.716	.781	.815
5	.590	.659	.734	.774
6	.531	.606	.690	.735
7	.478	.558	.648	.698
8	.430	.513	.610	.663
9	.387	.472	.573	.630
10	.348	.434	.538	.599
11	.314	.399	.506	.569
12	.282	.368	.476	.540
13	.254	.338	.447	.513
14	.225	.311	.400	.488
15	.206	.286	.395	.463
16	.185	.263	.372	.440
17	.167	.243	.349	.418
18	.150	.223	.328	.397
19	.135	.205	.309	.377
20	.122	.185	.290	.358

Figure 10-5

Composite Standard or Weighted Index			
	(A) WEIGHTING OR IMPORTANCE	(B) ACTUAL READING	(A x B) WEIGHTED INDEX
Complete order fill	25%	70%	.1750
Line item fill	15%	92%	.1380
On-time shipment/delivery	20%	89%	.1780
Accuracy of orders	25%	91%	.2275
Response to emergency, fill-in	10%	80%	.0800
Above minimum order	3%	60%	.0180
Other	1.5%	45%	.0068
Other	.5%	85%	.0043
	Index		.8276

Figure 10-6. Form for developing a single-number measure of customer service performance. To use: 1. List standards that are currently being used (or will be used) in the left hand column. 2. On the basis of 100% total for all standards listed, indicate in Column A the weighting (percentage of 100%) to be assigned to each standard. 3. When performance has been measured against each standard, indicate the actual performance in Column B as the percentage of standard actually achieved. 4. Multiply Column A and Column B and indicate the result in the right hand column under "Weighted Index." 5. Now, add all percentages in the right hand column; the total will be the single-number index of customer service performance. A score of 100% would mean that all standards had been met; a score of 95% would indicate that the most important—those with the greatest weighting—had been met. The score achieved in the illustration would suggest fairly low performance on a heavily weighted function, and reference to the individual data does indicate only 70% performance on the complete order fill standard.

ply give a broad reading of how "good" customer service actually is.

Even so, a single number rating may be required by management for reporting reasons or for charting on a graph. If so, the method demonstrated in figure 6 and the type of graph shown in figure 7 should be used for this purpose. Rather than simply averaging the percentages, this approach first allows for weighting each standard according to its importance to the company and then developing a composite single reading in which each element reflects that weighting.

Other Comparisons

By now, the manager has collected considerable data about the performance of the customer service department. Can it be used other than for measuring performance against standards?

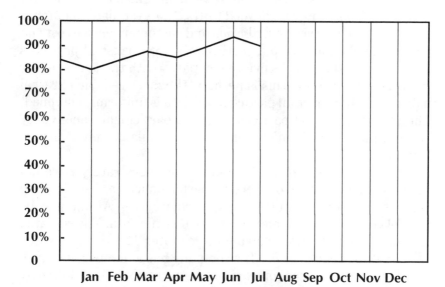

Figure 10-7. Charting customer service performance against standard using a composite or single-number standard of the type illustrated in Figure 6, page 158.

Indeed it can. There are several sources of data on performance by other firms in the same industry group, opportunities to estimate competitive performance, and possible internal comparisons that can be made.

External comparisons. In some industries, data on customer service performance is compiled by the trade association for the industry, sometimes by a publication or other third party, such as a doctoral candidate preparing a Ph.D. thesis. Care should be taken, however, to verify that similar measures were employed and the same words mean the same things. If the term "order cycle" is used, it should be defined as to when it begins and when it ends; otherwise comparisons don't mean anything. If the research doesn't distinguish between items shipped from stock and items made or finished to order, comparing order cycle performance will have little value. However, it is worth the effort to make a comparison wherever the numbers are truly comparable and the same things are being measured.

Participative studies. A database maintained by Herbert W. Davis and Company, Englewood Cliffs, N.J., tabulates a number of elements of physical distribution and customer service cost and performance annually, and participants are furnished printouts showing how their performance compares with the averages for their industry group. This is perhaps the most reliable external index available, since all participants' data is uniformly compiled. There is no charge for participating, and participants' anonymity is maintained. The detailed printouts are available only to participants.

Competitive studies. Although customers rarely have detailed statistical data on vendor performance, a few do keep records on on-time performance and order cycles. Also, it may be possible to survey customers for more specific data. The research techniques for this are explained in chapter 11.

Internal comparisons. If a company has a number of branch locations, performance comparisons between those locations may be the most reliable measure of all. First, the manager has complete access to all data and can guarantee its validity and uniformity. Besides comparing performance at the firm's different locations, the manager can insure that only comparable locations are selected, with comparable product mix and volume. Once the comparison has been made, any location varying significantly from the others should be scrutinized carefully. This goes for locations that are significantly better as well as those that are significantly poorer in performance. There is usually a good reason for the difference, but a better score doesn't always mean a more desirable situation. One firm found that one of its branch locations had an exceptionally low error rate—less than half that of other locations. When the manager was asked why the error rate was so low, the reply was to present a detailed description of procedures. But the procedures were essentially the same as at other locations. Further investigation revealed that a line supervisor at the outstanding location was, as one of

Item To Be Measured	Number	Percent
Total Orders Received		100%
Total Lines		100%
Total Dollars		100%
Orders Shipped Complete		
Orders Shipped Partial		
Orders Completely Backordered		
Line Items Shipped		
Line Items Backordered		
Orders Filled by Dollars		
Orders Backordered by Dollars		

Figure 10-8. Form for recording customer service performance in product availability. Standards for complete order fill, line item fill and dollar fill may be written in at the right to facilitate comparison of actual performance with those standards. The form can also be expanded to include internal order cycle, shipment standards, error rate and other standards conventionally expressed in percentages.

the workers there put it, "a real nut about mistakes—he'll go to almost any lengths to prevent them." It turned out that morale at the location was poor, and several key workers were on the verge of resigning. Overall productivity was lower than at other branches, and it appeared likely that it would continue to drop. The internal comparison had served its purpose by flagging a situation that needed correcting. But even then, the statistics did not mean what they appeared to mean. Of course, they *could* have.

And this is a major pitfall in all systems involving standards and measures of performance. Numbers are only numbers. Poor scores may mean that standards have been set too high to begin with, or that data may not have been gathered properly. Employees who are recording their own performance may be under-reporting for fear that if they do too well, standards may be raised and more will be expected of them. By the same token, high scores may well be a sign that standards are in fact too low. Then, there is always that happy circumstance when the numbers and the manager's instincts agree that the customer service department is indeed doing a fine job, and the customers have every reason to be as satisfied as they appear to be!

11

CUSTOMER SERVICE RESEARCH

Is customer service research worthwhile, or is customer service really an "intangible that can't be measured" as some executives say it is? A few examples should make it clear that not only can customer service be measured using standard market research and management science techniques, but also the investment will very often pay off in very large dollar amounts.

The high cost of customer service failures. Writing in the July, 1973 issue of *Harvard Business Review*, consultant Harvey Shycon described the results of research revealing that: (1) the average cost of a customer service failure, through delisting of product lines, came to $10,000; (2) that this type of "reprisal," as he called it, could come after as few as three or four failures; and (3) that the cost of a stockout in the food industry was about $50 per day, whereas the cost of maintaining sufficient inventory to avoid such stockouts was only forty cents a day.

Backorders cause customers to switch suppliers. A study by William D. Perreault, Jr. and Frederick A. Russ published in the April, 1976 issue of *Journal of Marketing* indicated that in purchases of electronic components, 32% of purchasing agents faced with a backorder situation at their vendors would simply cancel the order and purchase the components elsewhere. The study also revealed a great deal about buyer preferences in service.

Failure to respond to emergency service requests also costs business. The same study revealed that 42% of buyers would consider it justification for switching vendors if a vendor didn't respond the first time such a request was made; another 54% would change if the problem occurred several times.

Impact of a 5% reduction in customer service levels. Customers would cut back their purchases by anywhere from 7% all the way to 22%, according to findings in the landmark study, *Customer Service: Meaning and Measurement* commissioned by the NCPDM and conducted by the Ohio State University. The study, published in 1976, was the first major analysis of customer service practices and organizations in the United States.

Customer complaints and brand loyalty. For the first time ever, mathematical correlations between complaint handling and brand loyalty were established in another landmark study, *Consumer Complaints in America,* conducted for the U.S. Office of Consumer Affairs by Technical Assistance Research Programs, Inc. and published in 1979. Among the many significant findings of this important study was the fact that there is a remarkable degree of brand loyalty among customers who complain, even among those whose complaints are not satisfied. By contrast, nine out of ten customers who have problems but do not complain stop buying the product altogether.

Complaining customers who are handled well buy more! Another study conducted by Technical Assistance Research Programs, Inc., this time for Coca-Cola, showed a strong correlation between future purchases and a customer's feeling about the kind of response when they registered a non-product complaint, i.e., about advertising, contests, etc. The study came up with a number of useful statistics about word-of-mouth advertising and its effect on purchases by others, but the most striking finding was that customers who are completely satisfied with the company's response to a complaint (i.e., the way it is handled) are five times as likely to buy greater quantities of the product as customers who are not satisfied with the handling of their complaints.

Salaries, organization, telephone usage, incentive programs, productivity measurement and more. A number of research projects conducted by *Customer Service Newsletter* over the years have revealed important trends and applications in customer service management.

G.E. service beats advertising in market share growth. A meticulous four-year test conducted by General Electric dramatically demonstrated the powerful role of service in increasing market share in highly competitive markets. Described in *Marketing News* for June 24, 1983, the study revealed that two major service ingredients—readiness-to-serve (RTS) and quality-of-service (QOS)—are far more effective in increasing market share than substantial advertising outlays over a period of time. In brief, investing in more telephone lines and more skilled persons to respond to and handle customer needs brings in more business than investing in advertising.

Surprises. A company surveyed its customers to measure actual transit time of shipments as well as satisfaction with customer service, and was pleasantly surprised to discover that even though some customers were receiving consistently inferior and irregular transportation service, they nonetheless reported high degrees of satisfaction with customer service. Another firm surveyed customers and found out that only 21% wanted acknowledgments of their orders mailed back; at 1000 orders a day, the net savings would be $94,000 a year. Other companies were equally surprised at some of the findings of their particular customer service research—some pleasantly surprised, some less so, including a company that thought it was No. 1 with its customers when it turned out to be only No. 3.

These hard numbers underscore not only the *value* of customer service research, but also its importance in planning and managing the function. These examples also show that customer service research can be used for a number of different purposes, and that customers can be surveyed on a single point, or about a number of points. Perhaps the most important point is that the research doesn't have to be a major undertaking, nor highly formal. Obviously the integrity of data is important, and the objectivity of the research itself, but the majority of customer service research projects lend themselves to handling within the customer service department rather than turning over to the market research group or an outside firm. Not that there's anything wrong with either of these options, but they do tend to take longer and cost more. So the primary emphasis here will be on do-it-yourself approaches to this important subject.

Fact-Finding

"Research" is an elegant way of describing organized fact-finding or the gathering of information. A family shopping for an automobile may research different makes and models, deals and dealers, ease of driving and other features. A customer service representative handling a customer complaint will research it before making or suggesting a resolution. And of course there is the whole spectrum of scientific research ranging from the astronomical experiments of the early Egyptians to space exploration and the medical and scientific breakthroughs of the twentieth century.

What distinguishes research from idle curiosity is that it is *organized* and *purposeful.* There are two principal kinds of research. *Pure* research is an effort to increase knowledge in great depth about a given subject, with the objective primarily to obtain the broad benefits of having such knowledge. *Applied* research, as the name implies, deals with specific problems or situations with the objective of solving or improving them. Business research, including customer service research, will generally fall into the category of applied research.

Research is fundamental to good management. It is not a substitute for experience and is not intended to be. Good management requires accurate, objective information for decision-making, and research helps provide it. Because research is organized and objective, it protects the manager from the disorganized, subjective and sometimes distorted combination of half-facts and opinions that often masquerade as "experience." Experience is often a matter of finding what works by doing it wrong the first time; research helps find out what works right the first time.

Customer Requirements

Most of the subjects the customer service manager will want to research will deal with customer requirements and attitudes, or with customer service operations themselves. In the first category, the research objectives will include information of these types:

• Customer service features and levels customers really want and need; ranking of customer service elements in importance.

• Specific data about individual customer groups, and how their operations may impose certain customer service requirements. For example, firms with continuous process manufacturing may periodically require emergency shipments with lead times of eight hours or less. Firms requiring kanban or just-in-time delivery, as well as those ordering jobsite deliveries, impose special requirements.

• Data indicating opportunities for differential standards.

• Specific data about what kinds of service customers are getting from the firm, vs. the service they are getting from the competition; customer perceptions in general.

• Customers' suggestions for service improvements.

• Possible impact of changes in customer service procedures or levels on customers' buying habits.

• Customer acceptance of new policies on credit, returns, exchanges, minimum orders and other sensitive areas.

• Specific problems, including misunderstandings and misperceptions that relate to customer service and have not come to light before.

Informal Research: Customer Visitations

The distribution manager of a large Eastern manufacturing firm is responsible for customer service operations at the firm's regional distribution centers. He has set up a "dealer visitation program" whereby the managers at these regional distribution

Visitation Report

Dealer Visited: _____ Date: _____

City/State: _____ Time Spent: _____

Who did you talk with at the dealer's place of business?:

Name _____ Title

Who accompanied you? _____

Dealer Volume _____

Type of Operation: _____

General Description of Facility:

A) Items to discuss:

1) Inventory—How many lines does he carry and what is his average inventory level?

2) Order Placing—Does he consider our order personnel efficient, helpful, courteous and knowledgeable?

If he could change the procedure, how would he like to see it changed?

Does he like to know of item substitution if original item is not available?

3) Order Fill—What does he expect as a percentage of order fill?

What would he accept as a percent knowing most, if not all, companies have out of stock items, slow moving items, etc?

8) Adjustments—Is he satisfied with the time involved in receiving adjustment credits?

If not, why?

Does he always send claim forms at same time as adjustments are shipped?

9) General—What one thing would he like to see changed in our system which would most benefit him?

Does he deal with any supplier who has a central order department?

If so, what does he think of it? Is order fill better, delivery time better, better information on stock availability, etc.?

10) Other items discussed.

B) How does the dealer order?

1) On impulse

2) Weekly

3) After sale made on customer request

4) Other (such as because of discounts or unit quantities);

C) Does he have an inventory control system?

1) Did it appear to be effective?

2) Were you able to offer help?

3) If no system, does he believe it would be beneficial?

Figure 11-1. Dealer visitation report used by distribution center managers to record customer service related information about customer practices and requirements. Managers make up to three visits a month with combined goals of fact finding and

4) Backorders—How does he feel about backorders in general?

How long does he think it should take to fill them? How long is he willing to keep an item on backorders if it is:

a) A current item available from other suppliers?

b) A specialty item in tight supply?

Does he want backorders shipped when available or does he want a reconfirmation prior to shipment?

5) Delivery Time—Does he consider the time involved from when he places the order until received acceptable?

If not, what is wrong and what would he like to have?

6) Carrier—Does he specify carrier? (Who?)

Does the carrier give efficient service?

By changing the carrier, could we give better service?

Would he accept a change in carrier if he could get better service?

If not, why?

If he won't change, is he satisfied with the delivery cycle?

7) Invoicing—Does he have comments regarding our invoicing?

If so, what are the comments?

4) Were you able to offer any ideas?

D) What is his major brand?

E) What other brands does he warehouse?

F) What are some of his likes and dislikes about all his suppliers?

G) Do his other suppliers have:

1) Weight restrictions?

2) Unit restrictions?

3) Other (if able, give requirements);

H) How does the dealer rate us in comparison to his other suppliers?

I) Did you consider this visit worthwhile; why or why not?

J) Do you think the dealer appreciated your visit? Why?

To: _____ From: _____

SUBJECT: Dealer Visitation Schedule

I have scheduled a visit to the following dealers during _____ (no more than 3.)

Date	Name of Account	City/State	Volume

(Note: Send to Home Office prior to visit.)

goodwill, including cementing relations with key customer personnel. *Inset—* form used to notify management of visitation schedules planned. This type of informal customer research can be very effective.

centers are required to make up to three customer visits a month with the combined objective of developing personal bonds with key people at the dealer site and developing specific information that can be used to improve customer service. Figure 1 shows the "Dealer Visitation Report" that the manager fills out and files with headquarters after such visits.

Here is a sampling of the instructions the distribution manager gave his managers when the dealer visitation program was launched:

"During your visit, don't snub the dealer's workers. Ask if you can meet the people who order merchandise, the warehouse people who handle merchandise and others if necessary. Don't take a lot of their time, but be cordial; ask how things are going, and be sure to look around to see how things are done. These people can be the solution to some problems: yours or theirs.

"If you see where you can offer suggestions on how things might be better, don't push them. Be subtle, and offer your suggestions to the owner or manager.

"Try to see their inventory system, if they have one.

"Determine what makes them order. Is merchandise sold before they order? Do they have a service level system? How do they order: via phone, through salespeople, how? How quickly do they think merchandise should be shipped? What percentage of order fill do they consider acceptable? Would they prefer quick shipment with low order fill, or slower shipment with higher order fill? What do they think of competitive service?

"Some of this can be accomplished just through talk. Be courteous! Be a good listener. Be proud of who you represent. Write a thank you letter as soon as you return to your office."

An increasing number of companies are conducting some variation of this customer-visitation type of informal research. The emphasis is on fact-finding and at the same time improving ties with the customer. Most are not quite as highly organized as the excellent approach described here, but any kind of personal contact between customer service personnel and their customers is worthwhile. Some companies in fact have regular programs whereby the customer service reps themselves go out in the field, usually in the company of field sales personnel, to visit in person the customers they've known only via the telephone up to this point. It's a good way for customer service personnel to learn about and develop a feel for the customer's operations. It also transforms what's been a one-dimensional relationship into a three-dimensional one. Co-selling, as it's frequently called, also improves the relationship between the customer service rep and the salesperson in the territory. The rep also learns that selling isn't as glamorous as it's sometimes seen from inside the department, and a particular fringe benefit of these visits is that they're extremely good for the rep's morale.

Another type of informal research is to simply call customers on a periodic basis to gather basically the same type of information. This can be done either by the manager or by individual reps, or by both. One firm with a medium-sized customer service department has a requirement that each customer service rep call one customer a day simply on the basis of "Just calling to see how things are going, if there are any problems I can help you with." This helps measure satisfaction and at the same time uncovers any problems the customer may not have bothered to mention. It also helps the relationship with the customer. And while one call a day is not statistically significant, with 30 reps making such calls it comes to over 600 "visitations" a month.

Informal customer research of this type has many values, and every customer service manager would be well advised to conduct it on a regular basis. Even so, it should not be used as a substitute for formal research conducted with larger samples and in a standard, objective and scientific fashion.

The Three Types of Formal Customer Research

Formal customer service research is objective and it is also representative. It requires developing a scientific sample of customers, and standard interrogatories or questionnaires that will elicit reliable, comparable information from a large enough sample to be statistically valid. And of course it must have an objective that relates to the overall customer service mission.

The manager should take special pains to see that the objective of the research is set forth in very specific language. A great deal of thought should go into what *really* needs to be known, and what use the information will be put to. A major pitfall at this point is to go after information that is not what's needed, and to overlook information that is. Here are some examples of research objectives as they might be set forth:

• To measure our customer service performance against the competition with an eye towards adjusting those elements of customer service where the firm is outranked by the competition.

• To determine whether present distribution methods could be changed to direct plant shipment for selected customers without affecting overall service.

• To determine customers' ordering and inventory practices in order to develop a more responsive order system.

• To determine preferable modes of documentation and data interchange.

• To measure regional differences, if any, in perceptions of customer service and relative ratios of satisfaction/dissatisfaction.

Once an objective has been decided on, the next step is to decide what form the actual research will take. The three types of formal research available to the manager are: (1) face-to-face, in-depth interviews with customers, conducted by trained interviewers; (2) telephone interviews; and (3) mail surveys of customers.

Professionally structured and conducted personal interviews (as opposed to visitations of the type described above) are a superior method of research which is practically mandated when major changes in customer service practices or policies are being contemplated. A skilled interviewer can develop a great deal of information via probing that wouldn't come out in conventional surveying. The interviewer can also explain questions that the interviewee may not understand, or clarify the response to them.

Personal interviews that are undertaken in advance of telephone interviews and mail surveys can also be used to adjust and improve the questions and format in the later research. Terminology, for example, may mean one thing to the firm sponsoring the research and different things to the individuals being interviewed. Personal interviews would bring out this confusion where a mail survey would not. But the overall quality and reliability of the information developed from professional in-person research are justification in themselves. The one problem with personal interviews is that they tend to be expensive. A convenient rule of thumb is that a personal interview costs about ten times the cost of a telephone interview, and a telephone interview costs about ten times the cost of a mail survey—which costs about ten times the cost of the postage for each piece mailed. These costs include the cost of interpretation and tabulation.

Telephone interviews are basically the same as in-person interviews except that they generally can't be as long or detailed, and the person-to-person dimension is considerably less. This may restrict the amount of data and, to some extent, the quality. It is an excellent way to supplement personal interviews, or to validate or probe further into data uncovered in mail surveys.

Mail surveys are an excellent way of gathering a limited amount of information from a large number of people, but because there is no one present to prompt or explain to the individual being surveyed, they must be very carefully structured to avoid misinterpretation and their format must be carefully designed to facilitate completion. The response rates on customer surveys tend to be 20% and better—sometimes as high as 80%— but anything above 20% is sufficient. As indicated above, major changes would never be made on the strength of a mail survey in any event; personal and/or phone interviews would be needed to probe further and validate the findings of a mail survey. Another advantage of mail surveys is that they are fast and relatively easy to prepare and tabulate. They don't require professionals as personal and phone interviews do. The customer service man-

Pros

In-person interview
1. Effective
2. Probing possible
3. Interview/questions can be adapted to fit specific situation
4. Interviewer can clarify, request additional information
5. Completion rate is high
6. Visual aids can be used
7. Interviewee can look up information
8. Interviewer can maintain interest during long questionnaire

Phone survey
1. Almost as effective as in-person
2. Probing possible
3. Questions can be adapted to fit specific situation
4. Good for eliciting descriptive type information
5. Completion rate is high
6. Flexibility in format may result in additional, unexpected info
7. Interviewer can maintain interest during long questionnaire

Mail survey
1. Inexpensive (about $2 each)
2. Requires least amount of staff and time for administration
3. Can be done quickly
4. Can be anonymous
5. Answers tend to be more frank
6. Good for surveying relatively large numbers of customers
7. Good for comparing firm's performance with that of competitors
8. Respondent can look up info

Figure 11-2. Advantages and disadvantages of the different research metho

ager and staff can do the entire job, and they can segment their customer list and survey regularly throughout the year. And a mail survey is an excellent way to begin any customer research, particularly for the manager who has had limited experience in

---

Cons

In-person interview
1. Expensive (about $300-500 each)
2. Time-consuming
3. Should be conducted by trained market researcher, rather than CS dept. staff or company salesperson
4. Interviewee may be less than frank with interviewer, as a result of desire to please

Phone survey
1. Costly (about $50-100 each)
2. Should be conducted by person trained in the technique
3. Interviewee may be less than frank with interviewer, although this is less of a problem with phone surveys than with in-person interviews
4. Replies tend to be shorter than with in-person interview
5. Length of interview must be limited to 15-30 minutes in most cases
6. Interviewer cannot take into account facial expressions, gestures, etc.
7. Difficult to ask interviewee to look up info

Mail survey
1. Has lowest completion rate
2. Questions subject to misinterpretation by respondent
3. Probing not possible
4. Some questions may not be answered at all
5. Respondent's nonverbal communications cannot be taken into account

---

commonly used in customer service research.

this area. Since both telephone research and in-person research would normally be conducted by organizations or individuals skilled in these techniques, this section will confine its description to a mail survey of the type the manager might undertake as a first try.

A Model Customer Service Survey by Mail

• *Assemble backup information.* This will include records of past customer service performance, errors and exceptions reports, complaint files (statistical as well as actual letters or reports), other correspondence from customers and other departmental records. The views and experience of others should also be solicited.

• *Set survey objectives.* If there are problems of getting support for the survey or any other "political" matters to deal with, one of the approaches described in chapter 16 on improving public relations may be helpful, that is, by orienting your research project to what others see as their own primary interests. If these problems do not surface (and in all probability they won't for something as basic as a mail survey), then the manager should develop survey objectives as described earlier in this chapter—and with a great deal of thought.

• *Construct the survey sample.* Most companies have fairly large customer lists which it would be impractical to survey in their entirety. First of all it would be expensive, but more importantly it would likely bring distorted results. Pareto's Law, discussed earlier, means that 20% of a firm's customers account for 80% of its business. The firm will usually want to see that these important customers' needs are being met before it becomes involved with the 80% who bring in only 20% of the business. Thus a survey mailed to the entire list on a "one person, one vote" basis would find the responses skewed four-to-one in favor of the less important customers. In order to avoid this type of problem, a sample is constructed which represents customers in proportion to their importance to the company. This type of sample is shown in figure 3, where the number of customers within any revenue group to be surveyed will be determined by the percentage of actual revenue derived from that group. But that may not be enough; if the firm serves very distinct markets with different needs, it should make allowance for this in its sample—either that, or survey the different markets separately. If it's decided to survey across the board, i.e., use a representative sample, then a sample can be constructed using the form shown in figure 4. Here again, the number of companies in any

	Profile				
	Customer Analysis			**Sales Analysis**	
	No.				
Classification	**Customers**	**%**		**Sales**	**%**
"A" Customers: Over $100,000	500	2.5		$40,000,000	40
"B" Customers: $50,000-$99,999	1,000	5.0		$25,000,000	25
"C" Customers: $25,000-$49,999	2,500	12.5		$15,000,000	15
"D" Customers: $10,000-$24,999	3,500	17.5		$12,000,000	12
"E" Customers: $5,000-$9,999	5,000	25.0		$ 5,000,000	5
"F" Customers: Under $5,000	7,500	37.5		$ 3,000,000	3
Totals	20,000	100%		$100,000,000	100%

Figure 11-3. Form for stratifying customers by sales can also serve as a basis for constructing a sample for mail survey. In this example, assuming each customer group will be represented in the sample by a percentage reflecting its percentage of sales, Group A would have 40% representation, Group B 25%, Group C 15%, and so forth. In a sample of 1,000 customers selected for the survey, 400 would be from Group A, 250 from Group B, 150 from Group C, 120 from Group D, 50 from Group E and 30 from Group F.

market or industry group to be surveyed will be determined by that group's percentage of total revenues.

• *Determine sample size.* How many customers should be surveyed? This will vary with the size of the customer list, but in most cases it should not be necessary to mail to more than 1000 customer names in order to get adequate representation of the customer base and to insure a sufficient response to provide reliable information.

• *Weight or adjust sample as necessary.* If the sample is very small, it may be necessary to weight responses. For example, if there are not enough customers in a given group to fill out the sample, then the entire group should be included and their responses weighted proportionately. For example, in a survey mailed to 1000 customers, group "B" accounts for 20% of revenues but only includes 100 customers. In such a case, the sample should have 200 and this deficiency would be compensated simply by weighting each response from a member of this group—in this instance each response would be given double value, or counted

Profile		
Dollar Revenue By Major Grouping		
Classification or Channel	Sales	% of Total
2891 Adhesives		
2842 Cleaning Compounds		
2851 Paints		
2841 Soap, Detergents		
2893 Printing Inks		
0000 Others		
Totals		

Figure 11-4. Form for analyzing sales by market or industry group can be used for constructing a sample representing each market or industry group proportionately to sales revenue. (See Figure 11-3)

as two responses. In some cases it may actually be desirable to *under-represent* larger customers. This would be true in a satisfaction survey; larger customers are usually well known to all personnel and automatically get special treatment. Their responses would not necessarily be valid for "B" and "C" customers who might be getting inferior treatment and are too important to risk losng. In such a situation, the "B" and "C" portions of the sample would be increased, and the "A" portion decreased accordingly.

 • *Develop the survey questionnaire.* There is an infinite variety of survey formats. In a mail survey, the format should be as short and simple as possible. Lengthy questionnaires discourage responses, as do complex rating systems. Figure 5 is a survey that has been used successfully in a number of versions by companies of all types. It combines check-off answers with qualitative or open-end comments, and it is relatively easy to tabulate. Another version might use a multiple-choice format as shown in figure 6, or a more complex "agree-disagree" format of the type in figure 7. If the manager's concern is with competitive service, the survey form shown in figure 8 permits customers to rank both vendors and the importance of specific attributes. To minimize bias, this type of survey might be turned over to an outside research organization for mailing and tabulating, with the sponsor remaining anonymous.

 • *Avoid irrelevancies and ambiguities.* Customers should not be asked questions about age, salaries, etc. unless the information has a genuine bearing on the survey objective. If confidential information is requested, then anonymity for respondents must be guaranteed; even so, the response rate will probably drop. Questions should not be asked out of curiosity. Ambiguous terms that can be taken to mean different things should either be explained or omitted. "Order cycle" and "private fleet" are two examples of terms that were used on surveys, only to have it turn out that different respondents defined the terms quite differently. As a result, survey findings were meaningless and had to be discarded at a cost of several thousand dollars. Another example: "Who is responsible for purchases of product 'X'?" might appear to be a valid question, but in fact it has several

Customer Service Questionnaire

I. Customer service department
   a. Attitude of customer service reps
   b. Hours department is available
   c. Ability to handle various inquiries
   d. Follow-up after orders are placed

Excellent	Good	Average	Poor

Suggestions and general comments:

II. Distribution
   a. Delivery time
   b. Complete order ratio compared to competitors
   c. General rating from your viewpoint

Excellent	Good	Average	Poor

Suggestions and general comments:

III. Product quality
   a. Compared to competitors' products
   b. General rating from your viewpoint
   c. Today's rating compared to 5 years ago

Excellent	Good	Average	Poor

Suggestions and general comments:

IV. Additional comments—(but particularly *new* ideas and suggestions)

(Please use back if necessary and
 return in the enclosed envelope.
Thank you for your cooperation!)

Signed _____

Figure 11-5. A basic questionnaire used successfully by many companies. Note provision for both multiple-choice and open-end or essay-type answers ("Suggestions and general comments")

Dear Friends:

As the Customer Service Supervisor, it is my responsibility to see that your orders are handled in a prompt and orderly fashion to insure your satisfaction and goodwill. I personally feel we are meeting your needs but I am more concerned with *your* responses to our efforts.

Would you please take a few moments of your time to respond to the following questions to give us assistance in trying to improve this vital area of communication?

1. When you phone in a purchase order, do you find the person taking your order to be courteous and helpful?

        ( ) Always   ( ) Usually   ( ) Occasionally

2. When you phone into our switchboard, is your call handled in a quick and efficient manner?

        ( ) Always   ( ) Usually   ( ) Occasionally

3. When you have a complaint or problem, do you find Customer Service personnel to be attentive and understanding of your problems?

        ( ) Always   ( ) Usually   ( ) Occasionally

4. When following up on an order, do you find Customer Service personnel able to answer your questions to your satisfaction?

        ( ) Always   ( ) Usually   ( ) Occasionally

5. Do you find that Customer Service personnel can answer your technical questions to your satisfaction?

        ( ) Always   ( ) Usually   ( ) Occasionally

6. When we say we will call you back with information, do we call back soon enough to your satisfaction?

        ( ) Always   ( ) Usually   ( ) Occasionally

7. Do you find the customer information pages listing products you use to be of assistance to you when ordering?

        ( ) Always   ( ) Usually   ( ) Occasionally

8. Do you find our numbering system of products easy to understand?

        ( ) Always   ( ) Usually   ( ) Occasionally

9. Do you find our catalog and price pages to be easy to understand?

        ( ) Always   ( ) Usually   ( ) Occasionally

10. Do you have any comments to make in regards to our Customer Service Department?

Enclosed you will find a stamped self-addressed envelope for your response. I want to personally thank you for your cooperation in helping us provide you with better service.

Sincerely yours,

Customer Service Supervisor

Figure 11-6. Example of a self-contained, multiple-choice questionnaire which received an excellent 45% response from customers of a Midwestern manufacturer.

	Strongly agree	Agree	Neither agree nor disagree	Disagree	Strongly disagree
1. There is little red tape when I deal with _____					
2. I get accurate and timely response to my inquiries					
3. Your products are available to my satisfaction					
4. My order entry representative is courteous					
5. Claims are processed within a reasonable period of time					
6. You provide satisfactory technical assistance and information					
7. I often have to return items because of wrong material shipped					
8. I can obtain order status or product information with a single phone call					
9. I often have to return items because of damaged goods					
10. I am buying less from you due to the number of backorders					
11. I must wait too long to receive materials after ordering					
12. I get timely notice if my shipment date cannot be met					
13. I know my order entry rep by name					
14. Minimum order/item requirements are reasonable					
15. You meet promised shipping dates					
16. My complaints are adequately handled					
17. I can depend upon a consistent time period from order entry to shipment of goods					
18. Next-day service is essential for my business					
19. Emergency service is available upon request.					
20. Lead time for noncatalog items is reasonable					
21. It is easy for me to place an order					

Comments:

Figure 11-7. "Agree-Disagree" format in questionnaire is used by many researchers in preference to numerical rating systems which may confuse questionnaire respondents.

Attitudes of Buyers

We would appreciate your impressions of each supplier with which you are familiar. There are no right or wrong answers; these are only attitudes.

Please rate each factor for each supplier as follows: "E" – Excellent; "G" – Good; "F" – Fair (or average); "P" – Poor. Then please indicate, in the last column, the importance of each factor to you.

Factors	Company A*	Company B	Company C	Company D	Please indicate importance: High	Med.	Low
Price (lowest = "E"; highest – "P")					☐	☐	☐
Depth of product lines					☐	☐	☐
Product quality					☐	☐	☐
Consistency of quality					☐	☐	☐
Calibre of sales presentation					☐	☐	☐
Relationships with supplier's personnel					☐	☐	☐
Calibre of top management					☐	☐	☐
Competitiveness of supplier					☐	☐	☐
Technological expertise					☐	☐	☐
Appropriate location for communications & service					☐	☐	☐
Appropriate location for distribution					☐	☐	☐
Customer orientation (services, response to needs, etc.)					☐	☐	☐
Overall rating of suppliers					☐	☐	☐

*Original questionnaire listed names of actual companies.

Figure 11-8. Form for determining customer attitudes and ranking of vendors. Note that form also asks customer to rank each customer service element as well as the vendors performing it.

The Customer Service Corporation

221 National Press Building   Washington, D.C. 20045   202/628-8464

Mr. Philip W. Freeman
Purchasing Agent
Parkside Manufacturing Co., Inc.
4210 Parkside Boulevard, S.E.
Washington, D.C. 20045

Dear Mr. Freeman:

We at the Customer Service Corporation firmly believe that the quality of our customer service must be as excellent as the quality of our products.

We regularly employ internal measuring tools to determine how effective our customer service would appear to be. But . . . the ultimate measure is the rating that *you* give us!

For that reason, I'm asking that you please answer the brief questions on the enclosed Customer Service questionaire. Don't spare our feelings, either! We're looking for every area in which improvement can be made. Of course any additional comments you may care to make will be more than welcome.

A stamped envelope addressed to my personal attention is enclosed for your convenience in replying. I am looking forward to your reply with great interest, and be assured that it will receive our careful attention.

Many thanks for your help.

Sincerely,

JRB/es

J. R. Brainerd
Customer Service Manager

P.S. Please return the questionaire to me by April 15.

Figure 11-9. Personalized letter accompanying mail survey should be on good quality stationery and have appearance of individually typed and signed letter. Names on list should be carefully selected to reflect genuine buying influences in customer companies.

different interpretations: (1) who is the person who specifies the product; (2) who is the purchasing agent who approves or disapproves of suppliers; or (3) who is the buyer who actually negotiates the purchase but reports to the purchasing agent. In designing questionnaires where such ambiguities may arise, it's often desirable to include an open end question to the effect of: "Please explain why you answered as you did," or to specifically define what is meant by "order cycle," "private fleet," "buyer" and similar terms used in the questionnaire.

• *Avoid numerical rating systems whenever possible.* Asking respondents to rate customer service on a numerical scale tends to confuse them. It is preferable to use familiar words like "poor," "fair," "good," "superior," and, if a numerical rating is desired, assign values after the responses have been received and preparations are being made to tabulate the returns. Having assigned the values, the manager will know precisely what the numerical findings mean when they are printed out. Of course it can be just as meaningful not to assign numbers and to simply count responses in each category, which enables statements of this order: "10% of our customers rated us as 'poor,' 15% as 'fair,'

XYZ Manufacturing Co. Ltd.

We wish to improve the delivery of our products to you.
Would you please help us by completing and returning this postcard?

Customer . . . . City . . . .
Your Order. . . . . Number of Pieces . . . .
Date Shipped. . . . . Routed. . . . .
Date Received . . . . Condition . . . .
Comments/Suggestions. . . . .
. . . .

Acknowledged by . . . .   Thank you for your help.
                        Please Print

Title. . . . .   Traffic Manager

Figure 11-10. Postcard questionnaire accompanies shipment and is filled out and returned by receiving clerk, provides quick feedback on transit time and condition of shipment upon arrival.

50% as 'good,' and 25% as 'superior.'" In making presentations to others, this type of statement is likely to carry more weight than "On the average, our customers gave us a score of eight on a ten-point scale." Using numbers to *rank* things in order of preference—first, second, etc.—is of course perfectly all right.

• *Ask for signed responses when possible.* Signed questionnaires are preferable to anonymous ones for several reasons: (1) they tend to discourage exaggeration about service quality on

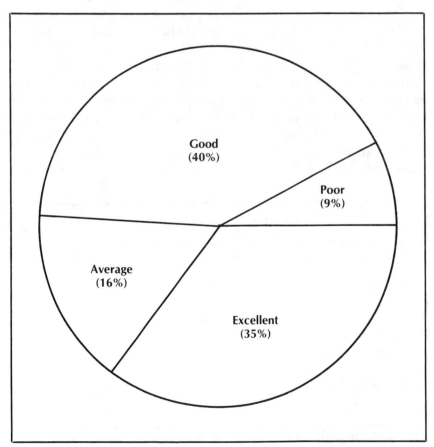

Figure 11-11. Graphic rendering of responses from questionnaire shown in Figure 5 shows results of total survey with all categories combined.

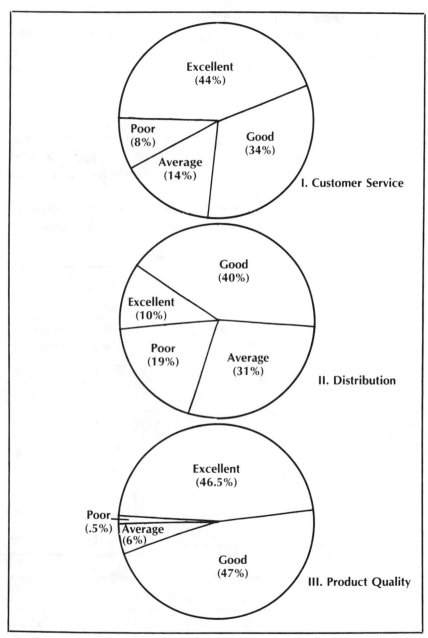

Figure 11-12. Rating results of the total survey by category.

the negative side; (2) they frequently uncover serious problems that a particular customer is having but never mentioned before; and (3) they enable a higher response rate, and therefore more valid findings, by simply following up on individuals known not to have responded. On the other hand, some customers may not want to be known as trouble-makers or to be identified as "the person who got Sam in trouble," and may avoid signing their names for that reason. Anonymity may be preferable in situations of this type and also where confidential information may be requested that would not be forthcoming if the individual and the company had to be identified.

● *Go first class in all respects.* Use a personalized letter of the type shown in figure 9; address the individual by name and

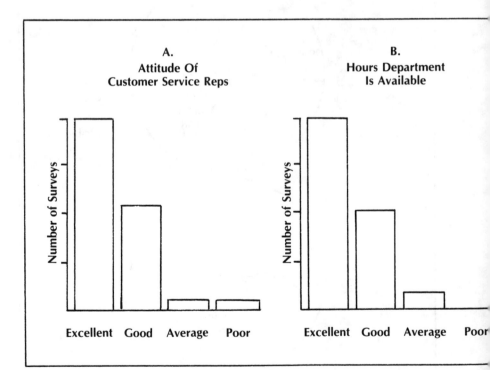

Figure 11-13. Customer service department rating by service element; other elements are shown in graphs in Figure 14.

title and have the letter signed personally or by Autopen or similar device. The customer should be made to feel that his or her response is important, and the quality of the letterhead, letter and questionnaire should bear this out. A No. 9 envelope should be enclosed for the response, with the name and address of the person who signed the covering letter printed on the face in typewriter type. Live postage stamps, preferably com-memoratives, should be used on both outer and inner envelopes. In the U.S. it has been demonstrated that a "flag stamp" on the reply envelope will actually increase returns by a significant percentage. Plate or tape addresses should not be used, nor should business reply envelopes for responses—they do not pull the way a live postage stamp does. Some surveys use incen-

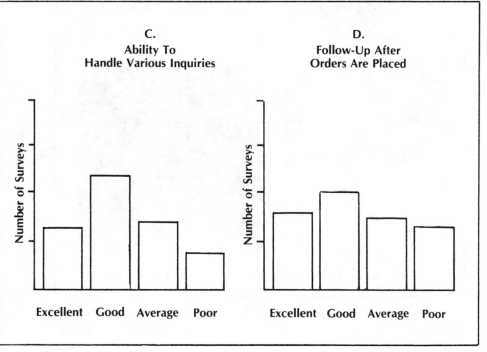

Figure 11-14. Customer service department rating by service element; see also Figure 13.

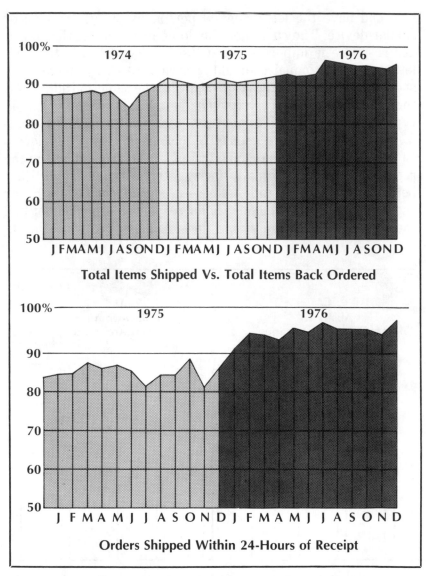

Figure 11-15. Illustrations from booklet entitled ''A Report on Product Distribution Performance'' sent by Devilbiss Corporation to its customers to demonstrate improvements in customer service. Booklet was printed in full color, had excellent response from customers and in addition won a design prize for its graphics.

tives—like entry of the respondent's name into a drawing for a calculator, or a dollar bill or something similar—but these should not be necessary. A promise to donate one dollar to a specified charity for each response received may increase returns slightly, although again most customers will have good motivation to respond if the survey is presented to them properly. If it is a signed survey, those who haven't responded can be followed up.

• *Ask relevant, readily answerable questions.* If respondents consider questions on a survey irrelevant, they may skip them or discard the entire questionnaire. The same will hold true if they can't readily answer questions; some will turn them over to someone else to research and respond, but many will simply decide it's too much work and jettison everything.

• *Survey the right people.* For some managers, this may be the most difficult part of the entire process. Whose names should be used? In some instances, the people who can provide the information may not be the real "influences" and therefore their needs and perceptions may be of limited importance. On the other hand, the influences themselves may not have the required information to fill out the questionnaire, particularly if it asks for specific information like transit time in detail. When information of this type is sought, it may be better to use a postcard survey asking only one or two questions and directed specifically to the receiving clerk. Figure 10 shows such a card, which moves with the actual shipment and is used to measure average transit times to customer locations. A frozen food packer uses a similar card asking the receiver to record certain load temperatures as shipments are received. The cards are printed on bright cherry-colored stock so that they can't be missed in the unloading process. In general, any questions about whom specifically to survey should be worked out in concert with the sales department. Of course in many cases the customer service manager will already know who the influences are and can simply use the customer database that already exists in the department.

• *Test the questionnaire.* It will usually be enough to mail out 100 or so of the surveys, using the actual "package"—letter, questionnaire and reply envelope—which will be used in the survey itself. Recipients should not be told it is a test. The returns will quickly indicate whether language has to be changed or other adjustments made. Unless significant changes are made in the questionnaire, the findings of this initial test can be combined with responses from the full-scale survey when it is rolled out. If the test suggests that the list may contain the wrong individuals, then this should be resolved and a new list tested. Returns from lists which will not be used should of course be discarded. The initial tests of any survey will also help turn up any potential problems in tabulation which may need correction before sending out the final version.

• *Present findings clearly when appropriate.* If the find-

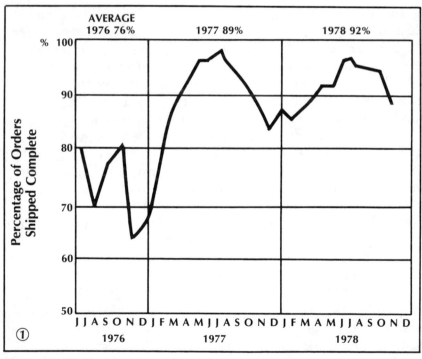

Figure 11-16. Ekco Products, Inc. informs customers about improvements in customer service via three-color graphs (reproduced here in one color) stressing customer service performance.

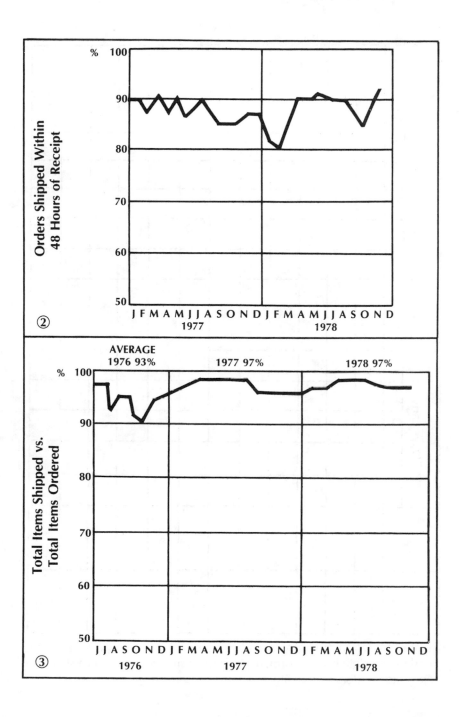

Vendor	Total Orders	Days Early					On Time	Days Late					Comments
		+5	+4	+3	+2	+1		−1	−2	−3	−4	−5	

Figure 11-17. Form used by chain food store buying headquarters to rank vendors on delivery performance. Some firms regularly furnish these reports to vendors as incentive to improve service.

ings are to be used entirely within the department, conventional tabulations are all that's needed. But if they are to be presented to others in the firm, some sort of graphic presentation will help get points across that might otherwise be lost. Figures 11 through 14 reflect charting of responses by the customer service manager who initiated the questionnaire shown in figure 5. He was quite concerned with bringing out and emphasizing certain specific findings and the graphs served that purpose quite well. An additional benefit was that the "comments" portion of the questionnaires contained some very persuasive information. Photocopies were made of these comments, accompanied by the signature of the respondent (in many instances somebody known to management) and bound into a booklet with the graphs. It was very effective!

• *Analyze findings objectively, follow up immediately on complaints.* Most of the findings of a basic customer service questionnaire will be self-evident in their numbers or what people actually say. If there are one or two responses that are extremely "off base," it may be preferable to discard them as unusable rather than distort the averages of the other responses. But this does not mean discarding unfavorable responses simply because they're unfavorable. In fact, sometimes unfavorable responses may be the customer service manager's most powerful weapon in selling management and others on the importance of making improvements in customer service. When complaints do surface in questionnaires, as mentioned above, they should be responded to immediately. Customers are often surprised, and almost always pleased, when they see this kind of prompt followup . . . and it very often helps avoid far more serious situations in the future.

• *Keep the faith.* From the customer's point of view, a survey of attitudes or satisfaction usually carries an implied commitment: a commitment that the vendor is making the survey in good faith and with every intention of making reasonable changes or improvements in service if they are needed. If this does not happen after serious problems have been revealed, then the company is likely to lose credibility with its customers, and perhaps some business as well. Of course there will always be some disgruntled customers who feel they aren't being listened to, and some companies deal with this by actually publishing and sending survey findings to their customers. Figures 15 and 16 show the formats used by two major firms to convey this information to their customers. Naturally a firm that did not get such good results might want to think twice about publicizing *their* findings—but on the other hand knowing that customer service scores are going to be published can be a powerful incentive to everybody in the department as well as in the company at large.

12

CUSTOMER SERVICE COSTS

In talking about customer service costs it's absolutely essential to distinguish between *customer service department operating costs,* which are the routine costs of equipping, staffing and running the department day-to-day, and *total customer service costs* which include departmental operating costs but also physical distribution costs and some other costs of selling. While it is true that changes in customer service levels are likely to impact departmental operating costs, there will be an even broader impact on transportation and inventory costs.

As one example, a decision is made to shorten the internal order cycle from 72 hours to 48 hours. This requires rearranging work practices in the department and hiring part-time personnel to handle the surges that previously could be leveled out by scheduling. This is a departmental cost. A much greater cost is incurred, however, on the physical distribution side. The inventory investment has to be increased substantially, and warehouse operating costs go up because, like the customer service department, the warehouse cannot balance the workload as effectively with the shorter lead time. Adding all costs together, the total customer service cost has increased significantly.

But there can be a bright side, too, when the manager recognizes these cost tradeoffs. A company decides to mount a major consolidation program. A basic requirement is some kind of regionalization of shipments, i.e., accumulating freight until there is sufficient volume to ship consolidations to each major market region served by the company. In this instance, the company determines that there will be sufficient volume to ship one consolidation a week to each of four major markets: West Coast, Midwest, South and Southwest; and twice a week to the East Coast. In order to distribute the workload in the warehouse and shipping departments, the company sets deadlines: orders for the West Coast must be received no later than Thursday noon in order to ship by Friday; orders for the South by noon Tuesday in order to ship Wednesday, and so forth. Substantial freight savings are generated through the consolidations, and by defining the regions in terms of volume it becomes possible to level the workload in the warehouse and actually cut overtime in half. The savings are attractive—well into six figures!

Does this affect departmental operating costs? Of course it does. A consolidation program doesn't run itself, so somebody has to be hired to administer it. Given overhead costs, salary and perhaps some added time on the computer and telephones, the total added cost is probably in the neighborhood of $30,000. The tradeoff is that the consolidation program is saving the company $900,000 a year in transportation and warehousing costs, so there's a net saving in total customer service costs of $870,000. The program is well worth while, but management must be willing to accept the fact that it has to spend money to save money in customer service as well as in other areas.

Although they're oversimplified, these two examples illustrate the potential cost impacts—negative as well as positive— that must be taken into account, both in administering the department and in setting overall policies and customer service goals. This chapter will deal with these two major customer service cost areas against the background of the unique economics of customer service—the provision of resources.

Basic Economic Concepts: "You Can't Do Business from an Empty Wagon"

Stripped to its barest essentials, business is a matter of providing *resources*—products, services, skills—with the expectation of a *return* which will provide sufficient margins of *profit* to justify the enterprise and make it attractive to its owners and investors. In government and non-profit undertakings, the return is generally stated in terms of *benefits:* economic benefits or social benefits, as the case may be.

It's axiomatic that in order to sell or deliver a product or service—a resource—the seller must have it reasonably available to the user. The old saying "You can't do business from an empty wagon" dates back to the time of itinerant peddlers traveling from town to town when a vendor's entire inventory might be aboard that wagon—and when a stockout very likely meant that the sale was lost forever and ever as the peddler moved on to the next town. The peddler was saying, simply, that he couldn't sell what he didn't have.

The peddler had to have his resource—his inventory—but it wasn't just a matter of loading down the wagon. After all, a one-horsepower mobile distribution center has a limited capacity! Too many of the wrong items and too few of the right ones could spell disaster: no oats for Dobbin and the poor farm for the peddler. Thus was begun the need for a *system for managing the resource.*

To underline the point that the resource doesn't have to be a tangible product, there's the case of Louie the Barber. Louie opened a small barbershop in the town of West Barrington, Rhode Island in the year 1930. He was the only barber in town, and business was good. And it got better and better. But then, Louie realized, there were times during the day when customers had to wait a long time, and some even stopped coming for this reason. So he hired another barber. Soon the word spread and he regained his lost customers and started getting new ones from the neighboring communities of Riverside and Bay Springs.

Business boomed for Louie, and at the going rate of fifty cents for a haircut and twenty-five cents for a shave, he was minting money. But the old problem started surfacing: people had to wait too long, and trade was beginning to drop off. So, he did the obvious: he hired another barber. But by this time he had to invest in another chair and accessories and enlarge his space.

Even so, he was happy to see that he didn't need any more chairs for customers to sit in while they were waiting. In fact the lines were much shorter, and Louie was pleased. Customer-oriented from the bone, he believed in the old axiom "Take care of your customers, and they will take care of you."

Imagine Louie's surprise, then, when after a few months he discovered that he was actually making *less* money with three barbers than he had been making with two, even though the three of them seemed to be keeping reasonably busy. At first he thought it was just a bookkeeping mistake, but when the situation recurred the next month, and the month after that, he came to an important conclusion: *he had reached the point of diminishing returns.* It was costing him more to provide the resource than the return warranted. He would either have to raise the price of a haircut and run the risk of losing some customers, or else let the third barber go.

Today's complex business enterprises face basically the same problems that perplexed the itinerant peddler and Louie the Barber in those faroff times: how much to invest in resources in order to bring the greatest return and assure the continuation of the business. This is the customer service manager's most important economic measure. Figure 1 illustrates the basic relationship between resources, service levels and profits. It reflects the experiences of both Louie and the peddler, and a good many others. It makes the point that if enough isn't invested in resources, then the enterprise won't get any customers; on the other hand, if it invests too much it won't make any money from the customers it gets. Another saying describes this situation: "You can't give away the store!"

Resource Case History No. 1: Bowser Won't Eat Kibble

What levels of service do customers really need? How much needs to be invested in order to assure their continued patronage? How much service can we actually afford to provide and still

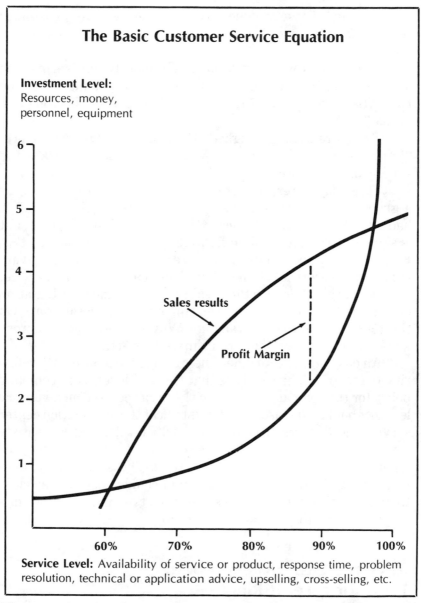

The Basic Customer Service Equation

Investment Level:
Resources, money,
personnel, equipment

6 –

5 –

4 –

Sales results

3 –

Profit Margin

2 –

1 –

60% 70% 80% 90% 100%

Service Level: Availability of service or product, response time, problem resolution, technical or application advice, upselling, cross-selling, etc.

Figure 12-1. Increasing customer service levels increases sales, but beyond a certain point the profit margin starts to shrink, to the point where the cost of rendering the service exceeds the return from rendering it.

make money? These are questions that perplex every customer service manager, and this case history illustrates a very common occurrence.

"But Bowser won't *eat* kibble!" The elderly gentleman in the sneakers and Chesterfield with the cane was getting red in the face. "If I can't get Ken-L-Ration he'll get sick! He won't *eat* kibble!"

The store manager sighed. He had been this way before. "Let me see what I can do, Mr. Wright," he said. "I'll talk to the zone manager. I promise you."

Three days later, the zone manager found himself looking at a graph labeled "Inventory and safety stock requirements." It had a remarkable resemblance to the graph shown in figure 1, but is shown in greater detail in figure 2-A. The graph showed that Ken-L-Ration and similar items were targeted for 90% availability at the store level, the equivalent of 90% customer service. The elderly gentleman in the sneakers was finding Ken-L-Ration on the shelf nine out of every ten times he went to the store. On the tenth trip it wasn't available. Why not increase inventory levels so it would be there ten times out of ten?

An easy question for the zone manager to answer. By referring to the graph, he could see that the 90% level set as company policy for the company's stores in the area required an inventory level of about 2,200 cases of safety stock at the distribution center serving those stores. To move to a 100% level in order to satisfy Bowser would require a 73% increase in inventory at the distribution center, from 2,200 cases to 3,800 cases. Clearly, dog-lover though he was, the zone manager couldn't see his way clear to making this kind of investment just to indulge Bowser's preference for Ken-L-Ration over kibble.

Resource Case History No. 2:
Let It Ring, Let It Ring!

The airline ad manager had a great idea for a campaign built around customer service: all phone calls to be answered and serviced live within 30 seconds. No long holds, no recorded messages, no queues. The idea had great appeal. Consultants were called in to determine what would be needed. They spent a considerable amount of time making observations. They massaged their numbers for a while, and then came back with the findings.

"First," they said, "the airline is already answering and servicing 90% of its calls within the 30-second limit. Indeed some calls are answered within five seconds, and a good many under 20. But if the airline wants to answer *all* calls within 30 seconds, it will have to look at the period between 12 noon and 3:00 p.m.

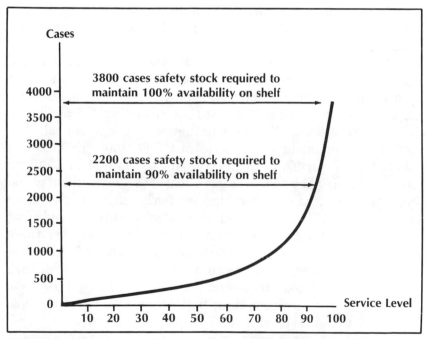

Figure 12-2-A. In order to be able to have a supply of Bowser's favorite dog food on the supermarket shelf every time the old gentleman in sneakers and a Chesterfield came in, the chain would have to increase safety stock in its distribution center by 73% just to go from the present 90% level of availability to a 100% level of availability.

when some callers have to wait as long as five minutes before having their calls serviced. These calls are queued and hear a recording telling them that they will be serviced in turn. Few complaints have been heard, although there are some hangups. There is no way of knowing whether these hangups call back later. Curiously, there is another peaking about 7:00 a.m., apparently from people calling before they go to work. Of course the full staff isn't on this early in the morning, and some of these callers, too, have to wait as long as five minutes."

The ad manager wanted to know what it would take to smooth out those peaks where delays occur so that the campaign could have complete credibility (and get by the Federal Trade Commission). "Sad news," replied the consultants, "it will cost you about a million dollars." The ad manager couldn't believe it. "A million dollars! That's more than the cost of the entire ad campaign!"

"But it's true, nonetheless," the consultants replied, and they called the ad manager's attention to the graph shown in figure 2-B. They pointed out that to be able to answer and service *all* calls within 30 seconds would require adding "X" additional inbound trunk lines, "Y" additional agents to handle the calls and "Z" more equipment in the form of CRTs, interline hookups, computerized tariffs. It all totalled up to more than a million dollars. "And," they added, "a good deal of that investment would be sitting idle and doing nothing for fairly long periods during off-peak hours." Sure, they could hire some part time people, but there was still the fixed cost of the underlying system. And there was another problem. Remember the ad campaign? Well, if it produced all the business the ad manager hoped it would, then perhaps it would take another million dollars to bring the system up to the point where it could adequately service all the additional calls that would be coming in.

Would the increased business justify the substantial investment in systems and people that would be required? That was up to the company to decide. But it seemed unlikely, simply on the basis that the added investment would see use primarily during peak hours and would be underutilized the rest of the time. The consultant's final recommendation: "Change your ad campaign slogan to read 'Nine times out of ten, we'll service your call within 30 seconds!'" Because, he said, if this brings in business, the cost of expanding the system at the 90% level will be far less than at the 100% level. The finding here, as with Bowser's Ken-L-Ration and Louie the Barber, is simply that the cost of improving customer service beyond a certain point may not be justified in terms of either increased business or return on investment.

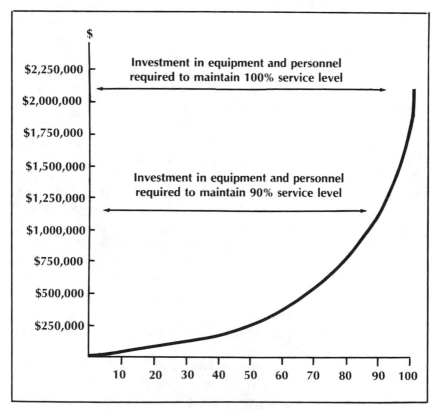

Figure 12-2-B. Is it worth an additional million dollars in order to be able to service all incoming calls in 30 second, with no holds or busy signals? This company decided there were better ways to spend the money.

Resource Case History No. 3:
An Artificial Hip Wings Through the Night

It is 11 p.m. at night. The telephone rings in the guard's hut at a plant in Los Angeles. There has been a serious accident on the freeway near Dallas and emergency surgery has been scheduled for 9:00 a.m. the following morning. An implant hip system is needed right away. How soon can it be shipped? The guard places the call on hold, calls a designated customer service rep at home. The rep consults her Airline Guide: "Tell them I'll get it on board American 526 leaving LAX 1:30 a.m. and arriving Dallas 6:50 a.m. their time. I'll be checking in at the plant in 45 minutes." She drives to the plant, is admitted by the guard, goes to the distribution center where she verifies, picks, packs and documents the order. Half an hour later, she's at the airport phoning the hospital in Dallas to report that the shipment is in fact on board American 526 and will be leaving on schedule. All in a day's work!

Is it expensive to render this kind of service? Of course it is! Yet some companies in the health care field regularly provide 98-100% levels of product availability and shipping. Can they afford it? Not under ordinary circumstances. But Americans demand high levels of health care and have demonstrated their willingness to pay for it. So in effect the high cost of rendering 100% customer service is simply passed along to the customer. A parallel situation exists in space technology and other high-tech applications where "redundancy" is a common concept—the provision of backup systems which will take over if the main system fails. These redundancies are expensive in money, but not in terms of the underlying investment in human lives and capital equipment that they protect.

In actual practice the economic principles demonstrated in these case histories are much more subtle and complex. For example, the zone manager might not be willing to underwrite the investment in 100% inventory of Ken-L-Ration for Bowser, but he would recognize the necessity of maintaining 100% inventory in staples like bread, milk, flour, etc. and other popular items, because customers will not deal with a store where these are not readily available all of the time. The airline might find that it could "educate" customers to call during off-hours, and the health care company could use a centrally located public warehouse service providing an emergency shipment service for computer manufacturers, oilfield suppliers and other companies requiring virtually immediate response to emergency orders. An important part of the customer service manager's job is to be aware of these alternatives and investigate their advantages and disadvantages.

Customer Service Cost Definitions

Fixed costs. For accounting purposes, fixed costs in customer service are essentially the cost of the underlying system: overhead, rent, data processing equipment, office furniture, files, etc. In the warehouse, fixed costs would be the warehouse itself, handling and storage equipment, heat, light and maintenance. Some accounting systems treat supervisory personnel as a fixed cost. Fixed costs are sometimes referred to as "noncontrollable" because they are essentially costs that have to be incurred whether or not the firm does any business. When a business closes down for the night, or a weekend, or for a prolonged period such as a strike, the fixed costs remain basically the same even though no work is being performed.

Variable costs. As the name implies, variable costs vary with the volume of work or business being handled. They include mainly labor costs, material costs and energy costs. In the customer service department, besides personnel there would probably be substantial telephone usage costs (the equipment itself would be a fixed cost) and computing costs. In the warehouse, labor costs, handling costs and energy costs are major variable cost components. An important variable cost that is sometimes overlooked is the cost of maintaining the inventory: capital costs, insurance costs, shrinkage or breakage, obsolescence, contamination, etc. These may run as high as 25-35% of the actual value of the inventory.

Interaction of fixed and variable costs. In the strictest sense there is no such thing as a "pure" fixed cost that remains the same regardless of how variable costs may vary. A good example is the warehouse. A 50,000 sq. ft. warehouse contains 50,000 units and has fixed costs of $50,000. The fixed cost assignable to each unit in that warehouse is $1.00. But business is increasing, and the firm decides to build a second warehouse, which it uses to store its increased production of the same product. The second warehouse is also 50,000 sq. ft. and has fixed costs of $50,000, but at the moment it contains only 25,000 units. If we consider the fixed costs of the two warehouses together (as we should, since the products stored are identical), the fixed costs for a total of 75,000 units are now $100,000, or $1.33 per unit.

A similar example occurs in the warehouse. Electric fork lift trucks have relatively high fixed costs but low operating costs in comparison to equipment powered by other means. Gasoline trucks have lower fixed costs but higher operating costs. Thus an electric fork lift may be recommended where usage is relatively high, and a gasoline truck where usage is intermittent. But if an electric truck is going to be used on a second shift it requires an additional battery, which is a high fixed cost. Thus the fixed cost of the fork lift truck, like the fixed cost of the warehouse, does in fact vary when a certain point of utilization has been reached.

In one company, the rapid growth of the business required increasing the number of customer service reps from ten to 22. This caused increases in both fixed and variable costs: mainly space and equipment costs plus labor costs. But there was an additional fixed cost that had been overlooked: the necessity of hiring an additional supervisor. While this is basically a fixed cost, it interacts with the variable labor cost by making labor more productive. The ratio of supervisors to direct labor employees varies from industry to industry. In customer service, many supervisors are actually working supervisors and may not be charged as a fixed expense at all. In this instance, the added cost of the supervisor was about $22,000 and this was allocated among all 22 positions, or $1,000 per employee. On a 50-week basis, this represented an investment of $20 per week; at average hourly rates in effect at the time, the justification for the supervisor was that the $20 per week per employee was more than offset by productivity gains of twice that amount, plus improved quality of work, fewer errors and better controls.

These examples illustrate the complexity and subtlety of customer service cost relationships. While the manager should not be overly preoccupied with the actual accounting methods employed in the company, he or she should make every attempt to identify both negative and positive tradeoffs of the kind illustrated here—and to see that others who are involved take them into account in planning policies and operations that impact on customer service.

Order Processing Costs

Order processing cost is usually treated as a variable cost that varies with the number of orders. Actually, it is a combination of fixed and variable costs. The fixed cost is the cost of the underlying equipment used to process orders, while the variable cost is the labor and associated communications. If a central computer is used, the company may "sell" its time to other departments, in which case computer usage is charged as a variable cost. This is true where an outside service is used for this purpose.

In looking at order cost, each order is also a combination. The fixed cost associated with every order is the cost of the order document, the cost of setting it up, sold-to and ship-to information, purchase order reference, terms of sale and other data. This information has to be entered on all orders, whether for $100 or $100,000, whether for one line item or for one hundred. To these fixed costs must be added the variable costs which are essentially the product descriptions or lines. Each added line requires either writing or inputting added data, adding a small variable cost usually termed an *incremental* cost. The cost of an added line can be measured in keystrokes required to input it, or the time required to write it. Usually this incremental cost is very small, because the major cost is in heading up the order—the fixed cost. In some cases, the customer service rep may have to look up or reference material for every additional line entered. There, the incremental cost would be larger.

Another point about order costs that is sometimes misunderstood is the relationship of order *value* to order *cost*. Does it cost more to process an order for $100,000 than it does to process an order for $100? The answer is no . . . and yes. In theory, an order for 100,000 units of a particular line item selling for $1 costs exactly the same, except for six keystrokes, as an order for one unit of that item. But in actual practice the dollar value of an order is often related to the number of lines in that order; the larger the order, the more lines, and therefore the higher the cost of order processing. There's also the factor that larger orders may require additional work in verification, special pricing and—unfortunately—backorders. Larger orders containing more lines run a risk of backordered items at a geometric rate; at a 90% line item fill rate, the possibility of having one or more items backordered increases from 10% with one line to 19% with two lines to 27% with three lines—59% with five lines and 65% with ten lines. (See figure 5, page 157 for a tabulation of the probabilities of obtaining a complete order at varying rates of line item fill.) In practice, order fill rarely drops this low because most customers tend to order the most popular items which are usually stocked in considerable depth very close to the 100% level.

Order Cost Components

There are two main ways to develop order processing costs. The first is simply to add up all costs of running the order processing section and then dividing by the number of orders processed. This will provide an *average cost per order processed*. This is reflected in figure 3, where all costs are simply listed, totaled and then divided by the total orders processed. There are advantages and disadvantages to this method. On the advantage side, it's relatively easy to calculate and if orders are reasonably comparable in number of lines, as is often the case, then the average cost will be fairly close to the actual cost. To determine whether this approach is applicable, the manager should make a frequency distribution by order size. If the majority of orders are grouped around a central axis, as shown in figure 4, then this particular method will provide a reasonably accurate reading of order costs. The disadvantage of this approach is that it may not be representative. If order size varies substantially as shown in figure 5, then the average does not reflect actual costs. In addition, the approach does not measure the actual cost of performing the operations but rather *assigns* a cost on the basis of

Table for Computing Average Order Costs

Cost Category	Annual Cost
A. Data processing equipment & peripherals	$ _____
B. Outside data processing costs	$ _____
C. Communications equipment & services	$ _____
D. Administrative personnel	$ _____
E. Order processing personnel	$ _____
F. Other personnel	$ _____
G. Office supplies	$ _____
H. Postage	$ _____
I. Miscellaneous or Overhead	$ _____
J. Total, lines A to I	$ _____
K. Total number of orders handled	No. _____
Cost Per Order (divide Line J by Line K) . . . . $ _____

Figure 12-3. This form will provide an average cost-per order but its validity as a measure will vary with the variation in orders. If orders are relatively similar in number of line items, for example, as well as exceptions and other items of cost, then the average cost per order will be a fairly representative figure. On the other hand, if there is considerable range in makeup in orders and in requirements placed on personnel, the average will not be very meaningful and in fact may cover up the desirability of reducing costs by having two different order processing systems for different types of orders or markets.

(Courtesy Herbert W. Davis and Company)

the total number of orders processed for a certain total cost. If this total cost includes other, non-order activities, then the true cost of processing orders will tend to be distorted.

A second method which comes closer to developing a true cost is to develop *standard costs* by actually measuring all the

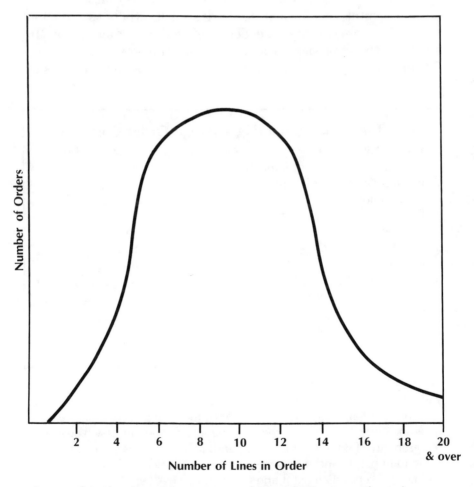

Figure 12-4. If orders are concentrated in a certain range (here they are mostly between 6 and 13 lines), an average order cost as developed by the form in Figure 3 will reflect the real cost of processing orders.

components that go into processing an order. This might be done in conjunction with industrial engineering staff, and could involve measurement of discrete items like keystrokes, motions of picking up and grasping a pencil, getting material from desk drawers, etc. Figure 6 shows an order cost analysis performed by this

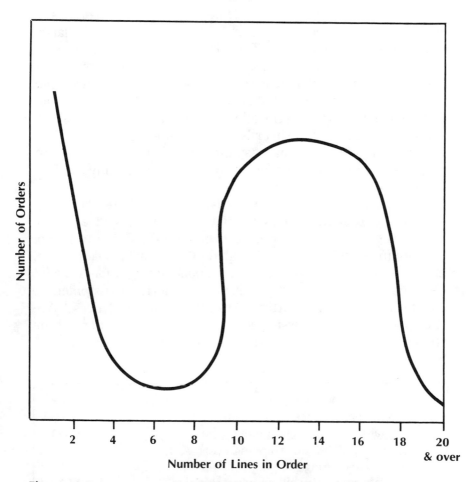

Figure 12-5. In a more typical distribution there are many orders for one or two lines, and then another concentration in the area of 10-16 lines. Many of these may of course represent the same customers ordering at different times and in different quantities.

general method. This approach would enable calculating the incremental cost of each additional line item on the order and then to develop standard costs for order processing based on order size. Orders from one to four items would be costed at "X" dollars processing costs, from five to nine at "Y" dollars, from ten to 15 at "Z" dollars and so forth, depending on the actual distribution. Or, the division might simply be made between very small orders of one or two lines, medium orders of ten or so lines, and large orders of anything over that. The advantage of the standard cost approach is in weighing pros and cons of different order entry systems; knowing what it costs to process an order with the existing system vs. projected cost for a new system is essential and must be related specifically to the operating costs of the equipment which are primarily the variable labor costs. The disadvantage of this approach is that it does not take into account costs *associated with* the order but not directly involved in processing the order per se.

For example, for every 100 orders entered there is a certain ratio of: (1) order status inquiries to be responded to; (2) errors to be corrected; (3) credits to be processed; (4) returns to be approved; (5) complaints to be handled; (6) internal queries (sales, credit, accounts receivable) to be responded to; (7) followups to be made with other departments; and (8) queries to customers to clarify orders or other matters. Are these part of order cost? Are they part of order *processing* cost? The answer really depends on the reason for taking the measurement in the first place.

Variable order entry and billing	$10.08
Fixed order entry (space/equipment).................	3.03
Total order entry and billing	**13.11**
For variable warehousing/shipping costs, add..........	15.05
For fixed warehousing/shipping (space, eqpt.)	5.01
Total order entry/billing whsg shipping	**$33.17**

Figure 12-6. Order cost analysis based on variable and fixed costs for company engaged in high-volume low-cost commodities. Cost figures are as of 1983.

If costs are being measured to determine whether improvements should be made to the order system, then these other costs should not be considered unless they would be affected by such improvements. A company may want to determine whether it should have separate systems, one for handling small orders of one or two items and another for handling all orders larger than that. Measuring the real-time costs of order processing may be the only way of making a sound determination. In addition, this standard cost approach will have relevance in extremely large and/or highly standardized operations such as in mail order, car rentals and reservation systems in general. One optical company servicing primarily optometrists is set up so some reps handle 300 orders—mostly one-item orders—per day per rep. These reps do not handle complaints or inquiries or larger orders, and thus standard or engineered costs are quite applicable to their operation, and must be used when changes or improvements are being considered.

On the other hand, if the company wants to know what ought to be entered as *order* costs (i.e., not limited to order processing), then it should just add up the costs of all order-*connected* activities including processing, and simply divide by the total number of orders as illustrated by figure 3. In fact, unless the customer service department is engaged in other activities which are not related to nor affected by orders, it would be acceptable to assign order cost simply by taking the total cost of running the department and then dividing by the number of orders handled. Some managers resist this approach on the grounds that it's not realistic; others counter with an example: if it costs $30 to process an order, and another $50 to process a complaint that arose out of that order, isn't the $50 part of the cost of handling that order? As discussed in chapter 9 dealing with productivity, it isn't usually practical to apply industrial engineering measures and standards to the entire range of jobs performed by individuals in the customer service department. It's more convenient, and realistic, to consider all these other activities as part of the order costs. And this is true even when order processing is done outside the department.

Should such distribution costs as order assembly, packing

and shipping be considered part of the total order cost? In some companies it is, in others not. If orders are roughly the same size and involve the same amount of handling, then these costs can be added in and then expressed like this: "This is what it costs us to get a customer's order through the system and onto the loading dock." Normally, transportation would not be included because it varies with distance. However, distribution costs are a part of the total customer service costs, including plant-to-distribution center costs, distribution center-to-distribution center transfer costs, and distribution center-to-customer costs. In short, all distribution costs incurred after the end of the manufacturing process are correctly stated as costs of serving the customer, whether this service occurs directly or indirectly. They are the costs of *being able to* serve the customer, in many instances, as well as the costs of actually serving that customer. If inventory requirements are overestimated and the leftover inventory has to be destroyed, that is a customer service cost. On the other hand, if an inventory is found to be defective or unsafe and has to be destroyed for that reason, the cost would not be charged to customer service but to manufacturing.

Complex Order Costs

While the approaches described above are suitable for measuring order costs in the majority of companies, and can be used for both tangibles and intangibles, i.e., for orders involving services as well as products, there are many situations such as custom products where they are likely to be too limited. For example, what does it cost to process an order for a metal building with floor space of 25,000 sq. ft.? A bank of elevators for a high-rise office building? A nuclear reactor?

In these and the majority of custom applications, customer service managers are likely to feel frustrated attempting to estimate the cost of actually processing an order, which would normally include the specifications, perhaps the bill of materials, transportation cost estimates and other elements. Yet a surprising number of these are machinable, i.e., with appropriate programming the customer service representative may have little more to do beyond entering specifications. Some companies which formerly used persons with engineering backgrounds for this part of the job have been able to turn the job over to persons with no engineering background, but with powerful computer support. An order entry system for an elevator cab, for example, is basically an interrogatory which asks the rep various questions about size, style, door opening, location of control panel, applicable building code, etc., and the computer does the rest, including a bill of materials and a cost estimate.

This does not mean that skilled customer service reps aren't necessary, because of course they are, and their skills must in some cases be in specific disciplines like medicine, chemistry, health care, metallurgy and others. But the development of appropriate computer programming simply releases these reps from many of the tedious manual chores formerly associated with processing orders—and makes them more readily available for person-to-person dealings which only they can perform. From an economic point of view, it may also be possible to do a better job with fewer people.

Problems of Order Cost Analysis

A typical problem awaiting the customer service manager is illustrated in the following case history, based on actual facts. The customer service manager had determined, some time ago, that it cost $40, on the average, to process an order. He had compared this figure with those for other companies and found that he was reasonably close to the average. What bothered him was that one day he realized that a significant number of orders processed by his department were for amounts under $25. Things came to a head when he did some quick calculations and discovered that in a two-month period he had spent some $40,000 to process $25,000 worth of orders.

The main options open to this manager in this situation were relatively limited:

- Increase the minimum order size to a level where all

orders would at least break even. A logical idea, except that most of the orders were for a single part for equipment the customer had previously purchased from that company that was now in a machine-down situation. The psychological effect of requiring a customer in an emergency situation to buy more than needed was felt to be undesirable and the company rejected the idea. The same would not apply to minimum orders in general, of course, where the practice is widely used and accepted.

• Use a separate batching system for processing small orders. This is standard practice in some situations, and simply means accumulating small orders until there are enough to process economically in one operation. In the present situation, it would not be acceptable because so many of the orders reflected machine-down stuations where order fulfillment time was critical.

• Simplify the actual process of ordering in small lots. This might involve an entirely separate system, or it might involve setting up a specific group to deal only with small orders. This had the most appeal, but at the time it appeared that there was not sufficient volume to warrant the considerable investment it would represent.

• Market a line of "parts kits" to equipment owners. This could be done at the time of sale or at intervals determined by the age of the equipment. One company has found this approach has worked extremely well when it is recommended to customers by field engineers repairing their equipment on-site. Of course it is a long-range measure whose effects would not be felt immediately and certainly would not cover all cases. But with the usage information that is usually available, sale of the parts kits would avoid a sufficiently large number of breakdowns and emergency situations to free reps and field engineers alike to service other accounts quickly and more effectively. The company decided to progress this approach, although it realized that other, shorter-term measures would also have to be taken. The parallel to this in ordinary stock situations, i.e., non-equipment environments, is to set up the customer's inventory and then maintain it for him or her either by direct replenishment (as with bread, magazines and rack items generally) or by furnishing an inventory management program with automatic reorder points.

• Give the parts to the customer free of charge. This seemed a rather radical approach, and at first management rejected it completely. The customer service manager suggested an alternative: identify the lower range of parts that are small in size as well as in value and set up a two-bin inventory control system. When a customer places an order for a single item in this category simply type up a combined address label-invoice with a standard shipping charge and ship the merchandise. Enclose a business reply envelope with a unique post office box or department number. Keep no record of the transaction, and send no followups. When payments are received, simply post them against the small parts account. When a bin is empty, indicate the usage and reorder. The likelihood is that 80-90% of customers will pay, particularly when they realize that unless they do the system will be scrapped and they'll have to go back to the older, slower method. Management was intrigued by both the revised suggestion and its potential for cutting costs, but it wasn't quite ready to buy. In common with many managements, it felt that what was basically an honor system wouldn't work, that customers would automatically take advantage of the system to cheat the company. In actual practice, this is seldom the case; the majority of customers are honest and will not violate honor systems. Those that do seldom constitute any significant threat to profits, and are usually found out in some other way anyway.

• Automate. The customer service manager was familiar with computer-to-computer ordering, and also touchtone order entry. Its principal applications were in captive systems where the company can write the rules, i.e., between the home office and branches, the customer service department and field sales personnel, etc. Could a system be set up between a company and its customers? Why not? Well, experience had shown that customers tended to resist placing orders via recorder, but then they'd never been given any particular incentive to do so. Supposing they were to be offered a special price, or some kind of "deal," if they would dial a special 800-number and enter single-item orders via touchtone? This is the way the company finally resolved the problem. It set up a separate, dedicated number for emergency (single-part) orders only. The phone went directly to an interactive voice synthesis computer which prompted the caller and offered a special on maintenance supplies. The special 800-number meant no waiting or no busy signals from lines tied up with lengthy stock orders. And orders placed before 3 p.m. were guaranteed shipment that same day. Customers accepted the new system, and with full utilization unit order costs dropped significantly because there was no human intervention until orders printed out in the warehouse. One of the tradeoffs with the old system was that it now became possible to process stock orders more efficiently because there were no emergency orders to "walk through" the system. This lowered unit costs on both sides. A more subtle gain was improvement in turnaround time and customer satisfaction.

This case history illustrates the complexity of order costs and the various kinds of tradeoffs that have to be taken into account. It also underlines the fact that management and other departments may resist changes that are too dramatic, but will very often buy what may appear to be "far out" ideas involving new technology.

Doubling Order Capacity
... But Not Costs

Every company's situation is unique. No two customer service departments have the same environment, the same conditions—the same problems. But the customer service manager should be sensitive to the right combination of circumstances that favors certain types of innovations.

This is reflected in the case of a company with three divisions served by a central customer service department. A year ago, it was a divisional customer service department. Management decided to consolidate order entry and customer service operations at the central point. Each division had its own field sales force, and effective with the consolidation all three field sales forces would be placing orders with the one customer service department. Would the department be permitted to hire more people? No, with the new computer system it shouldn't be necessary. Of course, the company would underwrite more phones and a reasonable amount of hardware if necessary.

The manager recognized the unique conditions, and this is the type of system that evolved: an 800-number for field salespeople's orders only, each sales group to telephone its orders in during designated time frames in order to balance usage of the system. The 800-number would consist of four trunks, each tied into a conventional recorder, with non-order calls—inquiries, problems, etc.—to be called direct to reps on different lines. Periodically, order entry personnel would remove the tapes from the recorders and input orders directly to the computer. Also included was a rollover or overflow system whereby when all four order lines are busy, additional calls will overflow and be picked up by customer service reps.

The key to this system is the economies of scale in batching all orders on tape, where they can be quickly input by experienced keypunch personnel at a much faster rate than if they were taken separately on an intermittent basis. The salesmen, being captive, can be trained to input information in a certain format and sequence. Meanwhile, the senior customer service reps are dealing with matters requiring higher levels of skill without the random interruptions of phone orders. This makes customer service reps much more productive, and it also makes the order taking process much more productive. How much more productive? Since the consolidation occurred, the same department with no additional personnel has actually doubled—increased by 100%—the number of orders it handles daily. The total investment: four trunk lines, and four tape recorders. And an understanding of what to do when the circumstances are right.

13

PROFIT LEAKS
...AND PROFIT CONTRIBUTIONS

Profit Leaks

• *Failure to properly define the customer service mission.*
When a company does not understand that a major goal in
customer service is *keeping customers* it may spend $100 to have
field sales personnel performing functions that the customer
service department could handle as well or better for only $20. In
actuality, the ratio is even higher when salespeople are performing service tasks that take them away from their primary job
of selling. As one example, many companies require their field
sales people to inspect and approve (or disapprove) returns at
customer sites. This is costly in terms of salespeople's time and
interferes with their selling time. Because it is a negative situation, salespeople tend to defer as long as possible their inspection visits to customer sites, and customers become understandably irritated at the long delays. When the salesperson does
arrive, it is already a negative situation and a negative selling
environment, more so if the return has to be disapproved. One
firm recognized this as a problem in cost as well as public relations, to say nothing of field sales productivity, and decided to
institute an "honor system" for returns. Under this system, when
a customer requests authorization to return goods, the customer
service department provides forms setting forth the criteria for
returns in three main categories—full credit; percentage credit;

and no credit—and are asked to decide for themselves whether their returns will qualify. The system has worked very well; customers have accepted the responsibility, field selling personnel have become more productive on two counts—more time to sell, and customers more inclined to buy—and the delays and resentment inherent in the old system have been done away with.

● *Isolated or non-linked customer service operations.* Failure of management to understand the tradeoffs between customer service and logistics, customer service and production, and customer service and marketing is often translated into paying out money needlessly for excessive small shipments, short production runs or total stockouts of critical parts, and expensive advertising campaign promises that the company may not be able to live with. One company which decided to market an install-it-yourself garage door opener did not involve the customer service department in any phase of market planning. The product went on the market, supported by heavy advertising investment. Within days, the phones in the customer service department were ringing off the hook: consumers who had bought the devices calling for help, explanation of instructions, or reimbursement for the plaster ceiling that had just been pulled out by their newly-installed garage door opener. Of course the customer service department was in no way prepared for this onslaught of calls and it had no in-house Mr. Goodwrench to send to the rescue. It was a costly lesson in unpreparedness which prior consultation with customer service could have avoided.

In a similar case, a major building products manufacturer discovered that the combination of delays and underproductivity in its customer service department were the result of a major national advertising campaign promoting products which were out of stock and would probably continue that way for 60 days or more. Customer service reps were tied up daily trying to explain the situation and maintain customer good will at the same time. This also meant neglecting some of their other work, and even more delays and customer relations problems as a result. And it was very costly in terms of lost sales and orders that would never be re-entered. Ironically, many other products which would have lent themselves just as well to such an ad campaign were in plentiful supply but were never promoted.

• *Too many customer service emergencies.* These are often symptoms of underlying system problems connected with availability of inventory. Figure 1 reflects some of the possible causes. Emergencies are expensive in several ways: (1) the vendor company may be expected to absorb the premium freight cost; (2) labor costs are higher than usual; (3) there is a much

---

Why Not Enough Inventory?

1. Corporate policy (e.g., turnover vs. stockouts).
2. Poor inventory planning and control system.
3. Misapplication of safety-stock theory.
4. Poor management of inventory control system.

Poor Sales Forecasting—

5. Misassignment of responsibility.
6. Poor system.
7. Poor information.
8. Failure to measure and monitor results.
9. Forecasts made too late.
10. Inadequate central warehousing.
11. Lead times too long.

Marketing Problems—

12. New items in line.
13. New kinds of promotions.
14. Promotions not planned early enough.

Procurement Problems—

15. Late receipts from vendors.
16. Quality not acceptable.

Manufacturing Problems—

17. Poor production planning and control.
18. Inadequate capacity.
19. Long manufacturing cycle times.
20. Late start on buildups.
21. Breakdowns.
22. Quality not acceptable.

Warehousing Problems—

23. Material "lost" in warehouse.
24. Too many warehouses.

Transportation Problems—

25. Breakdowns.
26. Uncertain transit times.
27. Loss and damage.

Other Causes—

28. Month-end peaks, sales contests, etc.
29. Poor allocation procedures when stock is short.
30. Catastrophe (e.g., fire, flood, strike, etc.).
31. Human error.
32. Failure to measure, monitor and identify reasons for poor performance.

Courtesy of Burr W. Hupp, Executive Director Warehousing Education and Research Council.

Figure 13-1

higher potential for error; (4) an emergency which is not handled well may cause loss of business; and (5) excessive emergencies cause stress and underproductivity and morale problems in the customer service department. Some emergencies can be anticipated, and prepared for. The machine-down situation can be mitigated when customers have parts kits or can procure them from a central stocking location within a few hours.

Sometimes, emergencies are not emergencies per se, but a form of expediting by customers to offset their own delays in placing orders. For example, a contractor is about to complete work on the structural components of a major convention hotel. Before too many months, the hotel will be open. But for now it's time to specify the locking systems for guestrooms at the hotel. Why wasn't the specifying done sooner? Well, it never is! So the lock manufacturer gets an order for several thousand lock systems for delivery in six weeks. Which means that in a few weeks an emergency situation will exist in the company and everybody will be so busy that nobody will ask the obvious question: If the marketing department was aware of this practice in the construction industry, why didn't it do something to educate customers—or make it worth their while—to place orders earlier? It does cost money to anticipate and prepare for emergencies. But the cost can be even greater in terms of loss of credibility and damage to the firm's reputation, and in specific lost sales and decreasing market share.

• *Inefficient operations in the department itself.* These are often part of the "backroom" image which some companies still associate with their customer service operations. Historically, the customer service department has gotten little attention in terms of both the physical environment and the incentives to employees to work productively and represent the company well. Many managers were promoted from the ranks, which is commendable, but without having any management experience or guidance, which is not. As a result, basic management techniques like assigning work, motivating and rewarding employees, and measuring and improving effectiveness may be relatively unknown to the manager.

Another problem is hiring and training of personnel. Unfortunately, the hiring job is often performed by personnel departments which tend to rank longevity on the job over specific skills needed in the job. The result of such practices can be a failure to get new employees with potential, and an excessive number of employees who have been there a long time but really aren't very good. These old-timers are also likely to discourage and alienate newcomers with good motivation and ambitions. The only lasting remedy for inefficient operations is a combination of improvement to the operations themselves, plus job upgrading, career pathing and creating a decent working environment. In short, a conscious effort to improve both the image and the reality of the customer service department.

   • *Treating symptoms rather than causes.* Bowing to pressure from its sales department, a firm opens a new warehouse in an area where customers have been complaining about poor customer service. But service doesn't improve. Customers continue to complain, and management fires the warehouse manager and customer service manager and hires replacements who do no better. Finally, management decides to look at the problem rather than the symptom. The symptom is poor service, but the problem or cause of the poor service is lack of inventory. Looking back, management can see that the problem never was lack of a local warehouse because the inventory problem existed long before the warehouse was built, and in fact was misread by sales and everybody else. Inventory problems have many causes, as reflected in Figure 1, but building a warehouse to solve an inventory shortage is like using gasoline to extinguish a fire: the inventory was already fractionated among six warehouses; adding a seventh merely fractionated it even more severely. With a new forecasting and inventory management system and using its own fleet of trucks, the firm can actually close down several warehouses and improve service to the point where customers no longer complain.

   Another example: customers complain because orders are late. Why are they late? Management doesn't know, but it orders the warehouse to ship sooner. The warehouse does as it is told, but now complete orders drop from 90% to 80% and customers complain even more. What management failed to understand, and didn't ask about, was the underlying reason for late shipments: they were simply being held for inventory. Shipping the orders sooner made the problem worse. In both examples, treating symptoms increased the cost but did nothing whatever to improve the level of actual service *or* customer satisfaction.

• *Multiple company contacts—multiple customer contacts.* This can be a particularly insidious problem. Customers who never talk to the same rep twice, or who have to talk to a number of different people in the company, often complain of their frustration. An even more serious result is several people working on the same problem without realizing it, or one person making a promise that the others aren't aware of and that can't be met in any event. The most common duplications of this type are likely to be between the sales department and the customer service department, but they exist elsewhere as well, and the results are just as costly. A corresponding situation arises when different people in the same customer company get involved with either the same or different people in the vendor customer service department. One company found that customers were exploiting the confusion of multiple contacts by filing excessive claims and making unauthorized returns, apparently on the premise that some would fall between the cracks to the customer's advantage.

On the vendor side, assigning reps either by account or territory—an individual rep or a team of reps—usually does a great deal to bring the situation under control. Some companies have been quite successful in asking their customers to designate a single individual and a backup for all their dealings. They have found that this has paid off, not only in sharply reduced calls from customer companies but also in sharply reduced error rates in their own. There is also considerably improved morale in the customer service department when reps find they are no longer being second-guessed or overridden by sales personnel or others outside their department.

• *Repetitive decision making—lack of decision rules.* This is perhaps one of the most pervasive problems in customer service, from the smallest of companies to the largest. One company with more than 59 customer service reps found that repetitive problems that cropped up daily were being again and again brought to supervisors for handling because the reps did not want to make what they felt were judgment decisions. Providing them with decision rules in the form of a simple checklist enabled them to deal with 99% of the problems without consulting supervisors and at far lower cost.

The most serious lack of decision rules seems to be in the area of refunds. In one company, refunds of as little as five dollars actually had to be approved by the executive vice president before they could be issued, and then only after they had passed through several other sets of hands in the company. At a conservative estimate, the cost of the decision—whichever way it went—was well over $100.

Some managers feel that if refund and exchange rules are too liberal, customers will take advantage of them. This is rarely if ever a significant factor. The few customers who do take advantage of liberal policies are usually a drop in the bucket compared to the savings that are generated by simply using decision rules that give the customer the benefit of the doubt and allow fast and automatic refunds up to a certain amount.

Another company found that salespeople were constantly pressuring customer service reps to make emergency shipments to "important" customers at company expense. Some cases were genuine emergencies, while others were not. The manager did not want to tell reps not to accept such instructions, nor did she want to continue footing the bill for emergency shipments where they were not warranted. So, she wrote a decision rule: "If the customer whom the salesperson says needs the emergency shipment is on our list as an "A" or "B" customer, make the shipment immediately; for shipments to any other classes of customers, the emergency shipment will be charged to the customer. Any exceptions will have to be handled directly with me by the salesperson." As soon as the policy or decision rule was instituted and salespeople became aware of it, the pressure on reps to make unnecessary emergency shipments dropped to almost zero. And a particular benefit was that genuine emergencies got serviced that much faster.

● *Burying customer service costs.* How many managements know what it *really* costs to serve customers? Not the so-called "cost-of-sales" heading, which is a hodgepodge of different costs including manufacturing expense, but a clear statement of all expenses incurred from the end of the production line until the product has been received and paid for by the customer, including all the administrative costs, fixed costs and variable costs, incurred along the way. It's pretty hard to control costs when you don't know what those costs are! Several variations on this problem are expressed below.

● *Overlooking measures of order and product line profitability.* In today's world of extreme product proliferation, sound marketing and customer service strategy calls for promoting, selling and shipping in optimum lots the most profitable lines consistent with volume requirements. But few companies appear to be sophisticated enough in their costing procedures—or, sometimes, to care enough—to be able to identify these lines and units of sale.

In many companies, lack of any communications between marketing people, on the one hand, and logistics people, on the other, can have near-devastating repercussions. In a typical situation, a company's marketing department sets a price break at 50 cartons, when a full palletload—the logical logistical unit for handling and storage—consists of 48 cartons. The cost of shipping two cartons loose is compounded by the fact that they have a much higher loss and damage rate than the palletized goods, and incur substantial administrative costs in claims, tracers and refunds. Distribution personnel tell marketing personnel, but all the ads have been published and all the mailers long since mailed and all the sales promotion campaigns and in-store merchandisers in place—and for every dollar it *ought* to be making, the company is only making 90 cents. A ten percent writeoff in a company with $400 million in sales is not an insignificant amount!

● *Overlooking measures of customer profitability.* Two customers with identical dollar purchases over a year may be making vastly different profit contributions. One buys consistently, in profitable lots; the other buys erratically, hand-to-mouth, often in crisis situations. One pays all invoices promptly; the other goes right to the edge before paying. Each brings in the same amount of revenue, but the company makes money on one and loses it on the other. But it's difficult to guess without having appropriate data, and the controller has to be persuaded to divulge the information—not always an easy job.

In one company, the customer service manager persuaded the controller to provide the data and, in studying two major customers, found that the costs of serving one, exclusive of overhead, were four cents on the dollar, while the costs of serving the other were *fourteen* cents on the dollar of sales. Why such a striking discrepancy? Among other things, Customer No. 2 required drop shipments at multiple locations plus a number of special services including lot segregation and sorting, stencilling and labeling, proof of delivery and other extra paperwork and communications.

It is not the customer service manager's job to dictate who will and who will not be served—but it *is* the customer service manager's job to let it be known what those costs are so that marketing management and top management can make enlightened decisions on whether the company should in fact persist in situations of this particular type, and, in general, on how to make the soundest decisions on investing the firm's marketing dollars.

Profit Contributions

They don't have to be dramatic or overwhelming, and they can work in a number of ways. Improvements in customer service can interact with profits in one or more of several ways:

1. In direct cost reduction; for many companies, a savings of five dollars is the equivalent of the profit on sales of $100.

2. In contributing to increased productivity of field sales personnel and thus to greater volume sales and increased profits.

3. In direct contribution to increased purchases by customers, and in the increased profits from those sales.

The customer service manager will find many opportunities to make profit contributions of all kinds, but one of the stumbling blocks will be the problem of determining beforehand whether service improvements will pay for themselves. Some of the case histories that follow will show how this can be determined. Major capital investments will usually be tested by ROI (return on investment) or discounted cash flow measures, but for everyday planning a pocket calculator and ordinary math are usually enough.

● *Physical distribution improvements for beginners.* Many firms are committed to shipping orders daily because of the nature of the business. Firms in the home heating and health care instruments business are examples. There are also firms which ship daily because customers ask them to, and firms which ship daily some of the time but not all of the time simply because it happens to work out that way. There is another dimension to this pattern, too: customers who place orders daily, and sometimes place a number of orders at irregular intervals during a single day.

There are many cost elements in situations of this type. Consider a company that may get as many as 15 to 20 orders during a single day from a single customer, and multiply this likelihood by its customer base of 2,000 customers, some ordering every day of the week. In some companies, urgency has priority over cost, so the orders are simply processed as they come in, sent to shipping and shipped out. Each of these shipments then moves at minimum rates. Separate packing and shipping averages four dollars per order, or $60-80 a day for an active account. By writing a program (not inexpensive) that will "trap" all the multiple orders from a single customer, one firm in particular was able to ship the combined orders in one or two cartons—and never more than three—at an average cost of $6.75 per carton. This translated to a maximum of one dollar per order and as little as thirty-four cents per order, or a minimum savings of three dollars per order. Multiply the daily savings from that one customer by the total number of similarly active accounts and it can be seen that the profit contribution potential in an apparently "minor" improvement can be very major, indeed.

In another situation, each order from a particular customer came with the notation "Immediately" in the "Ship Date" box on the purchase order form. Goods were sold FOB plant, so the vendor had no particular incentive to consolidate when orders came in on succeeding days. But the customer service manager decided to run a test. Shipments were going out to the particular customer four or five days a week in a weight range of 400-500 lbs., running up a freight bill of about $35,000 annually. The customer service manager showed the customer that by holding the orders until Friday and shipping at one time the freight savings would total about $15,000 annually. The customer was delighted at the prospect of saving $15,000, particularly since there was no service disadvantage. It turned out that the delivering carrier was holding all the week's shipments at the terminal and then delivering them together on Friday anyway.

In still another company, the distribution manager set up a consolidation program with a difference. To qualify for the program, orders from the South had to be placed on Monday, from the Northeast on Tuesday, from the Midwest on Wednesday and so forth. The incentive? If orders from the particular region were placed on the right day, the company would provide "free shipping," i.e., they would move in the consolidation but without charge to the customer. Orders placed at any other time would ship the regular way and the customer would be billed the regular shipping charges. The question is: how can a company make a profit giving away what it used to charge for, i.e., shipping? This company did! Order processing costs were running about $40 per order; with the new program average orders per customer dropped from 3.4 to 1.2. By rationalizing the flow of orders, the company eliminated virtually all overtime in the warehouse and shipping departments. True, it paid for shipping now, but this was more than offset by the other savings, and the net savings represented a handsome profit contribution. As a fringe benefit, it also went a long ways to reduce stress on customer service reps, which in turn contributed to better morale and improved productivity.

Then there was the firm that had a standard shipping day. "We'll ship your order by Friday or sooner," was the standard answer to all ship date queries. And it did. The agreement between the traffic department and the customer service department stipulated that the traffic department would accumulate freight and consolidate as many shipments as it could up to and through Friday, but that any shipments not consolidated by close of business Friday would have to be shipped out without further delay—in effect, the docks had to be cleared. The system works very well, and in practice many shipments do go out before Friday and are received sooner than expected. The savings of the program are simply reckoned by comparing average costs per hundredweight when all shipments went out individually with present costs when about 70% move in consolidations. It's a substantial amount.

• *Air freight applications in customer service.* Transportation is usually one of the most costly elements in the total customer service cycle. Companies usually distinguish between: (1) the need-now order, usually small and requiring immediate delivery at relatively high cost; and (2) the order-for-stock, which usually has little urgency and is typically sized to take advantage of transportation economies. Late deliveries are sometimes caused by carrier-induced problems like loss, terminal delay and misrouting, but most shipments that arrive late do so simply because they were shipped late. Late shipments arise from a variety of causes: lack of product to ship, backups in the warehouse and shipping department, and of course late placement of orders by customers. In such situations, many companies resort to air freight to pick up the slack as well as to respond to bona fide emergencies.

Relatively few companies, however, realize that air freight is often suitable for their *regular* deliveries. If built into an overall program involving inventory planning and warehouse management, air freight can sometimes offer savings over conventional surface delivery programs which may require substantially greater inventories and more shipping points. Air freight lends itself to products of relatively high value because it enables the firm to reduce the number of stocking points and save money in inventory, warehousing, packaging and other costs. These savings frequently more than offset the higher cost of air freight. A variation of this is to use air freight in shortage situations. Product is concentrated at a central location, thus eliminating underproductive safety stocks which might be dispersed at six to ten or more locations. More customers can be served from less total inventory, and more distant customers can be served by air at a net saving.

One application of particular interest to customer service managers involves warehousing of extremely high value parts at a central location at the airport in Memphis, which is roughly the geographic center of the U.S. in terms of deliveries. These parts are in the range of $5,000-25,000 and more, and usually relate to machine-down situations. When a call comes in to the warehouse from anywhere in the U.S., the part is drawn immediately from the warehouse stock and shipped out to the customer by the next available carrier—usually within several hours—to arrive at any airport in the U.S. in five hours or less. The cost of inventorying these critical parts five or six deep at the central location is far less than inventorying them two or three deep at 50 or more locations in major market areas where most computer and high-tech manufacturers have important customers. The cost of air freight is negligible in this context, and the system often gets the replacement part to the user just as fast as a local warehouse, and with considerably more reliability. A variation on this relates to the high cost of sending field technicians to remote sites where there are relatively few machines to service. In such cases, the Memphis location will ship out the needed parts and the specialized tools required to install them, while a specialist at the vendor's headquarters will walk the customer through the repair job via telephone.

• *Testing the validity of productivity improvements.* Many customer service operations run at about 70% efficiency because of the intermittent nature of the work and its frequent interruptions and changeovers from one job to another. This means that the true cost of labor is the fully distributed hourly cost of labor including allowance for fringes, etc., multiplied by a so-called "increase factor" (IF) to account for the 30% non-productive time. This IF is determined by dividing the actual percentage of productivity into 100. Thus the IF for 70% productivity is 100 ÷ 70 = 1.429, while the IF for 80% productivity is 100 ÷ 80 = 1.250. For a basic labor cost of $7.00 an hour, the fully distributed hourly cost including fringes is about $11.00 an hour. This means that hourly costs for a department with 20 reps earning $7.00 an hour and working at 70% productivity are actually—

$11 (fully distributed) × 20 persons × 1.429 IF = $314.38 per hour

Against this background, the manager wishes to test whether or not a full-time supervisor can be cost-justified. The full-time supervisor will have a fully distributed cost of about $15 per hour, and his or her job will be to plan the workload and maintain a good work pace. It's almost certain that the supervisor will increase productivity from 70% to 80%, and therefore the 80% IF will be employed—

$11 (fully distributed) × 20 persons × 1.250 IF = $275.00 per hour

This is an improvement of almost $40 an hour in productivity, or a net gain over the supervisor's salary of about $25 an hour, or $200 a day and $1,000 a week. Quite clearly, the investment would be justified.

A similar approach can be used to other investments in productivity including equipment, improved office layout, even "comfort factors" that have proven to contribute to increased productivity, such as office partitions and sound-deadening materials. The improvements need not be very large, and they can combine both tangible and intangible aspects of productivity improvement. One company found, for example, that its customer service reps spent an inordinate amount of time calling and re-calling customers—mostly brokers—whose lines were often busy. There was a substantial frustration factor which could be called an "intangible" but certainly inhibited productivity to some extent, but there were whole chunks of measurable, wasted, unproductive time spent just dialing phone numbers that rang busy. By installing equipment (at about $250 per phone position, at the time) that automatically dialed any one of 30 numbers at the press of a single button and had built-in memory for redialing, etc., the firm virtually did away with the frustration and in the process found itself saving over an hour a week per rep, thus paying for the machines in less than a year in "tangible" productivity improvements alone.

• *When customer service cuts contribute to profits.* Sometimes it's possible to improve customer service—and profits—by spending less money. One company was spending $40,000 a year in postage alone to notify customers when items on their purchase orders were not immediately available. Since customers weren't expecting speedy delivery (and didn't need it), the back order cards served no useful purpose. In fact, in some instances the out-of-stock items became available shortly after the cards were mailed and were shipped immediately by UPS—and arrived at the customer's location *before* the postcard notification! The postcard, when it did arrive, simply confused customers and irritated them because it caused more work. Eliminating the out-of-stock notification altogether eliminated confusion, annoyance and extra work for customers—but as importantly freed up some $40,000 for constructive uses . . . like profits.

A parallel situation occurred with a sporting goods company which set up an extensive public warehousing program so that pro shops at country clubs all over the U.S. could get almost immediate delivery when they ordered either single golf clubs or entire sets. Not only was the stock conveniently near by, it also reflected a high level of product availability and support for the pro by the company. Trouble was, the support was *too* good. Knowing they could pick up an order in no time at all, the pros didn't bother stocking the line at their pro shops. The absence of onsite stock resulted in lost sales, and proved the point that it's sometimes possible to improve profits by cutting back on customer service.

Nor does it always pay to charge extra for superior customer service. One company tried it and found that customers were buying only the items they couldn't get elsewhere; the bulk of customers' orders were going to companies that charged less and gave less in the way of service.

● *Coordinate lead times, units of sale, delivery and procurement.* Here's how one company does it: Customer service reps call customers by appointment. Because it's a very competitive business, the reps have to know beforehand what items the customers are likely to order, and—equally important—what items aren't in stock and what substitutions are available that can be recommended in their place. In addition to customer profiles, they also have schedules for the firm's fleet of trucks which are used for customer deliveries on the outbound run and purchased raw materials and supplies on the backhaul. Thus when the call is made, the rep has complete information on the probable order, plus inventory status and a delivery date. If necessary, substitutions are recommended and a delivery date is confirmed. Customers are impressed, and very few sales are lost. And the bottom line is that the company has made a substantial rebound from a staggering sales loss several years ago.

● *Take advantage of customer feedback.* Reps should be impressed with (and reminded of) the importance of feedback from their customers including: (1) offhand comments about future plans, job changes, new personnel, plant closings or openings; (2) significant changes in buying patterns, announced or otherwise; (3) information about competitors; (4) complaints about products or services; (5) potential hazards connected with products or services; (6) customers' friends who are potential customers; (7) suggestions for improvement or changes; and of course (8) compliments to the individual or the organization. These "attaboys" are very important and should be shared. Make it a rule that all feedback from customers be reported in writing. If customer contacts share confidences about their companies with reps, the first obligation of reps is to inform the manager regardless. It could have a bearing on their jobs!

● *Monitor order activity and content.* One major firm's

customer service department monitors orders constantly. The minute there is any significant increase over the original sales forecast, the data is fed back all along the line: to sales and marketing, production planning, procurement and production management itself. This allows enough time to decide whether additional manufacturing facilities should be brought on line. Traffic and distribution get the word so that they can consider such options as inventory centralization, longer lead times, etc. Fast, accurate feedback originating in the customer service department enables the firm to capitalize on unexpected sales growth.

Other firms similarly track reductions in order size and/or changes in order content, i.e., lines ordered. They do this both as a precaution against inadvertent ordering errors by customers and as a "flag" to the sales department to take action to counter declining purchases by the customer as necessary. In other companies the scrutiny of ordering patterns may be less formal, but it is no less critical. And the customer service department is usually the first to know and the most sensitive generally to this type of information.

• *Rationalize order sizes.* As indicated earlier, considerable expense is incurred when marketing, distribution and customer service fail to coordinate on price breaks or specials used in promotions and 50-carton prices are offered when a palletload consists of 48 cartons. The same holds true for everyday transactions; to the extent possible, the minimum order size ought to be determined as a combination of pricing policy, breakeven costs and the logistics involved. From there, price breaks would usually represent handling, storage and transportation economies: cartons, half palletloads, full palletloads, multiple palletloads, half truckloads, truckloads, containerloads and carloads. Or, for flowable products, by gallon, pound or ton and multiples.

But trade customs and sometimes just plain habit may interfere with such rationalization. From a logistical point of view, if 9-inch paper plates are packed 1,000 to a carton it would make sense to pack 11-inch paper plates 880 to a carton in order to be able to use the same size carton at roughly the same weight as for 9-inch plates. Whether or not customers can accept such innovation may be open to speculation, but the savings in packaging inventories, handling, storage and transportation would be spectacular.

• *Provide quality control data to concerned departments.* It may be a matter of component failure in equipment, or package design that results in freight damaged in transit. Or it may be more subtle, like packaging that stands up well in the air conditioned plant environment, and also in the three-high configuration in railcars, but won't withstand high-stacking in customers' 30-ft. ceiling warehouses in high-humidity Mississippi. Design features that make equipment difficult to service should be reported, as well as any unusual usage of certain parts or supplies.

• *Demarket uneconomic lines and customers.* While this is essentially a marketing responsibility, the initial push may come from the customer service department which is often closer to the action. Demarketing is a nice way of saying "drop," but it is usually undertaken in a "reverse marketing" context, i.e., customers are prepared for the idea, the company attempts to sell them on the idea, and alternatives are advanced: in the case of a product that's being demarketed or dropped, the alternative is often a higher priced version or a new model or a substitutable item; many companies see this as a marketing opportunity rather than a problem.

In the case of a customer who is about to be demarketed or dropped because of unprofitability, very often the customer is brought back into the fold via buying the product indirect rather than direct, or in some instances simply changed over from direct visitations by salespersons to telemarketing by inside personnel. One company has formed several thousand of its marginal customers into a "club" headed by a fictitious personality like Betty Crocker. These "club members" are regularly telemarketed, have their own 800-number to call and place orders with whichever rep is using the fictitious personality's name that day. It has been quite successful!

It goes without saying that in order to initiate demarketing—which is usually in the interests of the customer service department in any event—the customer service manager must have a firm grasp on customer service costs as discussed previously. And, in terms of demarketing individual customers, the manager should recognize that scattered among the smaller customers there are a number of customers with good growth potential who should be cultivated rather than demarketed.

Demarketing can also be applied to "problem" products or services which are difficult to obtain or provide to customers and are not important to the company's overall marketing effort. Generally speaking, a demand may persist for such products even though a satisfactory substitute exists. For example, a manufacturer of vacuum cleaners found that dealers ordering parts persisted in ordering metal fan blades which were difficult to obtain and had been replaced some years earlier by a perfectly satisfactory—and much less expensive—plastic blade. The company decided to demarket the metal blade by doubling its price—in effect, price it out of the market—and to its surprise saw a flood of orders come in at the new price from customers who assumed that the metal blade was now available as long as they were willing to pay the price. The result was that they had to "de-demarket" the metal blade, which was difficult to procure at any price, and soothe a lot of ruffled feathers at the same time.

There are instances where a product is readily available but is priced so low that it constitutes a "nuisance" or accommodation item. There are two courses open here. One is to raise the price so that people will either stop ordering it or pay the higher, profitable price (which often happens). The other is to simply give it away. Both approaches are used successfully.

14

THE FIVE
MOST COMMON ERROR SOURCES—
AND WHAT TO DO ABOUT THEM

Customer service errors can put companies out of business. A customer service rep took an order for a delivery of fuel oil to 172, Maple Ave. The driver read it as 1721 Maple Ave., several doors away from the Cranstons' house at 1727. Nobody was home at the Russo house at 1721, so the driver hitched the hose up to the filler pipe and started the pump. What he didn't know was that the Russos had converted to gas heat the previous spring, and removed their oil tank . . . but the contractor had forgotten to remove the filler pipe half-hidden in the rhododendrons. Result: several thousand gallons of fuel oil in the Russos' basement. Fortunately, there was no fire or explosion—but a damage suit that was more than the small, struggling fuel oil company could survive.

Or, consider the case of the keypunch clerk who transposed weight and quantity on an order for a custom-manufactured unit weighing in at $2,500 per unit . . . and the company found out a few months later that it had manufactured 40 more of the custom units than the customer or anybody else would ever need in this life or the hereafter.

Then there was the customer who ordered 200 units of P1270 when he meant to say P1280: he received a truckload of 20-ft. concrete inserts instead of the 24-lb. box of 1⅝-inch square end caps he was expecting. No damage per se, but a delay in getting the right product, plus the cost of returning the truckload of concrete inserts to the shipping point some miles away. Not quite so fortunate was the customer who ordered 1,000 rolls of specially-treated fabric, "40 x 30," when in fact she meant to say "30 x 40." In the particular industry, the convention is to list the width first *in inches,* and the length second, *in yards.* Her specification was handled as a 40″ width and manufactured accordingly. There was some salvage opportunity, but the overall loss was—well, let's say comfortably into six figures.

Perhaps the most bizarre of all are the customers who simply order the wrong things for no discernible reason, often claim that they didn't order them, and frequently get caught up in the machinery of returns and adjustments while in the meantime credit is in hot pursuit.

But one of the most common is likely to be the retailer who returns a product claiming it to have been returned by *his* customer as no good, defective and many other epithets. Perhaps it is a bicycle which the consumer attempted to assemble Christmas Eve whilst downing eggnog which led him to use a sledgehammer instead of a box wrench; perhaps even a pair of jogging shoes which only made it through two summers in Baja.

Would it have been possible to avoid these errors, and others like them?

Not by the most common method, which is to single out the individual who made the mistake and then try to persuade him or her to be more careful next time. The expression used in football is "Don't lose your concentration!" But the truth is that concentrating on the culprit does very little about the *causes* of errors. People do make mistakes, and they often make the same mistakes twice or three or four times; in fact, people have a predictable error rate. Which means that even after a talking-to and retraining, people are still going to make mistakes. In fact, errors by customer service personnel and warehouse workers or shipping personnel tend to be a small part of the error picture in many companies. And they have to be considered in the context of the other error sources as discussed below.

The Five Sources of Customer Service Errors

1. *Line personnel.* Customer service personnel and others directly handling customer accounts and orders *commit* mistakes but do not always *cause* them. Some of the errors they make can be traced to lack of motivation or identification with both company and customer. As the customer service manager of a major aluminum producer put it, "It's very difficult to get it across to people at the plant that a single day's output is one saleman's livelihood for an entire year—and if we blow it in any way we're taking the food off his table!" It's easy enough to blame personnel who make mistakes for having poor motivation or an "attitude problem," and wish they would take some pride in their work . . . but, regrettably, the customer service department in some companies is not a place to be proud of, or in.

Philosophy aside, what can the manager do about error-prone people in the customer service department? First of all, the manager should involve himself or herself directly in the hiring process. Skills should be tested in the specific areas where errors are made. People should be hired on the basis of proven qualification for the job, not on vague assessments of stability or longevity which personnel people sometimes favor for customer service jobs. If the manager is faced with the problem of incompetent people on the job, he or she must realize that incompetent people have to be dealt with wherever they are, and whatever the reason for their incompetence. If they can be retrained or transferred to less sensitive jobs, fine. If they cannot, then they should be separated from the department. Customer service is too sensitive an area to have bunglers who can't be controlled, regardless of how long-lived and loyal they may be. Beyond the damage they can do to customers and customer relations, the manager must realize that they can have a devastating and demoralizing effect on other employees in the department.

In actuality, incompetents are seldom the real problem. Most can be screened out before they come aboard. With good material to work with, and a combination of sound procedures, good training and effective supervision—plus positive motivation rather than intimidation—errors by customer service line personnel can be virtually wiped out. But some of the other sources may not be as easy and may take longer.

2. *Management personnel.* Management has the ultimate responsibility for a company's philosophy, its policies and its systems and procedures—and the resources that are committed to customer service. Some companies find that error rates go up sharply in the summertime, partly because some people are on vacation and partly because some are taking sick leave—they're sick and tired of working in a warehouse with no air conditioning so they stay home where it's cool. Those who are left on the job include summertime part-timers who don't know the stock, and as the volume of orders grows with fewer people to handle them, the error rate understandably climbs. Install air conditioning, as many companies have long since done, and the problem reverses itself. Over a period of time, the cost of the air conditioning is amortized many times over in improved performance.

Management can be the ultimate cause of errors in a situation of that particular type, or it can be a more general responsibility where management will not *position* the department where it has the status and image in the company to attract and motivate reasonably competent people who will identify with the firm. Again, management may simply refuse to pay sufficient wages, or to underwrite the cost of training. Quite a few managements frown on incentive programs for customer service reps, yet provide handsome commission and bonus arrangements for field sales personnel (and themselves). And of course management very often doesn't want to underwrite the cost of communications and data processing systems adequate to the customer service mission.

But perhaps the most serious management error is failure to appreciate the impact of many policy decisions they make on customer service and, ultimately, the company's profits. A management decides, for example, that credit is getting out of hand, and that terms are going to be a stringent 15 days EOM (end-of-month). Customers respond by delaying their orders until right *after* the first, giving them in effect 45 days and burying the department under a mountain of orders all marked "rush." Or, they'll simply wait until they actually need an item to order it. Result: more small orders, less lead time, errors in order processing, order assembly, shipping.

Management can also err on the side of too much customer service. If management insists on giving 100% customer service when other firms don't, customers will appreciate the service but they will start buying hand-to-mouth, i.e., without stocking anything beyond their barest needs. This will cost the company profits and significantly increase the workload in the customer service department and in the warehouse and shipping departments—more units of work to perform, but without any increase in overall sales volume. The result is predictable: an increase in errors as the workload becomes more uneven and difficult to manage. A subsidiary problem is that when a company gives better service than the market actually needs, customers very quickly get in the habit and come to depend on exceptional service—a habit that it's very expensive for the company to sustain over the long run, and yet one that's equally hard to break customers of.

It's not intended to use management as a whipping-boy for all problems that arise in the customer service department. It's an imperfect world, and managements have to deal with a wide variety of problems involving how best to invest the company's resources, how best to organize the company's activities . . . and how best to satisfy the board of directors and the stockholders.

It follows that errors of judgment made by management are in many instances made because top management did not get adequate or accurate information from middle management or had not been presented with a choice of alternative courses of action by those same managers. For example, the chief executive who orders same-day shipping because of the excessive complaints about late delivery he hears from customers. His own people do not present him the alternative of providing customers an incentive to order less frequently and in larger volume in order to avoid the high number of rush orders that originally precipitated the situation. Certainly there's a possibility that customer service managers raised in a tradition of being reactive but not proactive could be responsible for management misinformation or lack of information.

In short, the goal is not to blame top management for poor decisions, but rather to make middle management—including customer service management—aware of its obligation to help top management make good decisions.

3. *Systems and procedures inadequacies.* While faulty systems and procedures can also be characterized as people-problems, the responsibility is shared widely and here again the problem is to correct rather than assign blame. Many problems arise because programmers don't understand all the facets of the customer service operation, and managers don't understand all the facets of programming. "If I had my druthers," one manager said, "I wouldn't even *use* a programmer until that programmer had worked in a hands-on job in my department for at least a year!" Yet a programmer might equally respond: "If I had *my* druthers, I wouldn't even *talk* to a manager who didn't have at least one college-level course in programming!"

And the problem may be equally due to workers who use the system daily and are aware of its shortcomings but don't bother telling anybody. System inadequacies don't come to light until a serious error occurs, often at considerable expense. When one company changed from glass to plastic bottles, half a dozen people were aware that the computer was inadequate to preparing bills of lading because it hadn't been reprogrammed to reflect the correct "agreed weights" of the lighter containers. Yet none of the six notified the manager and as a result the firm spent over $40,000 in excess freight charges calculated by the computer before the system was finally corrected.

Many errors occur because procedures simply haven't been thought through in terms of the total system. As an example, the manufacturing department commonly stencils product information and descriptions on the heads of 55-gallon drums—a flat surface and convenient height for stencilling. As long as drums are stored on their sides, this system of identification works fine. But when drums are stood on end, palletized and stacked in the warehouse, the identification cannot be seen by fork lift operators and accordingly many mistakes are made in order selection.

Forms design is another common cause of errors. When forms are designed to capture information for a number of departments or purposes, the result is often confusion to the individual user who in some instances is working under conditions of poor lighting, noise and other distractions. In conjunction with forms design, poor handwriting is an extremely common cause of mistakes resulting from misreading or simply guessing at illegible words or phrases. Computer-generated documents like picking tickets can be formatted to the needs of the individual user, i.e., excluding non-relevant information and highlighting critical data like quantity, location, etc. However, shortcuts in programming like abbreviating product descriptions can be disastrous if they do not use the terminology familiar to pickers.

Most errors of the types mentioned here are the result of system fragmentation, i.e., split responsibilities with gray areas between those responsibilities. Giving customer service reps account responsibility is often an antidote to errors within the department, but the department should also have open channels of dialogue with other departments including credit, accounts receivable, shipping and warehousing. Working with the systems and procedures department in actual design of procedures can be an important plus, with one caveat: when procedures are designed with excessive steps or review stages in order to prevent errors, the opposite result may occur. That is, people will skip steps and perhaps make more errors than they would with less complex forms with fewer steps and a theoretically higher potential for error.

4. *Errors by customers.* "When I find out it's the customer who made the mistake, I relax!" This is a common misreading by customer service personnel, on several counts. Mistakes by customers are the most sensitive of all mistakes, and, far from relaxing, reps and managers alike should be making every effort to mitigate the damage and help the customer out of his or her predicament. The Golden Rule? More than that, there are very practical reasons for helping customers extricate themselves from situations they have caused:

• Many errors apparently caused by customers are in fact

the result of inadequate instructions by the vendor, poor communications or similar circumstances where the vendor is at least partially responsible.

• It may be difficult to actually determine who was in fact at fault when a mistake is made. The customer would not necessarily accept responsibility for an error even though there is nothing to suggest anybody else could have been responsible.

• The customer, in trouble in his or her firm for the mistake, may blame the vendor anyway and remove it from the account to demonstrate that corrective action has in fact been taken.

• If the individual who made the mistake in the customer company is disciplined or fired as a result, the vendor loses an important contact who is a known quantity. The successor may not be nearly as easy to work with, and may in fact assume that the vendor was ultimately responsible for the firing of his or her predecessor.

• The customer who does make a mistake and is helped out of it by the vendor becomes a friend for life . . . and an even better customer.

• A customer mistake often presents an opportunity to correct an ongoing source of difficulty in an amicable fashion.

A variation on mistakes by customers is mistakes by customers' customers. These are the most difficult and complex of all errors and usually but not always involve consumer goods. Problems arise in making the distinction between normal wear-and-tear, outright product failure, and misuse or downright abuse. It's not unheard of for the retailer and the consumer to "gang up" on the manufacturer and submit claims for refunds or replacement that do not appear to be justified. In the long run it may be preferable to make the requested adjustment with the knowledge that most claims are made in good faith and relatively few are downright dishonest. Because the manufacturer normally has little control over retailers and other entities in the distribution channel, consumer complaints often get mired down in excessive defensiveness, paperwork and sometimes downright incompetence at the retail level. The result can be outright consumer hostility directed towards seemingly monolithic and unresponsive manufacturers. In such situations, it may be better for the manufacturer to bypass the retailer and encourage direct communications from consumers via an 800-number, complaint hotline, warranty cards and similar means.

Whether the firm deals with other companies or with ultimate consumers, however, there is fundamental truth in the saying that "nobody ever wins an argument with a customer." It can be said similarly that by the time a problem has reached the proportions where it becomes necessary to argue who's responsible for it, relations with the customer are seriously strained and the entire account may be in jeopardy. If the dispute goes to court, the customer is as good as lost and the account might as well be written off. From the vendor's point of view, it's likely to be a case where it's wrong to be right.

5. *Errors by intermediaries: carriers, public warehouses, etc.* Here again, there can be a distinction between who *is* responsible for the problem and who *takes* responsibility for it. The most common example occurs when the firm sells FOB shipping point and freight is misrouted, lost or damaged by the carrier or carriers involved in delivering the order to the customer. If two carriers are involved, the problem becomes even more involved and complex, and if the customer discovers concealed shortages or damage after signing for the shipment it may be next to impossible to either establish responsibility or collect from the carrier. This is particularly true if the freight is prepaid by the vendor and later rebilled to the customer-consignee; the carrier has little incentive to settle expeditiously, particularly when consignees are small firms with little clout and no business potential for the carrier.

Although FOB sales establish the responsibility of the customer to file claims against delivering carriers in such instances, in actual practice the vendor's traffic department very often provides concrete assistance in such filings, and in addition uses its influence with the carrier to see that claims are resolved quickly and fairly. And since there is always the possibility that some claims result from poor loading, blocking or bracing—or even inadequate protective packaging—the vendor should review all these stages of the total order cycle. Up to a point no-fault compensation for concealed damage or shortages may be in order. When certain customers repeatedly claim shortages and abuses are suspected, just notifying them that their orders are being personally checked by the rep or manager and then tracked and monitored enroute is usually enough to bring an end to any abuses.

Most other third-party problems are not legitimately the concern of the customer. For example, products shipped to a public warehouse for distribution to a firm's customers are still under the control and ownership of the vendor, and any problems at the warehouse are the vendor's, not the customer's. (In certain types of operations, title to goods may pass from vendor to customer at the warehouse and without goods actually leaving the warehouse. There are also examples of consignment warehousing and field warehousing where title remains with the vendor but the customer has responsibility for protecting the goods. Such instances are a relatively small percentage of the total, however.)

Clearly, whenever a vendor uses a third party for whatever reasons the third party's performance reflects the good (or poor) judgment of the vendor and therefore should be a matter of No. 1 concern, particularly in the matter of resolving errors and disputes. The customer who is asked to deal directly with a third party with whom he or she has had no prior contact is likely to resent having to do the follow-up, and in any event will certainly take a dim view of the vendor in not avoiding such problems altogether or at least resolving them quickly when they occur.

Customer Service Department Liability for Customer Errors

• *Mis-specification by customer.* The simplest of these are cases where the customer specifies the wrong product, the wrong quantity or the wrong destination. The goods are usually returned to the shelf and replacements shipped to the customer. The customer normally pays the freight and a small restocking charge, although these may be waived in some instances. The problem becomes more complex with custom products manufactured to the customer's specifications, for example, printed materials, containers, custom assemblies and the like.

In a typical case, a customer's purchase order might call for 400,000 cartons printed with the customer's name and manufactured to certain dimensions. The purchase order is received and confirmed—and filled exactly as specified. Yet the customer refuses to accept delivery on the grounds that he *intended* to order only 40,000. Who's responsible? The customer says he has been dealing with the vendor for ten years and has never ordered more than 40,000 cartons at a time; it is incumbent on the vendor, he says, to take note of such an extreme variance from his "customer profile" and to call it to his attention. Some courts would be inclined to agree, but by this time the customer would be lost anyway. Certainly there's an implied obligation on the vendor's part to be familiar with customers' typical ordering patterns, ship-to-addresses and the like.

This type of problem may become more severe with increases in direct order entry by customers, either by a terminal at the customer site or via computer-to-computer ordering. This can be further broken down into direct and via a third party system. An order for 4,000 bicycles comes through as an order for 14,000 bicycles. Who is responsible for the error? Who is responsible for catching it and correcting the record before any harm is done? Generally, errors of this type will be caught by customer service reps familiar with the account, but if the data is handled only by key punch personnel, they are not nearly as likely to catch variances of this order. Clearly, it makes sense to develop systems aimed at avoiding such errors before they happen rather than trying to find the guilty parties afterward.

• *Errors in application.* This category of errors would usually include product liability cases arising out of misuse or abuse of the product by the customer. These often hinge on very subtle points having to do with how well the vendor has instructed the customer in use or application of the product. To illustrate just how subtle, to the courts there can be a world of difference between saying "Do not put the car in reverse while it is in forward motion," on the one hand, and saying more explicitly, on the other, "Do not put the car in reverse while it is in forward motion or severe transmission damage is likely to result." The point is that the manufacturer of a product is presumed to be the ultimate expert on product applications and may be held liable for damages resulting from failure to properly inform the customer on correct usage and the possible consequences of incorrect applications. In one interpretation of this, the vendor may be held liable to refund or exchange products damaged when customer attempts to follow—but does not succeed—instructions for assembling products that are shipped disassembled.

And although they do not usually come through the customer service department, there are some product liability cases where the customer is clearly at fault but the damages are awarded anyway. Such instances, unfair though they may be, underline the wisdom of re-examining all communications with customers so as to avoid such situations completely whenever possible. Additionally, when customer service reps are trained in complaint handling, specific attention should be given to identifying complaints which suggest a product liability situation—and then taking the requisite action necessary to place them in the hands of the upper-echelon persons with specific responsibility for handling liability matters.

In technical matters, the vendor is normally presumed to have superior expertise. This will usually be construed as an obligation to warn customers of potential hazards to persons or property, or to catch and correct obvious errors by customers that come to the vendor's attention. Even were the presumption not there, nor the construction, it would still be good business to do so!

Errors by Type, Cause and Cost

Companies differ considerably in their definition of what actually constitutes an error. Some companies will go so far as to treat an out-of-stock condition as an error, while others confine the definition to actual mistakes in entering and filling orders, providing wrong information to customers, etc. Many customers use the same routines for dealing with errors and adjustments which are not the result of errors; figure 1 is an example of one firm's classification by types. Figure 2 is a method for classifying errors by cause, dollar amount and percentage of total. Use of this form will enable quick determination of which errors are most serious in total dollars, as well as those which are serious because of frequency of occurrence rather than actual costs.

However, it should also be stressed that it is not always easy to tabulate errors by cost and arrive at a realistic number. An error requiring issuance of a credit for $100 doesn't necessarily cost the company $100 if it simply reflects refunding the customer sales tax that was incorrectly charged. On the other hand, the total time of the personnel involved in receiving, analyzing and issuing the credit may cost significantly more than $100. There may also be some residual effect of the incident on customer's attitude and subsequent purchases. Thus a lengthy credit processing cycle has a double disadvantage: it is likely to be expensive in and of itself, and costly in customer relations. Inasmuch as a credit typically involves the customer's funds or obligations, it should be issued in the fastest time. In addition, future customer purchases should be tracked to determine if they have been affected adversely or favorably. Some companies do this as a matter of course.

Generally speaking, the cost of errors in terms of lost business can only be measured on a case-by-case basis. Often it's the cumulative effect of errors over time that does the damage, rather than a single serious mistake. Billing errors which are quickly rectified will not drive customers away. Yet if they are repeated often enough, customers will eventually lose confidence and transfer some of their business elsewhere so as not to be

Customer Service Department Errors, Adjustments and Other Exceptions

Corrections

Product Errors

1. *Material billed not shipped*
   (Covers short shipments, items skipped when picking backorders, etc.)
2. *Wrong product shipped*
   (Product shipped is not product required or ordered by customer)
3. *Wrong quantity shipped*
   (Quantity shipped is not quantity required or ordered by customer)
4. *Material shipped to wrong address*
   (Material misdirected, customer reports non-receipt)
5. *Material shipped not billed*
   (Customer retains incorrectly shipped material and is billed for material)
6. *Material lost in transit*
   (Used when customer claims non-receipt of entire shipment/one or more cartons in multiple shipment)
7. *Material damaged in transit*
   (Used for issuing credit for material damaged in transit)

Billing Errors

1. *To cancel document*
   (Used when invoice/credit is issued to correct data processing and accounting records as a result of prior issued incorrect invoice/credit)
2. *To correct document*
3. *To complete document*
4. *To correct duplicate document*
   (Used when customer is billed twice for same shipment/or customer previously issued duplicate credit)
5. *To correct freight charged*
   (To correct freight charged to customer on a shipment)
6. *To correct tax charged*
   (When customer has submitted exemption certificate and has not been removed from taxable status; insufficient state sales or use tax charged on prior issued invoice)
7. *To correct pallet charges*
   (Used to cancel/correct charges made/not made to customer for pallets)
8. *To correct discount or allowance*
   (Used to correct improperly computed discounts, allowances, sales service commissions, etc.)

Figure 14-1. A typical listing of errors, exceptions, and adjustments. In normal practice, each listing is assigned a unique "error code" which will

Pricing Errors

1. *To correct price*
   (Price on invoice is incorrect)
2. *To correct bid price)*
   (Bid price on invoice is incorrect)

Other Adjustments

1. *Material picked up by our representative*
   (Used when a representative picks up material from an account as a result of a customer service, plant or sales error or customer's returning outdated, deleted, soiled, etc., merchandise)
2. *Material transferred*
   (Material transferred from a customer's location to another location)
3. *Material delivered by our representative*
   (Used when a representative delivers material to an account as a result of any customer service, plant, etc., error or when material is replaced not as a result of an error)
4. *Replacement material*
   (Used on a no charge invoice to replace returned goods, damaged in transit goods, etc.)
5. *State/city tax—not charged on past sales*
   (Used when a customer is charged for all back sales as a result of not having filed an exemption certificate)
6. *Return of pallets*
   (Used when a customer returns pallets for credit)
7. *Material destroyed in field*
   (Used when credit is issued to customer for material destroyed in field)
8. *Miscellaneous adjustments/allowances*
   Includes floor stock and retroactive price adjustements, coupon exemption
   (Used to cover miscellaneous adjustments and allowances)
9. *To credit standing order not shipped*
10. *Inventory adjustment*
    (Used by Inventory Control when issuing credit to add stock or when issuing invoice to deduct stock from finished goods inventory)

Returned Goods

1. *Credit for returned goods*
   (Material returned short-dated, defective, soiled, outdated, deleted, over stocked)
2. *Credit for returned goods (recall)*
   (Material returned as a result of product recall)
3. *Credit for material refused and returned*
   (Material refused and returned as the result of sales decision, e.g., account did not order merchandise)

be printed as an identifier in all documents pertaining to that transaction. This is one firms classification; others may vary.

overdependent on a single source prone to making mistakes.

The manager should make it clear to customer service personnel as well as those outside the department that there is no such thing as a "little" error. The examples cited at the opening of this chapter should make that point clear. But even unreported errors involving small amounts or minor matters tend to get blown out of proportion by customers, particularly if they are repeated. Moreover, what appears to one person as a minor error

---

Errors by Cause

1. Inadequate product information — salesperson, customer service rep or customer.

2. Inadequate customer information in files.

3. Lack of standard procedure for emergencies or exceptions.

4. Unsuitable or outdated order forms.

5. Special deals or packs.

6. Changes in packaging units, masterpacks.

7. Unstructured telephone routine; inadequate training.

8. Failure to monitor phone transactions and correspondence.

9. Confusing labels and markings on packages, including computer-generated labels or picking instructions.

10. Poor lighting or environmental conditions in warehouse.

11. Unreliable information systems.

12. Failure to follow established procedures; shortcutting.

13. Intervention by non-customer service personnel from sales, manufacturing, etc.

14. Lack of accountability (real or perceived) on the part of individuals responsible for errors.

Activity and Type of Error	Dollar Amount	Percent of Total Invoices
Office Errors:		
Incorrect customer billed	$ _____	_____%
Incorrect product billed	$ _____	_____%
Incorrect quantity billed	$ _____	_____%
Incorrect price billed	$ _____	_____%
Incorrect terms billed	$ _____	_____%
Other _____	$ _____	_____%
Warehouse Errors:		
Incorrect product shipped	$ _____	_____%
Incorrect quantity shipped	$ _____	_____%
Other _____	$ _____	_____%
General Errors:		
Billed but not shipped	$ _____	_____%
Computer errors	$ _____	_____%
Refused automatic replenishment	$ _____	_____%
Defective product shipped	$ _____	_____%
Unsubstantiated shortage	$ _____	_____%
Tax error	$ _____	_____%
Other _____	$ _____	_____%
Carrier Errors:		
Damage in transit	$ _____	_____%
Loss in transit	$ _____	_____%
Delayed in transit	$ _____	_____%
Other _____	$ _____	_____%
Sales Force Errors:		
Incorrect customer specified: Mail	$ _____	_____%
Phone	$ _____	_____%
Incorrect product specified: Mail	$ _____	_____%
Phone	$ _____	_____%
Incorrect quantity specified: Mail	$ _____	_____%
Phone	$ _____	_____%
Customer Service Rep Errors:		
Incorrect customer recorded: Mail	$ _____	_____%
Phone	$ _____	_____%
Incorrect product recorded: Mail	$ _____	_____%
Phone	$ _____	_____%
Incorrect quantity recorded: Mail	$ _____	_____%
Phone	$ _____	_____%
Customer Errors		
Mail	$ _____	_____%
Phone	$ _____	_____%

Figure 14-2. Form to help determine seriousness of errors by dollar amount as well as by frequency and type or source.

may actually have serious consequences for another. Some errors are virtually unavoidable, but even so are much more likely to be tolerated by customers from a vendor who has a good previous record of attention to detail and error-avoidance generally, than from a vendor who has already earned a name for carelessness and repetitive, though minor, errors.

Thus, accumulation of small errors can result in outright loss of a customer's business when the "breaking point"is reached—just as a single error of significant proportions can have the same effect. Recognizing this, some companies class an out-of-stock situation—i.e., shipping an incomplete order—as an error, knowing that in some industries two or three such shipments may simply cause the customer to turn elsewhere, to a more reliable source.

Between the two extremes of taking no action and ceasing altogether to do business with a particular vendor, customers have a number of different forms of "reprisal" they may use. One of the most common of these is to arbitrarily delay payment. Another is to increase inspection and rejection rates. Yet another is to arbitrarily make unauthorized deductions when paying invoices. A common practice among some disgruntled customers is to buy only low-margin items from a vendor in disrepute, that is to "cherrypick" such items and purchase the more profitable high-margin items from a competitor. There is some evidence to suggest that, once a relationship has been established with a supplier, a customer will not readily give up that relationship. But this may be a mixed blessing for the supplier. Reprisals taken by disgruntled customers who don't speak up but continue dealing with the supplier may end up costing more than outright loss of the business, to say nothing of the stress effect on personnel having to deal with such customers, and the long-range impact on morale and motivation—and error rate—in the department.

Strategies for Error Avoidance

• *Systems and procedures.* Given the versatility of computers, the most serious human input errors—i.e., those affecting quantity, weight, cost, etc.—can usually be prevented by writing appropriate subroutines or parameters. Similarly, subroutines can be written for common exceptions such as stockouts, applying consistent decision rules and avoiding the risk of judgmental errors by customer service personnel. As suggested earlier, procedures that are poorly thought through are a frequent source of errors. One reason for documenting errors as carefully as the forms reproduced here would suggest is to identify and correct as many of those errors as may result from systems or procedures design deficiencies rather than from human fallibility.

Several points about procedure should be mentioned here. When the customer service activity is fragmented among a number of people, there is likely to be a blurring of lines of responsibility and as a result an increase in errors of omission including failure to follow through. Additionally, procedures that are excessively complex invite shortcutting and increase the risk of errors. It's axiomatic that the complexity of the procedure should be hidden away in the computer and the visible parts made as "transparent" as possible to the individual employee. There is no need for the individual to manipulate or rearrange data or make repetitive decisions that can be programmed. At the same time, employees should be encouraged to remain flexible and use judgment in areas where computers have none.

With the increasing trend towards direct order entry by customers using onsite terminals, touchtone telephones or their own computers, additional constraints or safeguards may be necessary. In one recent transaction, a manufacturer's major customer entered a computer-to-computer order for 14,000 units of a particular item when the intended quantity was only 4,000. The size of the order was not excessive for that particular customer, and it might have gone through except that an experienced customer service rep recognized that no order of that size had ever been designated for the specific ship-to location and thus questioned the buyer by telephone. Errors of this type which cannot always be detected by routine programming will have to be taken into account as well as errors of substitution, transposition and the like which appear to "scan" correctly when input to the supplier computer.

It should go without saying that customer education in vendor procedures can help avoid many customer-caused errors. Where customers use vendor-supplied manuals, order blanks or other systems, such education may be relatively easy and well worth its cost. This point is discussed in greater detail below.

• *Training.* While the specifics of training are generally beyond the scope of this book, it is a matter of record that in many companies customer service training is often limited to having newcomers observe seasoned employees and then strike out on their own, perhaps with the aid of a procedures manual, perhaps without. In a recent meeting of customer service executives, fewer than 25% could report having such manuals for their customer service representatives. It is essential that employees not only have an objective step-by-step description of their principal duties, but also an understanding of the levels of performance—speed, accuracy, quality of work, etc.—that are expected of them. (It's assumed, of course, that employees have been hired on the basis of measurable skills or trainability in the work they will be performing.)

If existing personnel include suitable role models, then by all means they should be used to familiarize newcomers with the operation and to train them in specific techniques. But the training process itself should be monitored to make sure these trainers are not passing along bad habits they themselves have picked up, including over-familiarity with customers, shortcuts and the like. Some firms' training departments may be able to provide telephone training, and this is a good opportunity to introduce trainees to service observation or monitoring. By having them listen in on transactions being performed by experienced personnel in the company they will get used to the idea of being monitored, and can even anticipate one day being selected as role models to be listened in on by future newcomers to the department. There are also a number of off-shelf training programs in telephone techniques and customer service which can be administered to individuals or groups, and companies which provide in-house training in telephone usage.

Of course the telephone is only part of the total process, and the development of listening skills for this and other purposes should be an integral part of the total training. It has been the tradition to blame speakers rather than listeners for communications breakdowns, but more recently it has been observed that poor listening habits are even more to blame. Speakers typically speak at 150-300 words per minute, while the average listener can hear at the rate of some 600 words a minute. This disparity in speaking and listening speeds plus the habit of listening passively rather than actively is a principal cause of miscommunications. Some communications problems can be avoided by having personnel use standard interrogatories or prompts when receiving information from customers, as well as forms which provide for recording information in a systematic manner.

Many managers train their new employees through a step-by-step process of moving from simple to more complex jobs under the supervision of a senior employee. The important thing is that there be a formal training program to begin with, and that the department's budget and philosophy both provide for re-training as necessary to overcome lapses by individuals as well as to deal with new situations. The training period is also the best time to determine whether a new employee is in fact suitable, or whether he or she should be terminated or moved to other employment before entering into a position with such a high potential for serious damage from errors.

• *Observation and monitoring.* As noted above, a key point in error avoidance is systematic observation of customer service reps' contacts with their customers, both as to procedure and actual quality of the contact. The practice of service observation, as telephone monitoring is generally called, is widely accepted as a legitimate means of quality control and has no implications of "snooping" provided that it is restricted to business transactions between a firm and its customers and that it is done primarily for training purposes. It should be made clear to all employees that business transactions are subject to monitoring, and that this is a condition of their employment, much as materials produced by workers in the plant is subject to inspection for quality of workmanship. Manufacturers of service observing and other telephone equipment should be consulted. They can be very helpful in setting up systems that will be palatable to management and employees alike.

• *Suggestion systems, quality circles.* These can be excellent sources of ideas for error avoidance through improved procedures. It is important that both have credibility: that suggestions be quickly reviewed and responded to, and that ideas developed by quality circles and similar groups be discussed with the group and adopted when feasible. It should be noted that both suggestion systems and quality circles are expected to function as an employee activity without the participation of the manager until the time comes to accept or decline suggestions and recommendations. This is how they work best, but they will quickly lose their effectiveness if managers let their output pile up without taking action one way or the other. Also, it is highly desirable that persons making suggestions that are adopted—whether as individuals or as a group—be involved in the actual implementation of those suggestions when they are adopted.

• *Posting error rates.* If assignments in the department are relatively uniform, individual error rates may be posted on the bulletin board, preferably in conjunction with positive accomplishments. For example: errors per 100 orders taken, or some similar measure. Some companies prefer to say "98% error-free performance" rather than "a 2% error rate." Managers who have been interviewed do not feel that posting error rates has any significant demotivating effect on poor performers. One manager has even developed a humorous "award" for the individual making the most serious error during each month; the employee is required to keep the "award" plaque on his or her desk for an entire month. To make the practice more palatable, if there are no serious mistakes during a month, then the manager herself must keep the "award" prominently displayed on her desk—where it will be seen by other managers and top management itself—for the entire succeeding month.

• *Feedback of error causes.* An integral part of the training process is making workers aware of the causes of errors and how they can be avoided. This is just as important for errors that are caught in the checking process as for errors that get through. Many errors may be traced to changes in specification, nomenclature and packaging that have not been properly communicated, and provide a good opportunity to improve and reinforce that communication. Changes in pricing, discounts and terms of sale and of course special promotions may also fall into this category of "new" errors requiring special attention.

• *Analyzing checking methods.* Even work that goes through several checks may contain errors, and the fault could well be with the checking system rather than with individual checkers. End-to-end checking, i.e., one checker re-checking work already checked by another checker, does very little good and in fact may actually increase the error rate as each checker "relaxes" on the assumption that the other will catch any mistakes he or she has not caught.

• *Forms simplification.* The computer has done away with much of the need for complex and detailed forms traditionally used for capturing data, but even so a certain percentage of errors can be traced to forms which invite error: multipart forms which are often filled out by (dull) pencil, or forms that contain too much detail in too many places; forms that are obsolete and require crossing out or inserting new information; and forms that are too complex and find users' skipping items and in some instances guessing at information because they don't think it's important. Forms design should always take into consideration the environment where the form will actually be used, for example, under poor lighting conditions in a warehouse, in the cab of a delivery truck, in the noise and confusion of a receiving dock handling an avalanche of inbound freight.

Whenever possible, these problems should be addressed using computer-generated forms which provide information on a need-to-know basis. For example, an order blank mailed in by a customer may list items ordered in a random sequence. This is translated by the computer into, among other things, a picking document listing the items by location in pick sequence, so that the order picker can assemble the order in the most efficient manner and with the least travel. The order picker's document need not contain data about prices, shipping and invoicing, etc., thus minimizing the possibility of confusing irrelevant data with "working" data. The same basic data may be reconfigured for billing purposes, for inventory management, shipping control and other activities.

There are occasions where customers are asked to fill out extensive and detailed order blanks because it appears to be the best way to avoid errors of omission. When this is the case it may be necessary to sell customers on the benefits of using such forms. One company using such a form for metal clad doors has found it acceptable to customers because it does in fact help avoid most of the errors they had problems with in the past. Other companies have found their sales departments somewhat reluctant to ask customers to use such forms. One compromise adopted by some companies is a question-and-answer routine in which the customer service representative handles the form and asks the customer for the information in sequence.

● *Alternative methods.* Color coding has proved quite successful in error avoidance in some situations. Also, some computer applications using hand-held scanners and input devices have provided remarkably error-free order fulfillment and documentation in highly sensitive situations, for example in the health care field. Managers who have access to their firms' industrial engineering departments should request time-and-motion and procedural studies to determine whether simpler and less error-prone methods can be devised.

● *The working environment.* Closely related (and hopefully included in engineering studies) is the nature of the working environment in the customer service department. Noise and excessive activity are principal contributors to the error rate, and lack of sufficient privacy and/or individual "turf" is at least an indirect influence. Files and other sources that are inconvenient to access may cause some workers to guess rather than actually look up data. Conventional filing systems where needed files are frequently "out" (or misfiled) create a similar problem. Many firms are moving to microfiche and other forms of hard copy retrieval as a means of minimizing such problems.

● *Accountability.* Feedback of error causes to employees who make such errors must be supported by a system of accountability holding the individual worker responsible. One expert goes so far as to say that warehouse order assembly errors are often as high with checking and even double-checking as without it, but errors drop virtually to zero when a card is enclosed with the order bearing the order picker's name and photograph. "This device has been responsible," he says, "for an error reduction factor of such magnitude that orders are no longer checked. Customer complaints have fallen to the point of being almost non-existent." While this system does not necessarily imply that the employee is actually disciplined for any errors, the fact that he or she is personally identified to the customer may have an even greater deterrent effect. The same expert warns against identification by number rather than by name. "Numbers only provide continued anonymity," he says.

● *Customer training.* This is a subject broad enough for one or more books. As it applies to error avoidance, customer training relates to two main areas: (1) familiarity with the vendor's system of specification, ordering, nomenclature or whatever; and (2) use by the customer of internal systems which will avoid errors which might otherwise be transmitted to the vendor.

Many companies assume, mistakenly, that customers can understand and adapt to their systems and procedures without specific indoctrination. This can result in outright errors as well as disputed and delayed payments and in some cases actual lawsuits. One company, for example, specified "at once" in the "when wanted" column of its purchase order. The vendor delivered the product some 45 days later, and the customer refused to pay. When the case went to court the vendor won on the grounds that "at once" actually meant "as soon as possible," and that under the circumstances 45 days did in fact represent the soonest possible date the vendor could meet. And although the vendor won the case, it goes without saying that the customer was lost for good. A simple instruction to the customer on indicating a specific date or time frame would have avoided the problem altogether.

Vendor employees have been heard to complain that customers don't understand their own "responsibilities" in transactions, but it can often be established that no attempt was ever made to insure that customers were even aware that such responsibilities did in fact exist. A company switched from delivered pricing to FOB shipment, freight charges collect, and soon found customers making unauthorized deductions from invoices on the grounds of short shipments, damage and other problems that normally would be covered by claims filed directly with the carrier. However, customers had not been informed to this effect, and a further problem—this time in the vendor's procedures—surfaced to further complicate matters: mer-

Impact of Customer Service Errors

On Your Customers—	On Your Own Business—
1. Production downtime	1. Administrative costs
2. Standby costs for work crews, equipment	2. Communications costs
3. Lost sales	3. Extra shipping costs
4. Loss of advertising investment	4. Restocking costs, shrinkage
5. Potential FTC involvement	5. Delayed payment, cash flow
6. Potential product liability lawsuits	6. Lost sales—non-available product
7. Potential consequential damage suits	7. Lost sales—dissatisfied customers
8. Loss or alienation of customers	8. Loss of key salesmen, dealers, distributors
9. Morale problems with salespersons	9. Errors elsewhere in system
10. Additional administrative costs	10. Potential legal problems
11. Loss of market share	11. Loss of market share
12. Damage to image and reputation	12. Damage to image and reputation

chandise was traveling in sealed trailers and box cars under "shipper's load and count terms" so that actual responsibility for shortages was almost impossible to ascertain.

This same case also illustrates the type of problem that can occur when customers' internal systems do not contain sufficient safeguards. Some vendors faced with shortage claims from customers have discovered poor security at customer sites almost certainly suggesting theft by customer employees and/or carrier personnel—but difficult to prove, and yet costly and sensitive to

---

Seven Less Obvious Results of Customer Service Errors

1. Potential delisting. Distributor, dealer or retailer may decide not to stock some or all of a product line.

2. Potential future non-listing. Distributor, dealer or retailer may decide not to take on new lines introduced by the particular vendor.

3. Potential promotional loss. Distributor, dealer or retailer will not support vendor's products with advertising because of lack of confidence in availability.

4. Loss of field sales. Salesmen decide not to push products; lack of customer service support causes some to quit firm and possibly take some accounts with them.

5. Potential personnel costs. Cost of recruiting and training replacement salesmen (and customer service personnel) may run to $3,000 and more per person and will be compounded if underlying problem is not corrected.

6. Cost of replacing lost accounts. Double-penalty involved in loss of revenue plus extra costs of selling a new account. Cost of loss = 5 × annual revenue; cost of selling new account = 5 × cost of retaining through good customer service.

7. Possible increase in fixed costs. Added capacity or facilities may be required.

---

have to continue dealing with. Manufacturers of consumer products find frequent problems when customer records are inadequate to support product recalls or even to settle matters pertaining to warranties and adjustments. Yet most of these problems arise from poor management by customers rather than from deliberate intent.

Some companies have found that it very definitely pays off to provide specific customer training in records keeping, inventory management, economic order quantities and related areas because it cuts down on the types of errors resulting from poor planning and hand-to-mouth buying and other "crisis" events on the customer side. And this in addition to specific training in product use and application to insure that customers get best (and correct) results from their purchases, and to avoid dissatisfaction or lawsuits resulting from improper use or application. Some companies provide customer training free of charge; others charge substantially on the grounds that it's more effective because people pay more attention when they know what their training is costing their companies.

Case History: Reducing Departmental Errors by 75%

Customer service department errors were reduced by 75% at Carboline Company, St. Louis, Missouri, in a program reflecting a number of the principles outlined above. Kay Davis, Customer Service Manager, reported that the intensive error-reduction program was initiated by the Quality Circle group within the department, concentrating first on error-prone phases of order entry, including:
- legibility of handwriting
- product coding
- pricing
- quantities, i.e., transpositions and keystroke errors
- special instructions omitted or entered incorrectly
- sales splits regarding commissions
- invalid numbers for customers or colors

These error categories were incorporated in a checklist (figure 3) used to tally errors at each stage of order processing. Each time an error was discovered, a hashmark was made in the appropriate column. In two weeks of tracking 917 orders, 296 separate errors were found. The Quality Circle group proposed solutions ranging from a buddy system for checking errors to

Coordinator Checklist	1	2	3	4	5	6	7	10	11	12
Salesmen Error										
Customer Error										
Entry Error										
Plant Error										
Miscellaneous Error										

Entry Processing Checklist	1	4	6	9	10	12
Coordinator Error						
Salesmen Error						
Customer Error						
Miscellaneous Error						

Numbers in Checklist Column Headings Refer to These Types of Errors:
1) Coding
2) Shipping
3) Kit Size
4) Wrong Customer #
5) Color
6) Pricing
7) Special Conditions
8) Req. Date vs. Performance
9) Legibility
10) Quantity
11) Sales Split
12) Miscellaneous

Figure 14-3. Checklists used to log errors at key points in order processing sequence. Each checklist covered only error sources pertinent to the area being checked.

giving reps more time away from the telephones in order to concentrate better. The solution ultimately adopted was to redesign the order entry form to more closely fit the actual way in which orders are entered into the computer.

After the form was redesigned, a two-week test by the department noted a significant drop in errors, plus the need for some additional reworking. When this was accomplished, another drop in error rate—a cumulative total of 75%—was recorded. Further steps currently being contemplated include an on-line order entry system so that customer service reps can catch errors as they are taking/entering orders, an almost universal benefit of on-line systems. Additionally, consideration is being given to streamlining the 15-digit product code system which had accounted for some 27% of errors under the old method of entering orders.

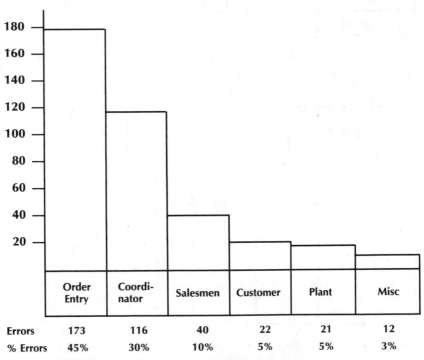

	Order Entry	Coordi-nator	Salesmen	Customer	Plant	Misc
Errors	173	116	40	22	21	12
% Errors	45%	30%	10%	5%	5%	3%

Figure 14-4. Chart showing errors by source based on checklists used over a two-week period.

15

CONVERTING GOOD WILL INTO PROFIT

Good will is worth more than a dollar. Accountants to the contrary, good will has a profit contribution potential far in excess of the traditional dollar. A landmark study conducted for Coca-Cola Co. by Technical Assistance Research Programs* established conclusively that consumers who felt well disposed towards the firm after making an initial complaint tended to significantly increase their consumption of Coca-Cola, while those who were less pleased showed a marked decline in their purchases of the soft drink. Other studies have shown that *loss* of customer good will results in partial or complete loss of business; consultant Harvey Shycon quantified the cost at $20,000 per incident as long ago as 1973.**

Beyond examples of this type, however, every customer service manager will recognize this type of event:

A manufacturer of electronic components has just filled a restocking order for one of its major distributors, with shipment promised for the next morning. An OEM customer calls in near-panic; if he can't locate a supply of Component "X" within hours his production line will shut down at a cost of $50,000 per hour. As fate would have it, the vendor's last available units of Component "X" are even now on their way to the shipping department to fill the distributor's restocking order. The customer service manager quickly puts a hold on the shipment and calls the distributor

---

* *Customer Service Newsletter,* Vol. 10 No. 1, January 15, 1982.
** *Ibid.* Vol. 1 No. 3, October 15, 1973.

to ask if he can tolerate a delay of a week or ten days so that the OEM customer can be accommodated. The distributor says "yes" and the vendor makes a sale . . . and a friend for life.

Events like this happen only because of customer good will, and it's good will that was not won overnight. It took a long time of keeping promises, understanding the customer's needs and meeting them, taking personal interest in the account, making the distributor feel "one of the family" and in general going the extra mile—it took all these plus exceptional customer service to earn the customer's good will. It took all these plus exceptional customer service to earn *credibility* with that particular customer, and confidence that he could expect similar support in a crisis from the vendor.

Of course, good will pays off in other than crisis situations. For example, a company decides to institute new policies on credit, minimum order size, lead time, returns and adjustment, consolidations, or other areas directly affecting customers. Acceptability of such policies will be enhanced or diminished, in many cases, in relation to the degree of good will that exists between the firm and its customers.

Quantifying customer confidence. One of the most common complaints registered by customers against their suppliers is failure to notify them (customers) promptly when a promise date can't be kept. Such failures over a period of time result in a sharp increase in the number of order status inquiries made by customers, including calls primarily to remind the vendor that on-time delivery is expected. Some companies find that 25% of inbound calls are in fact unnecessary calls of this type, i.e., unnecessary in the sense that the orders being inquired about are in fact on time and will ship on the promised date.

Unfortunately, it costs just as much to service an unnecessary order status inquiry as it does an inquiry about an order that is in fact delayed—five to ten dollars or more. Thus a company receiving 5,000 inbound calls a week can count on having to service 1,250 unnecessary calls at a minimum cost of perhaps $6,250, or $325,000 a year. For a company in the five percent profit category, this would be the equivalent of the profit on $6.5 million in sales. One company set out to eliminate these unnecessary inbound calls via a two-step process: (1) set up an improved early warning system to quickly inform customers of delays; and (2) identify the principal "needlers"—i.e., originators of unnecessary order status calls—and call them first to tell them their orders are in fact shipping on time. The combination of these two steps, the customer service manager felt, would cause customers to regain confidence that delays would in fact be communicated and that their check-up calls were unnecessary.

After about two months of operating in this fashion, the company abandoned Step 2—i.e., the calls reassuring customers that orders were on time—and maintained its practice of notifying customers about orders that would be delayed. Subsequent measures of inbound telephone calls showed that a 25% reduction of such calls was in fact achieved. A more subtle factor was that the existence of an early warning system for late orders acted as a subtle stimulus to on-time performance at the plant level where most orders were being delayed.

Although some managers claim that customer service contributions can't be quantified, the reason is usually that they have not attempted to use the same tried-and-true market research techniques regularly employed in marketing planning, forecasting, new product introduction and other areas of the business. Were they to do so, they would quickly realize that customer confidence and good will pay off in a number of measurable ways. The confident customer—

- is more likely to buy additional products in the line.
- is more likely to concentrate purchases with the vendor as a sole-source supplier.
- is more likely to be willing to take on or try out new or upgraded products in the line.
- is more likely to be willing to try new customer service procedures such as direct order entry via touchtone, use of recording devices, abandonment of acknowledgments, etc.
- is more likely to accept new policies on minimum orders, credit, lead times, returns, special charges for rush orders, etc.
- is more likely to tolerate occasional customer service

failures and to stay loyal in times of adversity.

● is more likely to be cooperative generally.

To quote the American Management Association: 60% of a firm's business comes from existing customers, and it costs only one-fifth as much to *keep* an existing customer through good customer service as it does to *get* a new customer through conventional sales effort. Clearly, the customer relations aspects of customer service play an important role in maintaining this equation.

Customer Training and Education

This subject was discussed in the previous chapter in connection with error avoidance. It has even broader ramifications in terms of positive contributions to customer satisfaction and the resultant sales growth, and it can be formal or informal, programmed or incidental to the conduct of the business.

The customer service department frequently has a specific responsibility to provide specific training to customers in use of equipment or applications of products. The long-term goal is to insure that customers use the products in the way they were intended and get maximum productivity and satisfaction from them, thus assuring future purchases of the same products as well as other products in the line.

When formal training sessions are involved, these are sometimes held at a training center at the vendor location, sometimes at the customer's site. Where such training used to be largely free, today an increasing number of companies are charging for it, on the premise mentioned previously that customers who pay for training will place a higher value on it and thus pay more attention to what is taught and recommended—and get better results from the vendor's products. Charging for training also makes it easier to deal with customers who prefer to do their own training and would otherwise ask for a rebate if training were "free" and they did not enroll their personnel.

Candidates: Blue-Collar to Top Management

Candidates for customer training can range from hourly maintenance employees all the way to top management of customer companies. For a fee, a manufacturer of water softening chemicals trains customer hourly employees in boiler maintenance; boilers last longer with proper use of the chemicals plus better overall maintenance procedures, and pleased customers continue to buy the product and specify it for new installations. Manufacturers of computers and other equipment have similar programs for the "hands-on" employees in customer companies. And of course operating or instructional manuals provided with equipment or products has the same general goals.

There is one important caveat, however.

Whether training is provided directly through actual instruction, or indirectly through manuals, the manager must be prepared to deal with problems of: (a) personnel turnover at customer locations, and (b) obsolescence of manuals and similar materials being used by customers. One company found that a customer's purchasing department had placed a hold on two orders totaling over $500,000 for additional equipment. The reason? Dissatisfaction with the unit already in place. Moving quickly, the manager was able to ascertain that the problem was not the equipment but a new employee completely unfamiliar with the equipment, compounded by missing pages in the operating and maintenance manual. Remedying the situation restored the customer's satisfaction and good will . . . and unfroze the orders. Meanwhile, the manager learned an important lesson—namely that customers don't necessarily inform their vendors of internal changes that may affect performance of equipment or products, in this case the departure of a skilled worker and his replacement by a worker without specific training on the particular equipment, aggravated by incomplete operating instructions.

And, although the preparation of operating manuals and product instructions is generally beyond the scope of this book, it should be observed that much of this literature is seriously in need of improvement, and some may in fact be inviting lawsuit because of its lack of clarity or detail, or in some cases omission of warnings about specific hazards from misapplication. Considering the amount of money that most companies spend in marketing products, it's surprising to find so many that do not make the relatively minor expenditures necessary to insure that customers quickly arrive at the best and most profitable use of these products so that they will keep coming back and buying more. Even at the consumer level, a surprising number of products sold at do-it-yourself stores contain little if any instruction on proper application, mounting, etc. As a result, customers are likely to make mistakes or encounter other problems which discourage them from further do-it-yourself purchases.

Besides training or instructing customer personnel in specific, hands-on applications of products or equipment, some companies also provide training in management techniques for both middle and top management. In such cases the motive of maintaining customer satisfaction with products may be overshadowed by an even stronger motive: *keeping customers in business.*

For example, a large chemical company discovered that many of its customers—smaller, family-type fertilizer manufacturers—were often shaky operations due to lack of know-how in such areas as inventory management, production planning, traffic and distribution, and credit and collections. The company reasoned that if it could help these customers in these areas, it would not only help keep them in business but also contribute to their growth—and thus stimulate their continuing and increased purchase of chemicals over the years. The firm set up teams of its own employees who served as consultants to these smaller customers . . . and succeeded in achieving both goals.

Although few programs are quite that comprehensive, a number of companies provide customer firms with specific training in inventory management including reorder points and economic order quantities. This benefits customers, of course, but it also benefits the vendor by improving customer ordering practices generally, cutting down the number of "emergencies" due to poor planning or inventory management, and improving sales at least to the point where customers maintain balanced inventories. And all programs of this type tend to "capture" customers by making them a part of the vendor's total system—even to the point where customers may have no interest in disinvolving themselves because of price advantages or other incentives offered by the competition.

Some companies go a step further and furnish the actual equipment for inventory control. A company manufacturing fasteners provides distributors with a two-bin inventory system which makes it almost impossible *not* to reorder in plenty of time, and at the same time assures that distributors are maintaining adequate inventories and not forcing all their stock back on the manufacturer. As an added embellishment, the firm provides customers with a chart showing equivalencies of its products to competitive products which are often asked for. By having the two-bin system with inventory already in place, the dealer-distributor can fill a majority of orders from the stock on hand, either directly by brand name and item number, or indirectly through substitution for a competing brand. This of course has the effect of motivating dealers and distributors to cut down inventories of competing products where there are such equivalencies, thus further increasing sales of its own lines.

Although it can be argued that "extras" and "frills" can add to the price customers pay for products, in actual practice most firms providing such extras are in fact quite price competitive or can point to improved sales or reduced costs—as in maintaining inventories of competitive products—as a benefit offsetting any added cost. What is more, companies are beginning to recognize that customer service is a marketing investment which should be assessed just like any other marketing investment, for example, advertising. Some companies have found that investing their resources in improved customer service won them a greater share of market than a far greater investment in advertising over a sustained period. In such cases, the customer service investment clearly represents the more profitable allocation of resources.

In this connection, it may be significant that a substantial amount of industrial advertising is about firms' customer service, sometimes in general terms, often about specific services offered. As an example, one firm's advertising highlights customer service personnel with photos and biographical plus skills data; another details the specific training customer service personnel receive to make them more useful to customers; and still another describes a resident computer program available to customers to help them determine which equipment is most suited to their particular needs. All are seen as part of the advertising mission of "selling by helping customers buy."

Even when customer service extras provided by some vendors are as slight as helping customers file freight claims, or calling customers occasionally just to touch base and make sure they're satisfied, the impact on customers can be substantial, particularly in the case of marginal or inactive accounts where salespeople rarely call. This probably relates to customers' perception of vendors as friendly, people-oriented businesses with their customers' interests at heart, rather than remote, monolithic and impersonal organizations.

Customer Service Responsibilities/Opportunities

While some managers may feel that the subject of customer training and education are beyond the scope or responsibility of their departments, in actual fact customer education can pay off quickly in reduced costs, greater efficiency and greater profit contribution in the customer service department itself. If customers can be motivated to use a recording system for placing orders, for example, it can increase the department's order handling capacity by as much as 100% with only minor investment in equipment. If customers can be educated in *how* and *when* to place their calls, investment in added facilities and personnel can be minimized or avoided altogether and the resultant savings added to the bottom line.

On a broader scale, educating customers in improved planning and buying will make it easier and less costly to meet their needs. In custom hardware manufacturing, it's been observed that architects typically leave specification of locks and door hardware until buildings are nearing completion. Then, there is great pressure on manufacturers to pump out the necessary locks and hardware so the finished space can be quickly leased out and start providing revenue. If architects could be educated—or helped—to specify locks and hardware earlier in the planning stage, manufacturers would have far less trouble in meeting want dates, manufacturing costs would be lower through leveled workloads, and building owners would be assured the earliest possible availability of income-generating space.

There are parallels in virtually every line of business. As another example, the poor image which has plagued the household goods moving industry has resulted almost exclusively from the fact that most family moves occur during the summer months—between the end of one school session and the beginning of another—and this places tremendous strain on service, equipment and personnel in organizations which often do minimal business during the rest of the year. The industry has done a remarkably good job in educating consumers in how to deal with the trauma of moving, and has been a staunch supporter of moves to make school a year-round affair—an eventuality which would make it far easier for the industry to serve customers better and which at the same time might significantly improve the quality of education available to their children.

In another example, a recent meeting of top executives of a major producer of business forms brought out the fact that nearly half the firm's multi-million dollar business consisted of "rush" orders, and perhaps as many as half of these were the result of poor planning rather than genuine emergencies as such. It further developed that in many years of business the firm had never actually researched its customers' buying practices or specific needs in terms of lead time and technical support. Behind this lay the fact that the company had never had a formal customer service department charged with developing such information and designing customer service programs accordingly. It follows that one of the first mandates of the meeting in question was to determine what the market actually needed—and how much of what it needed could be achieved through better customer education, and how much would have to be met through redesigning the service itself and perhaps increasing plant investment.

Significantly, the executives at this meeting accepted without argument the thesis that if they could help educate the poor planners and disorganized buyers among their customers they would almost immediately be in a better position to service those with genuine emergencies resulting from events beyond their control. And, through workload leveling, to have more capacity available to sell. Needless to say, the customer service department at this company has an exceptional opportunity to prove its worth . . . and an exceptional amount of top management support to help it do so.

Figure 15-1. Cards put out by Lederle Labs and parent American Cyanamid introduce customer service reps to customers. Cards give all necessary information about phones and emergencies. After receiving the cards, some customers even responded by sending photos of themselves so reps could see what *they* looked like!

282

New Customer Orientation

Although educating customers to mesh with the vendor's system goes on constantly with customers, it is particularly important in the case of new customers who are unfamiliar with the vendor's way of doing business. Particularly where customers are handled on a rotating basis, i.e., "next available rep," and thus may not come to the attention of any particular individual in the department, new customers are apt to feel that they are being treated somewhat casually. After all the wining and dining and attention from the salesperson on the account, it's somewhat of a let-down to be asked abruptly "customer number?" without any preamble, or to have one's lack of knowledge about the correct procedure for ordering, returns, etc., perceived as an annoyance rather than understandable lack of information on the part of a newcomer.

Some firms address the matter of new customer orientation by assigning a special customer service representative to "mother hen" all new accounts for several months. This generally speeds the transition from new customer to experienced customer, although on occasion customers who have been given the special treatment for several months are reluctant to give up their preferred status (as they see it) for treatment as an "ordinary" customer. The answer to this, of course, is that there should never be any such thing as an ordinary customer, nor should customer service representatives ever be permitted to lapse into thinking of customers in that way. Stories are told about customer service reps who complain that "Those customers can't seem to get it through their heads that we have to run a business here!" The attitude that customers have an "obligation" to their vendors is a closely related problem that is particularly likely to surface in recently deregulated businesses, franchise-type operations and other captive or formerly captive situations. This is a case where employee orientation and re-education should be undertaken immediately.

Customer orientation doesn't apply exclusively to new customers, of course, and it's a mistake to assume that because a customer has been a customer for some time he/she knows all aspects of the vendor's system. Very often, a particular customer deals with only a narrow area of the vendor's business and is unfamiliar with the rest, somewhat like a consumer who buys socks at a department store but is never encouraged to visit the furniture or major appliance departments. Thus customer orientation can range from the mundane to the unusual: educating the customer in whom to call for different types of problems, how to file a claim with a delivering carrier, how to format an order for placement by phone, how to get order status information by touchtone or terminal entry, how to package return goods, how to package and document an elephant for transatlantic shipment, etc.

Such orientation often takes the form of booklets, pamphlets, postcards and other types of mailing pieces. Some companies even publish mini-newsletters telling customers about various aspects of the customer service operation, and how they as customers can get the most out of it. A number send out postcards or folder-type mailings introducing their reps via photographs and brief messages; some send out mini-phone directories, or stickers with their phone numbers for customers to place on or near their phones. One firm's customer service department has been quite successful with a wall calendar carrying photos of all customer service personnel; the firm's salespeople frequently find the calendars hanging in the purchasing departments of customer companies.

Such materials can make a real dollars-and-cents contribution to the bottom line. Many managers feel that by sending photos of reps to customers they have succeeded in creating a better relationship—the customer can now see the rep as a three-dimensional individual rather than just a voice on the phone, and this in turn helps secure the account and increase its profitability over time. There are also instances where the cost of customer orientation by any other means would be prohibitively expensive.

Perhaps the most common example is in knowing whom to call about what. A major frustration for customers occurs when

XIDEX AIMS TO BE

THE (BEST) IN

SERVICE & QUALITY

If we miss the mark in any way
Please call:

Eileen Pendley: Lead Administrator
Linda Delsman: Supervisor Marketing Administration
Gary Lewis: Director, Marketing Services

outside California   **TOLL-FREE**   within California
800-538-1584   **800-672-1403**

We are available to serve you
6:30 AM – 4:30 PM
(Pacific Time Zone)

Figure 15-2. Flyer produced by Xidex to remind customers of department contacts and toll-free numbers, and the fact that toll-free phone hours are 6:30 a.m.-4:30 p.m. (Pacific Time Zone).

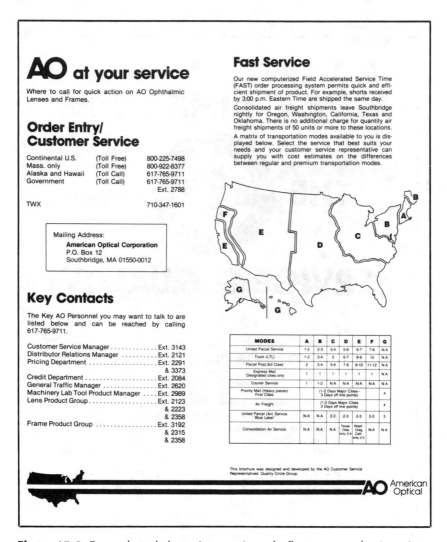

AO at your service

Where to call for quick action on AO Ophthalmic Lenses and Frames.

Order Entry/ Customer Service

Continental U.S.	(Toll Free)	800-225-7498
Mass. only	(Toll Free)	800-922-8377
Alaska and Hawaii	(Toll Call)	617-765-9711
Government	(Toll Call)	617-765-9711
		Ext. 2788
TWX		710-347-1601

Mailing Address:
American Optical Corporation
P.O. Box 12
Southbridge, MA 01550-0012

Key Contacts

The Key AO Personnel you may want to talk to are listed below and can be reached by calling 617-765-9711.

Customer Service Manager . . . . Ext. 3143
Distributor Relations Manager . . . . Ext. 2121
Pricing Department . . . . Ext. 2291
. . . . & 3373
Credit Department . . . . Ext. 2084
General Traffic Manager . . . . Ext. 2620
Machinery Lab Tool Product Manager . . . . Ext. 2989
Lens Product Group . . . . Ext. 2123
. . . . & 2223
. . . . & 2358
Frame Product Group . . . . Ext. 3192
. . . . & 2315
. . . . & 2358

Fast Service

Our new computerized Field Accelerated Service Time (FAST) order processing system permits quick and efficient shipment of product. For example, shorts received by 3:00 p.m. Eastern Time are shipped the same day.

Consolidated air freight shipments leave Southbridge nightly for Oregon, Washington, California, Texas and Oklahoma. There is no additional charge for quantity air freight shipments of 50 units or more to these locations.

A matrix of transportation modes available to you is displayed below. Select the service that best suits your needs and your customer service representative can supply you with cost estimates on the differences between regular and premium transportation modes.

MODES	A	B	C	D	E	F	G
United Parcel Service	1-2	2-3	3-4	5-6	6-7	7-8	N-A
Truck (LTL)	1-2	3-4	5	6-7	8-9	10	N-A
Parcel Post 3rd Class	2	3-4	5-6	7-8	9-10	11-12	N-A
Express Mail Designated cities only	1	1	1	1	1	1	N-A
Courier Service	1	1-2	N-A	N-A	N-A	N-A	N-A
Priority Mail (Heavy pieces) First Class	(1-2 Days Major Cities— 3 Days off line points)						4
Air Freight	(1-2 Days Major Cities 3 Days off line points)						4
United Parcel (Air) Service 'Blue Label'	N-A	N-A	2-3	2-3	2-3	2-3	3
Consolidation Air Service	N-A	N-A	N-A	Texas Okla only 2-4	Wash Oreg Calif only 2-5	N-A	N-A

This brochure was designed and developed by the AO Customer Service Representatives' Quality Circle Group.

AO American Optical

Figure 15-3. Reproduced above is a portion of a flyer sent out by American Optical's customer service representatives. This brochure (which was designed and developed by AO's customer service representatives' quality circle group) is an excellent example of how a vendor can inform customers of proper phone numbers, contacts, and shipping information. The back of this brochure gives policy highlights, backorder and returns information, and contains photographs of 12 customer service representatives.

they call a company about a specific problem but can't find anyone who can deal with it. After being transferred numerous times, they have still made no headway. And the account is increasingly in jeopardy. Several companies publish directories arranged by "problems," that is, the directory lists the type of problem and then indicates the individual(s) to call about it. One such directory contains the following:

- If you need help because you received the wrong material, were short material or what you received did not work, call . . .
- If you need help with return goods, call . . .
- If you need help concerning the status of a backcharge, call . . .
- If you need help with problems on a new product, call . . .
- If you need help with a problem and aren't sure whom to contact, call . . .

In all, the directory contains names and brief biographies of some 24 different individuals with specific responsibilities in customer service. The directory enables the customer to get to the right person faster and with higher levels of satisfaction. Equally important, it relieves customer service personnel of the strain of receiving calls from customers which they can't handle and have to transfer elsewhere, often by guesswork which doesn't turn out to be too accurate. In so doing, it also cuts costs within the department by a significant amount and at the same time increases overall productivity.

A similar function is served by a series of booklets published by a major railroad, the Missouri Pacific. In all, there are nine booklets covering such subjects as car ordering, billing systems, quality control, special services, automatic car location inquiries, intermodal services, international services and site location. Here again, an important economic function is served: the railroad maintains offices in many cities domestically and overseas, and shippers typically deal with these local offices. Yet many offices are relatively small and the cost of orienting customers in person or by phone to the many services offered by the line would be extremely costly and uneven at best. By publishing the book-

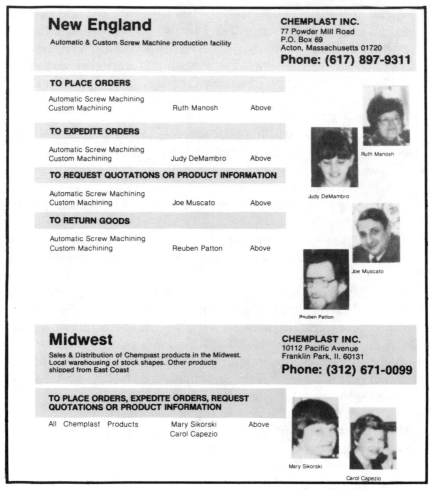

Figure 15-4. Reproduced above is a page from a mini-directory issued by Chemplast, Inc. The directory is introduced with "Chemplast will get the answer for you . . . fast," followed by this brief explanatory text: "Here's how it works: Personnel are assigned the job of getting out fast replies to every question. Write or call them directly. They are ready to help you. Direct your questions to the proper office and person for prompt attention." The directory gives locations and shows names, extensions and photos of individuals to call for such purposes as placing and expediting orders, requesting quotations, requesting specific product information, standard publications and samples, and returned goods.

lets and advertising them widely, the railroad performs broad-scale, uniform customer orientation and at the same time frees its local personnel for more productive work in actual sales as well as service operations requiring skilled personnel. In short, the railroad educates via "textbooks" rather than by tying up the time of its valuable contact personnel.

Telephone Contacts with Customers

For many companies, the principal channel of customer relations is the telephone. Indifference and often downright rudeness of switchboard operators, as well as inept referral of calls, is a principal source of customer irritation, even before the customer service department becomes involved. And even then, many customer service departments do not do a very good job in handling customer calls. While the subject of phone procedure within the customer service department is discussed in detail elsewhere, the problem of "switchboard-itis" should be mentioned here, in the context of customer relations generally. From the customer service department's point of view, it may be better to have a phone system in which calls come directly to the customer service department and do not have to go through the main switchboard. This doesn't solve the basic problem of poor switchboard procedure, but it reduces it by cutting down the number of calls that come to the switchboard and giving the operator(s) there more time to handle the calls that do come in and may need referral. It also takes the burden off customer service reps of having to compensate for prior poor handling of calls.

If direct lines can't be set up, one company's experience may be helpful. The firm hired an outside shopping service/market research firm and gave them a scenario about the firm's services and products. Shopping service researchers, posing as prospective customers, called a number of the firm's branches with inquiries about services, products and prices. Each call was taped by the shopping service, and a cross-section of tapes was compiled and played to a top management meeting considering a request for funds for training personnel in correct telephone procedure. Some of the calls were so atrociously handled that management needed no further persuasion, and authorized the expenditure within a matter of minutes. As observed elsewhere, an ongoing program of quality control via systematic monitoring is the only sure way of maintaining good performance once personnel have been trained, and there are no legal or ethical obstacles to doing so for purposes of training and retraining as necessary.

Figure 15-5. Reproduced above is a mailer sent out by Converse which contains a bright green label showing Converse's special reorder number. A legend on the mailer reads: "Peel this number and stick it close to your phone. The next time you need to order more Converse shoes you'll be glad you did. Because you can use it any weekday between 8:30 a.m. and 6:30 p.m. EST to get up-to-the-minute inventory info as well as details regarding all sales programs and promotions . . ."

Personal Contacts with Customers

In some companies, the customer service manager (and sometimes supervisory personnel as well) is required to visit a certain number of customers at their locations every month. In others, customer service reps themselves get an occasional opportunity to visit customers. All of these are among the most beneficial practices a customer service department can engage in—beneficial for the company, and for its customers, too. A visit gives customer service personnel a chance to see the customer on his or her own turf, to see problems at first hand, to understand needs, to get a "feel" for the customer's immediate environment. It also flatters the customer and puts him or her in the position of a host/hostess/guide/instructor, etc. to the visiting personnel, creating a merited sense of self-worth. In short, it's a highly recommended practice.

One firm is actually able to place its reps for two-week periods as assistants in the parts departments of distributors and dealerships for its farm equipment. There, the reps see at first hand the problems and pressures that their own customers experience daily: the irate farmer who's about to lose a crop for lack of a minor part, the problems created by errors and delay on backorders generally. The reps thus gain a better appreciation of the importance of doing their own jobs well, and the importance of being patient and understanding when their own customers seem irate and unreasonable after dealing with irate and unreasonable farmers across the counter.

There are also opportunities for personal contact when customers visit vendors' plants or headquarters offices. Although these visitors are often under time constraints, every attempt should be made to allow time for them to meet in person with the customer service manager, supervisors and individual reps handling their accounts. This meeting should be in the department, and after the usual "50-cent tour," there should be a brief meeting in the manager's office for dialogue about the account and the way it's being handled, with special reference to problems that are being encountered on either side. The practice is good for both the customer service department and the customer and makes subsequent dealings much easier for all concerned. It also contributes to the morale and self-esteem of individual reps to know that their company wants customers to meet them in person, and to be personally "showcased" in the customer service manager's office.

It should be a matter for serious concern any time an important customer visits the location and is *not* introduced to personnel, and a concerted effort should be made to avoid a repetition. One manager solved this particular problem by volunteering to have the customer service department provide guides for plant tours. Besides providing a pleasant break for the reps assigned to the task, it also assures ample exposure of the customer service department to the customers with whom its personnel deal daily. To dress the visit up, the manager in this instance also makes sure that the visitor's name is prominently displayed on a "welcome" signboard in the reception area.

Avoiding Disparagement

One of the worst things a manager can do in terms of customer relations—and certainly in terms of customer confidence—is to disparage his or her employees to customers. "Look at the kind of people we have to hire" is a thin excuse and demeaning to people who are usually doing their best under difficult circumstances. From the customer's point of view, when people can't perform the job they were hired to perform, it's a reflection on their management and on his or her management, not on the individual. It also suggests that the company doesn't care much about its customers in terms of the kind of people it hires, supposedly to help those customers.

The problem will sometimes arise when a customer will disparage a particular customer service rep, field salesperson or other department. Here again, the manager is on very sensitive ground. Disagreeing with the customer serves no useful purpose, but actually agreeing can have an even worse effect because it again suggests lack of concern for the customer. The best response when a customer actually criticizes an individual is to acknowledge the response but quickly move on to other topics: "I'm sorry; I'm sure he didn't intend it. But let me get some information from you so we can start resolving the problem. Can you tell me the order number?" A similar response would apply to criticism of a particular department: "I'm sorry; I know they've had a real overload in credit, and I'm sure the delay wasn't intentional. But let me get some more information from you so we can start straightening things out right away."

By the same token, the manager should set an example for the rest of the department—and the rest of the company, for that matter—in displaying respect for the customer . . . for *all* customers. Disparaging customers to employees, or permitting them to do so to one another, creates an unhealthy attitude throughout the department: a sort of "us vs. them" stance. The customer is not always right, but he/she is always the customer and the source of all revenues: paychecks, vacations, sick leaves . . . and a job that is as challenging and interesting as any in the company. Disrespect for customers should be as much a ground for dismissal as poor performance in any other aspect of the job, because customer service above all other jobs places the highest premium on attitude.

A Matter of Attitude

Indeed, the kind of customer good will that translates into profits often derives as much from perceptions of a vendor's attitude as from actual measurements of that vendor's customer service performance. This does not mean that customer service performance is unimportant, but rather points out that a good many customers do not actually *measure* customer service performance provided by a vendor, but *assume* it to be good, bad or indifferent based on overall impressions of the vendor's attitude.

It's of major importance that personnel be constantly reminded of this, and that their performance be monitored regularly to insure that every response to every contact—by phone, by letter or in person—reflect a corporate image of concern, interest in the customer and appreciation for his or her business. That same response should be warm, friendly but not overly familiar, and above all unhurried and reflective of willingness to help. Each employee should display respect for the company and for fellow-employees, and pride in the association. It's equally important to monitor contacts with other departments to insure that customer service personnel are giving and getting respect elsewhere in the company. The fact that an "inside" call can be recognized as such does not give either the caller or callee license to lapse from good manners.

The manager should also recognize that the quality of the training, education and general orientation provided customers—and to a considerable extent corporate policies on sensitive issues—can directly affect the attitude that customer service personnel display towards customers as well as towards others in the firm. Poorly-informed customers combined with policies that appear punitive can place great pressure on customer service reps leading to lapses in good manners.

Bearing in mind that calls about order status, corporate policies and even about applications and technical matters can all have a direct bearing on customers' ultimate satisfaction with products and future buying plans, the manager should make sure that the department is in fact equipped to handle such calls efficiently and that as few as possible are referred elsewhere. In fact, it should be decided as a matter of policy that except in highly technical matters all questions and answers be funneled through customer service reps along with the usual communications pertaining to orders, billing, etc. If this is established from the outset, the attitudinal problems that sometimes arise when reps are bypassed will be minimized, and reps will feel that they are part of the action, as indeed they are—an important part, at that.

Even more important, customer service reps who have been specifically trained in handling customers in sensitive situations are far more likely to get positive results in difficult situations

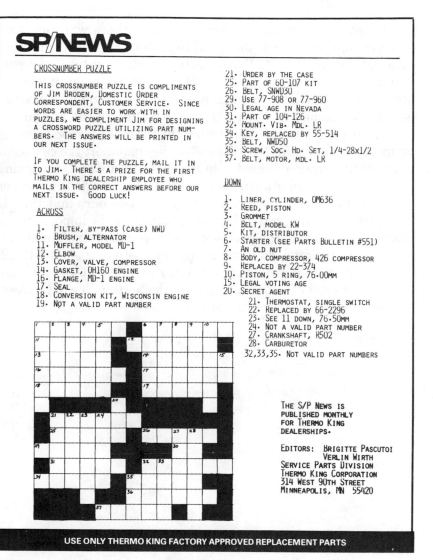

SP/NEWS

CROSSNUMBER PUZZLE

This crossnumber puzzle is compliments of Jim Broden, Domestic Order Correspondent, Customer Service. Since words are easier to work with in puzzles, we compliment Jim for designing a crossword puzzle utilizing part numbers. The answers will be printed in our next issue.

If you complete the puzzle, mail it in to Jim. There's a prize for the first Thermo King dealership employee who mails in the correct answers before our next issue. Good luck!

ACROSS

1. Filter, by-pass (case) NWU
6. Brush, alternator
11. Muffler, model MD-1
12. Elbow
13. Cover, valve, compressor
14. Gasket, OH160 engine
16. Flange, MD-1 engine
17. Seal
18. Conversion kit, Wisconsin engine
19. Not a valid part number

21. Order by the case
25. Part of 60-107 kit
26. Belt, SNWD50
29. Use 77-908 or 77-960
30. Legal age in Nevada
31. Part of 104-126
32. Mount. Vib. Mdl. LR
34. Key, replaced by 55-514
35. Belt, NWD50
36. Screw, Soc. Hd. Set, 1/4-28x1/2
37. Belt, motor, mdl. LR

DOWN

1. Liner, cylinder, OM636
2. Reed, piston
3. Grommet
4. Belt, model KW
5. Kit, distributor
6. Starter (see Parts Bulletin #551)
7. An old nut
8. Body, compressor, 426 compressor
9. Replaced by 22-374
10. Piston, 5 ring, 76.00mm
15. Legal voting age
20. Secret agent

21. Thermostat, single switch
22. Replaced by 66-2296
23. See 11 down, 76.50mm
24. Not a valid part number
27. Crankshaft, R502
28. Carburetor

32,33,35. Not valid part numbers

The S/P News is published monthly for Thermo King dealerships.

Editors: Brigitte Pascutoi
          Verlin Wirth
Service Parts Division
Thermo King Corporation
314 West 90th Street
Minneapolis, MN 55420

USE ONLY THERMO KING FACTORY APPROVED REPLACEMENT PARTS

Figure 15-6. Crossnumber puzzle using common part numbers was published in "SP News," a monthly dealer newsletter published by the Thermo King Service Parts Division, with prizes offered for the first correct answer submitted. The crossnumber puzzle is an effective way of involving dealers and customer personnel and educating them in part numbers, nomenclature, policies, and the like.

than engineers, production personnel and others who lack such training and who may in fact yield to customers on critical points where they should not. Particularly in policy matters, and particularly when there is "good news" for the customer in a policy interpretation, claim or similar matter, the customer service rep should be the one to convey that information to the customer.

There are several reasons for this: (1) if the supervisor or manager conveys the "good news" to the customer, the customer will feel that the rep cannot help and in the future will start going over the rep's head in all matters; (2) if the rep has done his or her job in explaining a particular policy to customers and then is "reversed" by the supervisor or manager, it is important for morale reasons that the reason for the reversal be explained, and that he/she be involved in informing the customer; and (3) it will enhance respect between the customer and the rep—and insure the continued confidence that goes to the bottom line in the form of quantifiable profit contributions.

16

IMPROVING THE CUSTOMER SERVICE DEPARTMENT'S PUBLIC RELATIONS

The quality of a company's customer service has a profound influence on that company's marketing success. Yet the customer service department itself often has relatively little stature and authority in its own right. Its value to the company and customers alike has always been the ability of its people to get things done working through other departments, usually on an informal basis. It could do a good deal more for the company's goals given a somewhat more formal mission, and the level of authority needed to carry it out. The manager has a real stake in this, and should give the department's public relations—particularly those within the firm—a high priority in the department's plans as well as daily operations.

The goal of this particular public relations effort by the manager should encompass three main points:

1. *Acceptance.* To gain a high degree of acceptance of the customer service department by other departments, particularly those with which it interfaces regularly.

2. *Support.* To achieve support for the customer service department—and specifically for its proposed programs, changes or improvements—among key influences in the firm, including top management.

3. *Visibility and image.* To increase the department's visibility and at the same time overcome its historical perception as the "order department," "complaint department," etc.

Incentives and the Concept of 'Turf'

The first step in cultivating and maintaining good relationships with other departments is to understand why those departments operate as they do, and what steps can be taken to surmount the roadblocks they sometimes appear to be placing in the way of the company's underlying customer service objectives.

First of all, it must be accepted that those roadblocks are neither deliberate nor capricious. In many companies the concept of customer service as a marketing strategy has not matured to the point where management sets specific customer service goals or standards for individual departments other than the customer service department. This means that the traffic or distribution department, for example, often sees its mission as using low-cost transportation whenever possible, with perhaps once-a-week shipments to major market areas. This is usually in direct conflict with customer service objectives of timely delivery to customers. Or, the warehouse manager's objective may be to minimize or eliminate overtime altogether, which means scheduling orders by size, location or other characteristics other than by customer service priorities. Similarly, production goals of minimizing unit costs via long production runs are often in direct conflict with customer service needs to quickly replenish out-of-stock goods customers are asking for.

Just as individual department heads are "rewarded" for achieving departmental rather than corporate objectives, so do their personnel tend to resist requests by customer service personnel to change orders, expedite, skip certain steps, rearrange priorities, alter conventional procedures, etc. Indeed, some personnel may even see customers as their "enemies" because they "interfere" with normal operations of the particular department. Again, it is relatively easy for individual workers to forget that they, too, have an interest in customer service and customer satisfaction that may take precedence over their immediate departmental goals. Even within the customer service department, personnel sometimes get so imbued with the notion

Doing the WORK

... but not the JOB

ARE you satisfied that you're prompt and punctual, complete your work accurately and efficiently on your own—and don't let anything interfere with your doing that work?

Well, it could just possibly be a case where you're doing your *work* . . . but not your *job*.

Is there a difference? You bet there is!

Work is the sum of the tasks we perform. The *job* is the *purpose* of our work. It is made up of many diverse elements with the overall purpose of *winning* customers and *keeping* customers by *serving* customers: with information, with expertise, with solutions, with a sympathetic ear . . . sometimes by making bad news palatable to them.

Doing our job, as opposed to doing our work, means going the extra mile on behalf of customers. Often this means disrupting our schedules, postponing tasks we had planned to complete today, persuading an irate warehouse manager to change an order that's all ready to ship—walking a customer's request through Credit, Quality Control, Accounts Receivable, Operations and other departments.

In short, doing our job means doing the *company's* job. It means helping the *company* achieve its goals of satisfying customers by serving them well. It's a job that's shared by everybody who works for the company. When we do that job, we may not always complete our *work* on time, or in the way we'd like to do it. But serving the company by serving customers is the best way we know of to be sure that we *have* a job to come to in the first place!

Figure 16-1. A common problem in customer service is that individuals in the firm tend to become so involved in their daily routines—their "work"—that they let it interfere with their *job,* which is to satisfy customer needs. This article from *The Customer Communicator* suggests one way in which customer service and other personnel can be reminded of the importance of maintaining customer orientation rather than just work orientation.

of doing their "work," i.e., the various tasks assigned to them, that they forget their *job,* that is the job of taking care of customers.

It is easy to see how department heads and personnel alike can develop a sense of "turf" and resist the introduction of new procedures or arrangements that either: (a) interfere with their goals, as they see them; or (b) appear to encroach on their authority in the firm. In this respect, the psychology of dealing with others in the company is no different from the psychology of dealing with customers and the general public. There are certain basic rules that apply across the board:

- Asking others to do something on the basis of logic is usually much less effective than appealing to their emotions.
- Asking people to cooperate is less likely to produce results than asking them to help.
- Asking people to accept a new idea is not nearly as resultful as asking their advice and letting the idea emerge.
- Asking people to support or endorse a major project is generally much less successful than asking them to support a small project and then a succession of more ambitious projects based on the success of the first.
- Asking people to understand one's problem is not nearly as effective as asking them what problems they have that one can assist in solving.
- Asking people to listen to an explanation never works as well as asking them to explain how and why they do things.

In short, the most effective psychology in dealing with other departments and personnel is to *involve* them in the customer service process rather than attempt to force it on them. Letting ideas originate with others, or introducing them in such a way that when they do surface they appear to be the other party's, is an effective road to involvement.

While meetings of departmental managers are common in most companies, few realize the potential of meetings between the rank-and-file personnel of customer service and interfacing departments. For example, training sessions or seminars set up by the customer service manager and conducted by the training department or outside specialists are often an excellent means for identifying problems and working out constructive solutions. Surprisingly, a number of roadblocks to effective customer service interposed by other departments are the result of poor communications and nothing else, for example:

Customer Service Rep: "If I could only get the status reports on Thursday instead of Friday, I'd have time to contact customers before the weekend."

Production Planner: "You never told me you needed them before Friday. Whydinchasayso?"

In some companies, joint meetings of this type are organized into role-playing and/or problem solving sessions. In a typical role playing session at one company which had just reorganized its customer service department, these three roles were employed:

Role No. 1: You are a salesperson who for a number of years has dealt directly with whichever department at the plant you felt could get the particular job done. Now you are in the process of learning that you can no longer call the plant at will; you must deal through the customer service department. You call a production assistant in an attempt to set up a short lead time for a favored customer and you are told that the assistant can no longer deal with you. Instead you'll have to call the newly reorganized customer service department and deal with someone there. You do not like this arrangement.

Role No. 2. You are the production assistant, and you have to explain to the salesperson why it is to his/her advantage to deal with Customer Service rather than with you as in the past. It is up to you to know exactly how the new department will work to the salesperson's advantage, and to be able to convince him or her of this fact.

Role No. 3. You are the newly appointed "account executive" in the customer service department whom the salesperson ultimately contacts. It is up to you to convince the salesperson that you can do as good a job as anybody else, and that he/she should trust you. However, you cannot give the sales rep a definite commitment to meet the desired date. Thus your credibility is at stake, and you must be able to get the salesperson to accept your handling of the matter.

Instructions: Role-player No. 1 calls Role-player No. 2 but opposes the suggestion to call directly to the customer service department. When that call is finally made, the salesperson continues to resist the new arrangement, until finally the customer service rep persuades the salesperson of the advantages of the new arrangement.

This type of role-playing can be set up with variations that reflect the situation in the individual company. A three-way session of this type should occupy between 20 minutes and one hour. The role-players should be selected from departments

---

How Logic Affects Interdepartmental Cooperation

Sales vs. Credit vs. Customer Service	**Sales logic** is that extension of credit will increase size of market and volume o purchases by individual purchases. Sales people are rewarded by commission as a percentage of sales, rather than profitability per se.
	Credit logic is that too-liberal extension of credit will result in serious collection problems and losses, and that soft policies may result in cash flow problems. Credit people tend to be judged negatively, i.e., the absence of large overdue receivables.
	Customer service logic is that credit problems interfere with the relationship with the customer and with smooth functioning of the department and should be resolved beforehand. Customer service people tend to be judged on the basis o perceived customer satisfaction.
Sales vs. Customer Service vs. Production Planning	**Sales logic** is that salespeople should sell what is currently saleable, i.e., what customers want and are willing to pay for. Sales people are motivated to make sales rather than to fulfill them.
	Customer service logic is to fulfill orders for service or product—to meet customer needs in a timely fashion. Customer service people are motivated to give customers what they want and are entitled to, within reasonable bounds
	Production planning logic is to minimize costs of setup and changeover by making production runs as long as possible and minimizing startup and shut down costs by accumulating orders until they are at an economic level. Production planning people are motivated by the basic economics of capacity utilization.

---

other than their own, and cast in roles with which they are not highly familiar. This approach has been used with considerable success in introducing changes in procedure which would normally meet resistance or prove difficult to justify. It is best to select individuals for the roles who have outgoing personalities and will enjoy playing the roles—and will do so with good humor. The manager or discussion leader should involve others in a critique afterwards: "Do you think Bill was right, Martha, when he said . . .?" or "What's another way Bill could have said 'no,' Martha?" are typical questions that can be used to start such a critique involving others.

Another approach is through a team-type exercise. In this,

Customer Service vs. Warehousing/Shipping	**Customer service logic** is that a change order by a customer should receive the same priority as the original order and be handled immediately. Customer service people are motivated by the importance of the account rather than order size or other logistics.
	Warehouse/shipping logic is that change orders should require recycling the original order so as not to interfere with smooth operations in the warehouse. Warehouse/shipping personnel are logistically motivated to maintain economic workflow and capitalize on economies of scale.
Customer Service vs. Finance vs. Distribution/Traffic	**Customer service logic** is to ship orders to meet customers' legitimate want dates. Customer service personnel judge themselves on line fill and complete order fill enabling immediate shipment.
	Finance logic is to minimize investment in finished goods inventory and accept some stockouts and delayed shipments as a matter of course. Finance personnel tend to judge themselves on return on investment (ROI).
	Distribution/Traffic logic is that accumulating orders until there is sufficient volume to obtain economical rates is preferable to the "penalty cost" of small shipments which would be required for immediate shipment. Distribution/traffic personnel tend to judge themselves on the basis of savings achieved in their expenditures for freight transportation.
Customer Service vs. Management	**Customer service logic** is to make significant investment in customer service personnel, communications and data processing, on the premise that customer retention via quality response will quickly justify the investment. Customer service people are highly motivated to identify customer service as a major activity within the firm.
	Management logic is to spend as little as possible on areas that have not been quantified in terms of ROI, or proven to have a specific, measurable impact on sales, negatively or positively. Management is motivated to take action only when it can be supported with hard data.

Customer Service Team Game

You have been appointed to a task force in your company with the specific mission of improving certain customer service operations that have come to the attention of management. Your task force is now in session, with these objectives:

1. Elect a chairperson who will lead your deliberations and will also present your group's recommendations to the meeting at large.
2. Discuss and analyze the specific problem assigned your team.
3. Draw up recommended solutions for formal presentation to the meeting when called to do so.

Bear in mind that the recommendations you are now working on are to management. You can recommend: new procedures or policies, training, new equipment, literature, etc.—anything you can cost-justify.

1. Communications problems—I. There are two phases to this problem:

a. Credibility. Mainly because of problems in the past, a number of your salespeople and customers refuse to believe you when: 1) They're told that their "request dates" will be met, and on the date requested; and 2) When told their request dates *cannot* be met. What can you do to improve this situation?

b. Saying "no" tactfully. Some customers (and some salespeople) make requests that have to be answered "no," either for legal reasons or because of company policy. This doesn't always set well, and your customer service reps have requested a special "scenario" to use in this situation. What do you recommend?

2. Communications problems—II. This problem also has two phases:

a. Bad News break. Your CS people are often given the unpleasant task of breaking bad news to customers about service failures, delays, missed dates, etc. that are beyond the control of the CS department. Your policy is to be as honest as you possibly can with customers in such matters, yet you don't want your CS people to appear to be passing the buck to other departments when they explain what went wrong, because that antagonizes the customers *and* the other departments. And yet many customers demand an explanation. How do you recommend these situations be handled?

b. Credit hold problems. Your CS reps have established some excellent working relationships with sales reps as well as key accounts. Yet every once in a while one of these key accounts is placed on credit hold—often for a situation they're not even aware of—and the individual rep has the burden of telling the customer that further product or service can't be provided because of the credit problem. Your task force is requested to come up with a better way for dealing with credit holds, particularly the "surprise" kind described here. Please outline your scenario or a specific procedure.

3. Errors in orders. Every order for product or service is checked twice, yet serious errors still get by. The supervisors say that the only way to solve this particular problem is to hire enough additional checkers to enable a third check of each order. Describe

Figure 16-2. Instructions and sample problems from "Customer Service Team Game" used in training sessions involving customer service representatives and personnel from other departments. Teams should be organized so that each includes members of other departments, and each team should be given a different

4. **Stress, morale and motivation problems.** This is a two-part problem:

   a. **Product and/or service availability** is extremely limited in some areas, and is likely to remain that way for some time. You sense that this will create a morale problem among your customer service reps because of the almost constant stress they will be under from customers and sales personnel. You are asked to make some specific recommendations addressed to this problem of stress. What are they?

   b. **Rude salespeople and customers.** Certain salespeople and customers (usually repeaters) are unwarrantedly rude and demanding to your reps, and are particularly harsh on them for matters beyond the reps' control. You don't want your reps to descend to this level, but neither do you think it's right to ask them to just sit there and take it either. You're afraid that if the situation continues your reps will develop a don't-give-a-damn attitude or will leave the company altogether. Your management has asked your group to recommend specific steps to deal with this type of situation, bearing in mind that important accounts as well as otherwise valuable salespeople are often involved and shouldn't be antagonized.

5. **Twenty questions.** Your company's customer service manager is concerned at the lack of feedback from reps about what they like and don't like about their jobs, their understanding of where their jobs fit in, and what improvements in procedures would help them as well as the company and its customers. Management has asked your group to frame a questionnaire containing at least 20 questions to ask reps with the goal of uncovering problems, misperceptions, inefficiencies, etc. It's expected that the manager will use the questionnaire to counsel reps where indicated, and to improve conditions or procedures as appropriate. Develop such a questionnaire and explain its logic.

6. **Dial-a-problem.** Your task force has been assigned the job of identifying the most difficult and costly customer service problem the company is now experiencing. Describe the problem in sufficient detail to cover its major points, and explain why it is serious and costly, with numbers to support your points. Then, recommend a solution.

7. **Service not fast enough.** Your "hit rate" on service is above standard—better than 90%—and yet Sales says that some customers insist on faster service, and say that if you don't start hitting the 100% mark you'll start losing important customers. By talking to customers, you find that they, too, think your service is slow and could stand improvement. You talk to your operations people about this at your management's request, and they go through the roof. To make improvements of that order, they say, would bankrupt the firm. It is up to your group to recommend a solution. What do you recommend?

8. **Major service failure.** Last week, a preplanned, prescheduled installation failed to be made and caused a plant shutdown. The president of the customer firm called your president and threatened the loss of an account valued in the millions. Checking reveals that a clerk had simply failed to follow through with the various people involved in the installation. It's not the first time he's goofed like this; apparently he has trouble understanding priorities. Your task force is asked to develop a complete scenario to deal with this situation from start to finish. What do you recommend?

problem. Teams should be given 45 minutes to an hour to deliberate and prepare their presentations. The program may also be conducted with exclusively customer service personnel, in which case the manager should assign team members so as to distribute leadership among the teams and also break up cliques or other groupings.

the group is broken down into teams of three to five persons each, arranged so that a typical team includes individuals from several different departments. Each team is assigned a specific problem involving some aspect of customer service and instructed to elect a chairperson to lead a discussion with his/her team about the assigned problem. Each team is then to develop a proposed solution for its problem, and make a presentation to the entire group. Presentations are discussed and critiqued by the entire group as in the case of role playing. If the total group is sufficiently small, the manager can decide beforehand on the composition of the individual teams and the specific problems to assign to them. If the company has recently experienced interdepartmental problems, these can be written up and used in the exercise. A typical set of instructions plus several problems are reproduced in figure 2.

The Roadblocker as Expert

A variation on this is to invite the head of a "problem" department to address the customer service group as a sort of "visiting expert." The customer service manager's approach is simply to invite the department head to "explain to my people how your department operates, and what they can do to make life easier for you." This is good public relations in itself; nobody objects to being considered an expert on a subject they're familiar with. Acknowledging this expertise will help establish the customer service manager as a person of judgment.

For this other department head *is* an expert, and the customer service manager and his/her staff will gain a great deal of knowledge and insight simply by listening to and participating in dialogue with this "outsider." Every advantage of the meeting should be taken, of course. For example, the customer service manager might hold an advance or warmup session with reps to prime them to ask questions about matters between the departments that concern them most. The idea is not to plant ideas or "rig" the seminar, but rather to insure that a genuine dialogue does develop and that reps do air their concerns.

Above all, the customer service manager should not suggest to reps in any way that the session is a subterfuge intended to "soften up" a manager who is creating problems for the department. Instead it should be presented as what it is: an opportunity to learn precisely why the department in question operates the way it does, and whether there are areas where the two departments can be more accommodating to each other.

Of course the same approach can also be used by the customer service manager in a one-on-one situation with other department heads or individuals in the company. But the manager shouldn't wait until there is a problem. Instead, he or she should pick a time when things are going well between the departments so that there won't be any question of ulterior motives. Certainly the new manager would automatically set up meetings with heads of interfacing departments to learn more about their operations. But the same general approach can (and should) be used even when all concerned have been in their jobs for some period of time: "Vern, how about giving me an update on your department? Maybe I can get a little more out of my people if I get a better understanding of what's new in your department"—or words to that effect. To repeat, the customer service manager should avoid whenever possible the appearance of forcing ideas on other department heads, or even expecting them to accept ideas and proposals based solely on customer service logic.

Maintaining High Internal Visibility

Most companies have some sort of employee publication, and it is an excellent place for the customer service department to improve its visibility and acceptance within the company. Two factors combine to make this so: (1) the editor usually welcomes newsworthy items from any source within the company; and (2) the customer service department typically has more "happenings" of general interest than most other departments. Special services to customers, participation in trade shows, development of new computer or communications systems—all these qualify.

Since complimentary letters from customers often concern an exceptional service rendered by a member of the customer service department, permission should be obtained to reproduce these in the company house organ. This is an excellent morale-booster for departmental personnel, and also an excellent publicizer of the value of good customer service. Photographs should be furnished whenever possible.

The company house organ can also be used to demonstrate the value of specific interdepartmental relationships. This is exemplified in Union Camp Corporation's house organ, a quarterly magazine for the organization's 15,000 employees worldwide, via a regular feature called "Face-to-Face." In this feature, an employee at one location nominates an employee at another location with whom he/she has had extensive telephone dealings but has never had face-to-face dealings. Photos of both employees are published, along with a commentary by the nominator commending the nominee for his/her spirit of cooperation, helpfulness in a specific situation, general attitude, etc. These nominations usually cross departmental lines, and the feature includes four or five pairings. The feature gets the highest readership scores of any article in the publication, and gets particular attention from management because it reflects peer judgments of and by co-workers.

A publication more specifically targeted towards Sales-Customer Service cooperation is issued periodically by the customer service department at Revlon. Called "Customer Service Newsletter," this publication is circulated exclusively to Revlon sales personnel in the field with the specific objective of facilitating the entire process of order entry and fulfillment. Much of the newsletter is devoted to explanation of procedures—formatting orders, the different types of invoices, how the management information system works. It recognizes that sales personnel can't be expected to know all the intricacies and variations of order entry, which are often complicated by the many promotions characteristic of the industry. So, it serves as a useful reminder and bridge-builder between Customer Service and Sales. It has achieved successful results, measurable in improved order accuracy, better relations, and participation—at Sales' request—by the customer service manager in regional sales meetings.

Newsletters or other publications of the customer service department need not be elaborately designed or produced. The main objective is to communicate. Typewriter type, clip art and home-drawn cartoons can be quite effective. Usually there is at least one member of the department with some writing skills, and another who can sketch or draw cartoons. In one firm's customer service department, the manager's secretary displayed a talent for designing posters conveying the customer service message to others in the company. In another company, customer service department employees were given buttons saying "Customer Service Makes It Happen!" Wearing these as they went about their jobs, on errands, to the cafeteria and elsewhere, they not only carried the message to others but also generated numerous requests for buttons from personnel in other departments. Still other companies pass out T-shirts, ball-point pens and similar mementos to help spread the customer service message.

10 Steps in Gaining Acceptance for Proposals

Bearing in mind that the easiest proposals to sell in the company are those that meet perceived needs, i.e., needs that are felt by others in the company, the manager should start with that premise and build credibility and acceptance on that basis. Here is a set of rules based on that premise.

1. *Identify the key influences.* Assuming that the proposal will involve some changes in customer service practices, the first step is to identify the individuals—department heads, product managers, etc.—who are in the best position to support and gain approval for customer service projects generally.

2. *Determine their customer service preferences.* Assuming the manager has drawn up a list of potential projects, he or she can poll these key influences to determine which of the projects appeals to the largest number of individuals. For example: improvement of order cycle time, error reduction, inside selling, substitution programs, etc.

3. *Draw up a "common denominator" proposal.* Based on polling, this would represent the type of proposal with the broadest appeal among the group of key influences.

4. *Maximize departmental resources.* Develop a proposal that will make the best use of the skills in the department and will not require drawing on persons from outside the department.

5. *Minimize encroachment upon others.* Invite suggestions from other departments but develop the project so that it does not appear to encroach on the prerogatives or "turf" of others.

6. *Assure acceptability to customers.* Before developing any proposal for change in customer service, make absolutely sure that customers will accept it. Otherwise, start again.

7. *Capitalize on opportunities brought about by change.* Key influences in the company faced with major change are more likely to be receptive to customer service proposals enabling them to deal more effectively with change. (See examples of such opportunities below.)

8. *Set modest, attainable goals.* Projects and proposals should be selected where chances of success are high, and expectations of others should be kept within reasonable bounds.

9. *Quantify and cost-justify.* Proposals that are supported with hard numbers demonstrating profit contribution, savings or other benefits are most likely to win approval and support.

10. *Build on success; increase scope of proposals.* Build credibility and acceptance through a series of small successes, with future projects becoming successively more ambitious.

Some Potential Projects: Opportunities Brought About by Change

For the customer service manager, some of the most critical areas of internal relations are those involved in gaining acceptance for changes in customer service policies and procedures. Some proposals are likely to be blocked internally on grounds that "customers will never accept it," or, simply, "it'll never work." Proposals for automatic refunds or credits often evoke responses like "They'll steal us blind!" or "Whaddaya want us to do, give the whole store away!" Old-timers are wont to respond with "We already tried it once, and it didn't work."

Most of these responses can be interpreted as plain old-fashioned resistance to change, but they must still be dealt with. For a main strategy in building the customer service department is to propose projects which have strong internal selling points. This includes the traditional sales strategy of overcoming objections. It also suggests proposing projects which have strong customer acceptance points and for that reason will also appeal to sales, marketing and product management people in the company.

Opportunities brought about by changes in the business environment are often excellent material for success-oriented projects. Some examples are listed below.

• *Rising costs.* Inside the company as well as among customers, the possibility of counteracting rising costs has wide appeal. For example: the company fleet is used for deliveries to customers, and the customer service manager proposes setting up an order schedule that will permit coordinating those deliveries with scheduled pickups of inbound freight—raw materials, components and other supplies. No question about it, the distribution executive and fleet management faced with rising labor costs will be quick to support the proposal because it will improve equipment utilization and turnaround and significantly reduce operating costs. Materials management and purchasing will support the proposal because it will hold down materials costs. And of course customer service will benefit from having a formal delivery schedule endorsed by the very departments with a stake in seeing that it operates consistently.

• *Energy shortages.* Recurring grid failures resulting in widely publicized power blackouts and brownouts have sensitized many managements to this particular problem. Some customer service departments have improved their stature considerably in their firms by proposing contingency plans for extended computer outages caused by such power failures or shortages. Most companies are more dependent on their computers than they realize. When management becomes fully aware of the potential impact of extended computer outages on order processing and fulfillment—and therefore on cash flow—they are likely to be unusually receptive to the customer service manager's proposal for contingency or standby plans. In fact, the manager may be asked to head up a contingency planning team. In one company, the manager discovered that the warehouse was dependent on computer-generated release numbers and that any appreciable amount of computer outage delayed shipments which were otherwise all ready to go. Development of a standby list of release numbers for use during such emergencies solved the problem—and won the support of the warehouse and distribution managers for further contingency planning by the customer service manager.

• *Natural catastrophes.* In many respects similar to the problems raised by computer outages, natural catastrophes often involve product damage or shortage, communications breakdowns due to weather, fire, earthquakes, etc., and personnel shortages due to inaccessibility of the workplace, illness and epidemics and the like. In snow belt cities, the customer service manager may be asked to set up a plan for transporting personnel in four-wheel drive vehicles.

• *Strikes and work stoppages.* Another area in which management is already highly sensitized and receptive to proposals which will minimize disruption to order fulfillment and cash flow. It is also an area with many opportunities for the customer service manager to develop contingency plans: when and how to notify customers; developing allocation plans for products in short supply and setting timetables for implementing them; planning alternate transportation and customer pickups; setting up shipments from alternate points or non-struck plants; developing substitution programs for short-supply products; and security measures as appropriate.

• *Product shortages.* Many customer service departments achieved significant stature in their own companies through their skilled dealings with the extreme product shortages of 1973-74. Some customer service managers also capitalized on the situation by impressing on their managements the urgency of upgrading information systems, communications and inventory management and forecasting programs—and got the hardware and software needed to do so. Outside the company, customers will naturally be concerned with the impact of shortages on their own operations, and thus will be receptive to any proposal that will help assure the uninterrupted supply of the products they purchase.

Interestingly enough, this same concern may overlap to products that are not currently in short supply. In a climate of widespread shortages, one manufacturer's customer service department persuaded customers to order twice as much half as often to assure a steady supply of a product that was in fact readily available. Another firm's customer service representatives regularly suggest to two-drum customers that they order four 55-gallon drums of product at a time, not only for the savings, but also to offset the consequences of a possible stockout or shortage situation. In both instances the vendor realizes substantial savings in order costs and handling.

Beyond such arrangements, however, the customer service manager should also look to the underlying causes of product shortages (figure 13-1, page 225) and, where possible, suggest means for eliminating such causes. Additionally, the manager is in an excellent position to recommend detailed allocation programs for products likely to remain in short supply for longer than 60 days, programs for centralization of inventories, barter arrangements, stock transfers from one customer to another, and similar arrangements. Naturally, such plans should be developed well in advance of the fact.

• *Delivery problems.* Many of these relate to: (a) the size of the order, or (b) the shortness of the lead time allowed. They often arise from changes in the economy which force customers into hand-to-mouth buying, i.e., forcing inventory back on suppliers and then delaying purchases until the last possible moment in order to remain as liquid as possible. Such problems may present justification for increasing lead time or minimum order size. Alternatively, they may present opportunities to assist customers with inventory management and production planning programs, as a number of companies have done, which also has the result of improving their purchasing practices. Where delivery problems relate to warehousing and order assembly problems, inventory shortages, loading dock congestion and the like, there is an excellent opportunity for the customer service manager to work with distribution and warehouse managers toward development of practices and policies which will level the workload and minimize these types of problems.

• *Changes in the marketplace.* Again, an area where management is likely to be already sensitized and receptive to proposals for dealing with specific problems. One example is changes in marketing channels. A cosmetics firm which had historically distributed through variety stores found that more and more of its product was moving through drugstore chains. This signalled the need for major revisions in lead times (shorter) and order quantities (larger), pricing schedules and customer service practices in general. Of particular interest to the customer service manager was the requirement for much faster and more accurate response on order status, shipment location and billing questions —providing an excellent opportunity for proposing (and gaining acceptance for) major upgrades to the order entry and information system. And for a considerable improvement in inventory planning. Another firm which had historically sold only to industrial markets found that more and more of its product was moving into consumer channels. Where in the past the company had largely dominated the market and "dictated" lead times, minimum order sizes and other terms of sale to its customers, in consumer markets it found that it was being dictated *to* . . . and that if it wanted to capitalize on this new and promising market it would have to make some fundamental changes in both attitude and customer service practices. And the customer service manager was quick to take advantage of the opportunity that presented itself.

● *Changes in lifestyles.* These may affect the marketplace in subtle ways. In the distilling industry, a downturn in the economy finds more people drinking at home than in bars. When they drink in bars they are more likely to order Scotch than blends, but for home drinking they are more likely to buy blends. The profit margin on Scotch is higher than on blends, so that there may be a need to increase minimum order size on blends in order to offset losses from reduced Scotch consumption. And then, readjustment must be made as the economy improves. Actually, the well-known volatility of the marketplace is often all the argument that's needed in order to gain management acceptance of customer service proposals to deal with or capitalize on this volatility.

● *Competitive changes.* A sure way to get almost anybody's attention in the company is to mention what the competition is doing. Yet often much of this is hearsay rather than fact. Given that it is now generally possible to measure a firm's customer service performance and expenditures against the averages for its industry group, this is often a near-perfect entree for proposals to upgrade customer service. While a great deal of attention is focused on front-end or before-the-fact marketing—research, new product introduction, advertising, test marketing and sales promotion—more and more companies are realizing the importance of competing *after* the fact, i.e., via customer service. And more and more companies are conducting ongoing research to determine where they stand relative to the competition in this respect, and where improvements are needed in order to maintain or increase market share. A 1983 study by General Electric* established conclusively the relationship be-

---

* Reported in the June 24, 1983 issue of *Marketing News,* published by the American Marketing Association, 250 S. Wacker Drive, Chicago IL 60606.

tween market share and quality of service vs. that of the competition, and showed that heavy front-end marketing, i.e., advertising, was far less effective in this instance than actual improvement of customer service performance.

• *Regulatory changes.* This is another area where management is already pre-sensitized and where there is likely to be a good audience for proposals addressed to those changes. These changes have broadened the range of both transportation and communications services available to the company, and these should certainly be exploited whenever possible. But these changes have also presented opportunities to customers, such as liberalized pickup and transportation rules generally, and some of these changes can have negative impact on vendor companies. Thus the customer service manager should consider proposals that both capitalize on the opportunities presented by regulatory changes and minimize the negative effects that may also result.

• *Technology changes.* New technology always has great appeal. This appeal should be exploited. Most customer service departments do not have nearly the levels of sophistication they need in information and communications systems as well as in actual software. It is almost always much easier to sell management on installing new equipment than on hiring more people. Preparation of a "wish list" should be one of the first priorities for the new customer service manager.

17

DEALING WITH SENSITIVE ISSUES IN CUSTOMER SERVICE

"The invisibles." It has been observed that most customers are aware of customer service only when it's *not* working—and have to be reminded when it is. As an example, years ago service personnel in a number of occupations wore black uniforms which did not show the dirt. A St. Louis businessman, Cherubino Angelica, pioneered the idea of wearing white uniforms that would *show* the dirt—thus enabling people to know whether the person waiting on them or taking care of them was in fact cleanly dressed. (By forcing more frequent changes of service apparel, this change benefited Mr. Angelica, too. He was the founder of the Angelica Uniform Group, Inc., which has since grown to annual sales of over $200 million.) A similar situation exists in the hotel industry. To emphasize that bathrooms have been cleaned, most hotels instruct housekeeping personnel to fold toilet paper and sometimes facial tissues into a point, thus indicating that the facility has been serviced.

These examples have a parallel in customer service, where personnel tend to be "invisible" as long as everything is going right. This can also result in their having little status with customers when something does go wrong and they—the reps—are suddenly placed in the limelight, so to speak. Increasingly, companies are preparing for this by "introducing" their reps before the fact via mailers, personal visits, assignment by account or territory and similar arrangements.

One customer service manager discovered to his astonishment that customers did not recognize the title "customer service representative," or the functions associated with it, even though they did know the *names* of the individuals they dealt with on an almost daily basis. The customer service manager decided at that point to change the reps' title to "Account Executive" and make customers fully aware of the range of services these individuals did in fact perform for customers. In this instance there was in fact considerable responsibility associated with the job, and the manager felt—correctly—that the title "representative" simply did not reflect that responsibility or the status of the job. Other managers may similarly feel that in difficult situations customers may prefer dealing with somebody who has higher standing in the firm. Sometimes, it may only require a *perception* of higher status.

In this connection, it is extremely important that customer service personnel themselves have a strong positive self-image, and transmit it to their customers as well as co-workers and others in the company. One customer service manager emphasizes this point and in addition requires personnel to observe a dress code comparable to what they would wear if dealing with customers in person. Additionally, she requires that when they answer the telephone they use their first *and* last names. "If somebody answers the telephone, 'Customer Service, Bill Smith,' " she explains, "that implies a certain level of accountability. If he answers it 'Customer Service, Bill,' that conveys a picture of somebody in the shipping room wearing a T-shirt and a folded hat made out of yesterday's newspaper."

Of course the surroundings in which people work will also have an impact on customer service representatives' self-perception. It is fundamental that these should be at least equal to offices elsewhere in the firm, with extra features as necessary to mask sound and provide ready access to information and communications equipment.

Training reps to deal with sensitive situations, and supporting them with sensible policies is of course fundamental.

The Value of Publishing Policies

It is naturally important that customer service reps be completely familiar with policies that are most frequently at issue—returns and exchanges, freight allowances, customer pickup, credit, deductions from invoices, telephone orders, emergency shipments, etc. But it is equally important that these policies be made known to customers *before* incidents arise where they may be called into play.

When customers have been put on notice, so to speak, and the policies themselves are reasonable, the majority of customers will abide by them. One manager observed that after she published a small booklet describing company policies and terms of sale and circulated it to customers, contraventions of policy by customer acts or requests for action dropped dramatically. She acknowledged that not all customers accepted company policies just like that. "But so many did accept them," she said, "that it was easy to deal with the others on an exceptions basis." This underscores an important point about policies: they need not be acceptable to 100% of customers. As long as they are acceptable to most, that's enough. It's far easier to deal with 10% exceptions than to have no policy at all and have to deal individually with *all* customers on a particularly sensitive issue.

Besides eliminating many stressful situations, publishing policies also benefits customer service representatives by enabling them to deal from strength when issues are raised that go contrary to policy. In the majority of cases the rep can handle the problem diplomatically and without escalating it to the supervisor or manager.

This is particularly true if the rep is given some latitude in actually invoking the policy. For example, a company has a policy imposing a five dollar surcharge on all orders phoned in for same-day shipment. The rep has the option of invoking the policy or not invoking it, depending on his or her assessment of the genuineness of the customer's need—or the customer's importance per se. The purpose of the policy is to discourage last-minute orders, and the rep may offer to delete the surcharge with the implied understanding that the customer will allow sufficient lead time on future orders. Or, the rep may simply decide that the surcharge is not warranted because of the circumstances or the size and importance of the account.

In other instances, the published policy may provide a basis for negotiation. One of the most common examples is equipment which is out of warranty and breaks down before a service contract has been signed. The manager may offer to perform the needed repairs free of charge provided the customer signs a service contract. In another case, the published policy may afford the customer service rep an opportunity to gain stature in the customer's eyes: "It's against policy to accept returns after 90 days, but I'm pretty sure I can get an exception made in your case." This can serve to solidify the relationship and at the same time reinforce the policy with the knowledge that an exception is in fact being made but may not be made in the future.

It is extremely important, however, that customer service representatives should not be called on to make judgmental decisions in complex situations. If the manager actually requires reps to make judgmental decisions in such instances then he or she has an implied obligation to back them up. If a rep offers a credit of, say, $300 because he or she has the responsibility to decide credits up to that limit and feels that this is an appropriate amount, then the manager has a clearcut obligation to back up the rep within the limits of the situation. If the amount is unacceptable to the customer, the manager may decide to offer a larger amount—indeed, the rep may even recommend it. However, if the manager decides $300 is too much and cuts the credit to a lesser amount, he or she has completely undermined the rep's credibility and relationship with the customer. This will also reduce morale to a shambles within the department.

In short, the customer service manager must first insure that policies are reasonable to begin with, and acceptable to a majority of customers, and that reps are completely familiar with interpretation and application of these policies, including judgmental areas. Many cases which at first appear to be judgmental can be simplified through the use of decision rules or trees, similar in format to equipment troubleshooting formulas or guides. These are particularly useful in warranty situations but can also be used to determine whether customers qualify for free exchanges or returns, refunds, advertising allowances and the like.

Exceptions to policies. Giving reps some latitude in making exceptions to policies can be an effective tool in morale-building as well as in improving customer relations. For example, car rental firms typically allow their agents to offer customers upgrades to the next size car when there has been a problem of some type. Often this is phrased as a "reward" to the customer: "You've been so patient that I'm upgrading you from a compact to a full-size car at the compact rate." Front desk personnel in hotels often have similar latitude in room assignments. In a manufacturing firm, reps may have latitude to make exceptions in the case of minimums, substitutions, surcharges and other matters. At the retail level, a higher-priced model may be offered at the same price as an advertised item which is not readily available; this is sometimes mandated by law, or as part of a consent agreement with the Federal Trade Commission.

"Overriding" customer service representatives. This is an extremely sensitive situation with respect to policy. In a typical case, the customer service rep has explained a policy on refunds to a customer—no refunds after such-and-such a number of days—and the customer has accepted the rep's explanation and the policy. However, when another customer in a similar situation is refused a refund under the same policy, he angrily demands to speak to the customer service manager who then makes an exception and in effect overrides the earlier decision by the customer service representative. At this point, the customer service rep complains that she has been "sold out" by her manager, and complains bitterly that if the company has policies it ought to either enforce them or scrap them.

Indeed the manager may have had a perfectly valid reason for making an exception in the particular customer's case. To avoid the rep's feeling of having been discredited, however, this reasoning should be explained to the rep in complete detail. The manager should also make clear the weight of responsibility that he/she is taking on in making the exception: the possibility of touching off a class action suit, for example. And whenever possible, the rep should be the one to convey the good news to the customer that an exception is being made in this particular instance. In this way, the customer service rep remains the principal point of contact and the customer does not feel impelled to deal with the manager rather than the rep on important matters. It follows that when there is "bad news" to communicate to customers in regard to applications of policy, it may be preferable for the manager to communicate the news directly to the customer. Here, the implication is that the customer service rep went to bat for the customer but the manager had to say "no"; this retains the rep's credibility and stature with the customer and yet makes it clear to the customer that an exception cannot be made.

The "Discovery Strategy." Regardless of how carefully they are phrased or explained to customers, some policies are likely to evoke strong, hostile responses from customers perceiving them as unfair or discriminatory. While it goes without saying that the best way to avoid hostility is to remove the causes, this isn't always possible, and one technique that often proves effective can be called the "Discovery Strategy." In this approach, the customer asks the rep about applicability of a particular policy to his or her situation. The customer service rep knows the policy and knows immediately that the customer is not eligible, but feels that to bounce back immediately with this information in a sort of rules-and-regulations response will simply anger the customer. So, instead of responding immediately, the rep says something to this effect: "Gosh, I really don't know all the applications, but let me place you on hold and check with my supervisor." After a suitable wait, the rep will return to the phone and say to the customer: "I'm terribly sorry, but under the policy you're not eligible for the refund. I'll be glad to read you the specific policy." This approach has the effect of softening the bad news while placing the rep in the position of messenger rather than policy-maker. For a further description of this process, see Figure 1.

She says 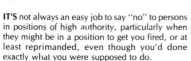 to the

TOP BRASS
and they LOVE IT!

IT'S not always an easy job to say "no" to persons in positions of high authority, particularly when they might be in a position to get you fired, or at least reprimanded, even though you'd done exactly what you were supposed to do.

That's the problem that faced Carol Brown, an attractive 22-year-old, when she was placed in charge of a major recreational facility—a complex of tennis courts—at a large army camp in the southeastern United States. Carol (not her real name) was told that rules for use of the facility, reservations, tournaments, and eligibility for lessons applied equally to all personnel, regardless of rank, and to their dependents. And she was expected to enforce those regulations.

"I'd never dealt with Army brass before," Carol admits, "and while most of them are willing to go by the rules, there are always a few—or their spouses—who'll pull rank on you at the slightest provocation.

"Of course, when the rules call for saying 'no,' I could do just that—say 'no'—and be hard-nosed about it, but I'm a realist. Some of those people carry a lot of weight around here and might influence my efficiency rating and my career. A 22-year-old civilian in an Army camp like this just isn't very important in the scheme of things.

"So I have to be diplomatic . . . and then some. I have to be able to say 'no' firmly and finally, and make them like it—and me."

How does Carol perform this miracle of diplomacy? We'll let her tell it in her own words.

"If you know the Army, you know there are rules for everything, and they're all written down somewhere. The first thing I did was to learn—inside out and backwards—the rules governing the use of the tennis courts. But a funny thing happened. When I quoted the rules, some of the folks got angry at me, and as much as told me I was a liar. When I showed them the particular rule in black-and-white, they got twice as mad, told me I was too smart for my own good, and went away muttering about turning me in.

"Of course, I didn't want that, but neither did I want to break the rules just to please the brass. So, remembering what they said about being smart, I decided maybe I should be a little less informed. That I should ask *them* to help *me*, so to speak.

"Just one day later, I had a chance to test my new theory. The situation involved the wife of a general who was in the Active Reserves. As a dependent, she wanted to sign up for tennis lessons we were offering. I knew that the general was not on active duty, and that therefore neither he nor his wife were eligible under the rules. But I knew, too, that both the general and his wife had a reputation for throwing their weight around. With him weighing in at 250 pounds, and her not much less, I decided I didn't want that kind of grief.

"So, instead of telling the lady she was ineligible, I handled it this way:

"Me: 'Let's see, General _____ is on active duty now, isn't he?'

"General's Wife: 'No, he's in the Active Reserves, but he's not on active duty right now.'

"Me: 'Gosh, I don't know what the regulations are on that. Could you help me look them up?' And with that I got out the manual, offered her a chair beside me, and started leafing through the book. I even let her 'find' the page that applied.

"When we got to the place saying that she was ineligible, I said, 'Oh, isn't that a shame! I don't know what to say. I wish I could make an exception, but if I did, the top brass would have me drawn and quartered. The only suggestion I can make is that you call me when you know your husband is going back on active duty and I'll make sure that you're at the top of the list for lessons.'

"It worked like a charm, and I've been using this approach ever since, varying it to meet different situations. I'm glad I learned early in the game that it doesn't always pay to be a know-it-all when you're dealing with important customers. A little bit of diplomacy can go a long way.

"By the way, the general's wife wrote a letter of commendation about me to the post commander . . . and she's *paying* me to give her tennis lessons in my spare time!"

Figure 17-1. Using the "Discovery Strategy" to say no to an important customer without creating antagonism is illustrated by this article from *The Customer Communicator.*

Policy Contingencies to Plan For

Every manager is of course fully aware that simply having a policy does not automatically insure that complaints or problems can be resolved by referencing that policy. Customers may not be willing to accept a particular policy, may dispute a particular interpretation that's being placed on it, may say that it doesn't apply to a particular situation, or may say that it's not legal and binding and that they are going to resolve the matter in the courts. In a case where a contract is involved, the customer may claim it's no longer valid. And, as always, the customer may simply decide that a policy is too distasteful, and simply decide not to do business with the firm. Unfortunately, many decisions of this type are made without informing the vendor of the reason so that it is sometimes difficult to quantify the effect of poorly thought out policies on overall sales and profits.

Thus it is important for the manager to identify beforehand the types of situations that are most likely to arise that have potential for seriously damaging customer relations. Here is a case history illustrating some of the subtleties in policy situations. The company sells liquid chemicals on an FOB shipping point basis. A customer has contracted to purchase a tank truck of a certain chemical that is shipped in molten form in insulated tankers. A common carrier tank line performs the movement, but upon arrival at the customer's location a leak is detected in the tank and the customer refuses to accept delivery, claiming possible contamination. Under the law, the customer owns the product, having purchased it on an FOB basis, and any claims lie with the carrier and not the vendor. But if the product isn't unloaded soon, it will harden in the tank and present a real problem and a potential three-way lawsuit. It's beyond the scope of this chapter to discuss possible solutions to this problem, and this example is used merely to illustrate the need for having contingency plans at the ready rather than having to develop them on an ad-hoc basis.

Here are some additional situations involving company pol-

icies that suggest advance planning in order to deal with potentially sensitive situations:

• *Price increases, announced or unannounced.* A customer
has just printed 500,000 four-color catalogs based on former
prices and demands price protection for the life of the catalog.

• *Discontinued item.* The company has decided to discon-
tinue a very popular but unprofitable item. Many customers
claim they were not formally notified and the company has an
obligation to fill their orders for a specified period of time.

• *Change in sale basis.* The company has decided to switch
from prepaid freight or delivered price basis to FOB plant shipment, freight charges collect or through consignee arrangement
with carriers, no exceptions. Many customers take strong exception.

• *Shortage.* The product is in short supply and an allocation
program has been implemented which some customers feel to be
unfair.

• *Warranty.* A product is out of warranty but the customer
demands replacement on the grounds that product was not manufactured properly to begin with.

• *Late time or jobsite delivery.* Construction materials are
delivered late to a jobsite and the customer threatens to sue for
damages including standby costs for work crews, cranes and
other rental equipment, etc.

• *Concealed damage.* Customer claims damaged product
after having signed clear bill of lading.

• *Shortage.* Customer claims shortage of a substantial
amount of material ordered but not delivered. The claim is
difficult to verify, and there is a suggestion that either the
customer is deliberately lying or that the shortages reflect thefts
at the customer location rather than short shipments.

• *Returns.* Customer wishes to return materials which
have passed the expiration date for returns.

• *Refused delivery.* Customer refuses to accept delivery of
a quantity of product which was manufactured to order on a
proper purchase order, properly acknowledged.

• *Repudiation.* Customer gives verbal instructions which

are followed but later turn out to have been in error. Customer now claims that these were not the instructions given.

• *Claimed commitments.* A customer claims that the customer service rep made an agreement—a commitment—to ship by a certain date, or at a certain price, and that the commitment wasn't met. The customer service rep, who has a reputation for honesty and forthrightness, says that no such commitment was made or even suggested to the customer.

Scenarios and scripts. Bearing in mind that these examples are only illustrative and not intended to represent a comprehensive list of the contingencies that might arise with respect to policies, the manager should draw up a list of contingencies relevant to the particular company and then develop a script or scenario that customer service representatives and supervisors can refer to.

The script or scenario should not be a "canned speech" which the rep simply reads to the customer, but rather an outline of points that should be made. If specific language or phrasing is important for legal reasons, then this should be noted. If particular techniques have proved effective in handling irate customers or cooling down potentially explosive situations, then of course reps should receive hands-on training, through role-playing and monitored on-job performance, in these techniques.

The truth but not the whole truth. It's often said that "the nice thing about telling the truth is that you don't have to remember what you said." But frankness can be carried too far. A customer calls and says, angrily: "You promised delivery by 9 a.m. today. It's now 4 p.m. Where's my shipment? What happened?" The completely truthful response might be: "Your shipment is still sitting on our dock. The driver showed up drunk and we couldn't send him out." Obviously, nobody would be likely to give this explanation but would say, instead, "We were short a driver, and the shipment didn't go out on time."

It's preferable that as many complaint calls as possible be handled exclusively by customer service personnel who are trained both in handling dissatisfied customers and in explaining or interpreting problems that have arisen affecting those customers. One of the dangers of turning calls over to personnel without such training is that they will tend to side with the customer. For example, turn the customer over to an engineer and the engineer is likely to say: "I've been telling them for five years they ought to redesign that part so it wouldn't keep breaking off like that!" Also to be avoided are attempts to reassure the customer that don't come off that way: "Well, the repairs *are* a little costly. But you can be thankful you have a Model J and not a Model K, because when that Model K blows, she *really* blows!"

As a practical matter, when the customer insists that they want to know exactly what happened, it is usually preferable to respond with a countermove of this type: "Well, I don't have all the details yet, but what I'd like to do is get some additional information from you so that we can start working on a solution." Similarly, it may be best to turn aside accusations of poor quality control, misinformation or whatever by saying: "I'm sorry you feel that way, it certainly wasn't our intention. But let me get some information from you so we can straighten it out."

If a serious question of credibility is involved and the customer accuses the rep or the firm of out-and-out lying, the rep may want to ask: "Can you tell me why you say that? We certainly didn't intend to misinform you, but if we did I'd certainly want to know about it." In general, however, it is best not to argue or dispute charges by the customer, and certainly not to dwell on drawn-out explanations of what actually happened.

Some questions are clearly not intended for answers. For example, the customer who asks, plaintively, "Why do you always botch *my* orders?" The temptation may be to say, "Oh, we treat everybody alike," but in actual fact the only practical response is to make the transition from negative to positive by saying: "It certainly wasn't our intention. Can you tell me what happened so we can straighten it out?"

What to Do When the Customer Is at Fault

Customer-caused errors represent one of the most sensitive and volatile of all situations likely to be encountered by the customer service manager. The initial problem is in determining whether the customer actually should have full responsibility for the error, or whether the vendor was somehow responsible for "contributory negligence." The most clearcut cases of these involve mistakes made by the customer that *could have been caught* by the vendor.

For example, a customer makes a mis-specification in a package dimension, resulting in a carton which will not palletize efficiently. Although the error was not discernible to the naked eye, so to speak, the packaging manufacturer offered a computerized dimensioning program whereby customers could test for the most efficient dimensions for use in their particular pallet system. Since this customer had already submitted dimensions, the manufacturer did not offer the program, nor did it attempt to test the dimensions for efficiency against the most popular pallet sizes. Who was at fault?

It's a difficult question to answer. Clearly the customer made the initial mistake, but the manufacturer compounded it by not testing it via a relatively simple procedure which was immediately available in-house. It might be comparable to a situation in which a physician writes a prescription including drugs that are clearly incompatible and dangerous to the patient; what is the pharmacist's degree of responsibility in compounding the prescription? Certainly the parties would both prefer to avoid the situation altogether regardless of the legal niceties that might be involved.

In a related type of situation, a customer made an error in specifying the reduction of a photograph to be stripped into a publication. Instead of reducing to column width of 2½ inches, the photo was reduced to one inch in width and centered in the column. When the customer complained, the printer responded: "Well, we thought it *did* look a little peculiar, but after all you're the customer and the customer is always right!" The customer disagreed with this view, and rightly so: if anything seems "peculiar" about a customer's order, it's incumbent on the vendor to contact that customer immediately to verify that this specification, quantity or whatever was in fact intended, and not an error on the customer's part. In this particular case, the customer gave the vendor the choice of doing the job over again properly and free of charge, or losing the account altogether. The vendor did the job over free of charge, and instituted internal controls insuring that questionable specifications always be questioned directly to the customer.*

Besides making sure that customers have the appropriate skills and information to order accurately, the customer service manager should review all catalogs, order forms, product sheets, policy statements and other communications to insure that they are not susceptible to multiple interpretations. A commonly-cited and somewhat humorous example is that of a householder who complained to a meat processor that the product spoiled, even though it was handled precisely in accordance with instructions. The processor sent replacement product, and this spoiled, too. And so did *its* replacement. Finally, the customer relations manager contacted the customer by telephone. "Did you place the product under refrigeration?" she asked the customer. "I certainly did," responded the customer. "The meat is under the refrigerator right now, just the way the package said!"

In another example, a well-known publisher offered a free trial subscription to a monthly book series using these words: "If you don't wish to continue, simply send us a postcard saying 'stop!' " As might be expected, the publisher subsequently received thousands of postcards, unsigned and bearing a single word: "Stop!"

Unfortunately, these are not isolated examples of mis-

---

* Seasoned buyers of printing will argue that if the customer had okayed a proof or blueline, then the printer had no further liability for the layout. Or, if the customer had opted not to see a proof or blueline in the interests of saving time, then the printer would not have been liable in this situation. Strictly speaking this is probably true, but in a legal setting much could be made of the fact that the printer acknowledged that the dimension seemed "peculiar" yet did not contact the customer—courts often will presume the vendor to have superior knowledge and skill to the customer, and this could certainly be argued in this case. Even if the case did go to court and the printer won, it would be a relatively empty victory since the account would have long since changed suppliers. In such cases it is far more productive to take countermeasures before the fact than to argue legal niceties after the damage has been done.

communication. Although catalogs and product sheet descriptions are usually carefully written to present the product in the most attractive light without misrepresentation, post-sale communications do not always get the same degree of attention. As a result, customers may misinterpret or misread instructions, invoices or other documents and take incorrect action accordingly.

Apart from the problems of customer-caused errors, miscommunications also incur other costs: the costs of servicing excessive numbers of phone calls or letters from customers seeking clarification (and followup calls and letters when a prompt response is not forthcoming); and the costs inherent in delayed or disputed payment on related invoices. In some instances, as many as ten percent of collection problems may be traced to miscommunications of some sort. Any investment of time and effort by the customer service manager that will reduce those miscommunications will be more than repaid by improved efficiency and productivity in the department itself.

Customer Errors: No Time to Relax!

Customer service representatives are likely to feel that they can relax just because it was the customer who made the mistake, rather than themselves. While it may be a good morale factor for them to know that for once they are not being blamed for a problem, in truth customer-caused errors often demand more of reps than those they make themselves. It does not take a great deal to acknowledge having made a mistake and then proceed to correct it. It takes a great deal more to correct or mitigate somebody else's mistake when there's no obligation to do so.

Yet there are several compelling reasons for making an extra effort to salvage such situations, and these should be explained fully to reps so that there will be no question as to what's expected of them—and the potential consequences to the company if they don't rise to the occasion. First, if it's a serious mistake the individual responsible at the customer company may actually be in danger of losing his or her job, or at least suffering some sort of discipline as a result. Second, the vendor may be blamed for the outcome, if not the error itself, on the premise that the error should have been caught or at least mitigated. Finally, there is always the possibility that the account will be lost—the individual responsible may fire the vendor from the account to cover up his or her part in the problem.

Under such circumstances, customer service personnel should be made aware of the importance of taking *any* action, however slight, that will help the situation. For example, if a customer faces a line shutdown because of a failure to order materials and the materials are no longer in stock, the manager and/or reps can contact other customers who may have stockpiled the materials and will lend or sell them on a short-term basis.* Or there may be alternate sources that can be recommended, or substitutable items. If it's possible to make a goodwill adjustment that will help the individual in his or her company, then by all means this should be done even when there's clearly no obligation to do so.

Find for the Customer When Possible

A basic premise of customer service policy should be that all policies should be interpreted in favor of the customer whenever possible. In other words, reps should be encouraged to "find for the customer" whenever there is anything at all in the firm's policies that will justify their so doing.

To managers and reps alike used to "defending" the company, this may take a little getting used to, but if policies have been drawn up equitably to begin with, no great expense will

---

* Note that in some industries it is an accepted practice for the vendor to "borrow" product that has already been committed to other customers for routine stock replenishment and to divert it to a particular customer who is in a crisis situation of this type, and to do so without having to request specific authorization.

accrue to the company—and there will be many benefits. Reps who understand that their job is to *help* customers get the best deal will be able to maintain a much more positive attitude and actually serve their customers and their company that much better. Customers who feel they are being treated fairly are likely to become better customers, and to more readily accept changes in customer service procedures and policies. They will also be more tolerant of customer service failures when they occur.

In this type of situation, the customer service department is analogous to an insurance agent who sees the agent's mission as making every effort to *find,* rather than deny, coverage for an insured who has suffered a mishap. While it is a fact that courts traditionally interpret gray areas in insurance policies in favor of the insured rather than the insuror, a conscientious agent will normally do so without even being asked. Similarly, when customer service representatives see themselves as customers' "agents," and at the same time supported by their own company, they will take a much more positive view of their jobs and perform them that much more effectively. And with very little danger of giving away the company.

Even so, there are sure to be some individuals in the company who will oppose any adjustment that the customer does not actually "earn" or "deserve." Their reasoning, which is quite understandable, is that any policy or goodwill adjustments not warranted by actual liability represent an admission of service failure, poor quality control or other lapses by the company. These individuals take considerable pride in the company and the quality of its products, and their own work, and bitterly oppose any actions that suggest otherwise.

To placate them, and at the same time avoid any issues of actual liability, goodwill refunds or credits to customers should be accompanied by a covering letter identifying the situation and including wording to this effect: "Because of the fine business relationship that exists between our two firms, our accounting office has been instructed to issue a credit (or refund) in the amount of $_____." This avoids the issue of responsibility altogether, but it also speeds the return of the firms to the desired posture of business as usual. Such adjustments should always be explained to personnel within the company who might otherwise feel that they were being blamed for problems not of their doing.

The Issue of Responsibility Within the Company

As suggested earlier, one of the most sensitive of all issues is the old familiar refrain of "Whose fault is it?" One thing is certain: it is definitely not the customer service department's mission to answer that question for the outside world. It will undermine customers' confidence in the company if customer service reps, in what is usually a genuine effort to smooth things out, side with the customer against a third party in the form of another department. "Well, Traffic just messed up your waybill, that's the best way I can put it." Or, "If those people in quality control had been awake instead of goofing off, you never would have had this problem." And, further, "The warehouse says the order's already shipped, and I guess we gotta take their word for it."

All these responses suggest the customer service rep is trying to say to the customer, "*I'm* on your side, even if all those other people in my company aren't!" But it is seldom interpreted this way by the customer, and often generates hosility. Because the customer sees the company as a single entity, not a collection of warring departments who aren't accountable to one another. Even though the problem may in fact have arisen in another department, it is far better to say: "*We* made a mistake—and *we'll* make it right."

And indeed it may be a good practice for the customer service rep to hold himself or herself accountable for errors that were actually made elsewhere in the firm. And for entirely practical reasons. Some of those errors very probably occurred because the rep did not follow through on an important matter. In many instances, personnel in other departments promise to take certain actions on behalf of customers but fail to take those actions. It should be impressed on customer service representatives that an integral part of their job is to see that those promises are actually kept. Being accountable directly to customers for whatever happens upgrades the customer service representative to an account executive relationship and also enhances the quality of follow-through in the department.

This of course does not prevent reps from acknowledging genuine problems such as work stoppages, computer failure, weather, illness, line down situations and other events that may legitimately be the cause of customer service problems. In so doing, however, the rep should be prepared to tell customers what countermeasures have been taken to mitigate the damage and speed the problem to a solution.

The Importance of Avoiding Defensiveness

All people have a natural tendency to go on the defensive when they are criticized. When a company's products or services are criticized, the firm's personnel see such criticism as a reflection on themselves. And this is both normal and healthy. Yet it must be contained. A defensive posture on the part of vendor personnel is almost guaranteed to intensify whatever problems exist and may in fact cause customers to escalate their demands and to be far less tolerant of problems in the future.

Even though it is not always possible to feel empathy for a particularly irate and abusive customer, all personnel should be trained to *practice* and *articulate* such empathy. The first step is to make every effort to identify with the customer's situation and say: "I can understand your feelings because I would feel the same way if I were in the same situation." The next step is to diffuse the customer's anger by taking tangible action to bring the problem to a speedy solution—with as little reference as possible to fault, blame and responsibility.

18

REALISTIC PERSONNEL POLICIES FOR THE CUSTOMER SERVICE DEPARTMENT

The manager's role. Few people in the company have a more critical one-on-one relationship with customers than the firm's customer service representatives. The customer service manager has direct responsibility for these reps. The reps must have both the talents and tools—and motivation and profit-mindedness—to maintain that customer relationship at a high, positive level in the face of frequently difficult situations. They must be resilient and resourceful and empathetic. They must understand customer needs and yet identify with their own company's goals—and be able to fit the two together. And they must bring it all to the bottom line.

If this is a realistic picture of what customer service reps *should be*—and it is—then the customer service manager's involvement should start with the development of personnel policies and hiring standards as well as actual job descriptions, and continue through actual hiring, training, compensation, incentives and motivation, promotion and career pathing.

Unfortunately, there are some companies where these functions are performed by the personnel department rather than by the customer service manager. This can seriously hamper the customer service mission, for two main reasons: (1) the personnel department does not always understand the true nature of the job, and what's needed to perform it well; and (2) the personnel department tends to give too much weight to job stability and longevity, and not enough to flexibility, personality, initiative and customer orientation.

Some companies and their personnel departments still consider the customer service rep's job as clerical. Customer service managers know better. Given the skills and responsibilities involved in customer service, to call a customer service rep a clerk is like calling an airline pilot a bus driver. If travelers felt this way, the airlines would do very little business, indeed. How many customers, with accounts running from the tens of thousands into the millions, would want to deal with vendors who staff their customer service departments with *clerks?*

The customer service manager has a direct stake in seeing that the clerk image is *not* perpetuated. And the only way to do this is through direct involvement in the entire process. This often requires upsetting conventional thinking and traditions about customer service personnel.

Longevity vs. upward mobility. In many companies, the customer service department was traditionally considered a dead-end. The emphasis was on hiring people who had little ambition, who would be willing to work for relatively little pay, stay in the job until retirement—and create few waves along the way. The main emphasis was on *continuity:* getting to know the product line, applications, company policies and, of course, customers and their needs. This is important, of course, but too often the price of continuity in one individual over a period of years is simple mediocrity. Sometimes it is worse: a hard shell of insensitivity to customer needs, exemplified in preoccupation with red tape and routines rather than with problem-solving. Also, the longer people work in the same jobs the more likely they are to resist change.

Ironically, longevity and high turnover often exist side-by-side in the same department. Promising younger people who are taken on board are quite likely to become alienated and disenchanted by the lack of opportunity and the attitudes of long-timers, including entrenched opposition to change. As a result, they depart the company for greener fields elsewhere, leaving the "lifers" more entrenched than ever.

This is not an indictment of longevity per se. There are plenty of people who stay on the job a long time, do a consistently good, professional job, and for valid reasons of their own prefer to stay in the job they have rather than move up and out of the department. But they have succeeded in spite of the tradition, not because of it. In other words, longevity does not necessarily equate with stagnation, but in many instances it does—not because of the people involved but rather because of the company policies that tend to actually reward stagnation while discouraging personal growth in the job.

For the real villain is often a company policy of providing ingrade salary increases for individuals based mainly on longevity. In a typical company, a very sharp customer service rep has been on the job for six months and is doing an outstanding job . . . until she learns that an old-timer who is doing the identical job (but not as well) is making twice as much money simply because she has been there for some 25 years. Unless the company can offer the younger rep a clearly defined career path, they will lose her and others like her, and the customer service activity will suffer accordingly.

Career pathing. An increasing number of companies today recognize that good people do not usually gravitate to certain behind-the-scenes occupations including customer service. From the company's point of view, a "good" employee is one who has skills, growth potential, good work habits and a sense of loyalty to the company. To attract people with these qualities to customer service occupations requires presenting a specific career opportunity.

As the name implies, career pathing implies a well-defined progression from, for example, customer service clerk, to assistant customer service rep, customer service rep, senior customer service rep, group or team leader, assistant supervisor, supervisor, assistant manager, etc. There may also be specialist and technical positions in products and applications, claims, import-export and special markets. The employee moves up in the career path as qualified, and if it is time for an employee to move again and no position is available in the department, then he or she is recommended for a step up to a job *outside* the department. While this loses a talented employee to the department, it keeps him or her in the company and protects a corporate asset representing a considerable investment that would be virtually impossible to duplicate from the outside.

More importantly, career pathing via the customer service department means upgrades company personnel gradually. The department is an incomparable training ground for almost every area of the company's operations. And the real benefit for the customer service department is that eventually it has "graduates" throughout the company—friends and cooperators who owe their advancement to that very department, and who can understand and accommodate its special needs.

A well-planned career path in the customer service department should take five or six years, assuming that the individual starts at an entry-level position. Some managers feel that a customer service rep's effectiveness begins to diminish at the six-year mark, so that career pathing can address this problem and at the same time provide excellent training for good people who are obviously an asset to the company and who are highly motivated towards its success as well as their own.

Electronic vs. human continuity. Does career pathing disrupt continuity? Very little. The traditional factor of personal continuity in the department is much less important today than it was even five years ago. The reason is that today's information systems enable extensive customer and product files with virtually instant callout of any segment of information needed to progress a transaction.

A callout of a customer buying profile is illustrated in figure 1. Such a profile can include buying history, credit record, discounts, lead times, names of key personnel and their hobbies or personal interests, willingness to accept substitutions—even such data as the width of alleys and locations of loading docks. The "prompting" ability that can be programmed into the computer enables a relatively inexperienced customer service rep to take custom orders that would ordinarily require somebody with an engineering background to interpret.

Some Suggested CRT Prompts for
Inside Selling Personnel

301/585-0730 (direct)   Acct. No. 5-032-717

Mr. Robert Arden   (Bob)   Ship to:
Purchasing Manager
Exclusive Manufacturing Co.   Same
8701 Georgia Avenue   Receiving hours 8 am-3 pm
Silver Spring MD 20910   Foreman: Tony Robinson

Purchases to date — This Year: $ _____ Last Year: _____
Most recent purchase — Date _____ Amount $ _____ Page _____

Purchasing Profile:

    Credit Rating: AAA
    Purchase units: Palletloads-Truckloads
    Returns to date: $275
    Frequency of orders: Weekly/Tuesday; occasional fill-ins
    Delivery requirement: 10 days; prefers McLean Trucking
    Other: pallets to be banded; no shrink wrap; will accept 10%
         substitutions; no backorders; inform by phone im-
         mediately of delays or other problems

Personal Profile:

    Active in NAPM, other professional organizations
    Raises prize-winning Afghan hounds
    Children: two boys, one girl, entering college 1984-86

Figure 18-1. Customer buying profile.

The computer is equally valuable for providing specialized product information such as substitutability of a product that is readily available for one that is not. Some programs will "sort" inventories and display substitutable items in descending order of similarity, showing both the similarities and dissimilarities and

Additional CRT Prompts
For Inside Selling Personnel

You're talking to Bob Arden, purchasing manager at Exclusive Manufacturing Co. A copy of his most recent order appears on page 3.

Our forecast indicates he is likely to order the following:

Item No.	Description	No. Ordered	No. In Stock	Substitutable Items/Count
_____	_____	_____	_____	_____
_____	_____	_____	_____	_____

Figure 18-2.

Jim, Exclusive Manufacturing has now placed a total of 1000 orders with us totaling $24.2 million. What acknowledgements? Automatic notification via electronic mail to regional sales manager, account manager, vice president sales, president's office. Any other special instructions?

Figure 18-3.

Any reason this order is smaller than usual? If known, enter reason code below:

Suggest you attempt order upgrade via the following:

    Special volume pricing:
    Deferred payment:
    New product:
    Substitutions:
    Potential future shortage:
    Other:

Figure 18-4.

the amounts of each item currently in inventory. A display of substitutable tires, for example, might be sorted on diameter and tread width, ply, belting, tread, cord, etc.

If inside selling and order upgrading are involved in the customer service rep's job, the computer can provide valuable help here, too, while reducing the need for extensive experience: showing price and weight breaks, even the approach to use with a particular customer. Figures 2 through 6 show some inside selling applications operating in a real-time mode that enable resultful direct selling even though the customer service rep may have limited experience with either the specific customer or with the firm's products.

What is important here is not the replacement of certain human skills by programmable software in the computer, but rather the flexibility accorded the customer service department to *hire and make productive use of good people* without having to sacrifice quality for the traditional and outmoded sacred cows of experience and longevity. In short, the old saying that "there's no substitute for experience" can now be answered with another old saying: "It ain't necessarily so."

Job Descriptions vs. Job Requirements

While it is very likely that job descriptions already exist for most if not all the jobs in the customer service department, only occasionally are there matching statements of job *requirements* beyond elementary clerical skills or educational levels. Figure 7 shows some typical customer service job descriptions based on a 1983 study by Customer Service Newsletter, and additional, more detailed job descriptions will be found in the Appendix. The job descriptions illustrated in this chapter are composites and do not necessarily apply to any single company or industry. They should be modified to fit the particular company's needs.

Particular attention should be given to the trend in some companies to redesignate the customer service representative as

---

This customer's order mix is just over breakeven. Your commission only 78 cents (only 1/2 bonus points). Suggest:

* Save money in actual machine downtime by ordering complete kits or assemblies rather than individual parts
* Set up two-bin system for expendables; offer assistance
* Offer our booklet on EOQ, inventory management

Figure 18-5.

Congratulations! This order brings you to Level C in the sales contest. You now have _____ bonus points and your overall standing in the group is No. _____. Complete _____ more sales like this and you will win the all-expense trip to Disney World. Here's your record so far:

Total Sales to Date $ ___   Total Bonus Points to Date ___

Total Sales Last Year to Date $ _____

Total Calls Attempted ___   Completed ___   Sales ___   Ratio ___

Your ratio of actual sales to complete calls is one of the lowest in the company even though your dollar volume is near the top. Are you calling some customers too frequently, and not spending enough time on others with greater potential? Suggest you review analysis on pgs. 13-88 showing your hit rate by account and dollar return per call.

Figure 18-6.

an *account executive.* This is particularly true where the rep has responsibilities beyond simply taking orders and following through on requests and inquiries. If the rep is involved with credits and allowances, allocations, deductions, returns, and special services, the account executive term is certainly more descriptive of the actual job. It also upgrades the relationship with the customer by saying in effect: "You are important to us and we have assigned an important person—an account execu-tive—to take care of you." Of course the customer service rep receives a similar message, so that the account executive title has great value as both a morale-builder and a motivator; it identifies the rep with the job the company wants done.

Given the existence of appropriate job descriptions and a career path which will attract skilled personnel, here are some of the job requirements and qualities that the manager should be considering in prospective employees.

1. **Educational requirements.** In many companies it sim-ply is not realistic to require college backgrounds of prospective customer service employees. While companies with a clearcut career pathing policy can attract college graduates on the basis of growth opportunities, companies without such opportunities would be well-advised to concentrate on skills and personal qualifications rather than educational attainments per se. There is reason to believe that a college graduate who takes a job in a customer service department *without* growth opportunities does so because he or she can't find a job elsewhere, and will leave as soon as a better opportunity presents itself.

Also, many companies offer educational opportunities via tuition refund and similar programs. Where this is the case, the customer service manager can encourage employees to take advantage of related courses at local institutions and community colleges. The value of a college degree per se is not nearly as great to the company as specific work-related education obtained off-job but interleaved with daily on-job experience. From the em-ployee's point of view, working toward a degree in this fashion is also an incentive to good performance on the job . . . and staying with the company.

Although possession of a college degree may have some correlation with motivation, it is not necessarily an indicator that the individual possesses or is trainable in the skills and qualities most relevant to the customer service job. To limit job applicants to those with college backgrounds or degrees may also limit the quality of personnel available to the department.

2. **Appropriate clerical skills.** Regrettably, possession of a

diploma of any kind is no guarantee that a prospective employee can read or write or exercise other skills required in the job. All applicants should be tested with approved tests, i.e., tests that

Customer Service Manager Has overall administrative and operational responsibility for the customer service department, including planning budgets, hiring and training of personnel, setting standards, monitoring performance, introducing more efficient procedures, writing and/or updating customer service manuals, and maintenance of customer files. Is responsible for customer relations and relations within the department; keeps abreast of and advises management of new technology and new management techniques applicable to the department. Implements policies, and recommends changes as appropriate. Maintains liaison with other departments such as marketing, sales, credit, accounting, traffic and distribution, production, QC. Has functional responsibility for receipt of orders, order processing, billing, returns, adjustments, product and other status inquiries.

Assistant Manager of Customer Service or Customer Service Supervisor Has functional responsibility, under the Customer Service Manager, for one or more areas of customer service, for example, order processing, and the customer. Serves as operating head of warranty administration. On behalf of the Customer Service Manager, performs actual liaison with sales, credit, inventory control, warehousing, shipping, trafic, data processing, and the customer. Services as operating head of the department in the absence of the Customer Service Manager. Occasionally delegated to perform special functions: customer research, preparation of the customer service manual, customer visits, etc.

Order Processing Manager/Supervisor *(Rank equivalent to Asst. Manager of Customer Service or Customer Service Supervisor)* Responsible for receipt of orders, order editing and review, credit check, order entry, manual or computerized systems, maintenance of records associated with order processing system: order status, inventory levels, backorders, order

Figure 18-7. Typical job descriptions.

under equal employment laws objectively measure the skills required for the job. Personality or IQ-type tests that are not relevant to the job should be avoided.

---

fulfillment ratio, etc. Responsible for training, motivation and supervision of order entry clerks and support personnel. Controls access to customer records and computer databanks, and maintains security as necessary. Supervises entry of new data, changes, product descriptions, weights, price information, etc. Responsible for order processing supplies, maintenance of equipment service contracts, etc.

Senior Customer Service Representative or Assistant Customer Service Supervisor Often functions as a team leader or account executive or working supervisor. Primary contact for customer, responsible for taking orders, handling routine inquiries and complaints, claims or credits and refunds below a certain dollar limit. Is expected to have extensive knowledge of account requirements and special situations, ability to cut red tape and get results for customers. Handles exceptions, substitutions, allocations and other special problems. Often possesses specialized technical knowledge about firm's products and their applications.

Customer Service Representative Receives and processes all incoming orders and prepares appropriate forms for pick lists, invoice generation, etc.; gives customers product availability and delivery information; initiates credit checks when necessary; advises supervision of unusual situations. The primary contact for customers for inquiries, complaints, product information and returns.

Order Entry Clerk Responsible for auditing and batching order entry documentation for computer output or, with on-line systems, enters orders on CRT terminal; maintains entry reports.

Customer Service Clerk Performs routine filing, clerical, typing and similar functions.

If legible handwriting is a must, the applicant should fill out the application blank in his own or her own handwriting, plus write an essay-type paragraph or two. If these are difficult to read, the manager can be sure that the applicant's handwriting will never be any better or more legible. And if any reminder is needed of the importance of writing legibly in customer service occupations, almost any manager will volunteer a "war story" of a multi-thousand dollar mistake that resulted when somebody read a "7" for a "1" or a "B" for an "8." If spelling is a must, the applicant should be given a spelling test. And the application blank itself should be checked for spelling as well as general neatness. If the job requires a resumé, then the resumé will tell a great deal about the applicant's accuracy, neatness, spelling and grammar. This can be discounted if it's obviously a professionally prepared resumé, although this will tell something about the applicant's resourcefulness!

3. Attention to detail. If the application blank is sufficiently detailed, it can serve as a test in itself. Certainly few things are more important in the customer service job than accuracy and adherence to procedures and instructions. However it is ascertained, this quality should be a central objective in the hiring process.

4. Motivation. This is particularly important because of the repetitive nature of the job and the frequent negatives encountered, plus the reliance the company must place on the individual to perform well on behalf of both customer and company with limited supervision. One test of motivation is the individual's interest in the job as manifested in personal appearance, punctuality for the job interview, interest in the job per se as opposed to emphasis on working hours, fringes, etc.

5. Resiliency. This trait is a strong plus because of the need to immediately bounce back from negative situations—complaints, backorders, errors, etc.—and project a positive, cheerful attitude on the next contact with customers and co-workers, often within seconds. By contrast, persons without the quality of resiliency often transfer the anger or emotion or general negativism to co-workers or subsequent customers they deal with.

6. Self-confidence and pride. Since customer service reps tend to hear mainly criticisms of product and service because that's the nature of the job, they must also have sufficient self-confidence and pride to overcome doubts about product and service quality that such criticism is likely to create. The individual with pride in company and work may sometimes overreact to criticism, but he or she will also prove willing to go the extra mile for customer and company in order to prove that the pride and self-confidence are indeed justified.

7. Ability to withstand pressure. Stress is inherent in the customer service job. If stress could be eliminated, it's likely that the job could be eliminated, too. Customer service seems to appeal to individuals who are over-achievers and thus have a tendency toward stress—but also the ability to deal with it. In rating applicants the manager should not let concern with stress overshadow other qualities to the extent of hiring phlegmatic or insensitive individuals who can't relate to or emphathize with customers. Instead, he or she should zero in on the applicant's understanding of the stressful nature of the job, and acceptance that it goes with the territory—and can be handled by that individual.

8. Ability to think-on-feet. This is particularly important because so much of customer service takes place on the telephone when there is little time to consider and evaluate responses beforehand—and when a statement, once made, is difficult to recall or amend. How can the manager tell when a candidate has this quality? One way is to fire some questions at him or her during the interview: "What would you do in a situation like this?" "Tell me about the most difficult situation you ever had to deal with on the telephone, and how you handled it." An articulate, detailed response reflects excellent thinking-on-feet ability. Too much deliberation will suggest that the candidate may be better suited for written communications.

A variation on this approach is to have two persons interview the applicant together in a sort of two-on-one situation, with both asking questions of the applicant. This approximates to some degree the pressure that customer service reps often encounter, and how well the applicant responds is a good measure of how well he or she will respond to such pressure on the job.

9. Credibility. One of the most important and most fundamental requirements of any customer service operation, credibility is doubly important in customer service reps. When reps cannot quickly achieve credibility with their customers, the burden must be assumed by others including the manager. This undermines the entire system and the entire departmental mission. And if lack of credibility undermines, the presence of credibility adds measurably to departmental productivity and particularly to customer acceptance of occasional failures, alternative solutions, and even major changes in customer service procedures and policies. In the interview environment, applicants who can hold their own conversationally and quickly achieve credibility with their interviewer(s) can also be expected to do the same with customers.

10. Personality. Will the applicant wear well? This is perhaps the most important question that the manager is faced with in terms of interpersonal relations within the department itself. It is largely a judgment call which tends to be biased by the manager's personal preferences. Perhaps the principal guideline in this respect is to remember that individuals who come across as real "personalities" in the initial interview may not wear well over a period of time in the actual working environment. Too much outgoing-ness, too much friendliness, too much exuberance—these may translate into what co-workers and customers alike perceive as aggressiveness, over-familiarity or a dominating attitude.

11. Team spirit. This is a valuable asset and one that is usually preferable to exceptional personal skills that exceed job requirements or might suggest personality clashes with others. At least a partial reading on this quality can be gotten by asking the candidate: "Tell me something about your last job and the people you worked with."

12. Telephone "projection." Customer service reps who cannot sell themselves over the telephone to customers and others within the company will have great difficulty in getting customers to accept negative or alternative situations, just as they will have great difficulty persuading other departments to jump into the breach to provide extraordinary service for a customer in trouble. Thus, assuming that the candidate will in fact be talking extensively on the telephone, it's an absolute "must" that part of the hiring interview be conducted over the telephone, and by the manager personally. Candidates who can't sell themselves to the manager over the phone at a time when it's important to their careers and when they are presumably at the highest levels of motivation, probably won't be able to sell themselves to customers or others in the company at a time when they're under equal stress but don't have the same degree of motivation.

The ideal prospect from a telephone point of view will have good telephone manners, clear speech and good grammar, knowledge of appropriate procedures, and above all the ability to come across as competent, sincere and concerned.

There are two main ways to set up the phone interviews: (1) Simply ask candidates to call for an appointment and use a standard script or set of questions with each caller; or (2) After the process of interviewing has narrowed the list down, ask each of the remaining candidates to call at a specific time (a different time for each candidate) to report whether they are interested in the job and, if so, why they should be selected for it. The second option provides an opportunity to measure punctuality and follow-through, and thus motivation as well. An applicant who does not call back at the agreed time is probably not right for the job on all three counts.

13. Trainability. Entry-level personnel may not have appropriate office skills, but if they are highly motivated and trainable they may be preferable to individuals with previous experience and set work habits which have to be "unlearned" before qualifying for customer contact. But the manager should be realistic about hiring people with limited basic skills; they may require extra training and both company and manager should be willing to make the commitment. And it is a good commitment to make; it is far better to pay to train somebody to be a productive worker than to sustain that person on welfare via taxes on the enterprise. The same is generally true of candidates with personality problems, although an even greater commitment may be required.

14. Growth potential, promotability. As mentioned earlier, more companies now recognize that the customer service representative *is* the company to most of its customers. It follows that they want these persons to project the most positive image of strength, professionalism, progressiveness, concern for customers, credibility and reliability and much more. And they are beginning to recognize that to do so they are going to have to recruit bright, motivated, upwardly-mobile individuals for this key job. Also, this has to happen fast, to overcome the cumulative effects of the relatively low status the job has had for so many years. Of course it follows that to attract upwardly mobile people, the department has to offer credible promises of opportunities for promotion and personal growth.

15. Loyalty. To be effective, a customer service representative must be able to maintain a high degree of loyalty to each of three separate entities which are not always in complete harmony: to the company, to the customer service team within the company, and to the customer. He or she must keep these loyalties in balance, never compromising the company, but always making sure that the customer's interests are represented well and fairly.

How can loyalty be evaluated in advance? The candidate should be asked about his or her current or previous employer, and his or her reasons for leaving. The manner in which the question is answered will reveal a great deal. Similarly, a prospective employee who is now working but can come to work on the new job "immediately," i.e., without giving reasonable notice to the present employer, does not rate highly for loyalty unless there are extenuating circumstances.

Special Employment Categories

1.Flextime. This is one of the most popular means of dealing with the workload imbalance—peaks and valleys—that is traditional in customer service activities. The term "flextime" is a contraction of "flexible time," and is basically what the name implies. In practice, employees are permitted to schedule their own starting and stopping times around designated "core hours" when everybody is required to be present. This usually works out to about two hours' flexibility either way, although there are some options allowing for four-day weeks. There is also built-in flexibility for personal business, doctor's appointments, etc., so that these can be conducted on personal time without a leave requirement or other penalty. Many companies report that flextime and its variations* have proven quite effective in customer service applications. An added benefit that is frequently cited is that flextime is an excellent motivator: people who feel that they have a voice in setting their own working hours have a greater sense of involvement and thus motivation.

2. Job-sharing and rotation. There are two versions of this. One is a single job held by two persons, one working morning and the other afternoon shifts, or some similar arrangement. The other version is where two people have two similar jobs but rotate specific assignments. For example, Rep A handles complaints in the morning and research in the afternoon, while Rep B handles research in the morning and complaints in the afternoon. In some companies, the time interval for job rotation may be longer: in one Eastern company, each rep rotates once a week to a telemarketing day during which he or she does nothing else while others handle his or her regular duties. In a West Coast company, the complaint handling job is similarly rotated. Both report that the system works well.

---

*Added information about flextime and its variations may be obtained from National Council for Alternative Work Patterns, 1925 K St. N.W., Washington, DC 20006 (202) 466-4467.

3. Permanent part-time. This has proven to be an extremely resultful approach to peak-and-valley problems in companies with extreme workload fluctuations that cannot be handled effectively with a full-time workforce. Apart from the direct economics there are a number of ancillary benefits: part-time people normally do not qualify for most benefits, so that the 30% to 40% expense that employers normally pay full-time workers for these are largely saved. Even more importantly, permanent part-time employees have proven highly motivated and highly reliable. It is not always easy to find a job that fits into personal schedule, and once such a job has been found the employee is highly motivated to retain it. Moreover, permanent part-time employees tend to be the exception to the upward mobility rule: even though they are normally not interested in specific career paths, they do not stagnate in their jobs but continue at high levels of performance. Studies of permanent part-time workers have shown, for example, that permanent part-time workers are significantly more productive, hour for hour, than full-time employees working at the same jobs.*

4. Handicapped workers. It has been well-documented that handicapped workers are highly productive in customer service jobs. Within recent years there have been dramatic equipment innovations permitting blind persons to access computers via vocal or Braille response terminals, and thus to service customers effectively by telephone. Comparable developments have made computers and word processing accessible to persons with severe physical handicaps or paralysis. The increased accessibility of the workspace to handicapped persons coupled with their increased mobility makes this a particularly attractive category from which to recruit effective customer service personnel.

5. Disadvantaged persons. As mentioned earlier, many companies make a commitment to hire and train disadvantaged

---

*National Council for Alternative Work Patterns, 1925 K St. N.W., Washington, DC 20006 (202) 466-4467.

persons in order to take them off welfare and put them in productive jobs. It is perhaps the most rewarding of commitments, and one that most companies can afford and should undertake. It is a much more meaningful contribution to the local community than gifts to charity. It's also much more difficult to sustain; which is why it is so important for *every* company to make the commitment regardless of whether it involves one individual or one hundred or more. And customer service, because of its team spirit and the innately supportive nature of its personnel, is an excellent place to start.

The Hiring Process

1. **Sources.** These may come from job posting, referrals by friends or relatives, advertising, employment agencies or other sources. Each has its pros and cons. Where it is possible, a relationship with a reputable employment agency—where the hiring company pays the fee—will often save time and money overall. This assumes that the agency has a good understanding of the department's needs and that it prescreens candidates and provides an adequate guarantee, i.e., that the employee stay on the job and prove satisfactory for a stated period of time, or the fee will be refunded. Advertising is frequently the least effective means of locating prospective employees. It may turn up people who are looking for work, or looking for a change, but it does not necessarily find the *best* people who may be available but not necessaily actively looking for new employment. Also, advertising often produces a high number of responses requiring extensive screening which is better performed elsewhere.

2. **Resumés.** The advantage of requiring resumés is that it makes the job of screening considerably easier, is faster and more effective than personal interviews, and will reflect the presence or absence of certain skills. Resumés also enable the manager to measure his or her judgment against that of the personnel department. As personnel expert Alex Metz points out, if the

customer service manager selects his or her top choices from among a group of resumés and then asks the personnel department to do the same, there is likely to be very little overlap. Given that, the manager is well advised to control not only who is ultimately hired for the job, but also who is actually *interviewed* before that hiring decision is made.

3. Onsite interviewing. This should be performed by the manager in conjunction with the assistant manager or supervisors who will be working directly with the new hire. The manager should of course make the final decision, but with due consideration to the recommendations of his or her staff. Since hiring new personnel is a relatively rare experience, managers should acquaint themselves beforehand with some of the basic interviewing techniques, but should not be overly concerned that they do not have the professional skills of the full-time interviewer.* Whenever possible, the applicant should have an opportunity to meet with line personnel, perhaps for lunch or during a break. This provides an opportunity to answer the applicant's most urgent question: "What's it *really* like to work here?"

4. Involvement of the personnel department. Where possible, the role of the personnel department should be mainly in formalizing the hire once the decision has been made. This means performing all the necessary documentation, apprising the new hire of benefits, etc. and performing whatever basic orientation the company provides. This is not to suggest that the personnel department be excluded from the hiring process but simply to emphasize the fact that customer service people are generally better qualified to hire their own people because of the specialized requirements of the job. Personnel people have broad experience in hiring clerical personnel, production personnel and other large-scale categories, but the selection criteria for these categories are generally not applicable to customer service skills. And, again, personnel specialists tend to overrate longevity and

---

*An excellent basic text for this purpose is *The Evaluation Interview,* 3rd ed., by Richard A. Fear, (New York: McGraw-Hill Book Company)

job stability to the detriment of initiative, customer orientation and other qualities that are so important in customer service.

Training: Quantity vs. Quality

Industrial and commercial customer service departments tend to be relatively small, to the extent that customized training programs are not always economically feasible. Unlike Sales, where an entire crew of recruits may be trained simultaneously, customer service people tend to be hired one or two at a time and are usually apprenticed directly into the work environment after receiving basic orientation on the company and its products or services. There are also some cassette programs on telephone technique, complaint handling, etc. which can be taken by individuals in a self-instruction mode. These can be quite helpful, even to persons with previous customer service experience.*

The main problem at present is that there is very little material available for continuous training, i.e., extended over a period of weeks or months. Several community colleges—Harper College in Palatine, Ill. and Middlesex Community College in Edison, N.J.—offer formal training in customer service techniques. Managers may wish to suggest similar curricula to community colleges in their own areas.** It is also likely that the International Customer Service Association will ultimately develop a prototype course in customer service skills.*** At the same time, improved management support of the customer service function will probably result in development of a wider range of packaged programs than is currently available.

---

*A comprehensive listing of training materials appears in the Appendix.

**Details of the Harper College courses, Customer Service Representative I and II, appear in *Customer Service Newsletter* Vol 12 No. 3.

***Clearly, membership in the International Customer Service Association should be considered a must for any customer service manager claiming a professional interest in the function, as well as any senior personnel with career potential and aspirations. Details on this organization appear in the Appendix.

At the same time, managers should take advantage of the wide variety of "one-shot" materials that are available. These range from single cassettes to booklets, motivational newsletters, training films with interactive workbooks, videotape presentations, and homemade or in-house live presentations. Although these vary in quality and are labeled as training materials, they should not be judged too harshly for their relevance to the particular environment. The manager should recognize that just the simple act of *paying attention* to employees and helping them improve their skills is one of the most effective incentives and motivators the department can offer its employees. One company with extensive branch operations circulates packaged programs to its branches. By the time a given program gets back to its original starting point there are always a few new people on board at that location to be trained.

Specific training techniques are beyond the scope of this book, and in fact there are many excellent texts on the subject readily available.* The manager who opts for on-job or apprentice-type training because there is no practical alternative should take special pains in selecting the personnel who will serve as trainers. Because they will also be serving as role models, the manager should impress on them the importance of training by the book—without the shortcuts or informalities that the trainer may have developed through some years of on-the-job experience. This is particularly important: line personnel serving as trainers and displaying sloppy work habits and a bad attitude will simply perpetuate these through their trainees. Personal observation by the manager and on-line monitoring of telephone performance of both trainer and trainee are an absolute necessity.

Improving the Working Environment

It goes without saying that a customer service department with physically unattractive surroundings is unlikely to attract

---

*A partial list appears in the Appendix.

top talent. Prospective employees who visit the department and find it down in the basement or off in a corner of the warehouse will apply for employment there only as a last resort. Existing employees who already work there will "live down" to the image they have been branded with. In short, the "ashcan image" that has characterized some customer service departments over the years is a surefire deterrent to prospective employees of the type *every* customer service manager should be searching out today.

Even without considering the future, poor surroundings tend to inhibit present productivity and they are often compounded by high noise levels, excessive traffic and inefficient layout. Improving these surroundings should be the point of departure for any effort to improve levels of morale and motivation in a department that has more than its share of demoralizing and demotivating situations to deal with on a daily basis year-round. This effort will be the subject of the next chapter.

19

IMPROVING EMPLOYEE MORALE AND MOTIVATION

Many customer service managers feel that the many negative situations encountered daily by their customer service reps are the primary cause of poor morale and lack of motivation in the department. While these are certainly a contributing factor, the root causes are often something much more mundane: the working environment itself, job design, policies, procedures and—yes—computer systems.

The previous chapter referred to the effect of a poor working environment on productivity as well as morale and motivation. Many customer service departments originated as clerical adjuncts to shipping and warehousing operations and were housed accordingly. They have long since outgrown the role, but not always the housing. This is beginning to change in some companies. In others, it's an excellent point of departure in persuading management of the need for parity between customer service and other departments. Since it's often easier to sell management on cosmetic improvements than on fundamental changes in departmental relationships, the customer service manager may find it opportune to present a detailed proposal involving new layout, partitioning and soundproofing, and decor and appointments suitable to the importance of the job.

Acceptance of this proposal will lay the groundwork for future, more pervasive proposals. Thus, if at all possible it should be prepared with professional assistance and presented with professional renderings. And the layout should take into account two primary concerns of customer service personnel—ample workspace, generally a No. 1 consideration, and privacy without isolation plus a sense of personal space.

Even so, the manager should be wary of "efficient" layouts which place all desks close together, without dividers, to improve the workflow and facilitate consultation between workers. This tends to dehumanize the function, and while it may be necessary to pair some personnel because of the nature of the work, any advantages of an open-space environment are likely to be illusory and more than offset by disadvantages measurable in lost productivity due to noise, interference, traffic and other factors. Although open space does improve the span of supervision in warehousing and shipping operations, this is not a major factor in customer service, where electronic supervision via the computer is more practical.

What about colors? Most companies have relatively conservative color standards which are generaly imposed by management as a reflection of its own tastes. Consultants on office design report that color preferences of employees are in fact quite different from those of their managers but are seldom taken into consideration in planning. It may not be worth the effort to attempt to change existing color standards, but this difference in color preferences should be a useful reminder to the manager that reps' outlook may differ significantly in other respects, too.

Assessing Internal Perceptions

Some morale problems arise in the customer service department simply because people do not understand their jobs or where the department fits in. Managers have a tendency to assume that reps have the "big picture" when in fact they often have a very narrow and frequently distorted view of what they do. Ask reps the purpose of their jobs and they will often respond in terms of the paperwork they handle: "I take orders over the telephone"; "I issue credits"; "I process claims." Seldom do they see themselves as the major link between their companies and their customers, with a specific mission of customer retention and account growth. Seldom do they see themselves in an account executive capacity, although this is often what they are.

Since some morale problems can arise from something as basic as an individual's inability to identify or feel the relevance of his or her job, it can be very helpful to the manager to find out what reps' perceptions actually are, and to correct or clarify where necessary. Figure 1 is a questionnaire used by one firm's customer service department to "quiz" its employees about their particular perceptions. It turned up some surprising facts: first, that most customer service personnel did not understand the departmental role, then that they had a poor perception of their own jobs, and finally that many felt that their principal problem was with other departments.

While the questionnaire did uncover some very real customer service problems that needed to be dealt with, it also showed the manager and staff what needed to be done to get personnel really involved in departmental goals and working as a team rather than as individuals. One of the most common complaints was the sense of going it alone: "I care, but nobody else does. If everybody cared as much as I do, we wouldn't have any problems." A combination of individual counseling and procedural changes brought about visible improvements in both morale and output.

Some of the complaints about other departments turned out to be justified, and the manager committed to improve these problems—and made good on the commitment through diplomatic discussions with other department heads. As often happens, these other departments frequently had no clear idea of what was needed from them because nobody had ever told them.

Motivators, Demotivators and Burnout

"Customer service is stressful work. It's a succession of negatives. It's discouraging to hear so many no's all day long. It's demotivating. What can I do to motivate my people in the face of all this?"

This is the question most frequently asked by customer service managers who see the stresses of the customer service rep's job as the main obstacle to productivity. "What can I do to prevent burnout?" is another frequently asked question.

The view that customer service work is exceptionally stressful and demotivating is popular but not proven. Without realizing

---

1) What percentage of contacts is by phone and what percentage by mail?

2) Who usually places the order (purchasing agents, field sales reps, end users, etc.)?

3) About how many orders do you handle on a typical day; a slow day; a very hectic day?

4) What type of orders (small, large, a mix) do you handle on a typical day?

5) How can we measure the quality and level of service our reps provide?

6) How could a rep or his or supervisor know he or she is more effective in dealing with customers than six months ago?

7) How could you tell if he or she were *less* effective?

8) Please list things (in terms of behavior) that a good rep would do.

9) . . . that a good rep would *not* do.

10) Reps have access to the following records (list):

11) What are the most frequent problems or the most troublesome things a rep deals with?

12) What skills are helpful to a rep in dealing with customers (check those that apply: remaining calm, listening, showing awareness, showing sensitivity to a customer's needs)? List others.

Figure 19-1. Questionnaire used by one firm was designed to bring out customer service employees' perception of their jobs, as well as to uncover problems that might otherwise go unobserved. The questionnaire was administered to reps, supervisors and managers with upper level employees getting additional questions about complaint handling and employee relations.

it, managers sometimes project their own views onto their reps. Yet a survey of these same reps will usually reveal that most are well-adjusted, happy in their jobs and on the whole more highly motivated than most of their peers in other departments. Certainly, they feel some stress. But stress is present throughout the work day. Many reps report that they would feel more stressed working at a repetitive production-type job than in their present setting with its constant change. And indeed it's often pointed out that the diseases usually associated with high stress—heart attack, ulcers, alcoholism—are as prevalent among blue collar workers as among any other segment of the work force.

Another factor that is sometimes overlooked is that customer service personnel tend to be overachievers, individuals to whom stress is normal and even desirable. Overachievers tend to view problems as challenges and solutions as achievements. When they are frustrated, it is more often because they don't have the proper tools for problem solving than because of the problem per se. So there are often stress factors in policies and procedures, and in the workplace itself, but not necessarily in the nature of the work itself.

There are likely to be personal factors as well. Overachievers need to have recognizable achievements. They would prefer doing an entire job and seeing the results than performing one step of it repetitively. They also need recognition for their achievements, but a certain amount of freedom from close supervision. Thus the customer service manager may be the main influence in motivating customer service workers, simply through his or her ability to influence the working environment, to change frustrating policies and procedures, and to design work that is satisfying and recognizing achievement as it occurs.

The two most important rules for the manager in this respect are: (1) workers must know specifically what is expected of them; and (2) they must receive immediate feedback on how well they are achieving these goals. Recognition should be immediate. A figurative pat on the back, a word of thanks or congratulations at the time of the achievement—these are more powerful incentives than a plaque or trophy given at the annual banquet six months later. Many managers say that an occasional dinner, tickets to a baseball game or similar forms of recognition are preferable because they can be given immediately and informally.

Surprisingly, salary is not a major motivational factor for most workers. Money is a form of recognition, but it is the status that money conveys that counts rather than the money itself. Thus it is important that customer service salaries be competitive within the company, but not necessarily within the geographical area.* Beyond this, the manager who pays close attention to the four main motivators—achievement, recognition, work itself, and responsibility—will be in control of the psychological environment and can turn to the work itself and the physical environment in the workplace.

Parity of Physical Surroundings

As mentioned earlier, it is essential that the customer service workplace at the least be on a par with other departments in terms of space per worker, decor, furniture and the like. In some respects it should exceed the standards for other departments: carpeting, soundproofing and partitioning are particularly desirable because of the typically high noise levels and distracting activity. If flextime and part time workers are employed, the layout should accommodate the fluctuating workload without disrupting ongoing activities.

Whenever possible, the customer service manager should have a "prestige" office, outside and preferably a corner. Given the choice between an onsite cubicle close to the day-to-day activity and a more remote, luxury-type office, the manager

---

*Although it is true that salary generally ranks quite low as an actual motivator to productivity, it is clearly an important consideration in hiring new personnel. Additionally, a salary survey conducted in 1983 showed that salaries for customer service representatives appeared to be national rather than regional, that is where there had previously been significant regional differences in compensation, by 1983 these differences had all but disappeared. The survey is reported in detail in *Customer Service Newsletter,* Vol. 11 No. 10, October 15, 1983.

should select the luxury office even though it may be less convenient. The reason for this is simply that it is important to employees to establish the status of their manager as being on a par with, or perhaps a notch above, other managers. Also, there should be no need for the manager to be immediately in the midst of departmental activity. The manager's job is to plan and manage, not to have "shirtsleeves involvement" in the daily routine, nor to be too readily accessible to front-line personnel.

The department itself should not be a thoroughfare, yet at the same time it should not be remote from other departments and the reception area. The department should definitely *not* be placed in the warehousing or shipping area simply because it is sometimes involved with these functions. It is equally important that it be accessible to *other* departments, perhaps more important. Certainly it is important that the department have visibility, and this means proximity to other departments and their executives, including top management whenever possible.

Given these basics, what should the department look like and how should it be furnished? First, a general rule: the department should project professionalism, competence, efficiency and productivity both in the way it is laid out and in its actual decor. For the specifics, this is clearly an area where professional guidance is needed. The customer service manager has one advantage here, however. That is that he or she can call the customer service managers of some of the larger office furniture manufacturers for general ideas and suggestions, and possibly visit some actual installations and talk to other managers onsite. The manager should definitely take advantage of the willingness of other customer service managers to share useful information of this type.

Dress Code

A reasonable dress code is basic to an image of professionalism. Workers who dress in blue jeans and T-shirts do not reflect professionalism, and will quickly be equated with "touch" laborers and custodial personnel. If the working environment is poor, it is all the more important that personnel look *better than* their environment so that the manager can impress management with the necessity of upgrading that environment.

It follows that pride in self that is reflected in personal appearance is fundamental to pride in job and department, and pride in the firm and its services and products—and the quality of its customer service.

Work Design and Job Enrichment

As it applies to customer service work, job enrichment is a means of designing work in such a way as to provide some of the job rewards other than money referred to earlier. For the existing customer service department, this often means rewriting job descriptions and reassigning responsibilities. Of course job enrichment should not be interpreted as simply assigning additional work without improving the basic quality of the job. Some examples of job enrichment applicable to customer service are listed below.

- Changing the customer service job from simply order taking to total account responsibility for selected accounts.
- Enabling individual customer service representatives to develop "specialties," so that one might become a specialist in export matters, another in claims, another in technical applications, another in returns and so forth. This encourages reps to turn to their peers for special assistance rather than to supervisors or the manager, and it reinforces the concept of the team which is so important in customer service.
- Eliminating some of the usual signoffs or review and control steps from reps' work—credits and adjustments, for example—and increasing their levels of accountability and responsibility.
- Involving personnel in more complex and mind-stretching tasks, for example, analyzing accounts for profitability.

- Involving reps in specific management tasks such as preparation of budgets.
- Permitting employees to make decisions that affect their own working conditions: flextime, job sharing, part time, etc.
- Developing new skills: inside selling and telemarketing are particularly appropriate for many departments at this time.
- Offering field assignments providing customer contact, a particularly valuable activity for all concerned.

Participative Management and Quality Circles

Customer service is exceptionally well suited to constant improvement and upgrading through participative management, quality circles and similar approaches. All have a basic premise that workers have input to management decisions in one or more of several ways as listed below.

- Through an organized procedure whereby workers in a task force-type group formulate recommendations for improving productivity, cutting costs, changing procedures, etc., and submit these recommendations to management.
- By managerial delegation of broader responsibility for decision-making to front line personnel.
- By managerial affirmation that customer service representatives are expected to depart from company policy when they are genuinely convinced that it is in the company's interest to do so, and without necessarily consulting others.
- By requiring personnel to make independent decisions affecting their hours of work as in flextime, workspace arrangement, job rotation, participation in field visitations to customers, telemarketing and other activities.

Quality circles were originally developed in the U.S. but were popularized in Japan and then reimported to the U.S. They are a form of participative management whereby employees meet at regular intervals and through an organized procedure develop ideas for improved quality of output, improved efficiency and productivity, and improved interdepartmental transactions. In some versions, the manager participates and may serve as facilitator, i.e., as a sort of parliamentarian rather than actual chairperson. In other versions—and these seem to be in the majority—the manager does not participate at all.

There are many other versions, of course, of participative management. Most have excellent potential as motivators and morale builders because they give the individual employee a sense of self-worth: a sense of belonging and contributing. They are also an excellent means for gaining credibility and acceptance for ideas that might be resisted if the manager introduced them unilaterally. Some managers report that well-motivated quality circles, operating without managers' participation or intervention, have generated excellent ideas that they—the managers—had wanted to put into effect but had hesitated for fear of the resistance they expected to meet.

It goes without saying that participative management programs must ultimately produce some rewards for employees. The rewards do not have to be monetary, however, nor do they have to involve special privileges. The greatest reward any employee or group of employees can have is to see ideas or recommendations being actually accepted and put into action. Whenever possible, the employee or employees responsible should be directly involved in the actual implementation of the recommendation or proposal.

Communications and Information Systems

It has been stressed throughout that the customer service department is the "nerve center" of the organization. Much of its activity is concerned with securing and communicating information. And inadequacies in the supporting systems can be strong demotivators. Poor or malfunctioning systems hamper productivity and demoralize workers. The list below suggests some basic requirements for such systems:

- Reliability of performance and freedom from mechanical defects.
  - Speed and ease of access.
  - Flexibility, user-friendliness.
  - Adequacy of programming.
  - Customer-orientation rather than program-orientation.
  - Timeliness of updates and other information.
  - Safeguards against major errors.
- (For communications systems) automatic dialing or redialing where appropriate.
- (For computers) availability of special programs for substitutions, special "prompts" for telemarketing, etc.

It follows that high usage telephone systems should incorporate a fair system for distributing calls and measuring productivity by type of call as well as by number and duration. Support equipment like Telex, facsimile transmission, microfilm or microfiche should meet equal criteria. Customer service personnel work with communications and information systems almost constantly and are highly motivated to respond with speed, accuracy and completeness of information. And become extremely frustrated when they cannot. Continuing problems with systems are an important demotivator.

One example of this is the typical batch system, where customer service representatives have limited access or can only input orders during certain hours of the day. In some companies, this means that all orders must be entered into the system before noon or 1:00 p.m.; orders received later either must wait until the next day or else be "walked through" the system by the individual rep. This is time-consuming and interferes with other work: still another source of frustration.

In short, customer service representatives see themselves as having a primary mission of helping customers by providing and transferring information. Anything that interferes with that process, whether mechanical failures of telephone or computer systems or inadequacy of programming, will frustrate that mission and dampen the enthusiasm of those charged with carrying it out.

Job Rotation

Job rotation can be a particularly useful way of maintaining high morale and interest. There are several versions. In its most basic form, the individual performs one job in the morning and a different job in the afternoon. For example, in one firm where customer service personnel are highly skilled in electronics applications, half of the group handle phone inquiries in the morning while the other half are researching inquiries made the previous afternoon. In the afternoon, personnel who handled calls in the morning turn to research on the calls received at that time, while the other group takes over the telephones. The rotation provides a healthy variety, since the reps find the calls somewhat stressful and the research enjoyable by contrast.

In another firm, customer service reps handle orders and simple inquiries four days a week and on their fifth day handle complaints, rotating days so that there is always a complement to handle complaints. Here, telephone orders are preferred to complaints, and yet there are few enough complaints so that one or two persons daily can handle them. The individual employee knows that he or she will be handling complaints only one day a week. In yet another firm, reps each have one day per week for telemarketing, rotated in similar fashion so that others will handle their regular accounts during their telemarketing day. In this instance, the telemarketing day is seen as an incentive, something to be looked forward to as a break from the regular customer service duties.

Expanded versions of job rotation involve placing the individual in another job for a period running from several weeks to a year or more. Sometimes, headquarters personnel can be rotated to a branch or field warehouse or to another job at headquarters. In a few instances companies have been able to place personnel at a customer location—for example, at a distributor or dealership—where they will gain priceless experience and renewed motivation through better understanding of how their performance impacts customers and others in the field.

Contests and Incentive Programs

Contests and incentive programs have proliferated widely in customer service departments in recent years. Unfortunately, there have been almost as many failures as successes—mainly because the managers who started the programs did not realize that running a customer service incentive program is likely to be a full-time job and should be assigned to somebody who can devote the necessary time to it.

Programs which depend on voluntary nominations of individuals for outstanding performance do not work especially well for customer service activities. Good customer service performance is not necessarily dramatic or spectacular, and some contests reward "newsworthy" deeds rather than consistently good day-to-day performance. One company with an otherwise excellent program saw its program lose credibility when it started selecting persons whose accomplishments made good press releases but did not make any significant contribution to the firm's customer service performance.

Not surprisingly, money does not seem to be any more of a motivator than contests which offer primarily recognition—a plaque and dinner with the president of the corporation, for example, or "team" productivity contests between different branches of a firm or teams within the customer service department. As mentioned earlier, immediate recognition in the form of praise or thanks for a rep's performance is often the best motivator of all. In one firm, the customer service manager informally awards two plaques each month: one designates the individual as "Customer Service Rep of the Month," and is kept on the individual's desk during this period. The other award is designated "Goof-Up of the Month" and is similarly placed on the desk of the individual who made the most serious error during the preceding month. If no serious errors were made during the previous month, the manager must keep the "Goof-Up" award on her desk for the entire month. Here it is seen by management and other department heads and of course is a source of amusement as

This year will present to each of us new challenges, old problems, but unique opportunities. It will be a year of economic slow down which has the "experts" telling us opportunity will be less, and they are probably right. You can be assured that our marketing people will make every attempt to keep us competitive, and our manufacturing people will put out the best quality material they can. So where can we make our contribution? By offering the best possible service we can; in fact, we should strive to have our service integrity second to none.

To help us achieve this goal at **all** branches, we are announcing a new quarterly Customer Service Incentive Contest, starting January 1. The details are listed below:

Eligibility

a) All branches.

b) The office manager and the entire staff will be able to participate.

Standards of Competition

a) Service Integrity—35 percent weight of importance.

The composite score from the monthly reports will be used, i.e., calculate total orders shipped, repromised, and missed for the three months. If more than one plant has a 100 per cent rate, then each will be ranked number one. The next highest plant will be number two, etc.

b) Productivity—30 per cent weight of importance.

This will be calculated by dividing the total number of orders shipped per quarter, by the number of office personnel, including the office manager. Part-time hourly employees would be considered 1/2 person. Head count totals will be given to me each quarter by the RPOD Personnel Department. The plant with the highest productivity will be number one, next highest number two, etc.

c) Returns & Allowances—20 percent weight of importance.

This will be a percentage calculated by dividing the dollar value of "Service" error C&A's by the total dollars shipped for the quarter. The branch with the lowest percentage will be number one, next lowest number two, etc.

d) Cost Per Order—15 percent weight of importance.

This will be the total of the controlled variable cost divided by the number of orders shipped. The lowest cost will be number one, next lowest number two, etc. The variable cost used will be:

1. Salary labor	5. T&E.
2. Social Security.	6. Taxes
3. Pension	7. Sundries
4. Group Insurance	8. Telephone & telegraph

Below is an example (using just six branches) of how the tabulations and standings will be calculated:

Branch	Service Integrity (.35) Standings	Score*	Productivity (.30) Standings	Score*
A	5	1.75	6	1.80
B	12	4.20	4	1.20
C	3	1.05	5	1.50
D	2	.70	10	3.00
E	8	2.80	9	2.70
F	14	4.90	3	.90

*The score is found by multiplying the number in the Standings column by the weight given that category. For example, 5 x .35 = 1.75.

Branch	R&A's (.20) Standings	Score*	Cost Per Order (.15) Standings	Score*
A	3	.60	2	.30
B	18	3.60	9	1.35
C	8	1.60	6	.90
D	11	2.20	16	2.40
E	4	.80	3	.45
F	6	1.20	11	1.65

*The score is found by multiplying the number in the Standings column by the weight given that category. For example, 3 x .20 = .60.

Branch	Total Points	Final Standings
A	4.45	1
B	10.35	6
C	5.05	2
D	8.30	3
E	10.10	5
F	8.65	4

The calculation ("score") is simply the final standings of each category times the weight of each category. The points in each category are added into one grand total. The branch with the lowest number of points is first, the branch with the next lowest points is second, etc. It will be done this way each quarter. To determine the annual winner, the total points for all four quarters will be used. This way, a branch may not be a quarterly winner, but if it is always near the top, it may get rewarded for its consistency.

Quarterly Awards

1st Prize:
Incentive check for Office Manager	$100
Incentive check for Office Personnel	75 each
Awards Dinner, including spouses, for all eligible people	
Quarterly plaque	

2nd Prize:
Incentive check for Office Manager	$ 75
Incentive check for Office Personnel	50 each

3rd Prize:
Incentive check for Office Manager	$ 50
Incentive check for Office Personnel	25 each

Annual Award (Branch of the Year)

Branch of the Year Dinner which includes all office personnel plus invited branch, district and headquarters personnel, including spouses.

Cash Incentive—Office Manager	$150
Cash Incentive—Office Personnel	100
Plaque	

The contest will be controlled at headquarters. In case of ties, the branch with the best service integrity wins. If still a tie, the best productivity wins, etc. If a tie still exists after all four categories, then the branch that shipped the most orders wins. If a tie still exists after this, a toss of the coin will determine the winner.

In addition to the above awards, all winners will receive much recognition in various company publications to credit the high esteem of these awards.

This contest is designed to not only reward the managers, but also to reward everyone who is part of the "service team." Service integrity can never be achieved without those people who perform the day to day tasks of handling customer calls, invoicing, inventory control, traffic scheduling, production planning, etc., or the people who put a smile in their voice when the customer calls. Our sales plan is ambitious and we are asking our salesforce to continue to make our business grow. We can make a significant contribution to a successful and profitable year by offering our customers the service integrity needed to give us the competitive edge. And we can have fun doing it.

Figure 19-2. The Model Customer Service Incentive Contest reproduced here is based on materials furnished through the courtesy of Doug Doherty, Manager, Customer Service, for Owens-Corning Fiberglas Corporation, Toledo. All proprietary information has been deleted, and numbers and locations are fictitious and for demonstration purposes only.

well as actual motivation to other personnel in the department.

An incentive program between groups could follow the lines of the program depicted in figure 2. In this case, the contest is run between the branches of a firm with customer service representatives at multiple locations, making allowance for differences in operations and sales volume. This program has several advantages over programs directed mainly at individuals. It avoids the problem of the different levels of visibility and responsibility of different people in a given department. It also compensates for differences in both volume and value of work performed. Most importantly, it fosters the team spirit that is so fundamental in customer service. In this particular company, the program has recently been enhanced by expanding it to include warehouse personnel at the participating branches.

As a general recommendation, the manager should start with a modest program which can be monitored easily, and which should run over a sufficiently long period to establish credibility. The program should above all be fair, and the prizes or awards suitable but not excessive. Hopefully, the individual has already been praised for the specific accomplishment, so that the award ceremony itself should be staged primarily for its value as a motivator of others—and a reminder throughout the company that customer service is indeed the business of the business.

All This—and the Hawthorne Effect

It is a fact well known to industrial psychologists that almost any attention paid to workers will result in improved performance. This is called the "Hawthorne Effect" because the underlying research was performed at the Hawthorne Works of Western Electric Company in Cicero, Illinois. Researchers concluded that workers responded as much to the actual attention they received as to what was done when different work environments were created: changes in the lighting level, for example— raising light levels increased productivity . . . but so did lowering light levels! This fact can be particularly valuable to the customer service manager because there are so many different facets of customer service where changes can be instituted or tested without a major commitment. This fact alone will be motivational per se, and it should establish and maintain the manager's reputation as an innovator as well as motivator in the most important area of the firm's business.

20

CUSTOMER SERVICE COMMUNICATIONS: TELEPHONE SYSTEMS AND PROCEDURES

Communications to and from the customer service department typically represent over half of a firm's total communications. A typical customer service representative has 15 to 20 times as many customer contacts, hour for hour, as anybody else in the company. Management may spend hundreds of thousands of dollars for "public relations" but in truth few things affect a company's standing with its customers as profoundly as those hour-by-hour contacts with customer service personnel.

Whether or not it is specifically assigned, the customer service manager has a direct responsibility for the quality and efficiency of those communications—and, through them, for the firm's public image as well as its bottom line. And the manager should recognize that the most efficient communications are not necessarily the best communications, and vice versa. In short, communications should meet quality standards that satisfy company objectives—and have a price tag consistent with the quality as well as the company's budget.

As an example, one company with an advanced call management system and some 50 customer service reps handling routine transactions was averaging an incredible 300 telephone transactions *per rep* daily, when it decided to test whether or not a cash incentive would increase the number of calls handled. Indeed it did; some reps actually increased the number of calls handled to more than 400! The only flaw was that the quality of

Setting Standards of Performance for Customer Service Communications

At Bendix Automotive Aftermarket, Jackson, Tenn., Customer Service Supervisor Harley Allen has developed a unique set of standards for internal customer service department operations—and an equally unique method of rating individual employees' performance against them.

The eight standards shown as A through H in the accompanying table are assigned weights or values in terms of their relative importance to the firm's overall objectives. These weights or values add up to 100, so that in effect anyone doing a perfect job would get a score of 100. In practice, each employee rates himself or herself against each individual standard; earning 10 points out of a possible 15, for example, or 6 against 10 and so forth. These scores are then added up to provide a composite number representing the employee's over-all score against a possible 100.

At the same time, Harley makes an independent rating of the employee's performance against the same standards and similarly determines his or her score against a possible 100. He then compares his determinations with those of the employee, and decides whether any adjustments should be made.

Total Value	Standards: Procedure or Activity	Self Score	Supv. Score
15	A. All telephone calls are answered within three rings accurately and courteously, with no complaints received resulting from the quality of the service rendered.	_____	_____
15	B. All telephone callback messages will be returned within fifteen minutes of the original call.	_____	_____
20	C. All callbacks to be made at the time promised whether or not there is anything new to report.	_____	_____
10	D. 90% of inquiries to be handled while the customer is on the phone.	_____	_____
10	E. All status reports or open order reconciliation reports will be completed and returned within five working days.	_____	_____
10	F. 90% of inquiries on order status to be answered within two hours with the balance which would include tracing and expediting of shipments within four hours.	_____	_____
10	G. Respond to request for shipping promise in accordance with the type of promise needed. Emergency (4 hours); Special Handling (8 hours); Standard Request (24 hours).	_____	_____
10	H. All written correspondence will be processed and mailed within five working days from receipt of request to contact customer.	_____	_____

the transactions deteriorated so badly, with reps hustling from one call to the next, that the incentive system was quickly abandoned.

Setting Communications Objectives

This incident underlines the importance of setting specific objectives for customer service communications in terms of both quality and productivity and then designing the system accordingly. The first step is to identify specific communications needs.

One customer service manager, faced with the problem of handling a substantially increased workload of telephone orders, correctly diagnosed the situation as requiring not more people, but rather a system that would make better use of the people-skills already present in the department. He recognized that taking orders by phone does not in itself require exceptional skills, but that follow-up calls related to those orders often do require such skills. And for every 100 calls placed by phone there may be as many as 20, 30 or more additional calls from customers about order status, billing, errors, returns, applications and other matters.

This manager said to himself: "If I hire more people to take orders, I'll be adding a double burden to my existing staff: training the new personnel, plus handling all the additional followup calls they will be generating." He realized that an ideal situation might be to have the new people do nothing but take orders and have his present people do nothing but handle inquiries and exceptions. But he also realized that management would not approve that kind of budget. So he did the next best thing: he "hired" four state-of-art answering machines and four dedicated trunk lines terminating at the machines. He set up schedules for order placement to balance calls to these machines so that they would rarely all be tied up at the same time. When they were all tied up, the call would roll over to a live human being. Otherwise, all orders would be recorded and the tapes removed and transcribed as input on a regular schedule. This

A Checklist of Customer Communications

1. Inbound—From Customers

☐ Inquiries about product availability and price
☐ Inquiries about product features and applications
☐ Inquiries about order status and delivery
☐ General inquiries; explanation and clarification
☐ Order placement
☐ Change orders
☐ Complaints
☐ Trouble reports: loss, damage, errors, malfunctions
☐ Requests for return authorization
☐ Requests for credit or adjustment
☐ Unauthorized deductions, chargebacks
☐ Miscellaneous communications including emergencies

2. Outbound—To Customers

☐ Inquiry response: product availability and price
☐ Inquiry response: product features and applications
☐ Inquiry response: order status and delivery
☐ Inquiry response: general*
☐ Order acceptance and confirmation, including changes
☐ Complaint handling and resolution
☐ Dispatch or resolution of trouble reports
☐ Authorization for returns, credits and adjustments
☐ Queries to customers: order clarification
☐ Queries to customers: acceptability of substitutions, split shipments and other variances
☐ Notifying customers of credit holds
☐ Telemarketing: to regular customers, marginal accounts, non-customers

* In many companies the customer service department acts as a clearing house for queries of all types; when the switchboard does not know where to route a particular call, it will usually give it to the customer service department. Some of these calls will be handled by customer service personnel, but others will be transferred to the appropriate departments.

- ☐ Notifying customers of delays, errors and other problems
- ☐ Exceptions reporting to customers, verbal and written
- ☐ Policy and procedure guides, printed
- ☐ Telephone and personnel directories, printed
- ☐ "Meet the People" and memento or reminder mailings, newsletters
- ☐ Miscellaneous spoken and written communications and forms

3. Internal—Interdepartmental

- ☐ Contacts with credit department about customer credit status
- ☐ Contacts with accounts receivable about invoices, deductions
- ☐ Contacts with production planning about schedules, availability
- ☐ Contacts with quality control about product defects
- ☐ Contacts with shipping and warehousing about order status, changes, emergency shipments, etc.
- ☐ Contacts with traffic about routings, claims, shipment location
- ☐ Contacts with purchasing about resale parts availability
- ☐ Contacts with legal department about claims, liability and special situations—pricing, pickup allowances, liability, etc.
- ☐ Contacts with executive department about major policy matters
- ☐ Contacts with personnel department about personnel, compensation, training, etc.
- ☐ Contacts with administrative department about information systems, communications, procedures
- ☐ Contacts with sales departments about pricing, order status, delivery, expedites, special situations and general customer service matters

4. Other Communications

- ☐ Contact with customers through participation in co-selling or visits to customers with sales personnel and others
- ☐ Conducting plant tours for customers and other visitors
- ☐ Field assignments of reps as counterpersons at branch locations
- ☐ Participation in trade shows, public seminars and similar events
- ☐ Participation in professional organizations

would mean that reps would be freed up for problem-solving and other activities where their considerable personal skills would find good utilization. They would be more accessible to customers because they would not be tied up taking lengthy orders, line by line. And without the inherent pressure of constant blinking lights of calls on "hold," they would be more likely to do a more thorough job on the exception-type calls they would mainly be handling—thus resolving many problems at the outset and avoiding others in the future.

This particular installation was so successful that the department actually increased its order-handling capacity by more than 100% without adding a single person to the staff. The four trunk lines and associated answering machines represented a relatively minor investment which was more than offset by improved productivity in the department. Much of the credit should go to the manager for understanding that the problem went far beyond simply handling more orders, that it really concerned the quality of the follow-up phone calls associated with those orders and beyond that the quality of customer communications generally.*

Another example of setting objectives concerns a firm with some 25 customer service reps already handling exceptions— inquiries and complaints—exclusively, with all orders handled by a separate group. The firm's customer service executive estimated that if each exceptions call could be reduced one second in length, the company would save $3,500 annually in total expense. But the executive was quick to point out that the objective was not to save money per se, but rather to insure that calls were the right length—no longer than necessary, and no shorter. It was pointed out that in some instances, supplying information not asked for by the customer might take a few seconds longer but

---

*It should be emphasized that recording devices are not necessarily suitable for all order entry applications, but in this situation they were. At this writing there is still some resistance on the part of customers to the impersonality of recorders, but this is rapidly dissipating with the proliferation of this type of technology generally.

could very well eliminate the need for a callback to or from that customer at a later date.

Here again, a central issue was the quality of the telephone transaction—in this instance, its completeness. The manager emphasized the importance of call format, i.e., getting and giving information in a standard sequence so that nothing would be overlooked, as a way to reduce costs while actually improving the quality of the customer service itself. At no time was it suggested that personnel eliminate any of the normal conversational courtesies; most experts feel that a friendly attitude on both sides facilitates communications and that brief pleasantries are well worth the time they take. On the other hand, there is no courtesy in a disorganized, sloppily managed telephone transaction which leaves one or both parties ill-informed and likely to make costly mistakes.

Certainly a major concern of the customer service manager should be the image projected by the department's communications, both spoken and written. Given that the department has a mission *to keep customers and increase the volume of their purchases,* rather than simply to fulfill orders, every contact with a customer should have as a central objective:

- To project the image of a company that cares for its customers
- To project the image of a company that is staffed by professionals
- To project the image of a company that values its reputation
- To project the image of a company that takes pride in producing quality products and/or services, and stands behind them for that reason
- To project the image of a company that appreciates every piece of business it gets, no matter how small or difficult it may be
- To project the image of a company that is friendly and helpful, and is never too busy to help a customer
- To project the image of a company that people like to do business with, because it is such a rewarding and satisfying experience

Few things are more important than winning customer confidence, and few avenues are more readily available for this purpose than the telephone. Telephone training in itself is extremely important to overall efficiency and accuracy, but even more important is training in telephone *attitude*—the projection of qualities that facilitates the communication and at the same time creates a strong bond with the customer that manifests itself in repeat and increased business.

It follows that communications objectives should also bear down on actual *function:* what the communication is expected to accomplish, and the best way of accomplishing it consistent with the type of image the company wishes to project.

Communications as a Reflection of Corporate Image

1. Attitude and tone. Given the volume of telephone calls handled daily in almost every type of business establishment, it is understandable when switchboard operators and reps alike sometimes lose sight of corporate goals and project an image of impersonality, impatience, irritation and sometimes plain rudeness.

Sometimes this is a matter of language; just as often it is a matter of procedure. For example, a customer says to a customer service rep: "Oh, I forgot to tell you. It's a different 'ship to' address." The rep, replying on the spur of the moment, responds: "You should have told me that first!" Now the customer is annoyed, and retorts: "No, you should have asked me first!" The customer is right; under the "rules of the game," the vendor is expected to lead and control the telephone transaction. The customer cannot be expected to know each vendor's unique format and procedure. In another example, the customer reads off a list of parts, laboriously reading and repeating the part numbers one by one. After the list is complete, the customer service rep, noticeably annoyed, asks: "Why didn't you tell me you wanted the complete clutch replacement kit?" To which the customer, equally annoyed, fires back: "Why didn't you ask me?"

Again, the customer is right; the vendor's telephone ordering format or interrogatory should anticipate such situations.

Perhaps one of the most pervasive attitude problems in telephone communications is the phrase "You'll have to . . ." This is used in varying contexts such as "You'll have to take that up with the credit department," "You'll have to send us the packing list," "You'll have to send us a certified check," etc. Here it is not the words themselves so much as the implication that the customer service rep is "commanding" the customer to do certain things. Actually, repeated use of the phrase "you'll have to" has even deeper implications in terms of attitude: after a while, reps begin to believe that the rules-and-regulations of their firms' policies and procedures are in fact sacred and unchangeable and customers are compelled to abide by them. In actual practice this is of course not true, and the attitude should be a matter of concern to the manager as of course it is to customers.

Sometimes, the underlying responsibility is the manager's: first, for not training personnel in acceptable language; second, in excessive fixation on rules and regulations rather than on meeting customer needs. Acceptable language to overcome the "You'll have to" syndrome is simply substitution of phrases like "would you please," or rephrasing to include a benefit for the customer: "If you'll take that up directly with the credit department, I'm sure you'll be able to resolve the matter quickly." Or, "If you'll send us the packing list, we'll investigate your claim right away."

A variation on this is the "don't" syndrome. "We don't accept open account orders from unrated firms"; "We don't accept orders after 4:30 p.m."; "We don't give refunds." All of these are "confrontational" types of responses, and can be softened considerably simply by substituting "can't" or, better, "we're sorry that we can't," as in these examples: "We can't accept checks"; "We can't handle orders after 4:30 p.m."; "We regret that we can't give refunds," etc. In some instances, a reason or benefit may be included: "Because these are sale items, we can't give refunds"; "To keep our prices as low as possible, we ask that payment be included with order." Naturally, where there are specific governmental regulations involved it is perfectly acceptable to say: "Federal law requires that I ask you (advise you, etc.) . . ."

These illustrations show how easy it is to change the language. But changing the attitude may take longer, because it often pervades the entire organization from management on down: an attitude that the customer is an adversary to be defended against rather than an asset to be nurtured and protected. One unfortunate result is that newer employees tend to develop an "all or none" attitude and apply rules across the board without regard to who the customers are. For example, placing Sears Roebuck on credit hold; or applying a minimum order charge to a follow-on order placed by a customer who forgot to include a $3.00 item with an $11,000 order.

2. "System attitude." Even without people, a poorly-conceived or managed telephone system can project an attitude of indifference. For example, an answering machine that places callers on lengthy holds to the accompaniment of music or repeated mumbling of an indistinct message—clearly a lie—that "your call will be handled shortly." While there are some highly creative applications of telephone answering devices available, relatively few appear to be used in customer service departments today. The most common is a recording device for handling overflow orders or callbacks, but even many of these are poorly programmed and tend to produce many hangups because they intimidate or offend callers. Some organizations use the "hold" period to familiarize the caller with specials, ordering procedures, or alternate phone numbers for specific types of calls. Many systems now in place and using 800-numbers suggest that customers might wish to call back during off-peak hours in order to receive immediate attention and faster service.

Additionally there are a number of third-party telephone service firms which handle overflow calls on a demand basis; that is, when the vendor's lines are all blocked with incoming calls and calls on hold, subsequent calls automatically roll over to the third party's system, where they are answered in the vendor's name. This type of system is most effective where a company has dedicated phone numbers that are used exclusively for handling orders, so that the rollover and subsequent order-taking can be "transparent," i.e., appearing to the caller to be performed by the vendor company itself rather than by a third party.

The state of the art in telephone systems is such that the most aggravating problem—lengthy holds—can often be significantly reduced via use of appropriate technology. For example, one company found the answer in installation of an automated call routing system whereby callers were automatically connected to the right regional desk as determined by call origin. This cut average wait time for callers from one minute to just over five seconds. Another company found that a similar system increased call handling capacity by almost one-third; this is another way of saying that wait time was reduced commensurately.

"System attitude" is likely to be particularly associated with calls where the customer is paying for the call, as for example, a call to a switchboard where the customer is placed on hold and watches the expensive minutes tick by. Some companies compound this perceived attitude of indifference by not permitting switchboard operators to take callback messages when internal lines are busy. Some switchboards compound it further by taking messages but not passing them along in timely fashion, and sometimes by not passing them along at all. This can reach the point of absurdity; in one company, a customer returning a call to an executive is told that all the executive's lines are busy and no message can be taken, not even one indicating that the executive's call was returned!

Sometimes the solution to the customer-paid call which is placed on lengthy and aggravating hold is surprisingly simple: ask customers to call during off-peak hours. One company found that in addition to calls on hold at the switchboard, many other calls were being blocked because all inbound trunks were tied up. It printed a few thousand flyers saying to customers: "For better service, please have your customer number and all item numbers ready, and if possible phone before 10 a.m. and after 3 p.m." The flyers were simply enclosed with orders being shipped, and the effect was immediate and dramatic—enough customers decided to call the customer service department during off-peak hours that the problem of holds and blocked calls during peak hours was virtually eliminated. The total cost was in the neighborhood of $30 for printing, as opposed to hiring additional personnel and installing more trunks, at a cost that would have run into the tens of thousands of dollars.

West Coast firms with a majority of customers in the East have a similar problem. The "window" during which their Eastern customers can call them is relatively small, and tends to coincide with the times they receive calls from local customers as well. By requesting customers in the different time zones to call during specific time frames, such firms have largely overcome the problem, which involves actual productivity as well as customers' perception of system attitude.

Other state-of-art applications that can be used to improve communications include voice-activated answering devices, interactive systems that prompt the caller by asking specific questions, and actual order systems employing touchtone telephone systems. Voice recognition systems which can recognize and respond to words and phrases are now available for limited applications, and their use will undoubtedly broaden dramatically in the near future.

Although many managers still feel there is considerable resistance among customers to the "depersonalization" that such technology represents, in actual fact they are probably projecting their own misgivings more than their customers' resistance. Generations currently in and entering the workforce are completely at home with the new technology via video games and home computers and the proliferation of automated systems in virtually every aspect of daily life. There is also considerable pressure to make better use of people—which implies using fewer people but paying them more—and relegating to machines the routine and often boring or degrading jobs that machines do best. Considering that robots are about to play important roles in daily life as babysitters, for example, who can protect latchkey children better than pets do and at the same time teach them a foreign language, there is no reason to believe that the same levels of automation will not be widely evident in customer service communications.

The key of course is making communications serve customers by being both palatable and customer-oriented. At the beginning, banks found that customers preferred dealing with live tellers to using bank machines. However, when they realized that the bank machines were generally faster for routine transactions and could be accessed at odd hours, they quickly gained in popularity. The same is true of automated communications systems, and the manager should stay constantly abreast of the many alternatives to voice-to-voice, person-to-person communications for routine transactions. Not with the goal of reducing personnel involvement in customer service, but rather with the goal of actually increasing it by zeroing in on people-to-people transactions which further the customer service mission of keeping and growing with customers.

Analyzing Telephone Requirements

Given a commitment to excellence in telephone communications, and an awareness of what is available, the manager faces a major task in actually defining what the telephone system should include and what standards should be established. Fortunately, the job is considerably simplified by the availability of practical systems for measuring existing traffic including wait times, blocked calls and call abandonments or disconnects by the customer.

Thus, decisions should be made covering each of the following aspects of telephone response:

1. How quickly the phone should be answered. Note that there are two aspects to this: the time that elapses, or the number of times it rings before there is some kind of response—switchboard, a person in the department, a recorded message, etc.; and the interval until the caller actually *reaches* a person who can help him or her. Many firms set their standards for answering within four or five rings; yet meeting these standards doesn't mean much if the caller is immediately placed on hold for an indefinite period. Callers paying for the call would often prefer not to have it answered until somebody is actually available to help them.

2. Allowable number of calls in queue, and maximum allowable hold. These are calls that have actually entered the system, but have not necessarily been responded to by a human being.

3. Allowable level of disconnects by waiting customers. This refers to customers who have gotten into the system, but are now tired of waiting and hang up.

4. Allowable number of blocked calls. These are calls that do not get into the system because all incoming lines are tied up, in many instances by calls that are on hold.

5. The likelihood that callers who disconnect or whose calls are blocked will call back. This is difficult to estimate, but there will be some basic differences between customers and non-customers (with established customers more likely to call back, albeit with some irritation) and between paid and toll-free callers (with the toll-free callers more likely to call back).

6. Policies and procedures affecting length, frequency and timing of calls. Each year-end a major branch of a postage meter firm is deluged with calls from customers wanting to know how to change the date on their machines. This blocks calls from other customers requiring repair service on vital equipment where downtime is critical; the firm might be able to avoid much of the problem (and the expense) of handling so many calls through the expedient of an instructional enclosure with the previous month's rental invoice, or some similar approach. Of course the firm might also consider using an "overflow" third party service where calls would automatically switch over when all trunks were busy.

7. The extent to which customers' present calling patterns can be modified. That is, the extent to which customers can be persuaded to call at different or off-peak hours. In some instances, simply asking customers to do so will find a sufficient percentage doing so to balance the call load; in others, it may be desirable to offer a specific incentive like faster service.

At this juncture, the customer service manager has the underlying information needed to determine what the general configuration of the telephone system should be, including actual call capacity for present demands as well as future growth. It's assumed that the manager will first do as much as possible to smooth out call patterns in order to get maximum utilization with the minimum numbers of both personnel and units of equipment, recognizing that even under the best conditions it may be necessary to have some part time personnel plus equipment that is used mainly during peak periods.

It's also assumed that the manager will have considered such alternatives as different lines for different types of calls, for example, trunks answered by a recorder for short and uncomplicated orders, trunks answered by people for longer orders and inquiries of all types. Finally, it's assumed that the manager has looked at other events, as in the case of the postage meters, that can influence phone traffic and may be handled in different ways to reduce that traffic. (Note that even the actual placement of phones can affect equipment and personnel requirements; if phones are too far from files or other references, travel time back and forth will stretch the queue and slow response time significantly.)

The basic procedure for deciding how many phones to have, and how many people to service them appears in this book's Appendix. Most telephone organizations and interconnect firms will provide substantial assistance in these areas. While it is impractical to describe here all the options that are currently available, certainly it will pay the manager to visit other installations and find out at first hand their pros and cons for customer service applications. For example, whether calls should go through the switchboard, or directly to the department—or directly to specified individuals within the department. Or, whether it will pay to have calls "pre-routed" by origin; in this application, all callers nationwide call the same number, but are routed to different extensions (and sometimes to different geographic locations hundreds or thousands of miles apart) depending on the point of origin of each call.

The Issue of Toll-Free Numbers

Although a large majority—84%—of manufacturing companies surveyed in October, 1983 were found to have toll-free inbound telephone lines, there was still considerable question about their actual value. For example, more than half the companies with toll-free lines had found it necessary to impose restrictions on their use, as shown in the following data:

Do not have toll-free number 16%

Have toll-free number with restrictions. 45%

Have toll-free number, no restrictions . . 39%

Some typical restrictions included use of the numbers for order placement only, for calls to designated departments only, for use by sales reps only, for use by customers only (and sometimes by designated customers only), for calls about problem products only, and during specified hours only. There may also be restrictions on the actual length of calls as well.

Many of these restrictions have been imposed in an attempt to minimize "trivial" or unnecessary calls that would not be made if the caller had to pay for the call. For example, one company found that its branches were making use of the firm's central toll-free number repetitively during the day for matters of routine internal business, and in the process cutting their own telephone costs—but also blocking calls from the very customers for whom the number had been intended. For similar reasons, many companies designate their toll-free numbers as nontransferable: that is, the lines terminate in the customer service department, and callers who wish to speak to other departments must call them directly or through the company switchboard at their own expense.

There is some disagreement about these restrictions. Some managers argue that if a customer is given a toll-free number for order placement, that same customer ought to be able to use the same number for order status inquiries, complaints and other calls. Other managers argue that if they opened up their toll-free numbers to all calls, the lines would be so choked with trivial calls that often the important ones would not be able to get through.

It is certainly a fact that the availability of an 800-number generally produces a sharp increase in the total number of inbound calls, although there is some question as to how much it produces in the way of additional business. The mail order industry is an exception here: studies have shown that toll-free numbers do increase business, particularly in the fact that orders coming in this way are larger, dollar for dollar, than orders coming in by mail. At the same time, a few upscale firms with extremely loyal followings appear to have decided that toll-free numbers do not make that much difference.

Meeting the Competition

For most manufacturing firms, the issue of whether or not to have a toll-free number is decided rather simply: what is the competition doing? Firms that sell through distributors have found that, given a choice between a vendor with a toll-free number and one without, the distributor will usually call the vendor with the toll-free number. This is because distributorships are usually hands-on entrepreneurships where the boss has made it quite clear that every opportunity to save shall be capitalized on: a penny saved is a penny earned. In larger organizations such as are found in the original equipment market, buyers are more remote from management and in any event tend to be driven more by overall economies in laid-down costs than by incidental savings in the cost of order placement itself.

Are the Economies Real?

But the real issue in toll-free numbers is whether there are in fact any real economies for the customer. First of all, it's basic that all costs are borne by the customer in the end anyway. Regardless of whose phone bill they show up on, the customer is paying for those toll-free lines just as surely as if they showed up on his or her regular monthly phone bill. What is not quite as obvious, however, is the fact that the toll-free numbers may actually be *increasing* costs for some customers:

1. By making it too easy for personnel to call vendors, the toll-free numbers encourage inefficient ordering practices and frequent phone calls. The cost of the time itself of the personnel involved can be significant over and above the purchasing diseconomies of unplanned buying.

2. Customers with well-organized buying practices who make few calls on the toll-free number are actually penalized, because they must also pay part of the cost of the extra lines required when other customers make excessive use of the system, often on trivial matters.

A major concern for some customer service managers is this entire issue of whether "the bad drives out the good," so to speak—whether by encouraging trivial calls, toll-free numbers may block out calls of greater importance. It's universally true that publication of a toll-free number will be followed by a sharp increase in the number of calls received, and that this in turn often requires installing additional trunks with additional personnel to handle the increased volume. Some managers feel that this is desirable. "We want to *hear* from our customers," they say. "We *need* to hear everything that's on their mind. And we have to give them an opportunity to sound off, to ventilate, or we may lose them. So, we make it easy for them to reach us."

Other managers are not as optimistic. One company, recognizing the special needs of the first-time customer, decided that such customers should be given every encouragement to phone if they encountered any problem whatsoever with their first order. This company felt, rightly, that the first order is often a test and that if the first-time customer is not genuinely encouraged to ventilate any dissatisfaction whatsoever, he or she may end up being a last-time customer as well. Thus, the toll-free number was prominently displayed on the packing slips accompanying all first-time orders, and customers were urged to call to voice any disappointment with their orders.

It was a great idea, but what the company had not taken into account was the fact that the toll-free number was already overburdened with other calls. When first-time customers called with a problem, they often got busy signals, which increased their dissatisfaction and in some cases lost them as customers. They felt, with some justification, that the company didn't really want to hear from them and that the toll-free hotline was just another gimmick. For the company, the ultimate solution was to install a toll-free number for the exclusive purpose of serving new customers, an expense which management was somewhat reluctant to underwrite. Fortunately, the manager had data to show the beneficial effect of complaining on repeat business vs. the amount of business lost when complaints are not actually articulated (see chapter 24 on complaint handling).

It seems inevitable that most larger companies doing business nationally will ultimately install toll-free numbers for their customers. Equally, however, customers will ultimately come to the realization that they are paying indirectly for these numbers and will impose restrictions on their own personnel on excessive use adding to the cost of such service and also interfering with their own productivity. An educated guess today is that many of the vendors' restrictions on toll-free numbers will ultimately be abandoned as well. Even today, companies which do not publish their toll-free numbers find that they quickly become known and used for purposes for which they weren't intended. And it's not easy to tell callers—customers and non-customers alike—to hang up and call back at their own expense.

How Long Will Callers Hold?

Some companies impose strict standards on how long a customer will be permitted to hold before the call is handled or a callback message is taken. These standards are usually less than a minute. Other companies set no limits, but expect the operator to cut in every 30 seconds to ask if the customer wishes to continue holding. When customers pay for their own calls, the abandonment or hang-up rate goes up significantly after the first 30 to 45 seconds. On toll-free calls, callers will stay on the line quite a bit longer—up to three minutes, and sometimes five if contacted by the operator at frequent intervals. Some other findings:

• Callers will hold longer for a named individual than for a department.

• Although many companies take callers' names for call-backs, the customers often call back before there has been an opportunity to return the call. This is particularly true with toll-free numbers.

• Irate customers will sometimes hold for an exceptionally long time, but become progressively more irate as they do.

• A caller will remain on the line longer "if there is a sense of being helped."

• Potential customers and non-customers will generally hold longer on an 800-number than regular customers, who will simply decide to call back later.

• Persons filing claims or with other beneficial interests in the call will often stay on the line for lengthy periods, but as noted above their irritation quotient tends to increase com-mensurately. By contrast, hotlines that are answered promptly tend to defuse complaints quickly; it's been well established that the speed with which a company acknowledges and responds to a complaint is often more important than the actual resolution of that complaint.

Outbound Telephone Calls

Outbound telephone calling presents a somewhat different situation from inbound. First of all, it is more subject to abuse by company personnel: calls to friends and relatives, "dial-a-porn" calls and similar undertakings have been widely reported. On the other hand, many of these abuses are relatively easy to control via access or authorization numbers and similar devices. Many companies have found that news of the pending installation of measuring and monitoring devices usually produced an immediate drop in the volume of personal calls.

Of course outbound calls are easy to track and cost out, simply by reviewing the telephone bill. But this can be deceptive. One company was concerned with the size of its outbound telephone bill, and in particular the large number of calls originating in the customer service department and lasting longer than three minutes. So the controller's office started circulating copies of the phone bill with calls longer than three minutes highlighted with a fluorescent marking pen. Shortly thereafter, the number of calls over three minutes dropped almost to zero—but the total number of calls increased dramatically. Customer service reps, clocking their calls, were simply saying to customers—"Oh—my three minutes are up; hang up and I'll call you right back!"

This suggests also that in reviewing outbound calls, the manager should weigh the pros and cons of discouraging such calls vs. actively encouraging them. For example, customer service reps who are discouraged from making outbound calls to customers may decide not to call when potential problems arise, or when there are questions about orders or other instructions from customers. These errors of omission are usually far more expensive than the telephone "savings" that motivated them in the first place.

There are also tradeoffs between inbound and outbound calls in another respect: continued failure to contact customers about delays and other problems quickly results in loss of confidence on the part of customers, which in turn is reflected in a dramatic increase in the number of *inbound* calls, many of them unnecessary, about order status and similar subjects. Thus it's possible that a 5% cut in outbound calls may actually result in a 25% increase in inbound calls; the savings in outbound calls are completely washed out by the cost of servicing the increased volume of inbound calls that result.

It is important that customer service personnel be as well trained in *making* calls as they are in *receiving* them. Indeed, in some respects outbound calls may require greater skills, for example, in breaking bad news to customers. But reps should be made aware that the main costs of the call are not the line charges per se, but the combined costs of their own time plus the positive or negative results of the way in which they actually make the call. In notifying a customer that an order has been significantly delayed, a skillful caller may persuade the customer not to cancel the order but to wait until it is filled or to substitute another product. A less skillful caller may see the customer erupt into anger and cancel the order, and perhaps future orders as well.

Because outbound calls are generally more controllable than inbound, it is also easier to make determinations about paid vs. toll-free lines on economic grounds. A company with a high volume of outbound calls in a telemarketing or inside selling application, or in calls to branches and sales offices, can forecast overall call volume as well as call duration and call destinations with reasonable certainty, and can then compare the various telephone services available as to economics and other features. Companies with a high volume of calls to a relatively small group of customers—brokers or manufacturers' agents, for example—may want to install automatic dial and re-dial systems to avoid the frustrations to reps inherent in dialing and re-dialing access codes, area codes and telephone numbers that may run into as many as 18 or 20 digits.

Which System to Choose?

At this writing, following shortly the breakup of AT&T and deregulation of many aspects of telephone service, there are many options available in both service and equipment. It is beyond the scope of this book to review what is currently available, or to make recommendations. In fact, there is considerable literature on the subject, including several magazines and a number of newsletters. Generally speaking, the customer service manager will be only one of a number of people who will be involved in the selection of a company's system. Even so, he or she should make absolutely certain that the interests of the customer service department are actively represented and its needs clearly defined before any final determination is made.

The manager should also be aware that today's order entry and telephone systems are in many cases transitional, and that state-of-art developments within the next few years are likely to have far-reaching impact on the way the business of the customer service department is conducted. Any investment in systems today should take this into account, and should have sufficient built-in flexibility to accommodate such future changes.

Why Did the Customer (o

In customer service circles, it's referred to as "abandoning the call": a customer or prospective customer places a call to a vendor and can't get through to the customer service department—and at some point hangs up without completing the transaction.

Although we can measure the number of calls that are abandoned within a given time-frame, we have no certain way of measuring how many of these call back later vs. how many don't call back, or call a competitor. However, we do have some statistics on callers who get to the switchboard but no further. In one study, 46% of the callers who got that far and left their names for a callback were found to have changed their minds in the interval between placing the call and being called back, usually the same day.

Lost sales are of course a very real cost of blocked or abandoned phone calls, but there are other, more subtle costs that have to be taken into account as well. These would include more irate customers to deal with—and more time required to deal with them, thus blocking more calls—more emergency situations escalated because customers couldn't get through to report them while they were still manageable, and extreme wear-and-tear on all personnel involved.

Why Did the Customer Hang Up? These are the Apparent Reasons:

Possibility No. 1: Phone rang an excessive number of times without being answered.

Possibility No. 2: Trunks or direct lines busy.

Possibility No. 3: Placed on hold (or in queue) for an excessive amount of time.

Possibility No. 4: Disconnected or left on dead line too long in process of being transferred.

Possibility No. 5: Transferred too many times.

Possibility No. 6: General disgust at manner of treatment.

Now for the Real Reasons

1. Phone rang an excessive number of times without being answered.

    a. Switchboard. Combination switchboard-receptionist function may interfere with prompt servicing of calls as well as walk-ins. Or, personnel at switchboard may be tied up trying to answer questions from callers. This could reflect insufficient training, lack of monitoring or supervision, or failure to provide switchboard with information about ads, promotions, specials or other matters customers are likely to call about. It may also reflect inadequate information on whom to call and other matters in company advertising, catalogs and mailing pieces.

Prospective Customer) Hang Up?

b. Branches or extensions. Phones may be unattended because personnel are at files or answering other extensions. May reflect lack of suitable call distribution system, lack of supervision or measurement of response against standards.

2. Trunks or direct lines busy.

a. Call volume. Overall volume of calls may be too great for existing trunks, suggests need to measure call volume and percentage of calls made that did not get through due to busy signal. If call volume fluctuates during day, problem may be due to "bunching" of calls at certain times, potentially remedied by balancing call load by one or more of several methods (restricting inbound calls from field sales personnel to slack periods, preinforming customers of best times to call, etc., limiting outbound calls on dual-use trunks.)

b. Excessive holds. Many calls that are blocked—simple inquiries, short orders—could have been handled except that trunks and/or branches were tied up by calls on hold, either awaiting person called or while rep researches subject of call, perhaps using another line which then registers busy as well. Cumulative amount of hold time in a department with 20 reps may run as high as 10 or 12 hours of dead hold time, suggesting lack of suitable standards for when to hold and when to call back. More serious underlying problem is lack of on-line information systems reflected in excessive search time while callers are placed on hold.

c. Unsuitable phone procedure. Lack of scenarios, scripts or formats for routine calls may result in too much time given to repetitive situations. Untrained personnel using unstructured routine may generate additional calls for information omitted from initial call. Errors and omissions caused by unstructured routine or lack of training ultimately generate a high volume of additional calls.

d. Wrong medium. Telephone often being used for communications which have limited time-value and do not require actual presence of person being communicated to. Alternatives, telex, electronic mail, conventional mail.

e. Miscellaneous. Use of phones for personal calls, 20 persons making one six-minute call per day is two hours of phone time. Sometimes reasons are subtle: one company set a standard of outbound calls not to exceed three minutes, as a call neared three minutes, the rep would inform the

Continued on overleaf

Why Did Customer Hang Up? *(Continued from page 401)*

customer, disconnect and then call back—total phone time and cost would have been less on a single call properly structured.

3. **Placed on hold (or in queue) for an excessive amount of time.** All reasons cited above, plus:

   a. **Prior communications failures:** Customer was not given adequate information at time of purchase, misinformation on applications, uses, etc.; situation generates many new phone calls.

   b. **Service failures.** Late shipment, errors or damage in orders, etc., resulting in order status inquiries, claims, complaints and related calls.

   c. **Lack of analysis of call subjects:** Certain categories may be capable of handling via recording, schedules, instructions for obtaining permits, routine notification of hours, alternate phone numbers, etc. Use of dedicated lines (and preinforming customers) for such matters will remove overload from regular lines and reduce overall costs by not requiring "live" participation by personnel. Analysis of call subjects will identify opportunities for such prescreening.

   d. **Absence of system for callbacks.** Use of a recorder or live personnel for screening and arranging callbacks would permit quick turnover of queue, callbacks during slack periods or at time convenient to customer and thus much greater utilization of lines. (Note: callbacks must be made within specified standards.)

4. **Disconnected or left on dead line too long in process of being transferred.**

   a. **System problem.** Transfers difficult to make.

   b. **Personnel not properly trained.** No procedures.

   c. **Failure to follow through.** Rep does not verify that party receiving transfer is in fact available to receive transfer, or that line is covered or free.

5. **Transferred too many times.**

   a. **Uninformed/untrained personnel.** At switchboard or in departments, personnel who are not adequately informed on company resources or who are not trained to identify subjects of calls may transfer calls without realizing that the person to whom they are being transferred is no better qualified than they are. (Some companies deal with this problem by requiring the individual answering the phone initially (other than switchboard) to obtain the needed information and call the customer back within an agreed time.)

   b. **No directories.** Directories furnished to customers telling them whom to call for what will help avoid misplaced calls, excessive transfers, internal directories will help the switchboard as well as departments in this respect.

c. Unwillling personnel. Some personnel may be unwilling to take responsibility for specific responses to customers. This category includes personnel who consider it "not my job," and those who transfer calls simply to get rid of them.

6. Customer's general disgust at manner of treatment.

a. System. A slow or inadequate information system frustrates customers as well as customer service personnel, may result in friction between the two.

b. Policies. Unreasonable callback policies irritate customers. For example, some companies' switchboards will not take callback messages for unanswered or busy extension, some require customers to call back at their own expense, etc.

c. Attitudes. Whether it's real or perceived, many personnel contacted in the course of phone transactions come through to customers as indifferent, uninformed and uncaring.

d. Image. If the manner of treatment represents the company's attitude towards its customers, towards quality control, fair treatment, etc., customers may decide that it is not the type of company they want to deal with.

And . . . Some More Real Reasons

a. Failure to monitor and observe transactions. There is no substitute for first hand monitoring of the quality of phone service in the real-life setting where both sides of the conversation can be heard. Standard rating forms should be used and performance reviewed with the individual reps in a nonthreatening environment.

b. Failure to supervise. This is one of the most costly of all problems, often a result of the "working supervisor" concept, where the supervisor is so overloaded that he/she cannot adequately supervise.

Weigh Cost of Holding v. Staffing

Besides being an irritant to customers, excessive hold on the telephone—even 800-numbers—can be expensive in terms of lost business as well as the actual telephone time. At a certain point, it's less costly to staff than it is to keep customers on hold, says Calvin A. Finke, Customer Service Manager of Physicians Mutual Insurance Co., Omaha. "When we determine our staffing requirements, we use an average speed of answer (hold time) 10 seconds," he adds. "With the present rate structure of in-WATS, call waiting is expensive. Our cost-per-second is 4.6 cents. When your cost for call waiting exceeds your hourly pay rate, consider increasing your staff."

Checklist of Professional Telephone Techniques

☐ **Know sources of information and approval, including—**

- Customer files
- Departments, individuals and other resources
- Procedures, policies and terms and conditions of sale
- Credit matters
- Returns, refunds, claims and credits
- Emergencies and exceptions
- Organization and lines of authority and approval

☐ **Be familiar with appropriate scenarios/scripts/routines—**

- Troubleshooting decision rules, interrogatories
- Current promotions, new product introductions, specials, etc.
- Do-it-yourself scripts based on your own experience and comparing notes with others

☐ **Be familiar with principal types of calls, including—**

- Routine requests (orders) for product or service
- Routine requests for product or service information
- Routine requests for technical or application information
- Special requests: policy interpretation, followup, order status, etc.
- Complaints: service, product, price, personnel, billing errors, etc.
- Emergencies and exceptions

☐ **Set general objectives for all calls—**

- Image of company to be projected
- Interest in customers, recognition of their importance
- Maintaining customer satisfaction and revenues
- Doing the job professionally, and with professional satisfaction

☐ **Answer the telephone professionally—**

- Decide beforehand that *you,* not the caller, will control the transaction
- Recognize that every business call is a *communication* with a purpose, not just a conversation
- Pick up or connect *after* one ring when possible (picking up too soon startles the caller, interferes with concentration)
- If you're busy, allow the caller to state his or her business before putting on hold

- Announce your name slowly and clearly to set up concentration
- Identify company, division, department or specialty as appropriate
- Use pleasant, animated conversational tone

☐ **Respond to the caller as an individual—**

- Repeat name, verifying pronunciation and spelling if necessary (don't be embarrassed to ask!)
- Use name frequently in conversation, but avoid over-familiarity and "talking down." Don't use first names unless you have a clear signal to do so
- Get caller's name, address and phone number (and company or department) as early in the call as possible
- Respond to inquiries or complaints with warm expression of interest and willingness to help. "I'll be glad to help you with that, Mr. Brown!"
- Emphathize with callers who are upset; exhibit concern: "I can understand why you feel the way you do; I would, too." Or, in extreme situations: "Gosh, you must feel terrible." Respond to direct attacks or exaggerations with: "I'm sorry you feel that way. Let's see what we can do to resolve this." Or, "We certainly didn't intend to inconvenience you; let's see what we can do to make things right."

☐ **Identify and analyze; determine course of action—**

- Identify call by type and response category
- Identify caller by class, i.e., customer, non-customer, size and location of account, etc.
- Determine what specific information is required from customer to progress the transaction
- Whenever possible, get information first-hand from the individual with the actual problem or application
- Use combination of closed-end and open-end questions: *Closed end:* "What model do you have?" *Open end:* "Please tell me how it happened," or "How did it happen?"
- Determine whether there is a standard course of action that can be taken, i.e., automatic refund, return authorization, etc.
- Advise customer of the next step to be taken; be sure that the customer understands

(Continued on overleaf)

Telephone Checklist *(Continued from page 405)*

☐ **Transfer and refer as appropriate—**

- When you are clearly not qualified (or don't have the authority) to handle the call
- When the proper authority is known and available (when not, offer to call the customer back with appropriate information, set a time, and call back at that time)
- When you are certain the customer's need will be met by the person to whom you're transferring the call—and that the call won't simply be retransferred to somebody else.

☐ **Rephrase and paraphrase customer statements to define scope of call—**

- (Inquiry) "You want to know _____"
- (Problem) "In other words, _____"
- (Request) "You would like us to _____"
- (Complaint) "As I understand it _____"
- Confine discussion to the agreed subject, restate key elements to ensure that you both understand

☐ **Repeat and verify names, numbers, dates, dimensions, etc.—**

- Use Able-Baker-Charlie alphabet to verify spellings
- Spell out proper names as necessary
- Always include dates: "Next Tuesday, March 11."
- Verify sizes and dimensions, always mention unit of measure: inches, centimeters, feet, ounces, pounds, kilos, etc.
- Verify packs, packaging, colors, finishes, specials, etc.

☐ **Bring transaction to a conclusion or resolution—**

- Avoiding "commanding" customer; instead of saying "You'll have to _____," say "Would you please _____?" or "If you would be willing to _____, I'm sure we could resolve the matter quickly."
- Provide information or instructions to customer as appropriate.
- If the customer is placing an order, enter it and thank the customer, confirming ship date and pricing as appropriate.
- In other matters, explain to customer what happens next, set timetable

for further action and then follow through to make sure timetable is met
- Thank caller; wait until he or she hangs up before disconnecting.

☐ **Use special strategies for special situations—**

- Address callers' needs and interests, and phrase responses or requests in terms of benefits to customer
- Use "forced choice" strategies for negotiating delivery dates, quantities, complaint resolutions and sales: "Would you prefer delivery on the 18th or the 25th?", "Would you prefer a half-pallet or a full pallet?", "Would you prefer to take an automatic refund of $25 now, or file a claim for the $35 and have me process it through regular channels?"
- Don't be reluctant to engage in "small talk," but make it brief!
- When customers insist on "talking to the boss," tell them you will relay the message, and if that fails, ask the boss to let you transmit the ultimate response to the customer. (This is so that the customer will continue to call you, not the boss.)
- Identify sensitive situations involving important customers and/or liability situations and refer them upwards as appropriate.
- Learn to control and limit over-talkative or "lonely" customers without offending.
- Follow through, report back even when there's nothing new to report.

☐ **Avoid these telephone don'ts—**

- Don't snatch up the telephone, it isn't going anywhere.
- Don't pick up and immediately place customer on hold.
- Don't snarl, growl, snap or slur your speech when answering.
- Don't display boredom, irritation or impatience.
- Don't argue or make defensive statements.
- Don't anticipate questions or jump to conclusions.
- Don't pass the buck.
- Don't blame the computer.
- Don't start sentences or explanations with "You'll have to . . ."
- Don't use colloquialisms or jargon unfamiliar to the caller.
- Don't take it for granted that the customer understands you.
- Don't "accuse" customers: "You should have told me that!"
- Don't hang up or disconnect until after the caller does.
- Don't drop the phone into its cradle.

21

COMMUNICATIONS—
INSIDE SELLING AND TELEMARKETING

Customer service departments have done considerable selling
over the years, but it has generally been informal and randomized. Customer service reps taking orders might occasionally
suggest increasing order size to take advantage of a price break.
Or, they might recommend a substitute product in place of one
not currently in stock. A senior rep might know some customers
who would buy seconds at a discount or refused shipments or
surplus inventory. And even though the terms "customer service" and "inside sales" were used more or less interchangeably,
it was generally understood that selling as an organized, structured activity was the responsibility of the field sales department. Indeed, the relationship between the "inside" and the
"outside" was often strained and frequently characterized by a
"hands off my accounts!" attitude on the part of field salespeople.

Several events have significantly changed this state of affairs. One has been a sharp increase in field selling costs, estimated in 1984 to be $250 per field sales call on industrial or
commercial accounts. Some firms have been faced with the alternative of eliminating field sales calls on smaller accounts altogether vs. contacting these same customers by phone at considerably lower cost per contact.

Another changing circumstance has been the fact that fewer
and fewer field salespeople actually write orders. Most orders go
directly from customers to the customer service department, and

in fact may be "negotiated" between the customer and the rep in matters of deliveries, split shipments, substitutions and the like. As many of the traditional administrative functions have been shifted from Sales to Customer Service in order to free field salespeople for more selling and less paperwork, inside personnel have developed account knowledge and rapport with customers to the extent that it is easy and natural for them to do suggestion-type selling or order upgrading.

A third significant event impacting inside selling has been the development of computerized, sales-oriented information systems. These have been particularly notable in helping reps offer substitutions for items ordered but not in stock. Substitutability programs have become a major selling tool in com-

---

Economics of Inside vs. Outside Selling

It's generally accepted that most outside salespersons can consider it a good day's work when they have made five sales calls. A great deal of their time is spent traveling between calls, and then waiting for persons to be available. Additionally, in many instances they may have to call on a number of different persons in one company. By contrast, an inside salesperson contacting customers by telephone can complete anywhere from six to 12 calls in a single hour. This difference in productivity is simply a matter of logistics; it takes considerably less time and effort to reach people on the telephone than it does to visit them in person.

This does not mean that contacting customers by telephone is a *substitute* for visiting them in person; it is simply a more productive way of making the contact. And it is often suitable for accounts where the economics no longer warrant personal visits—where the sales results of personal visits do not pay for the cost of making the calls. Even so, there are accounts where for reasons of size, sensitivity or growth potential, personal calls are mandatory. By using telephone selling, or a mix of fewer personal calls and increased phone contacts, to secondary accounts, sales personnel have more time to devote to key accounts where they are most productive in actual sales results—and where only they can do the job.

petitive situations where an entire order may be lost if acceptable substitutes cannot be found. This is true in the tire industry, in the computer chip industry, health care, grocery products and many others. In some industries, programming may permit substitution of a more expensive item at the same price merely to keep the sale: substituting a 12-ply tire for a 10-ply, for example.

Other aspects of these information systems have been customer profiles permitting comparison with previous orders and flags identifying customers who will buy seconds and/or refused shipments if the occasion arises. In some businesses with a high volume of customer calls—like orders for air freight or parcel pickup—the customer profile on the computer will carry data like location of loading dock, width of alley, names of persons to ask for, etc. In one firm, the agent uses the time normally required to enter this data for a version of inside selling: suggesting regular daily pickups, introducing a new service, cross-selling other services, etc. From this type of base it is possible to develop on-line selling programs which provide specific "prompts" to the inside salesperson as the order is being entered. Here are some possibilities:

"Mr. Brown, I notice that you're not ordering end caps this time. Was that an oversight, or did you mean not to include them?"

"Ms. Green, this brings your orders with us this year to over one million dollars. I just want you to know how much we appreciate your business . . . and I think you'll be hearing shortly from our president!"

"Mr. Ballou, I've got a truck going to your area Monday. If you can up your order from 7,500 to 10,000 lbs. I can give you the truckload rate."

"Ms. Oliver, I see you've had eight fill-in orders in the last month where you had to pay premium transportation charges. Could I suggest increasing your regular orders by ten percent so you'd get the price break and at the same time wipe out those premium charges? I calculate a savings of close to $5,000 a year."

The computer may also provide prompts to the individual

rep indicating sales to date, commission or bonus points, or overall sales performance:

"Increase this order from $7,500 to $10,000 and you will be at Level Two in the sales contest."

"Your ratio of closes to calls is very low; suggest you follow outline B on overcoming objections and making closes until ratio improves."

"The commission on this order is only $1.65. Suggest you attempt upgrades in A and B Category items."

Telemarketing in Consumer Markets

Many people associate inside selling or telemarketing with fast-talking, "boiler room" salespeople selling securities, cemetery lots, real estate, dance lessons and the like. Actually, this is a very small and non-typical segment of total telemarketing activity, and, as the examples suggest, is confined mainly to consumer products. It should be established at the outset that telemarketing is a legitimate, ethical activity that is being used by many reputable companies in conjunction with other marketing tools. One of the most widespread uses is to convert inquiries generated by space or electronic media advertising into sales. On high-ticket items, this may be a two-step process; the objective of the telemarketing call is to set up an appointment to visit real estate, attend a product demonstration, etc., where salespeople will be on hand to do the actual selling.

Telemarketing is also widely used for subscription renewals to both consumer and business publications, and it is seeing increasing use to "reverse" cancellations of such subscriptions, as well as cancellations of memberships in collectible programs like those offered by the Franklin Mint, book clubs, etc. And of course telemarketing can be used for screening purposes, i.e., to determine which prospects on a list should be followed up more closely, and which should be removed from the list as being not potential customers. Telemarketing may be used by department stores to notify certain customers that a particular type of merchandise they have expressed interest in has arrived; it may also be used by dentists' offices to remind patients that it's time for their annual checkup. Indeed, the call reminding the patient that he/she has an appointment is a form of telemarketing in itself.

In short, telemarketing in consumer markets is almost any use of the telephone to promote, advance or solidify sales, including actually closing sales and taking orders. Telemarketing personnel are hired primarily for their sales skills and customarily paid on a commission basis as an incentive to productivity. The ratio of calls to closes is an important measure of such productivity, and is watched closely, particularly with relatively low-ticket items where selling costs must be kept to a minimum. Telemarketing personnel generally do very little account servicing beyond taking orders, and often their knowledge of products or applications is limited to the particular script or scenario in use at the time. In most instances, the customer is not known to the telemarketer except as a name on a list, and the emphasis tends to be on one-shot sales rather than repeat business or long-term relationships.

Inside Selling and Telemarketing In Industrial and Commercial Markets

As the examples of consumer telemarketing suggest, inside selling and telemarketing in industrial and commercial markets are considerably more complex and varied. A great deal of the actual selling activity takes place directly in conjunction with account service activities, and it is often done by persons trained in customer service rather than in selling techniques. And it usually covers a much broader range of items, often in the thousands. There are five main categories of such selling activity:

1. *Reactive—regular accounts.* This consists mainly of suggestion selling in connection with telephone orders being placed by regular accounts: order upgrading, substitutions and

the like. Virtually all customer service departments perform some selling of this type, although in many it is more or less at the discretion of the individual rep.

2. *Proactive—order-taking only.* This involves calling regular customers, often by appointment or at a regular time, but only for purposes of taking orders and not selling as such. In some companies, this activity may be supported with data on available substitutes for items the customer normally orders that are currently out of stock.

How Telemarketing Can Reduce Total Selling Costs by 50% (Also see chart on page opposite)				
Account Category	No. of Accounts	Call Frequency	Cost/ Call	Total Cost
A & B	2,000	12	$250	$ 6,000,000
C & D	5,000	6	$250	7,500,000
E	10,000	2	$250	5,000,000
			Total	$18,500,000

Figure 21-1. Before. With field sales calls only, a large industrial company might schedule 12 calls per year on each of its top (A & B) accounts, 6 calls per year on each of its medium (C & D) accounts, and only 2 calls per year on each of its 10,000 small accounts. At an average cost of $250 per sales call (the generally accepted figure for such a firm in 1984), the total selling cost would be $18.5 million per year. Even then, coverage of accounts in the medium and small categories is relatively ineffective, particularly where there may be significant competition.

Account Category	No. of Accounts	Call Frequency	Cost/ Call	Total Cost
A & B	2,000	12	$250	$ 6,000,000
C & D (visit)	1,000	6	$250	1,500,000
C & D (phone)	4,000	12	$ 14	672,000
E (phone)	10,000	6	$ 14	840,000
			Total	$ 9,012,000

Figure 21-2. After. The same company with its sales call patterns reconfigured with the addition of telemarketing to medium and small accounts. Note that the 2000 top (A & B) accounts are still receiving 12 visits a year each from field sales personnel, while the top 1000 medium accounts are still receiving 6 visits each. The other 4000 accounts are receiving no visits, but instead 12 telemarketing calls per year, actually doubling the previous rate of contact with the firm. The 10,000 bottom accounts have also been cut off the call list, but are now receiving 6 telemarketing calls per year, or three times as many contacts as in the past. The total saving to the company in this reconfiguration is almost $9.5 million, assuming a cost per telemarketing call of $14 (a 1984 figure which may vary from company to company depending on the length of the call, skill levels of personnel, etc.) Of course, the company may elect to reinvest some of its savings in greater call frequency for top accounts, more phone contacts with smaller accounts, etc. Also, it should be stressed that classification of an account as "A & B," "C & D," or "E" does not necessarily reflect that account's actual purchases. A very large company which is currently buying only very small quantities but has the potential for very large purchases would probably be classed as an "A" account. A small company with good growth potential might well be classed as a "B" or "C" account.

3. *Proactive—selling to regular accounts.* This version usually involves initiating sales calls to regular accounts, usually smaller or marginal customers, with specific sales objectives rather than simply order-taking. This would also include such selling activities as introducing and selling a new product, often in conjunction with an advertising campaign. It may also include special promotions, sales of overstock items and the like.

4. *Reactive—non-customers.* Here, customer service reps handle inquiries generated by advertising with the objective of converting them to sales or, in some instances, arranging appointments with field salespersons, setting up demonstrations, etc.

5. *Proactive—non-customers.* This form of inside selling or telemarketing consists of initiating calls to non-customers with a specific sales objective.

Many inside selling and telemarketing programs in customer service departments combine two or more of these categories. Perhaps the most significant difference between companies is not so much in the specific kinds of inside selling they perform as in the degree to which they do it as a formal, organized activity with specific marketing objectives.

Approaches and Techniques

Recognizing that in most instances industrial and commercial firms are looking at repeat business, the actual approaches and techniques will vary considerably from company to company as well as from customer to customer. Here are some of the more widely used approaches:

1. *Order upgrading.* This has several dimensions. It may consist of suggesting an increase in order size to take advantage of price breaks; often it involves suggesting add-on items. Add-on items can be intrinsic, like glue for glue guns, or non-intrinsic, like extension cords.

2. *Special-of-the-week.* This is often a form of order upgrading. After the customer has placed his or her order, the rep

will introduce the special-of-the-week and suggest adding this to the order.

3. *Specific products.* These may be offered as specials, or they may represent overstock items or slow movers. New products being introduced by telemarketing would be included in this group.

4. *Offering substitutions.* Generally speaking, this refers to suggesting a substitute for an item which a customer has ordered but which is not currently available. In some cases, the recommended item may be directly substitutable—i.e., the same item but with a different trade name—or functionally substitutable, a nylon gear in place of a metal one, white-coated electrical cord in place of brown, etc. Or, the recommendation may involve a higher-priced version of the same item, the deluxe version over the standard. In some cases, the substitution may refer to order configuration, units of sale, or means of transportation: shipping product in multiwall bags instead of drums, shrink wrapped pallets vs. loose cartons, tank truck vs. rail tank car, etc.

5. *Refused shipments.* Where a customer refuses to accept delivery on an order (for whatever reason), it is often more economical to sell the order locally at a discount than to pay transportation charges back to the point of origin. Some customer service departments maintain geographic files of prospective buyers of refused shipments, and telemarket specifically to them. This is also used with perishables; a firm selling nursery stock or house plants maintains such files and if a shipment is refused by the ordering retailer, can usually find a quick sale nearby at a discounted price, while the product is still saleable. To return the perishable stock to origin would result in substantial loss.

6. *Freight savings.* This is simply calling customers or prospects to tell them when a pool truck will be going to their area so that they can place orders and take advantage of freight savings.

7. *Seconds.* This involves calling to sell products or materials which are outside of normal specifications because of color variations or other irregularity, but will otherwise perform satisfactorily.

8. *Customers with declining purchases.* A frequent target of inside selling and telemarketing in industrial and commercial organizations is the account whose purchases are markedly down. Often there is suspicion that a competitor is making inroads, but there is also the possibility that the account has been alienated by some previous problem(s) which can be rectified. One company discovered that declining purchases were actually the result of insufficient contacts by the vendor, and thus instituted a telemarketing program designed specifically to remedy this situation. In the process, it restored a sales decline of close to $20 million.

9. *Customers on allocation or blanket purchase orders.* Tracking customer purchases against their actual commitments is a particularly valuable telemarketing activity when products are in short supply and have been placed on allocation, or where special pricing has been set up for customers based on blanket purchase orders covering a specified volume of purchases. A similar application is to monitor customer participation in consolidation programs based on agreed cutoff times for entering orders.

10. *Contacting customers in advance of price increases.* The objective here is often not to make sales per se but rather for public relations purposes, i.e., to avoid antagonizing customers who might later claim they had not been notified of the price increase. But it may also be an effective gambit for selling to non-customers.

11. *Selling production capacity available on another customer's order.* This is similar in some respects to selling a refused shipment, except that it represents an order that has not actually been produced. Particularly in custom operations where machine time may be a critical item, having files available showing potential customers for that capacity can lead to a quick sale with no loss of profits.

12. *Opportunistic selling.* One firm knows from its daily contacts with the marketplace which items it has in ample supply that its competitors don't. Each customer service rep initiates two phone calls to non-customers, using this approach: "You've

probably been having trouble locating a source of [product type]; we have an assured supply, and I would be glad to take your order. How much do you normally require?"

13. *Customer retention strategies.* Some aspects of inside selling or telemarketing are more oriented towards customer retention than to actually making a sale. This would include a whole category of calls initiated to customers when there is a customer service failure or other problem, and the goal is to persuade the customer to accept an alternative and not cancel the order. It would also include cases where the customer has in fact cancelled the order and the goal is to persuade the customer to cancel the cancellation, i.e., reverse the decision and allow re-entry of the order.

Why the Customer Service Department?

There is no basic rule which says that the inside selling and telemarketing activity has to be part of the customer service function. But in many industrial and commercial firms it is located in Customer Service because it works best that way. For example, a firm which has a large number of small or marginal customers it can no longer afford to call on combines tele-marketing with normal customer service activities to keep these customers on the books. Where a salesperson formerly called once or twice a year, the customer service rep now phones at least once a month at far less total cost—and usually far better results. The phone calls amount to perhaps $100 a year or so vs. $250 for a single call in person, and $500 for two calls a year. More import-antly, the regular phone calls establish *continuity* and identify the company with the customer's interests.

One company which was concerned that customers being changed to telemarketing accounts might resent the change found to its pleasant surprise that the customers felt pleased to be the center of this much attention and as a result increased overall purchases significantly. Another found that customers preferred the brief phone call to personal visits, simply because they

Checklist for Setting U

YES	NO		**I. Feasibility**
☐	☐	1.	Does the company's marketing situation and/or product mix genuinely lend itself to an inside selling activity?
☐	☐	2.	Can a need be demonstrated in terms of lost business under existing conditions, reduced customer contact, high cost of field sales or other sound reasons?
☐	☐	3.	Does the customer service department have the basic resources—skills, product knowledge, customer data, and time—to do the job on a pilot basis without extensive additional investment or recruiting?
☐	☐	4.	Is there a reasonable possibility that management will support the project, at least to the extent of giving it a fair trial?
☐	☐	5.	Is there a better-than-even chance that, even under adverse conditions, the program will produce measurable benefits for the company?

II. Justifying and Selling the Program

☐	☐	6.	Have hard numbers been developed for present and future field selling costs and comparative inside selling costs?
☐	☐	7.	In anticipation of the inevitable question, has a list been worked up of *other* companies with successful inside selling operations in the customer service department?
☐	☐	8.	Is there genuine logic for setting up the activity in the customer service department rather than as a separate selling entity, and have all those points of logic been fully developed for use in justifying and selling the program?

an Inside Selling Function

☐ ☐ 9. Have all possible objections been identified and appropriate responses or strategies for dealing with them been developed?

☐ ☐ 10. Has a less ambitious program been developed to offer as a compromise or substitute if the initial proposal appears headed for trouble?

III. Operational Planning

☐ ☐ 11. Have the scope and mission of the inside selling activity been fully defined and formalized in writing, with particular attention to interfaces with other selling arms of the firm?

☐ ☐ 12. Have the individuals been identified who will be actually performing the inside selling function?

☐ ☐ 13. Have they been trained and/or provided with scripts, scenarios and other sales materials; and have firm procedures been developed for keeping them abreast of promotions, deals and new product introductions?

☐ ☐ 14. Have the specific accounts been identified who will be contacted, purchasing profiles developed, and a system of assignment or responsibility developed for the reps who will be contacting them?

☐ ☐ 15. Have the space, furniture and equipment to be used in the inside selling operation been identified and cleared for this use, and any additional equipment been placed on order?

☐ ☐ 16. Has a plan for compensation, bonus or other recognition been developed and approved?

☐ ☐ 17. Have plans been made for supervision and performance measurement or rating of individual reps?

☐ ☐ 18. Has a contingency plan been developed, or sufficient flexibility built into the program, so that it can be expanded rapidly—and kept within the

(Continued on overleaf)

Inside Selling Function Checklist *(Continued from page 421)*

(Continued from page 421)

YES   NO

jurisdiction of the customer service department—if management decides to do so on the basis of initial results?

☐   ☐   19. Has the planning considered the desirability of pre-notifying customers—particularly those who have been contacted in person by field sales reps up until now, but from now on will be contacted primarily by inside selling personnel?

☐   ☐   20. Has any necessary budgeting been performed . . . and expenditures kept within that budget?

☐   ☐   21. Has a timetable been developed for implementation—including design and procurement of forms, computer software and the like—and is that timetable being met?

IV. Implementation

☐   ☐   22. Are reps' sales contacts with customers being monitored regularly and systematically to determine adequacy of reps' training and possible need for additional training or support materials?

☐   ☐   23. Is customer response, reaction or degree of acceptance being recorded as one measure of the impact of the program?

☐   ☐   24. Are practical measures of productivity being applied, such as completed calls per day (or other time segment), total dollars sold per calls made, and similar measures?

☐   ☐   25. Are high-potential contacts being regularly referred to the appropriate field sales entity for possible followup in person?

☐   ☐   26. Is the overall *tone* of the program consistent with the image the company wishes to project; is the program itself *professional* and *ethical*?

V. Results

☐ ☐ 27. Does the system of recordkeeping permit quick and easy readout of results at any given time?

☐ ☐ 28. Is management being notified, regularly and in concise language, of these results and plans for dealing with any problems that have arisen or for adapting to future trends or conditions?

☐ ☐ 29. Are program results being measured in terms of return on investment, discounted cash flow, opportunity cost—or whatever measure management prefers?

☐ ☐ 30. Do the results clearly and unequivocally support continuation and/or expansion of the inside selling program?

☐ ☐ 31. Assuming the program has been successful so far, have additional plans been developed for expanding its scope to additional areas such as disposition of surplus inventories, seconds, refused merchandise at remote locations, and similar special situations?

☐ ☐ 32. Is the inside selling program being perceived by employees as a legitimate career path in the company and, where job openings are posted, attracting applicants from other departments?

☐ ☐ 33. Is it helping the customer service manager achieve greater stature and an improved future—and improved income—in the company?

SCORING: Clearly, any customer service department which can answer all 33 questions listed on this checklist with a resounding "yes" is in excellent condition and has a definite success on its hands. For firms which are just entering an inside selling program, the answers to the last dozen or so questions lie mainly in the future. But if you are at the stage in your planning or thinking where you can answer "yes" to the first 21 questions, then the chances are quite good that you, too, will have a winner on your hands.

represented less of an intrusion. A third company found that customers were particularly pleased to be assigned to an "inside person" at the vendor firm to whom they could turn for help in emergencies or other problem situations.

Managers also see inside selling and telemarketing as an excellent motivator for their personnel. At one company, for example, each customer service rep performs telemarketing and inside selling duties one day per week. Others in the department handle his or her accounts on this particular day. The manager reports that it's an excellent motivator, and it doesn't happen so often that reps become bored. If reps don't wish to participate, he adds, they are not required to, but there is no commission or bonus or other special consideration for those who do. Here again, the customer service department is well-suited for telemarketing because reps have extensive knowledge of their own products as well as customer requirements and special applications.

There are situations where setting up a full-scale telemarketing operation does not necessarily require doing it in the customer service department. In fact, there are cases where it may be contraindicated. One instance might be where personnel may deemphasize their customer service activities in order to spend more time on selling. Another might be just the opposite, spending too much time on customer service and not enough on selling. Actually, the question of priorities should be decided by the manager rather than left to the individual rep. The customary requirement is that each rep make a specified number of telemarketing calls each day in addition to his or her regular duties. Observation of the rep's handling of regular account service calls will quickly reveal whether they are suffering; and the rep's actual sales record will tell the rest.

Conflicts With Field Sales

It is true that there are frequent conflicts on this subject with the field sales department. Often, field salespeople feel that their "turf" is being threatened and persist in this feeling even when told that the effort will be confined to accounts which they are presently not even calling on. If it is proposed that customer service reps receive commission on their sales, this aggravates the situation. But even where sales people would receive commission on those same sales they may not be agreeable to an inside selling or telemarketing program handled by anybody other than themselves.

The most successful customer service telemarketing activities have been those where Sales is involved in organizing the program and is a vigorous proponent on its behalf—and where field sales personnel receive some sort of commission on all sales. The sensitive issue of whether the rep himself or herself should receive commission is more difficult, because customer service reps often consider that they are entitled to a commission because they are in fact selling. Indeed, reps often feel that field selling is a "soft" job consisting of entertainment, fat expense accounts, and easy sales with extravagant commissions; they feel that if they are to engage in any version of selling, that should at least entitle them to some semblance of a commission.

What reps seldom understand (and what the manager should clarify for them) is that there is a vast difference between sitting in a comfortable office and opportunistically making sales, on the one hand, and the "real world" of field selling which involves relatively little luxury and entertainment, and a great deal of hard work, disappointments from sales not made, separation from family and other problems. Also, reps should realize as a fact of life that many managements consider the customer service rep's job as mainly clerical; management may need to be shown that reps can sell before they are willing to accede to any suggestion of a commission basis for reps on inside selling or telemarketing programs. And even then they may not agree to commission basis inside selling or telemarketing except by bona fide sales personnel.

Of course there are a number of companies where sales people work on straight salary. Although the "turf" issue may have to be resolved to the satisfaction of field sales personnel, the commission issue is not a factor. Another approach is to provide reps an incentive in the form of a bonus-point system, or to offer catalog items based on reaching specified levels of sales.

The notion that inside selling or telemarketing as a "break" from regular customer service routines is an incentive in itself should not be carried too far. The more frequently it is performed, the sooner the novelty wears off and the less of a motivator it becomes. If reps do not get significant results in the form of sales, they are likely to be discouraged or demotivated. If too much pressure is placed on them to make a certain number of calls within a specified time frame, yet without added pay or commission, they may simply decide they don't want the job. On the other hand, reasonable results and sufficient rotation with other duties may in fact be excellent motivators.

Which raises an issue of extreme importance in any inside selling operation: the quality of the customer list that is used as the basis for calling. Clearly this is not an issue if the selling activity is confined to simple order upgrading on orders phoned in by existing customers. But it becomes more significant when outbound calls are involved. One company's customer service department became involved in a new product introduction using names of marginal and inactive accounts furnished by the field sales force. Almost immediately it discovered that the list was out of date, some of the firms no longer in business, and a number of the individuals retired, deceased or no longer with the companies listed. Another company, given a list of "prospects," discovered after a week that its reps had made virtually zero in sales. Both situations were extreme demotivators. In the first, the reps had to spend so much time cleaning up the data on the list that they were discouraged before they even got to the point of making a sales presentation. Fortunately, the list finally did get cleaned and reps actually made almost twice as many sales as had been projected.

In that particular instance, the list had been given to the customer service department by the sales department in good faith. It was out of date simply because few calls were being made by the sales force on the companies listed. In the second instance, however, it appeared that the sales department might have deliberately set out to sabotage the inside selling effort by providing a list of known non-buyers, firms that had not purchased the products in the past and could not reasonably be expected to do so in the future. Certainly the customer service manager should personally examine the calling list and determine whether it is valid, or the extent to which it needs to be brought up to date. If indeed it does require revision, the job should be given to an outside service specializing in this type of work; it is not cost-effective to have reps attempt to clean lists and telemarket at the same time, and it also limits actual sales results.

Training and Performance Measurement

How much training—and what kind—is necessary for a successful inside selling and telemarketing activity in the customer service department? To a large degree this will depend on the extent of the program. Simple order upgrading and related types of suggestion selling are relatively easy to undertake with minimal training. One company set up a program whereby each rep suggested, on each order received by telephone, that the customer order one additional carton of product "just in case you run short." This produced an added $1 million in sales for the year with virtually zero training or instruction requirement.

Another company approached the order upgrading potential by designating one rep to undertake it on a pilot basis within certain limits. If an order was within 200 lbs. of the next price break, the rep would point this out to the customer and suggest ordering the larger amount. Soon the 200 lbs. limit was extended to 300 lbs., and eventually to 500. Within several months the rep had progressed to the point where she had achieved several hundred thousand dollars in added sales, and other reps were introduced into the program using the same techniques. For a more ambitious program involving a new product introduction, yet another company set up a formal training program using actual scripts and pairing customer service reps in a "buddy system" for practice. The scripts were prepared by the sales department, and the teams worked with them about an hour a day for several weeks. At the end of this time they went online calling customers, made some modifications in their scripts, and continued on to get exceptionally good results in the program.

The most significant factor the manager has to deal with in instituting an inside selling and telemarketing program using existing customer service reps is overcoming a "fear factor" whereby many reps are so used to simply taking orders that they have many different reservations about actually initiating and conducting sales calls. This situation has to be dealt with and it may in fact develop that some reps simply are not going to succeed as telemarketers, even though they may perform satis-factorily in all other respects. In the case of long-time reps who are close to retirement, the best response may be simply to wait it out. With others, though—particularly with good workers—the manager should actively help them to overcome their fears and reluctance to make the transition from taking orders by tele-phone to making sales by telephone.

Part of this process is simply coming to the realization that there is no "mystique" attached to selling, that selling in fact is nothing more than an extension of what they have been doing all along—selling by *helping customers buy*. This is particularly true in industrial and commercial sales where it is not so much a question of *whether* to buy, or even *what* to buy, but more often *from whom to buy it*. And here is where a customer service activity with a good record of helpfulness to customers has an advantage over telemarketing and inside selling activities using non-customer service personnel: customer service people have a degree of customer orientation and understanding that cannot be duplicated by any other type of experience, including sales itself.

In talking to reps who harbor fears about selling, the more common reservations concern that selling is "pushy" and aggres-sive, that instead of being friends with their customers as in the past, they'll now be adversaries, and that somehow selling isn't exactly ethical. All these views are out of date and in fact they're probably cover-ups for the most basic fear, which is fear of failure, of being turned down too many times. Sound counseling—plus a few successes by the rep himself or herself—should help overcome most of these inhibitions in any event.

Although it is not essential, it is certainly appropriate to use outside specialists to train personnel in telephone selling techniques, particularly if the manager has limited experience in this area. There are a number of firms and individuals who provide both consultation and training services. Many of these individuals also conduct public seminars which provide a good introduction to the subject plus a chance to evaluate the individual as a potential consultant and/or trainer.

Naturally performance records should measure personal productivity as well as actual sales achieved, that is, the number of calls attempted vs. the number of calls completed, the number of sales actually made, and the dollar value of the sales. It may be desirable to reduce these to ratios if personnel spend differing amounts of time in the activity. Also, it should be remembered that a larger volume of sales isn't always the result of better selling; the individual may have a better territory or a better list of accounts.

The Do-It-Yourself Pitfall

The biggest pitfall awaiting the do-it-yourself manager seeking to set up an inside selling/telemarketing activity in the customer service department is the problem of setting sales objectives which are reasonable and against which performance can be measured—and which can't be shot down by others in the company who may be opposed to the inside selling program.

Most persons unfamiliar with sales tend to oversimplify sales objectives, which are often quite complex. A typical approach to increasing sales is to develop new applications for a product and sell the application which will in turn increase demand for the product. Yet some firms find themselves developing new applications for products which are already in short supply: in effect, they work at creating a demand which they will be unable to fill. Another firm with better controls will set sales objectives to "demarket" low margin, high-volume items and concentrate instead on high dollar density sales. Some firms have done this and increased profits substantially while actually reducing overall sales volume.

These examples illustrate the point that sales objectives often involve much more than simply persuading the customer to say "yes." Particularly in inside selling and telemarketing it is important to set objectives that are both realistic and meaningful. A number of examples have already been cited in the area of substitutions and disposing of surpluses of one kind or another. One firm takes this approach a step further by using its substitutability programs as an "inventory-leveler." That is, when shortages start to develop in some lines and surpluses in others, it tries to marry these up so that items in oversupply are recommended, whenever possible, as substitutes for items in short supply. The system won't work with all products, but has proven quite successful for the firm in question.

The ideal way to test inside selling and telemarketing is in selling a product that is not available through other channels. Thus sales that are generated are directly traceable to the inside selling and telemarketing effort and can't be shrugged off as the result of field sales, advertising or other marketing efforts. When this cannot be done, the manager should decide specifically what the department's sales objectives are going to be, which customers are going to be involved, and how records can be set up whose integrity can't be challenged.

This is particularly important in the case of order upgrading, where it may be argued that overall sales volume has not been increased but rather shifted around, or that a substitution is no assurance that the sale would not have been made anyway after the substituted item had again become available. In these cases, records reflecting actual account growth can be particularly useful in making the point that the inside selling and telemarketing effort is paying off in both near-term and long-term benefits.

Finally, of course, the manager should be able to quantify the bottom-line contribution by showing the real cost of the telephone selling activity vs. the dollars realized. This should be an attractive number. If it is not, then this may be one of those relatively few instances where an inside selling and telemarketing activity may not be feasible for the customer service department. But it also illustrates the importance of not being overly ambitious, nor making a large investment in a telephone selling activity without first testing it and then selecting specific objectives from the many available.

Given such objectives, given careful preparation and practical measurement of both performance and results, given appropriate training and supervision, customer service personnel can make a substantial contribution to the firm's bottom line through a combination of increased sales and more profitable or less costly sales procedure.

Inside Selling: As Easy As A-B-C—A Guide for Customer Service Representatives
Step 1: Set Objectives

a. Know your objectives in general terms; be prepared to modify them for specific calls.
b. Be fully informed of special objectives in effect.
c. Be fully informed of current promotions, ad campaigns.
d. Know your products/services.
e. Equip yourself with forms, scripts, etc.
f. Know standards, record-keeping requirements, etc.
g. Know procedures, contingency plans.

Step 2: Identify Yourself

a. Announce your name slowly and clearly to set up concentration.
b. Identify your company and products/services as appropriate.

Step 3: Make Interest-Gathering Statement

a. Name of company where appropriate.   *(Continued)*

---

b.   State objective clearly: "May I have a few minutes to accomplish this objective?

Step 4: Maintain Continuity

a.   If customer wants to postpone, give closed choice of date, time.

b.   If customer indicates no interest, ask qualifying questions.

Step 5: Ask Probing Questions

a.   Suspected benefits: "If I could show you how to save $-----, would you -----?

b.   Use closed-end questions (yes-no) to maneuver prospect.

c.   Use open-end questions to qualify prospect.

Step 6: State Benefits

a.   Know difference between features (product characteristics) and benefits (satisfaction, convenience, profit to customer).

b.   Stress benefits over features:

*"The large tank enables you to travel 400 miles between fill-ups."

*"The 'miracle fabric' will save you hundreds of dollars in dry cleaning costs!"

*"The four-station model enables you to do the complete job in a single pass with half the labor cost."

Step 7: Watch for Buying Signals

a.   Application questions by the prospect: "What's the maximum sheet size it'll handle?" "How long does it take to dry?"

b.   Installation questions: "Does it require a dedicated line?" "How much floor space does it require?"

c.   Price and minimum order questions.

d.   Questions about terms, cash discounts, etc.

e.   Questions about delivery.

f.   Questions about returns policies, warranties, etc.

g.   Note that any objection might actually be a buying signal. "I've heard that you're having quality control problems" may actually mean, "I'd like to buy your product, if you can reassure me that you DON'T have quality control problems." Again, "I don't think you can meet my service needs" could be another way of saying, "Convince me that you can and I'm sold."

Step 8: Anticipate Objections

a. Look at them as milestones telling you you're on the way to closing the sale.

b. Be formally prepared to respond to them with appropriate scripts or scenarios.

c. But *don't* suggest objections to the customer: "You're probably worrying about quality control; well, let me assure you—" The thought may never have crossed the customer's mind, but now it's firmly planted there!

Step 9. Respond to Objections

a. Restate the objection in your own words to confirm it.

b. Anticipate the standard objections and appropriate responses:

*Postponement Objection: "I'll need some time to think it over."

*Need or Suitability Objection: "I'm not in the market," "Not interested," etc.

*Cost Objection: "I can't afford it," "Your price is too high," etc.

c. Phrase your confirming statement as a question where appropriate, and use this as a "bridge" to restatement of benefits:

You: "As I understand it, you feel it's too much money to be spending in today's economy, right?"

Prospect: "Yes, you're right."

You: "If I could show you how to actually *save* 10 percent on this transaction, would you be interested?"

d. State additional benefits: "Our projections show that spot-buying of product is likely to cost you 10% to 15% more than if you order in economic lots now."

e. Indicate any additional incentives provided by management.

(Continued)

433

"I'm authorized to offer you a 10% discount if you'll enter an order for at least -----."

f.   Where appropriate, dispel the objection directly: "No need to worry about its suitability for *your* application, Mr. Jones. The Navy has had several hundred in continuous use for more than 10 years!"

Step 10: Prepare Close

a.   Test with a closed-end, forced choice question: "Do you prefer the red or the blue?" "Would you use the two-station model or the four-station unit in your operation?"

b.   Ask for the order directly where appropriate: "Why not let me enter your order now (and add a benefit) so you'll receive it in plenty of time for the -----?"

c.   Use a closed-end, forced choice question: "Shall I write you up for the two-station or four-station model?" "Would you like us to ship the order to St. Louis or Chicago?"

Step 11: Use Non-Sales Closes

a.   Forced choice—appointment: "Would you prefer our representative visit you in the morning or in the afternoon?" "Would you prefer the 12th or the 15th?"

b.   Forced choice—trial order: "Would you prefer to try out the institutional pack or the retail pack?"

c.   Forced choice—demonstration: "Should we demonstrate the equipment here or at your location?"

d.   Forced choice—references: "I can give you the name of some other users—would you prefer to talk to distributors or manufacturers?"

Step 12: Follow Through on Delivery

a.   Enter orders promptly.

b.   "Sample" occasionally for service levels.

c.   Keep up-to-date on all forms and reports.

d.   Compare notes with others.

e.   Remember that good service is taken for granted—and you are "it"!

22

COMMUNICATIONS—
THE WRITTEN (AND PRINTED) WORD

A major manufacturer sends out one million postcards a year confirming customer orders. At 1984 postal rates, this represents a cost of $130,000 for postage alone; depending on how the cards are processed, filling them out, metering and mailing may add another $40,000 to $50,000 annually. Given such costs, there are two separate issues: (1) whether the postcards are necessary at all; and (2) if they are necessary, is the firm getting full value for the amount it spends for this particular mode of communications?

There's a very good possibility that neither question has been asked for years, and probably a 50-50 chance that the postcard is unnecessary and in addition is written or phrased so as to annoy or confuse some customers. Many firms have discovered, for example, that orders are received by customers several days before the confirmations themselves arrive in the mail. This may confuse the issue of whether or not the order has actually been received, and it's one more piece of paper to deal with. One company surveyed its customers on the question and found that a scant 25% wanted confirmations; the other 75% preferred eliminating them altogether.

While legal departments tend to feel that confirmations are necessary to protect the vendor because they restate the terms of sale on the vendor's form, in actual practice only a handful of disputes with customers ever get to the point where the written confirmation is used as a legal instrument. In other words, most vendors will try to settle with customers short of going to court because they know that once they do go to court they've lost the account in any event. The principal type of situation where written confirmations are important would involve big-ticket orders with special conditions attached by the customer, or major custom work which is usually covered by contracts in any event. In the first instance, a customer specifying job site delivery within a certain time frame would receive a confirmation setting forth any obligations on the customer's part, such as a 24-hour telephone contact, and exceptions on the vendor's part, such as strikes, etc.

Other Costs of Written Communications

The examples given above deal only with confirmations. What about notifying customers when an item ordered is back-ordered and shipment will be delayed? Most customers would want to be notified, and most companies would want to notify them. But one company found it was taking so long for the backorder notices to reach customers that on numerous occasions the backordered items had been received back in stock, shipped and actually received by customers *before* the backorder notification was received in the mail! This exercise was costing the company some $80,000 a year in postage, and it was also causing considerable confusion among customers.

Another example: a large organization found that it was sending out large numbers of followup letters a year explaining previous letters which the recipients hadn't understood. By rewriting—and simplifying and clarifying—the models or guide letters used for the initial letters, it was able to eliminate a total of 56,400 followup "letters of explanation." A parallel experience shared by many companies is an excessive number of phone calls from irate customers confused and irritated by their bills. Quite often redesign of the invoice format so it can be more readily interpreted, or enclosing a key or guide to the bill (as some utilities do) can cut the irate phone calls by 50% or more—and also result in faster payment by customers.

Written communications are costly. In 1984 it was estimated that the cost of an average letter was between $7 and $8, including the time of the originator and the typist plus associated materials and postage costs. In the organization referred to above, the development of 40 form letters to cover different situations replaced 60,000 individually written letters a year. Assuming the cost of a word-processed form letter to run about $1.50 including postage (and it's often less), this represents a net saving of $330,000 annually. One of the largest savings was in reduction of management dictating time by some 75%.

This is a very important point in written communications. Quite often, there is a significant hidden cost in correspondence representing the time of the individual who may compose the letter or, if not, make a policy decision or interpretation that is conveyed by the letter, even though somebody at a lower salary level may actually compose, write and sign the letter. The repetitive decision-making involved is costly, and in many cases can be eliminated by establishing decision rules which say, in effect, "For Situation 1A (equipment out of warranty two months or more), use letter 2B." Many word processing units today are equipped for much more sophisticated letter-writing, of course, including using specified paragraphs, and with internal personalization such as recipient's name, department, company name, location, volume and type of purchases, and similar information. Some word processed letters going to consumers go into such details as names and ages of children, names of neighbors, even names of pets!

With all the sophistication available in word processing and computer-generated letters, however, the manager should not get carried away by ambitious thoughts of "pushbutton letter writing" to cover every situation. In general, word-processing letter banks are more suitable to consumer situations where there is a high volume of correspondence on a relatively small number of situations. Industrial and commercial situations are more likely to require individually written letters. Where they do not require individually written letters, it is often easier—and usually quite acceptable—to send the customer a preprinted form letter with variable information filled in by hand, and hand-signed by the customer service rep.

The key to the acceptability of such preprinted form letters

---

21 Tips for Effective Business Letter-Writing

1. **Select appropriate medium.** Choose among conventional letter, form letter, printed acknowledgments, telex or other hard copy media.

2. **Assemble all materials.** Stationery, memoranda, correspondence, files, job jackets, invoices, etc.

3. **Make a topical outline.** The Detail in the outline will vary with the complexity of the letter, but exclude non-essentials.

4. **Format the letter properly.** Follow company style. If no standard exists, consult a standard secretarial text for appropriate headings, margins, etc.

5. **Address the addressee properly.** Doublecheck name spelling, company name and address. Do not omit "Mr.", "Mrs." or "Ms." Also, be sure to use the individual's correct title. This is important!

6. **Identify the subject.** Use "Re:" or open with a simple declaratory sentence.

7. **Be specific.** In referring to earlier correspondence, don't just say "In reply to your letter . . ." Instead, say "In reply to your letter of August 20 about our returns policy . . ."

8. **Avoid lengthy, awkward openings.** Eliminate phrases like "With reference to the above-captioned subject," "beg to advise," etc.

9. **Avoid circumlocutions and redundancies.** Do not use "It is the opinion of the writer" for "I think." Eliminate meaningless phrases like "At this point in time."

10. **Use "we" and "I" properly.** Never use "we" to avoid using "I." Never say "the undersigned" instead of "I." Permissible: "I think that we will be able to ship November 1."

11. **Use everyday language, declaratory sentences.** Minimize use of lengthy words. Keep sentences to 25 words or less, paragraphs to three or four short sentences.

12. **Format letters of instruction or explanation.** Depending on com-

---

lies in two specific areas: (1) the fact that they convey needed information to the customer faster than if an individual letter had to be written; and (2) they are clearly written, understandable and not offensive in tone. Form letters that are used to respond to customer inquiries but are delayed more than a few days are

---

plexity of subject and detail required, use numbers and letters for main topics and subtopics. Summarize.

13. **Use separate enclosures for extra emphasis.** If the subject lends itself, write it up separately in report format and use the covering letter to summarize and emphasize key points.

14. **Give extra attention in writing letters of apology.** Answer customers' complaint letters promptly; if the matter is complex and requires research, acknowledge the complaint immediately and promise a followup shortly (and keep the promise). Avoid admissions of liability, but: 1) show concern for the individual's state of mind; 2) express regret for the individual's inconvenience; 3) explain mitigating circumstances where appropriate, but avoid any appearance of defensiveness; 4) explain the action to be taken, and the timetable; 5) show positive results in avoidance of recurrences; 6) ask for another chance, or more business.

15. **Quit while ahead.** Don't repeat, except to summarize key points of longer letters. Don't wander. Stop when it's all been said.

16. **Close the letter properly.** Follow company style; use your title and provide a phone contact—extension or direct number, as appropriate.

17. **Use a P.S. as a final attention-getter.** "P.S. I'll be leaving on vacation Monday the 21st, so if you'll contact me before then I'll be able to handle your order personally."

18. **Proofread both letter and envelope.** Correct and if necessary retype. Paper is cheaper than a poor impression on customers.

19. **Check enclosures.** Make sure that what was requested (or what your letter says is enclosed) is in fact enclosed, up-to-date and accurate.

20. **Save and circulate relevant letters as guides.** Exchange or circulate letters dealing with complex or sensitive subjects so that new letters won't have to be written from scratch when similar situations arise in the future.

21. **Write first, phone later—or vice versa.** Make sure that important letters are received and actually get read, allow for clarification. Or, alert customers to a letter that's on its way to assure that it won't be overlooked.

likely to offend most customers. The same is true of form letters that are not responsive to the customer's inquiry or that can't be understood or that imply that the customer is at fault.

Despite their impersonality, form letters have numerous advantages for the sender, over and above dollar savings. One of the most important is that form letters allow the manager to delegate many of his or her "fire-putting-out" duties and devote the time and effort to more important tasks of planning and managing the department. Form letters also represent an excellent way to control communications; instead of having to review voluminous reading files, the manager can devote his or her attention to the really critical communications that genuinely require management involvement, judgment and decision making. Finally, form letters insure uniformity of language and avoidance of admissions of liability or similar unintended and unwanted statements in correspondence.

Importance of Language and Format

It's unfortunately true, as suggested earlier, that a significant percentage of the customer service department's workload is created by communications breakdowns over which the manager may have little if any control: advertising, catalogs, product sheets, order blanks, etc. To the extent that the manager can identify such communications breakdowns by source and persuade the departments involved to clarify language, illustrations, policy statements, etc., personnel can be assigned to tasks that are more productive and profitable than correcting avoidable errors or misunderstandings.

Many customer service managers find, for example, that customers' purchase orders often omit critical information such as orientation on equipment (controls on left or right, top or bottom, front or back, etc.), colors of trim, voltage requirements, etc. They also find that language and terminology used by customers may be subject to misinterpretation. And they dream of the day when *all* customers would use a standard order blank which would eliminate all such problems and the delays, call-backs, extra work and frequent customer complaints that often result.

It doesn't happen frequently, but occasionally customer service managers are able to persuade their sales departments *and* customers that the use of a standard, company-provided order form will not only avoid errors and misunderstandings but will also save time and money for all concerned. One company, a manufacturer of metal doors, did just that. Working with the sales force and with distributors, the customer service manager developed a 17-part order form—17 different sections, *not* an original and 16 copies!—and showed those same distributors how use of the standard order form would cut the total order cycle by two to three days. Learning how to use the form took some time on the distributors' part, but since they had been consulted in its design and had to format the information in some manner any-way, it was felt that they could be persuaded to substitute the form for the purchase order formats they had been using in the past. It took some one-on-one selling to individual distributors, presenting the form strictly in terms of benefits to them, but at the end of six months nearly all of the firm's several hundred independent distributors were using it. And everybody was benefiting.

Appearance of Written and Printed Communications

In written (typed), word-processed and printed com-munications, the first thing the customer is aware of is the overall appearance of the document or piece. In some respects, the appearance may outweigh the actual content of the com-munication because the appearance may be what decides the customer to read further—or to put the piece to one side. So, appearance is fundamental in every letter, form letter, form, postcard, shipment enclosure or whatever.

The appearance of its communications says a great deal

about a company and, as its most frequent communicator, about the customer service department itself. And it is particularly important that the customer service department's communications reflect accuracy, precision, attention to detail, consistency and neatness and orderliness—all the things customers value in customer service. A neatly-typed letter with no evident erasures or strikeovers gets a plus mark for the writer and the company, simply because there is so much business correspondence today that does not meet this basic standard. A form letter which is brief, understandable and to the point—and neatly presented—also rates a plus. The same is true of postcards and even the handwritten notes that some departments use effectively to speed communications. Forms and checklists mailed out

---

Turning **NEGATIVES**

Would you tell your beloved that his/her face would stop a clock? Of course not! But if you said "Time stands still while I gaze into your eyes" you'd probably win a few points! In the same way, there are right ways and wrong ways to present bad news to customers, for example. . .

- **Don't vs. Can't.** These terms crop up frequently in attempting to explain company policy to customers, particularly new customers. *Wrong:* "We don't extend open account credit to unrated firms." *Better:* "We can't extend open account credit to unrated firms." *Best:* "I'm sorry, we can't extend open account credit to unrated firms. Shall I send you a credit application?"

- **Have to vs. Will You.** One of the most common traps that company personnel fall into is in interpreting policy in a "rules-and-regulations" tone of voice. *Wrong:* "You'll have to take that up with the credit department." *Better:* "That's handled in the credit department. May I transfer you?" *Best:* "If you'd be willing to talk directly to the credit department, you'll save time and get the matter resolved that much sooner. May I transfer you?"

- **You vs. We.** Using the pronoun "you" in negative situations sometimes sounds as if we're accusing the customer of a crime. *Wrong:* "You didn't give us the order until Thursday afternoon, and there was no way we could get it out

---

into **POSITIVES**

Friday." *Better:* "We didn't receive the order until Thursday afternoon, and just couldn't get it out Friday." *Best:* "If we'd received it Wednesday instead of Thursday, I'm sure we could have gotten it out Friday. Would it be possible to set it up that way next time?"

- **Feature vs. Benefit.** Just citing a policy or terms of sale may turn a customer off—that's the feature part of it—but very often if we can translate that feature into a benefit for the customer it will become more palatable. *Wrong:* "We ship FOB plant, freight charges collect." *Right:* "We ship FOB plant, freight charges collect, so that you can use your own carriers or use your own trucks to pick up."

- **Small vs. Large.** There's a tendency sometimes to quote the minimum order or the lowest price, but it's much harder to start from the bottom and work up than it is to start from the top and work down! *Wrong:* "Our minimum order is 12 cases." *Better:* "You get the palletload rate for 48 cases." *Best:* "There's a big price break at 48 cases, and we ship them as a palletload so you save money in handling and storage as well. May I enter your order?"

- **Take vs. Enter.** The phrase "take your order" has a connotation of a carryout or pizza parlor. It can also sound as if we are taking something away from the customer. "May I enter your order?" sounds not only more professional, but it also suggests that we are entering it on the customer's behalf, as of course we are.

to customers will also get good grades provided they are well-designed, understandable and well reproduced.

On the negative side, poorly-typed letters with obvious erasures or strikeovers may suggest to customers that the company is as sloppy in its manufacturing and quality control processes and customer service as it is in its letter-writing. The same is true of form letters and printed forms and communications which have been over-reproduced on office copiers to the point where they are grey, spattered and half-legible. Many of today's office copiers make excellent, clear forms and form letters if good, clear originals are used. But when copies are made of copies, and copies of those copies, eventually the result looks cheap and second class. A company that spends millions of dollars attracting new customers and cuts corners on its customer service communications to new and existing customers is sending an additional and unintended message to the effect of "once we have you as a customer, you're not very important to us." Even the most minute communication from the customer service department to customers sends its own message about the company and the department, particularly to those increasingly large number of customers for whom the customer service department contact is the *only* contact they have with the company.

Questions of Tone and Attitude

The next thing the customer notices, after the physical appearance of written or printed communications, is the tone in which it is written or the attitude it reflects, as the customer perceives it. Form letters and checklists often refer to negative situations, and their writers sometimes adopt a negative tone: "We are returning your order for the reason checked below," followed by a list of possible reasons, including "You did not enclose a check," "You failed to specify a model number," "You sent the order to our New York office when you should have sent it to your local distributor," and similar statements sounding more like accusations than acknowledgments of welcome business.

Simple rephrasing would take out much of the sting: "Thank you for your order. We regret that we cannot fill it at this time for the reason(s) checked below." And then: "Payment was not enclosed as per our terms of sale; we will be glad to ship as soon as we receive your check for \$_____;" "In order to properly service your order, we will need the model number; please write it in the space provided and return this sheet to us so that we may ship it to you right away;" "Your order was received at our New York office and we ask that you redirect it [or we have redirected it to] your area distributor whose name appears below." In the revised versions, the accusatory tone has been largely eliminated and phrases have been added indicating appreciation for the customer's business rather than annoyance that the order has not been submitted properly.

Another form of "accusation" frequently crops up in correspondence responding to a customer complaint, when the letter-writer uses phrases like "you said," "you specified," "you told us." These are likely to be interpreted as overly defensive at a time when the concern should be with solving the problem rather than blaming the customer for it. Clearly, phrases like "according to you" or "you allege that" have no place in correspondence between the department and customers. When the issue is likely to be sensitive or controversial on the issue of responsibility, the defensive, accusatory language should be neutralized. Instead of saying "you said," "you specified" or "you told us," the letter-writer can simply say "it was our understanding that . . ." and then make the transition to the proposed solution to the particular problem. Except in genuine liability cases (which would normally be reviewed by the legal department in any event), it's more important that the letter reflect a genuine concern in resolving the problem first and apportioning costs or responsibility later. Or, if it's necessary to spell out specific costs to be borne by the customer, doing so in the most palatable way possible. (This subject is dealt with in detail in the following chapter on complaints and complaint handling.)

In a similar vein, customer service people sometimes become over-imbued with the "rules-and-regulations" approach and as a result are likely to communicate with customers in a dictatorial manner: "You will have to take that up directly with the credit department;" "you must submit the request in writing;" "you will be required to submit proof of purchase." It is much easier to simply say "please take the matter up directly with the credit department," or—better—include a benefit: "If you will take that up directly with the credit department, I'm sure the matter can be cleared up quickly." Or, "please submit proof of purchase so that we can expedite your refund." Business and commercial customers, in particular, are not impressed by statements beginning with the phrase "It is our policy that . . .," and some may even respond angrily by retorting "It is *our* policy not to accept *your* policy!" In short, while policies and procedures are an integral part of the customer service activity, it is important that customer service personnel understand that such policies are not the law of the land, and should not be presented to customers in that light. Of course, if there are legal requirements involved, it is easy enough to say "We are required by law to . . .."

Where written agreements or contracts are involved, it is not always diplomatic to address the subject of disputed invoices with phrases like "according to the terms of our agreement, you are required to . . ." If the customer has a bona fide complaint, citing the agreement will only fuel the fire further. It is always possible that the customer is right, agreement or no agreement, and it's a fact that relatively few agreements are enforced via the courts. It's also a fact that customers who are antagonized by the tone of such correspondence will frequently go over the heads of the customer service department and get their way anyway. It's a basic rule of customer service that there are very few policies that apply 100% across the board; there are always a few customers who are important enough to be treated as exceptions to the rule. If policies are formulated and presented in such a way that 90% of customers will accept them, then it's relatively easy to deal with the other 10% on an exceptions basis. This is why it's important (a) that policies be inherently fair; and (b) that they be presented in the most inoffensive and neutral way in both printed and written materials.

Meaning, Verbiage and Understanding

Many problems of written and printed communications occur when managers forget that the ability to write clearly and understandably is as much a professional skill as the ability to prepare a corporate balance sheet. The result is often pure gobbledygook. Here is a verbatim quotation from a form letter received from a Fortune 500 manufacturer's service department:

> In an attempt to minimize any possible misunderstanding and to facilitate the implementation of the system, a brief description of how it will affect you, our valued customer, will be necessary.

The writer, who was trying to explain a new telephone system to the firm's customers, clearly had a problem communicating because he was not entirely sure what he wanted to say or how to say it. Translated into basic English, and with a 75% reduction in verbiage—from 31 words to 8—the statement would read: "Here is how the system will affect you." Excessive verbiage like this is often a sign of uncertainty or indecision, like speakers who repeatedly clear their throats and flounder through their presentations.

In this particular instance, the explanation that followed the muddled introduction was even more muddled. Users of different types of equipment were given different numbers to call, effective on different dates in different counties, and as a result some customers were completely confused. Had the manager thought about it before plunging ahead with his communique, he would have realized that separate notices to the different types of users in the different areas would have taken a little longer to prepare but would have avoided a barrage of phone calls from customers seeking an interpretation of how the letter applied to them personally.

There is a parallel situation with written and printed instructions accompanying products which are shipped disassembled, and with operating, installation and instruction manuals generally. If they do not convey the message in a language and

The phone is handy...
...why write a
LETTER?

1. When you want a clear, unassailable record of what you said.

2. When you want to think a matter through, and writing it out helps you organize your thoughts.

3. When you want to make sure you have the recipient's complete attention. A letter can be set aside and read when the recipient can give it full time and attention.

4. When you want action.

5. When you want to be sure you are understood.

format that is understandable to the customer, the department will be swamped with unexpected phone calls which it may not be able to handle. A company which introduced a line of do-it-yourself garage door openers referred to earlier learned this the hard way. Within two days after Christmas (when the units were first introduced) the manufacturer's customer service department received a barrage of telephone calls from homeowners who couldn't get the openers to work even though they had followed—they thought—the instructions enclosed with each unit. The problem was compounded by the fact that the department was completely unprepared to answer the homeowner's questions because this type of situation had never arisen before. And, in the effort to help the homeowners solve their particular problems, customer service personnel were tying up all the inbound trunks so that regular commercial customers—distributors and retail chains—were unable to get through to place orders. All because of inadequate printed instructions!

Clearly the customer service department is not always consulted when instructions of this type are being written. But where the possibility exists that simple miscommunication can have such a costly impact on regular customer service operations, there are persuasive arguments for having the customer service manager review *all* printed communications that are sent to customers, regardless of where they originate.

There is also the question of *internal* miscommunication. The most common example is when customer service reps are not advised of special deals, promotions, pricing arrangements or exceptions for certain customers. A customer calls in to order merchandise under the promotion, or at the special pricing, and the customer service is completely unaware of either. Some managers wince when they recall how reps have placed major customers on credit hold because they had no written instructions to the contrary, or because their customer service manual was not clear on the subject.

Thus there are miscommunication errors where there has been no written communication at all, and errors where the communications have not been fully understood by those to whom they were addressed. In the first instance, it is largely up to the customer service manager to find out about promotions, deals, special pricing and so forth . . . and *communicate it in writing, in clear and understandable language, to customer service representatives.* In an ideal world, all other departments would communicate clearly and completely and well in advance of all such events. But in the real world they seldom do, and the customer service manager can't afford to wait around for the millenium. If the information is not forthcoming in a timely fashion, then he or she will have to take the initiative and set up the channels of communication that make it happen. It isn't easy, but it is necessary, both for smooth functioning of the department and for the morale of its people.

Basics of Written Business Communications

"The written word, unpublished, can be destroyed, but the spoken word can never be recalled." The poet Horace said it 2,000 years ago, and it is just as true today as then: written and printed materials can be reviewed, examined, analyzed, tested, clarified and refined before they are ever sent on to customers. All nuances of meaning, all possible misunderstandings, all ambiguous words or terms—these can all be taken care of well before the communication is put in final form and sent on its way. And they should be, because written and particularly printed communications are often reserved for the most important messages, or those that are going to be circulated to the most people—and where the most damage can be done by misinterpretation. It is also true that anything in print is usually considered "official"—the company's final word on a policy, terms of sale or whatever. Thus the printed word is likely to be scrutinized very carefully, and relied on by customers in their dealings with the company—all the more reason that such materials be carefully screened for meaning and possible misinterpretation before being released. This should not be taken to mean that all printed materials should be submitted to the legal department for review (although this is certainly advisable in the case of major policy statements or liability situations), but rather that every reasonable attempt should be made to assure that they can be under-

OFFICE COPIER PLUS STOCK ART = EFFECTIVE COMMUNICATIONS

Illustrations -- photographs, diagrams, cartoons, sketches, and so-called "stock art" -- have a number of practical uses for customer communications. Instructions for the use and maintenance of products, installation, testing and the like are more readily understood when illustrated. And cartoon and comic-strip sequences have proven quite effective where there may be language or comprehension problems, or a broad spectrum of persons of varying levels of literacy who must be addressed. Labels identifying hazards or hazardous materials fall in this category and are sometimes a customer service responsibility. Step-by-step illustrations that show customers how to pack materials for safe return help avoid loss and damage and later arguments about product condition of returns. Quality of illustrations is not as important as function. Sometimes, sketches by members of the department with an artistic bent are quite suitable. Sometimes stock art -- also known as clip art -- will do the job very effectively at a cost of fifty cents or less per illustration. With an office copier, scissors and pastepot, eye-catching communications are easily produced. This illustration was produced using a typewriter, copier and all stock art.

stood by the persons to whom they are addressed. This leads to the following basic rules for written or printed communications:

1. *Define objectives and scope.* The writer should ask: "What is the purpose of this communication?" "What should it include—what *must* it include?"

2. *Define audience, informational need, skill or understanding level.* This is basic to what will be covered, the language that will be employed and the way the information will be formatted. A communication directed to hyperballistics engineers would conceivably be quite different in many respects from one directed to customer service reps without engineering backgrounds. The same may be true of messages directed to dis-

---

Charts, Graphs Add Interest to Communications

TELEPHONE CUSTOMER SERVICE
1983 CALL TYPES

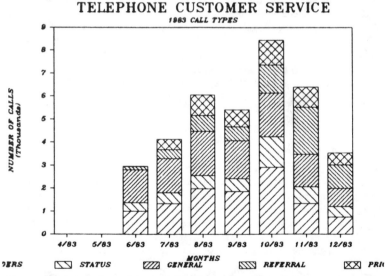

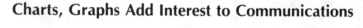
?ERS   STATUS   GENERAL   REFERRAL   PRI(

Charts and graphs, either hand-drawn or computer generated (as these were) can add considerably to the interest of the printed page while also serving to summarize information that is described in greater detail in the text. This is particularly true when there are

---

tributors, as contrasted to communications to retailers, where the business context and language are entirely different.

3. *Consider different messages for different audiences.* If the communication is intended for a number of significantly different audiences in terms of interests, need-to-know and educational levels, consider framing a separate message for each audience in the language and format best suited to it.

4. *Decide what* not *to include.* Information that is not directly related to the purpose of the communication is very likely to confuse the reader, or possibly get the message set aside altogether as irrelevant.

5. *Identify and emphasize key topics.* Capitalizing, under-

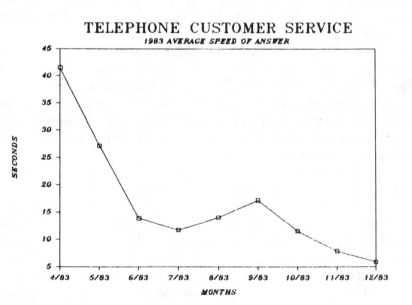

TELEPHONE CUSTOMER SERVICE
1983 AVERAGE SPEED OF ANSWER

relationships between a number of variables like cost, service levels, sales volume, etc. The illustrations reproduced here reflect changes in telephone customer service over a period of time. *(Courtesy Data Systems Group, Texas Instruments).*

lining, boldfacing or highlighting with color will draw attention to main topics and enable the recipient to quickly grasp the overall significance of the message.

6. *Break complex subjects down into numbered steps or subtopics.* Solid masses of type tend to be intimidating and discourage readership. Breaking the page up makes it more interesting and easier to read—and also easier to check back to previous points.

7. *Use diagrams and illustrations where appropriate.* These always add interest. Even amateur cartoons or hand-drawn stick figures can sometimes get a message across more effectively than words alone.

8. *Use language appropriate to the audience.* If the communication is addressed to a broad audience, highly technical terms and trade jargon should be avoided. If it's necessary to use such language, follow it with one- or two-word lay definitions in parentheses.

9. *Verify for relevance.* Communications that are going to be widely circulated should be tested beforehand on a sample of the audience to insure that they are in fact relevant and understandable to that audience. It is extremely important to the customer service manager to remember that customer perceptions and interpretations may be sharply different from his or her own perceptions!

10. *Keep it short.* Long memos or communications tend to discourage readership. Good communication thrives on brevity, but this does not mean that key information should be left out. Customers and others receiving communications are subject to frequent interruptions from telephone calls, visitors, etc., and the briefer the message the more likely it is to get read and assimilated in one pass the way it was intended to be. Messages that get set aside because they seem too long or complicated may get buried.

11. *Define all units of measurement.* Inches, feet, pounds, centimeters, millimeters or whatever should always be set forth clearly. Do not rely on industry conventions where "30 x 40" is known to one and all to mean "30 inches wide by 40 feet long."

There is always at least one customer (and sometimes many more) unaware of this usage or meaning.

12. *Be consistent in usages and units.* Serious communications breakdowns result from minor inconsistencies, like saying on one occasion "24 20-ounce cans" and on the next "24 1 lb. 4 oz. cans." The writer knows both mean the same thing, but a few readers may not. And in a case where the first usage appears on the customer's order and the second on the shipping documents and cartons received at the dock, the computer may reject the shipment as unordered merchandise.

13. *Circulate on a need-to-know basis.* Too many memos or other communications to people who aren't directly concerned, and they will soon start to ignore all such communications.

14. *Hold sensitive letters or memos overnight before mailing.* Written documents can be edited, reviewed, refined and polished—but once they've been sent they become part of a permanent file or record . . . as many a manager has learned to his or her embarrassment and sometimes regret. Memos written in anger or for internal political reasons often look intemperate or ill-advised in retrospect. Responding in kind to angry customer letters may make the writer feel good, but they should be held over at least 24 hours or until the writer has cooled off sufficiently to re-read the letter objectively. Setting correspondence aside this way for later review is often a wise move—and frequently saves the company postage as well. Of course if there's any doubt about whether a letter or memo should be sent, an opinion should be sought from somebody who's not directly involved.

15. *Use "cc's" and blind copies appropriately.* A "cc" ["carbon copy"] at the bottom of a letter or memo, followed by the names of one or more individuals (and their titles where relevant) puts everybody named on notice that the subject concerns them or is of interest to them. In correspondence with customers about adjustments or other action to be taken as the result of a complaint, the "cc" device at the bottom of the page is a very effective way of letting the customer know that others in the company have been put on notice about the problem and the action to be taken; in this type of communication, including the titles of the

"cc" names gives added strength and emphasis to any commitments made by the writer. So-called "blind copies," i.e., copies sent to others without any "cc" or similar notification to the recipient, should be used very sparingly because they can lead to embarrassing situations. It's also risky to use blind copies for political reasons, for example, writing a memo to another department head that makes him or her look bad and the writer look good, and then sending a blind copy to upper management. This usually backfires on the writer.

16. *Remember the basic rule of* all *communications has a special significance for written and printed communications.* The rule is "Do not communicate so that you can be understood; communicate so that you cannot possibly be misunderstood." The special significance for written and printed communications is the statement by *Newsweek* magazine several years ago that "About 23 million American adults, as well as an estimated 13% of 17-year-olds, are functionally illiterate."* At this writing, those 17-year-olds are now 23 years old, and some of them are quite likely your customers . . . and perhaps even your co-workers.

---

*November 6, 1978 issue.

23

THE HOW AND WHY OF SETTING COMPLAINT POLICIES

"Those who buy, support me. Those who come to flatter, please me. Those who complain, teach me how I may please others so that more will buy. Only those hurt me who are displeased but do not complain. They refuse me permission to correct my errors and thus improve my service."

These classic words were spoken over a century ago by the great merchant prince, Marshall Field, whom many consider the father of modern day customer service. (Stressing customer service in his Chicago department store, he introduced such "radical"—for the time—policies as liberal credit, the one-price system and free return of merchandise. And he was the first to have a department store restaurant for the convenience of shoppers.)

What Marshall Field was describing, of course, was an unchanging law of customer service that even today, more than 100 years later, many people in business management cannot seem to grasp: *a complaint is a profit opportunity, pure and simple.* It is an opportunity to retain customers who might otherwise be lost, at considerable expense, and to improve the service or product so that additional customers will be attracted—additional revenues and profits. Marshall Field knew it by instinct; today, there is quantified research to prove the point.

The TARPS Studies

Two landmark studies in the field of complaint handling were conducted by Technical Assistance Research Programs, Inc. Washington, D.C. The first of these was conducted for the U.S. Office of Consumer Affairs, Department of Health, Education and Welfare. Titled "Consumer Complaint Handling in America," the 1979 study established firmly the value of actually *making it easy* for customers to complain: customers who have a problem with a product of value (over $100) but do not complain, are only half as likely to rebuy that product as customers who complain but don't get satisfaction, who in turn are only about one-third as likely to rebuy the product as customers who complain and get satisfaction. Here are the actual percentages:

Category	Percentage That Will Rebuy
Had problem, did not complain	9.5%
Complained but did not get satisfaction	19.0%
Complained and got satisfaction	54.3%

These numbers will naturally vary with the dollar value of the product or service in question, but what is truly significant in these findings is that there is a measurable dollar value to the simple fact of getting customers to complain. It's greater if the complaint can be satisfied, but still significant even when it can't. Most companies have data on account value—how much it costs to get a new customer, how much the customer spends, what it costs to lose a customer, etc.—and thus it is a relatively simple matter to determine what it's worth in dollars to make it easy for customers to complain.

In 1981, the same organization conducted a study of the economics of complaints for the Coca-Cola Company, and the findings again demonstrated both the direct and indirect impact of complaint handling on sales volume:

1. *Direct impact.* 75% of customers who complain and are dissatisfied with the way their complaints are handled either buy less of the product or stop buying it altogether. (See Table 1.)

2. *Indirect impact.* Customers dissatisfied with the way

their complaints were handled tell 9 to 10 others about their negative experience. Customers who complained and were completely satisfied with the way their complaints were handled told only half as many people, 4 to 5 others.

The study demonstrated that the way complaints are handled thus has an immediate effect and a long-range effect on sales, first with the complaining customers themselves and later with others whom they influence. The study concluded that negative word-of-mouth cancels sales about twice as fast as positive word-of-mouth closes them. Since poorly handled complaints generate twice as much word-of-mouth as well-handled ones, this means that bad complaint handling is four times as important in stopping sales as good complaint handling is in creating them. Coca-Cola addressed this by increasing the ratio of satisfied customers: "During 1980," the report explained, "1.56 customers were gained as a result of positive word-of-mouth for every customer lost because of negative word-of-mouth."

Table 1. How Customers' Satisfaction Levels Influence their Purchases

Satisfaction Ratings	Buy More	Buy at Same Rate	Buy Less	Don't Buy
Completely satisfied	9.9%	84.0%	5.2%	0.9%
Response Acceptable	2.7%	59.6%	31.5%	6.2%
Not Satisfied	2.5%	22.2%	44.4%	30.9%

Customers who are completely satisfied are almost five times more likely to buy more than customers who simply find the complaint handling response "acceptable," but what is even more significant is that the "defection" rate—buying less or not at all—is from six to thirty times as great in the "acceptable" and "not satisfied" categories, according to a study commissioned by the Coca-Cola Company and conducted by Technical Assistance Research Programs Inc.

Translated into integral numbers, Coca-Cola demonstrated that by strengthening the complaint handling function it could gain three customers for every two it lost, a healthy ratio indeed! And while these studies relate to consumer products, it is much easier for industrial and commercial firms to track purchasing patterns of individual customers, and indeed with many it's standard procedure to monitor closely the subsequent purchasing levels of any customer who has complained. As for the comparability of consumer buying behavior and that of professional purchasing personnel in businesses, a study by Prof. Alvin J. Williams of the University of Southern Mississippi reported in the May 2, 1981 issue of *Marketing News* established that complaining patterns among industrial or organizational buyers are similar to those among consumers, except that industrial buyers tend to complain more often, suggesting that professional buyers are more likely to give vendors a second chance.

There are reasons other than complaints for cutbacks in purchases, but even so it is not difficult to establish cause-and-effect relationships when poor handling of complaints is at fault. Naturally, it can't be ignored that the *cause* of the complaint— the customer service failure or whatever—impacts future sales, but experienced managers also know that prompt and creative handling of genuinely serious complaints can often turn them into long-term gains rather than losses.

This is particularly true in the case of complaints where it turns out that the customer is at fault and the company has no liability. There is a tendency on the part of customer service representatives to breathe a sigh of relief and relax their efforts to find an acceptable solution in such cases. This is a serious error in judgment, because customers who feel that they have been or are likely to be "abandoned" when *they* are the ones to make the mistake will quickly become alienated and find a way of paying the vendor back. By contrast, customers who are at fault but get constructive help from the customer service department nonetheless tend to show their appreciation by becoming even better and more profitable customers in the future. The subject of what to do when the customer is at fault will be discussed at greater length in the next chapter. In the meantime, the economics speak for themselves when more than a few buyers will readily acknowledge that their jobs were saved for them by quick-thinking customer service reps who did *not* relax when they found the customer was wrong but instead went above and beyond the call of duty to help the customer salvage whatever could be salvaged from the situation.

"Reprisals" by Customers

Another reason for tracking customers' post-complaint purchases is that negative reactions by customers take different forms that aren't always immediately discernible. Contrary to popular belief, cutting off the relationship with the vendor is relatively rare, and usually done only as a last resort. Yet the "reprisals" that customers do undertake are sometimes more costly than actually losing the account. In this respect, Prof. Williams' study confirmed what many customer service managers have learned from painful experience: that the first response to poor handling of a complaint is that the customer starts splitting orders with other vendors. Managers report such other types of reprisals by customers as slowing down payment of invoices; ordering only low-margin or difficult items, the so-called "dogs"; making excessive demands and quibbling about minor items; sharing negative experiences with other customers and prospective customers at industry meetings and trade shows; and other obstacles to a profitable business relationship. One costly response that a number of managers have commented on is that when complaints aren't handled responsively, customers tend to lose confidence in the vendor and thus call much more frequently to check order status and verify delivery. This adds customer service costs simply in terms of servicing the added volumes of telephone traffic.

It shouldn't be assumed that complaints have to be serious before they have a monetary impact. A Midwestern manufacturer sent its vendors a checklist of situations which, if not remedied, would cause a significant delay in approval and payment of their invoices. These included:

☐ No vendor packing list included with the shipment.

☐ Packing list enclosed, but references an incorrect P.O. number.

☐ Packing list enclosed, but no P.O. number referenced at all.

☐ Vendor did not include customer part numbers on packing list or invoices.

☐ Shipment includes parts not listed on the P.O.

☐ Shipment includes parts in excess of quantities on P.O.

☐ No "Certificate of Compliance" included in the shipment.

☐ Short counts in shipments; wrong items shipped.

☐ Vendors shipping against cancelled P.O.s.

☐ Materials drop-shipped from a secondary source do not include proper documentation or prime vendor identification.

☐ Multiple shipments and invoices against small dollar items without prior authorization by buyer.

This particular company was being straightforward with its customers, pointing out that the time required to resolve these matters would inevitably delay payment of invoices. Other companies might be less direct. Unfortunately, messages like this often don't reach the right people in the vendor organization: Accounts Receivable, Shipping, Sales itself, and sometimes the Systems and Procedures people who designed the system to begin with.

One unfortunate byproduct is that when payment on an invoice is being delayed while a complaint is being resolved, somebody neglects to inform the credit department and the customer is either placed on credit hold or the account starts receiving the cycle of collection letters. And it is often very difficult to stop that cycle once it's started. What's the actual cost in dollars? A retailer requested a duplicate copy of a lost invoice from the vendor and while waiting started receiving collection letters. The request was repeated several times, and some six months later the duplicate invoice was finally received by the customer and paid. In the meantime, however, the customer had completely suspended doing business with that vendor . . . and had had plenty of time to find a replacement.

In a case where the customer was partially at fault, a distributor drew up and mailed two separate checks to a vendor to cover two separate invoices. The customer enclosed both checks in one envelope, but omitted one invoice copy. Several weeks later, the distributor started receiving collection letters for the invoice which had been paid but no copy had been included in the envelope. The distributor's accounts payable department investigated, discovered what had happened, and wrote a mild letter of complaint explaining that payment had long since been made and with the letter enclosed a copy of the invoice as well as a copy of the cancelled check, front and back. Still, the collection letters kept coming. The sad ending of this story is that not even apologies from the credit manager as well as the vice president of sales at the vendor company could convince the distributor to resume doing business with them.

But . . . Don't Give Away the Store!

None of the above is intended to imply that complaints should be automatically resolved in favor of the customer just to get back to business as usual. The company is not a charitable organization; it is in business to *make* money, not give it away. What is important is that complaints be handled *well* and handling complaints well means handling them fairly and—particularly—handling them *fast*. A study by Dik Twedt of the University of Missouri reported in the April 6, 1979 issue of *Marketing News* revealed that it is the speed of response, rather than the actual content of that response, that carries the most weight with customers. Interestingly enough, other than in extreme cases, the severity of the problem being complained about did not appear to have any direct correlation with the degree of dissatisfaction of the complainer.

Even so, different types of complaints do suggest different kinds of responses. A complaint charging a major customer service failure on the vendor's part requires an almost immediate response—yet it is essential to research the complaint before responding. If the complaint is put in a queue with other complaints waiting to be resolved, the problem will certainly get worse . . . and possibly extremely expensive. If it is given priority over the other complaints in the queue, then *they* are likely to escalate. It sounds like a no-win situation!

Actually, there are several possible solutions. The alternative to actually resolving a complaint quickly is to *acknowledge* it quickly. This can be done by phone, mail or Mailgram. The customer is thanked for letting the vendor know about the problem and assured that action will be taken as quickly as possible. Depending on the nature of the complaint, this may buy as much as a month of time, although sometimes it may be only a few hours. A main purpose of the swift acknowledgement is to reassure the customer that he or she is not being "stonewalled," and that the vendor does in fact care and is set to take action quickly.

In the case of more serious complaints where responsibility has not been established, there should be clear guidelines as to how far the company will go, and how much it is willing to spend, to resolve such problems *before* responsibility has in fact been determined.

As an example, cost of downtime in an automobile assembly plant can run as high as half a million dollars an hour. A plant is about to shut down because a large shipment of components from an outside vendor—tail light assemblies—has not arrived and cannot be located. It's not clear whether the shipment was purchased FOB shipping point or FOB delivered, which would be a major determinant of responsibility. At the moment, the only way to avoid shutting down the assembly plant altogether is to charter an airplane and fly a planeload of parts from the vendor's plant some 1,500 miles distant . . . at a very hefty price. Question: should the plane be chartered and the shipment made? And if so, who will pay the freight bill? The customer service manager has about five minutes to decide!

Most managers would understandably seek a commitment from the customer to pay the air freight bill if it later turned out that the vendor had in fact been blameless. Yet even without such a commitment, some managers would proceed with the air freight movement anyway on the premise that, whatever the cost, the consequences of *not* doing something would be far greater. This is an extreme example, of course, but it has many parallels in smaller-scale complaints that occur routinely. Some managers have a blanket policy which says, in effect: "If delay will make the problem worse, we'll concentrate on solving the problem first—getting the customer back in business—and worry about who pays for what later."

There are a number of grey areas in such situations, however. A manufacturer of printing equipment was authorized by a customer to retrofit certain presses, with the work to be done on a weekend. The technicians arrived on site to do the work, and found it necessary to spend half a day cleaning the equipment before the retrofit work could begin. This added substantial cost to the final invoice, and the customer refused to pay on the grounds that the cleanup work had not been authorized. The vendor pointed out that it would have been impossible to perform the retrofits without the cleanup, and the technicians assumed, logically, that this was part of the job they were supposed to perform. Who paid? At this juncture, it's still in negotiation. But the example does serve to underline the desirability of having written policies to cover the most customary contingencies—not to serve as alibis, or "I told you so's," but rather to avoid disputes altogether by spelling out *beforehand* the respective responsibilities of the vendor and the customer.

What Most Companies Don't Know About Complaint Costs

In most companies, the main emphasis is on how much the company pays out to settle complaints. There is a tendency to overlook other costs associated with complaints, direct and indirect. Yet any balanced analysis of complaint costs would have to include these elements:

1. Administrative costs of handling the complaint. Most companies do not separate out the costs of the personnel involved, the costs of maintaining files, research, telephone and correspondence costs, etc. They also tend to overlook the cost of the management time that's often involved when complaints escalate, and what it costs when other departments become involved. These costs tend to be buried in departmental and corporate general expense, and nobody thinks about them much. By one estimate, a single four-drawer file represents administrative expense of some $1,500, or over $2,000 if the cost of the file and the space it occupies are included. It also contains several hundred misfiles representing an administrative expense of about $300 for searching, procuring duplicates, etc. And with all that, 85% of all files are never referred to again, and 90% are dead after three years. Most managers will accept an estimate of order processing costs of $40-$50 per order (1984 figures), and chances are that a typical complaint costs even more to handle when it goes through conventional administrative processes: starting a file, conducting an investigation, verifying proof of purchase, warranty or returns policy applicability, submitting materials to Quality Control, and perhaps going through an appeals-type process before the complaint is finally resolved.

2. Out-of-pocket costs of settling the complaint. These are direct payments, refunds or credits to the customer after the complaint has been judged valid and an acceptable settlement made. In some cases, these are spelled out in the terms of a warranty: after one year, the settlement is "x" percent of the original purchase price, after two years "y" percent and so forth. This is common in products like tires and batteries. Or, company policy may specify deductions representing handling charges, restocking charges, cleaning or refurbishing charges and the like. Many complaints, particularly those involving large dollar amounts, are negotiated individually.

There are also different authorization levels: in a typical company, the computer will automatically allow deductions by the customer up to a preset dollar limit—normally in the range of a dollar—while the customer service rep can offer the customer adjustments which in some companies are limited to $5 or $10 but in others range as high as $300 or $400. The department head may have signoff authority to $1,000, and beyond this point upper management is likely to be involved. Of course, each added step adds a degree of cost, and a certain amount of delay—sometimes a great deal of delay, which may have a cost itself in terms of customer good will.

3. **Indirect costs such as lost business or increased costs of doing business.** Sometimes these costs may be quite subtle. If a feeling develops that a company doesn't stand behind its products, that company may have a great deal of difficulty selling new models or designs to its existing customer base. It is not very difficult to assign a dollar cost to customer disaffection, but some managements are reluctant to do so. Yet the numbers are very clear: the American Management Associations says that it costs five times as much to *get* a customer as it does to *keep* one that is already on board.

Most companies know—or should know—their customer acquisition costs. They should also know their customer turnover or longevity rate. In other words, if it costs $1,000 to acquire a new customer, the company can in theory spend up to $999.99 in settling complaints for that customer and still come out ahead . . . *if* not settling the complaint well would result in the loss of that account and the need to replace it.

One consumer publications company found that it was spending $8 to acquire each new customer, but only $1 in administrative cost to handle each complaint that came in. It also determined that customer turnover was too high, mainly as a result of the highly routinized, impersonal way complaints were being handled. The company determined that it was losing 40% of its customer base each year, in effect, turning over its entire customer base every two and a half years. If it could extend this to three, three and a half, four years, the profit contribution would be enormous. These numbers justified a two-pronged investment program in improved complaint handling: (1) correcting some of the situations and policies that caused complaints in the first place, often involving misposting of payments and misdirected collection efforts; and (2) upgrading and personalizing of the complaint handling function itself, including training of personnel in more empathetic responses to complaining customers.

A final type of indirect cost of complaints that must be considered is the potential for retaliation by disgruntled customers via the courts or legislative process: either through punitive lawsuits, or pressing for regulatory legislation. These costs can run into the millions.

The Case for Automatic Adjustment

Most complaint handling arrangements assume that it's necessary to have certain policies and procedures to safeguard the company from paying out excessive amounts of money in settlements when it is not obligated to do so: the don't-give-away-the-store-syndrome referred to earlier. There is also a feeling that if adjustment policies are too liberal, customers will take advantage of them—"Steal us blind" is the way it's often expressed.

The "safeguard-the-company" assumption often ignores the fact that the direct cost of handling and investigating complaints below certain dollar levels almost always exceeds the savings that are derived from investigating them and declining to adjust those that are not justified. In other words, it costs more to run complaints through the administrative mill than it would if they were simply paid without question. Which leads to the second assumption, the steal-us-blind view: the fear that once the word gets out that a company makes automatic adjustments without investigating, customers in swarms will be taking advantage of the policy and registering unjustified complaints in order to receive refunds or other adjustments they aren't entitled to.

This second assumption is more difficult to deal with because

The Non-Dollar Costs of Ineffective Complaint Handling

In some companies, complaint handling is seen as a nonproductive, cost-adding activity that contributes nothing to the company's bottom line. As a result, there is very little effort to systematize the complaint handling activity and make constructive use of the wealth of useful information to be found in customer feedback in the form of complaints.

In one extreme case, a company received an unusually high number of returns of a particular product. Customers complained that it was incorrectly described in the catalog. Customer service representatives were observed saying to these customers. "You'd be surprised how many people make the same mistake that you made!" And while they were thus offending customers they were at the same time making no attempt to relay the information to the company's catalog department where the problem could be rectified. Such companies pass up opportunities for improvements in product or service design or delivery, better and more understandable documentation, rewriting of offensive policies—and other changes which would make the product or service more salable to more people, and in greater volume.

A surprising number of decisions to change sources of supply are based, not on the severity of a specific complaint to a vendor, but rather on the vendor's perceived ineptness in handling the complaint, or insensitivity to the subject of the complaint and the inconvenience to the customer. "I just got tired of the constant hassle," said one excustomer to his former vendor. "Not that your people didn't try. But every time we went for an adjustment, or a credit, or some other routine matter, it was like trying to bat a Kleenex out of Comiskey Park!"

it has emotional overtones: people don't like to feel that they've been taken advantage of, even though it doesn't cost them anything. Thus managers and employees alike are likely to resist the idea of a policy of blanket adjustments when they know for certain that some of the customers seeking such adjustments are deliberately taking advantage of the company's liberal policy. Indeed, if they are not instructed otherwise, many new employees will automatically assume that all complaints are to be "stonewalled," that is, deliberately delayed, tied up in red tape and otherwise resisted—just to protect the company from its predatory customers. And it's not surprising that they feel this way, because a number of managements do, too.

Yet in spite of these sentiments, the facts are almost always otherwise. Relatively few of a company's customers—most managers agree that it's usually well below 10%—will deliberately try to get adjustments, refunds or comparable arrangements they know they're not entitled to. And this percentage doesn't appear to vary significantly with the degree of liberalness of the company's policies on such matters. It's often overlooked that the vast majority of customers who purchase goods or services do so because they genuinely want them and in many cases need them. They have certain expectations from those goods or services, and if those expectations are not met they feel that they are entitled to some adjustment by the vendor—particularly if the vendor is seen as having created those expectations.

For example, take the case where vendor advertising says, in effect: "This new product will double your fastener sales. It will be supported by radio, TV and trade paper advertising. Be sure to order extra cartons to meet the increased demand!" Customers over-order in reliance on the advertising; when the product does not sell—for whatever reason—they feel, with some justification, that they should be able to return the excess product for full refunds. And most vendors will make it relatively easy for customers to return products or obtain satisfactory adjustments or credits in such cases. If they didn't do so, their sales effort and advertising alike would quickly lose credibility *and* effectiveness!

However, not all cases are quite as clearcut. When is the expectation the direct result of the vendor's sales and sales promotion representations and promises, and when is it due mainly to wishful thinking on the customer's part? Under both the Uniform Commercial Code and common law itself, vendors have certain responsibilities toward their customers, and one of the best known is the "implied warranty" doctrine which says that products must be able to do what by their nature they are supposed to do: a canoe must float, an airplane must fly, a typewriter must type, a book must be readable and contain all its pages, etc. Similarly, products that move in commerce must be "merchantable," of a quality and in a condition that's considered commercially acceptable or salable. If these conditions are not met, the customer must be "made whole" again.

This is an oversimplification of what has become a very complex process because of the involvement of numerous state and federal agencies. There are even distinctions between what constitutes acceptable "puffery" in advertising and sales promotion, on the one hand, and what constitutes a genuine advertising claim or sales representation that customers would be expected to rely on in purchasing a product or service. For example, if a horror movie promises that "It will make your hair stand on end," it would be very unlikely that any court would entertain a suit against the film-maker from a patron whose hair did *not* stand on end as a result of seeing the motion picture.

On the other hand, if the advertising of a training film promised that "Productivity of your personnel will improve at least 25% in three months," the law would strongly support any manager who had purchased the film and then found that it did not increase productivity to any appreciable degree. And through all this, the basic fact remains that the overwhelming majority of customers seeking adjustments do so because they genuinely believe they are entitled to those adjustments both morally and legally, not because they are looking for "freebies." And this is equally applicable to retail customers, i.e., consumers, as to commercial customers.

Naturally, there are some exceptions, some companies that

may be particularly susceptible to fraudulent claims. Furniture manufacturers and retailers are often prime targets of such claims. A customer will write from Milwaukee that furniture purchased in St. Louis and manufactured in North Carolina collapsed after only four months' usage. It is very difficult to establish all the facts, and if the companies involved are not watchful, they are likely to find themselves paying out substantial refunds to customers who are not entitled to them. But these cases are usually the exception rather than the rule, and it is not too difficult to identify would-be defrauders by name, telephone number or zip codes pinpointing "repeaters" who are the primary offenders in any event.

In commercial relationships a customer service manager who feels that certain customers are making repeated and unjustified claims of shortage is understandably reluctant to openly confront customers and accuse them of attempted fraud, particularly when there may be no hard evidence that they are doing so. These situations can usually be handled on an exceptions basis. Once a particular customer becomes a "suspect," all orders for that customer are checked twice, or cartons may be weighed to insure that they match standard weight for that type of shipment. In some cases, the customer service manager may personally supervise order assembly and packing and sealing. If the claims of shortage persist, the manager may then ask permission to send an inspector to the customer site to witness unloading of the carrier equipment on arrival. The offer is seldom accepted—but the shortages often stop when customers and their personnel become aware that they are under scrutiny. In the relatively few cases of bonafide but repetitive shortages, the customer will be as anxious to get to the bottom of the problem as the vendor. Cooperative investigation may uncover a dishonest driver or, in some cases, dishonest personnel in the customer's receiving warehouse who are siphoning off goods and then reporting them to their own managements as short count deliveries.

In some instances, the vendor may prefer not to investigate repeat claimants, but simply to drop them as customers on a no-fault basis. One company with a very large force of independent field sales agents employs such a policy. If a particular agent claims non-delivery, or shortage upon delivery, the company automatically replaces the shipment or the short items without charge to the agent—and it will do so up to four times within a given time frame, regardless of the size or dollar value of the shortage. After the fourth time, however, it simply cuts off the agent. It does not accuse the agent of any dishonesty, and indeed there may be none. It simply says that the relationship is no longer profitable, which is true.

The case for a policy of automatic adjustments is logical and persuasive. But perhaps the most compelling argument of all concerns the negative effect of red tape and delay on the 90%-plus of customers with bona fide claims who are quite likely to take offense at extensive delay and red tape, and particularly at what it suggests: that their claims may not be bonafide and that they themselves may be perceived as dishonest. And this is exactly the kind of impression that some companies' complaint handling policies create. Either this, or a variation which comes across to customers as "If we stall you long enough, or make it difficult enough for you, you'll get tired and give up—and we'll keep your money." An insurance company which sends first one form, and then another, and perhaps a third form, to claimants is seen by these customers as simply doing whatever it can to delay payment of the claim on the premise that the longer it can delay payment, the longer it can derive income from that sum of money. And while it may be true that discouraging complaints and claims, or making them difficult to pursue, may actually save money for the company, it's been well established that customers who are discouraged from complaining cost the company far more in lost business than those who feel their complaints will receive courteous attention and prompt action.

The Economics of Automatic No-Fault Adjustment

How high—or how low—should a company set its dollar limits for automatic adjustments? This will depend on how that particular company views the costs and benefits associated with the no-fault, automatic adjustment approach. The legendary L.L. Bean sporting goods firm has a policy of replacing or refunding on any item for any reason and at any time, in other words a virtually unrestricted refund policy if customers are dissatisfied for any reason whatsoever. At the other extreme, a manufacturer of jet engines may take a much narrower view of what conditions will warrant an automatic no-fault adjustment. Yet the jet engine manufacturer may actually pay out thousands of dollars more, claim for claim, under its automatic adjustment policy than Bean does under its far broader policy. (It should also be mentioned that both Bean and the jet engine manufacturer can point out that their customers are rather exceptional and would on the whole be quite unlikely to file false claims.*)

Actually, the mathematics of automatic adjustments are rather easily demonstrated. If a company determines that it costs $10—a very low figure—to process a complaint through the

---

*The story is told about the Bean customer in Alaska who filed a claim for non-delivery of several shirts he had ordered. Bean promptly shipped a replacement, no questions asked. When the spring thaws arrived, the melting snow uncovered the original shipment where it had been dropped by a bush pilot, and still in perfect condition. The Alaskan promptly mailed Bean a second check paying for the "lost" shipment.

Figure 23-1. Breakeven chart shows amounts that company can automatically pay out without losing money at varying validity or "customer honesty" levels when the cost of investigating complaints is known. Most managers agree that an 80% validity level is reasonable, and that a conservative estimate of the cost of investigating a complaint would be $20. Thus using this chart and finding the coordinates of a $20 investigation cost and an 80% validity level, the company could pay out all claims of $100 or less without investigation and still break even. Additionally, when all smaller claims or complaints have to be investigated before adjustment is made, the process is often offensive to bona fide complainers, who see the delay and red tape as a form of "stonewalling," or discouraging complaints. Of course, the payout is not necessarily in the form of direct payment to the complaining customer, but may also include expenses incurred by the customer service department in "making the customer whole."

conventional processes and if it can assume that at least 80% of the claims or complaints it handles are bona fide and will eventually be paid anyway, it can use a simple equation to determine the breakeven point of investigating complaints as follows:

To automatically pay out 100 claims at "X" dollars each: 100X

To investigate 100 claims at $10 each: $1,000

To pay out 80% (80) claims at "X" each: 80 x X

If the company now says that it is willing to pay out as much in automatic adjustments as it would pay to investigate each

Automatic Complaint Settlement Breakeven Points						
Cost of Investigating a Complaint	Amount That Can Be Paid Out Automatically By Claim validity or "Customer Honesty Level"					
	90%	80%	70%	60%	50%	40%
$10	$100	$50	$33	$25	$20	$10
$20	$200	$100	$67	$50	$40	$20
$30	$300	$150	$100	$75	$60	$30
$40	$400	$200	$133	$100	$80	$40
$50	$500	$250	$167	$125	$100	$50
$60	$600	$300	$200	$150	$120	$60
$70	$700	$350	$233	$175	$140	$70
$80	$800	$400	$267	$200	$160	$80
$90	$900	$450	$300	$225	$180	$90
$100	$1000	$500	$333	$250	$200	$100

complaint and then pay each complaint on its merits only, it would arrive at an equation like this:

$$\begin{aligned}
\textbf{Investigate and Pay} &= \textbf{Pay Automatically}\\
\$1{,}000 + (80 \times X) &= 100X\\
20X &= \$1{,}000\\
X &= \$50
\end{aligned}$$

In other words, given a basic cost of investigating claims of $10, the company will do as well by automatically paying out all claims up to a dollar limit of $50, as shown in the following comparison:

*To investigate 100 claims at an investigating cost of $10
each, and pay out 80 at $50 each* = $5,000

To automatically pay out 100 claims at $50 each = $5,000

To be sure, there are some administrative costs associated with automatically paying all complaints without investigation, but these would generally be incurred anyway. There is also a difference in the cost of writing 100 checks vs. having to write only 80, but this is more than offset by the cost of notifying 20 claimants that their claims will not be honored. If the company sees there is long-range benefit in settling complaints quickly over and above the administrative savings, it may set its automatic adjustment level at the actual breakeven. If it is more conservative, it may set it at one-half or two-thirds breakeven. For example, if breakeven is $50, then it may set the automatic adjustment at $25 or $35 to be on the safe side.

Non-Money Adjustments

Although most of the examples in this chapter have assumed some sort of payout, either in actual cash or credit, or in the replacement of a product, the scope of automatic adjustments will also include actions taken by the vendor which have a measurable cost but which do not necessarily result in a direct payment to the customer. One instance of this would be the earlier example where the vendor opted to pay the cost of air freight to avoid a shutdown of the customer's assembly line. Another might be price protection for a retailer who had printed a catalog in reliance on current prices, only to find that prices had been increased the day the catalog went in the mail. While the vendor's price lists might proclaim the conventional "All prices subject to change without notice" in bold face type, some manufacturers would protect the retailer at the original prices for the life of the catalog. Or, the vendor might elect to absorb the costs of warehouse overtime, telephone calls to alternative sources and similar expenses. One company uses a parallel approach in its substitution policy: if the particular item a customer wants is not available, it will substitute a higher-priced item at no additional cost.

The customer service manager should also recognize that there may be conflicts with other departments when automatic adjustment policies are adopted. For example, if the company adopts a policy of automatically replacing products which customers claim are defective, production and quality control personnel may feel that it's being implied that they are at fault. Engineering personnel, in particular, have been known to take such claims as a personal insult to their professional skills. It is important that such individuals be made aware that it is a no-fault policy and defects will be charged to them only when and if the products in question are actually tested against the company's standards.

And the fact that a company has a no-fault policy with regards to customers does not mean that it is barred from establishing responsibility for its own internal purposes. A company which produces personalized stationery which is sold through department stores has a no-fault policy whereby it automatically reprints any order the customer says is in error. Even so, it also backtracks to determine where the error actually occurred and keeps records accordingly. In some instances, the order was entered incorrectly by the order-taker or keypunch clerk; in others, typographical errors were made in the typesetting department. Company errors are charged according to the firm's standard practice. If the customer is determined to have been at fault, obviously nobody in the company is charged with the error. If a particular customer makes repeated errors, it's a sign to reeducate the customer in correct order procedure— if many customers make errors, the fault may be with catalogs and order blanks.

Investing in the Complaint Handling System

The final economic factor to be considered in complaint handling is the investment in the complaint handling system itself. Too many companies think of complaint handling in terms of out-of-pocket costs, or the costs of curing symptoms rather than eliminating causes of dissatisfaction with the way complaints are handled. As discussed in Chapter 22 on written and printed communications, a company that is willing to spend a fair amount of money to train personnel to handle customer complaints about billing may not realize that for a lesser amount of money it could redesign the billing forms so that customers could understand them and thus would not be registering so many complaints.

Actually, training of personnel is often a very minor aspect of the entire complaint handling process. The need for exceptional complaint-handling skills in customer service personnel is usually inversely proportional to the quality of the firm's products or services and the reasonableness of its policies towards customers on returns, errors, exchanges and disputes . . . and the speed with which personnel are able to respond and the extent to which they can resolve them without putting the customer through extensive red tape.

From the company's point of view, the major investment expense in setting up an effective complaint handling system will involve three main areas:

1. Investment in improved design and quality control of the service being offered and the manner in which it is delivered to the customer.

2. The development of management information systems and communications enabling fast, accurate responses to inquiries and retrieval and transfers of information essential to timely and effective complaint handling and resolution.

3. The cost of systems personnel and consultants to develop the underlying procedures and supporting policies.

Effective complaint handling begins long before the telephone rings or complaint letters start arriving in the mail. It begins with a management philosophy, translated in specific

---

Losing the Sale . . . But Keeping the Customer

If the customer is clearly dissatisfied with the product, what's to be gained by refunding his or her money? It can be argued that it's like throwing good money after bad, because the customer isn't ever going to buy the product again anyway.

That may be true, but what about other products offered by the company? The fact that the customer is dissatisfied with one particular product does not necessarily mean that the customer is dissatisfied with the company itself. Recognizing this, many companies make it a practice in such instances, first to issue the customer a prompt refund and to ship a complimentary sample of another (and often unrelated) product in the company's line.

The logic is sound. The customer whose claim is honored promptly and courteously is favorably disposed toward the vendor in any event, and the free sample is seen as an unexpected and welcome gift. One meat packer finds in dealing with complaining consumers that it pays to offer something of substantially greater value than the item that was originally complained about. If a customer complains about the taste or quality of the bacon, the company will send the customer a refund plus a small ham. It has proven an excellent way of keeping customers as customers that works equally well in the industrial environment: a customer who is dissatisfied with a particular piece of equipment is given a generous trade-in on a higher-capacity and more productive unit, and remains a customer . . . and grows as a customer and opens more locations and buys more equipment.

---

policies enforced companywide and supported by the type of commitment of resources described here. For the company that is genuinely concerned with being the best and at the same time being profitable, this investment has a double payback: an un-paralleled quality control system in the form of direct feedback from customers, with appropriate internal communications "con-nections" to insure that the feedback is used constructively to improve services and products; and improved profitability through reduced customer turnover and higher levels of cus-tomer retention and increased sales volume: growing with sat-isfied customers.

24

ORGANIZING THE COMPLAINT HANDLING SYSTEM PROACTIVELY

What to do is far more important than what to say. Many companies overemphasize the *reactive* part of complaint handling—the "what to say when the customer says . . ." part—and pay relatively little attention to actually organizing a *total complaint handling system* that will serve these important goals for the company:

1. Conform with company policies on complaint resolution.

2. Meet company standards for timeliness and speed of resolution, and actual amount of settlement.

3. Maintain good customer relations and meet marketing objectives of customer retention, repeat business, increased sales and account growth.

4. Operate at the least cost and highest productivity consistent with overall company goals.

5. Generate the least stress for personnel actually handling complaints in typical "confrontational" situations.

6. Provide feedback from customers that can be used constructively to improve services and products, correct misapplications and hazards and otherwise protect and enhance the company's standing with its customers and in the marketplace generally.

In short, scripts or scenarios for dealing with customers in specific complaint situations are only one element in the total complaint handling process or system. Managers and reps alike tend to dislike complaint handling per se because of the under-lying negatives and unpleasantness of the complaint situation—being confronted by a displeased and sometimes angry customer. Yet a well-organized complaint handling system, supported by fair policies, will remove many of those negatives and much of that unpleasantness. Reps who know that they are supported by the right tools for complaint handling will have more confidence in the complaint situation in the same way that a surgeon with the right instruments knows that he or she can exhibit greater skill in a difficult procedure. And both know the virtual impossibility of "going it alone," i.e., without the organized support of others doing *their* jobs the way they're supposed to be done. The tremendous sense of frustration that customer service reps often feel in complaint handling is that they *don't* have this kind of organized support. If management has a negative view of com-plaints, it's natural that others in the company will see this and quickly adopt the same view themselves—executives, depart-ment heads, specialists, supervisory personnel. These are the people reps have to turn to in resolving complaints, the people whose quick response and cooperation is essential to fast com-plaint resolution. These are the people who *really* have a nega-tive view about complaints—and nobody told them to have that negative view; it just came naturally when they saw the absence of a specific management commitment and an organized system for handling and resolving complaints fairly and quickly . . . with a specific definition of their roles in the total process.

Basic Requirements of An Effective Complaint Handling System

1. **Management commitment, appropriate policies and standards.** This was discussed in detail in Chapter 23.

2. **Effective methods for measuring performance against standards.** These concern mainly logging complaints and track-ing them through the system. Depending on the number and kind of complaints handled, a form similar to that shown in Figure 1

will often serve the purpose of making the initial entry of a complaint that is telephoned in or otherwise reported verbally.

Customer Inquiry Form

Remarks

Caller	Phone

Account
Name

Invoice   Order   P.O.
Number   Date   No.

Type of Inquiry	Loc. A	Loc. B	Loc. C	Loc. D
☐ Shipping Info.	☐	☐	☐	☐
☐ Delivery	☐	☐	☐	☐
☐ Invoice	☐	☐	☐	☐
☐ Back Order	☐	☐	☐	☐
☐ Mis-Shipment	☐	☐	☐	☐
☐ Request for Return	☐	☐	☐	☐
☐ Other Sales Lead	☐	☐	☐	☐

Complaint
Attributed to:

Immediate
Action Taken:

Corrective Action
Recommended
or Taken:

Analysis   Order Date _____   Shipping Date & Carrier _____
                Delivery Date _____   Order Cycle Time _____

Inquiry—File by Type   Submitted by _____

Figure 24-1. Form used to record customer inquiries and complaints that come in by phone. Format of the form enables customer service rep to structure the call and record information in a logical fashion.

When customers enter complaints by letter or by use of forms they have developed specifically for this purpose, the complaint form may be attached to the customer document (or a copy of it) and it may be forwarded to the departments involved. Each complaint should be logged as received, and "aged" at predetermined intervals, i.e., tracked to determine its progress through the system. Complaints that are still open should automatically be treated as exceptions and reported to the next level of management as a matter of company policy.

3. **A practical method for identifying serious complaints immediately upon their receipt.** The seriousness may be because of the nature of the complaint itself, i.e., personal injury or other hazard, violation of law, effect on the customer's operations, or total dollar amount; or it may be serious in the sense that it involves a major customer, even though the complaint itself may be relatively minor. Complaints that fall into this category are always given exceptions or expedited handling to avoid their becoming even more serious through delay or mishandling by inexperienced personnel.

4. **An effective information system, preferably on-line and real-time.** This is the heart of the complaint handling system. It should enable reps to quickly ascertain status of orders and backorders, historical and profile data on customers, inventory availability, and items potentially substitutable for lines currently not available. As many systems are, the system should be capable of accepting corrections and updates to customer files, including credits or refunds meeting automatic adjustment criteria. The data retrieval system would probably include microfiche for bills of lading and similar paperwork, where examination of original documentation may be needed to support or disallow claims, unauthorized deductions and the like. The system will also contain such features as automatic lockout of credit hold on invoices that are being disputed by customers. That is, if a customer delays payment on a particular invoice on the grounds that it is inaccurate, the system will not permit Credit to take any collection action while the matter is still unresolved.

5. **Timely carrier reports on shipment status.** Regardless

of the mode(s) used to ship goods to customers, all carriers should be capable of providing prompt, accurate and up-to-date reports on such shipments. This should also apply to the company fleet where it is used for such purposes.

6. An organized procedure for cradle-to-grave handling of complaints. This should be diagrammed in flow chart fashion as reflected in Figure 3, and supported by detailed procedures covering each major step.

7. Specific accountability for followup on promises. Perhaps the most critical stage in the entire complaint handling process is the period immediately following agreement by the customer to a proposed settlement of the complaint or claim. Prompt adjustment is imperative; any delay will be seen as a lack of good faith and may actually result in a new and more severe complaint. Thus it is essential that the system incorporate speci-

---

Dear Customer:
We recently handled the matter you reported to us about _____
_____ and now
we would appreciate hearing from you again. Your responses to the following questions will greatly assist us in measuring our service.

1. Did you receive a reply as promptly as you felt you should?
   ☐ Yes ☐ No Comments _____
2. Was the explanation understandable to you?
   ☐ Yes ☐ No Comments _____
3. Did the letter give a complete explanation?
   ☐ Yes ☐ No Comments _____
4. If you returned a product, was a replacement (refund) sent?
   ☐ Yes ☐ No Comments _____
5. If this was a follow-up from earlier correspondence, was this prompt enough and the information complete?
   ☐ Yes ☐ No Comments _____
6. Is there anything else we should know about?
   _____

Figure 24-2. Basic questionnaire form mailed to customers to determine customer satisfaction with the handling of the complaint.

fic requirements for followup on such promises, and direct accountability when this is not done.

8. **Provision for feedback on customer satisfaction and buying habits after complaint resolution.** Complaints well handled will usually have a positive effect on customer purchases. Tracking of customer performance after the complaint handling cycle is through will help identify successes in this area as well as specific procedures where improvement may still be needed, for example, in excessive forms to fill out, delays in issuing refunds, problems with the credit department not being informed, etc. Some companies simply mail a questionnaire to each customer after complaint resolution to determine customer satisfaction with the actual handling of the complaint rather than the outcome itself. A basic questionnaire form used for this purpose is shown in Figure 2. Tracking of purchases may be somewhat more complex, but the data moves through the customer service department as orders are entered, and can usually be extrapolated without too much difficulty.

The Groundwork:
Making It Easy For Customers to Complain

Having learned that customers who have problems but don't complain may not remain customers for long, many companies have recognized the value of telling customers *how* to complain: where to write or phone, what information to include, what documentation to have available. In a large organization, telling customers beforehand which department to contact for a particular type of complaint or problem, as well as what information to provide, can substantially speed up the entire process; first by minimizing the number of people who have to handle the complaint before it gets to the right person; and second, by getting the appropriate information on the first contact and avoiding the delay inherent in having to re-contact the customer for additional data. It should also be pointed out that when it's necessary to go back to customers for additional information, some will interpret this as stalling on the complaint; it's far better to impress customers *beforehand* with the need for providing complete information of specified types.

One company may publish different phone numbers for different types of complaints: (a) freight loss and damage complaints; (b) complaints about errors in orders or billing; (c) technical, quality control or applications complaints. A major elevator company publishes a booklet containing the names and extensions of its customer service specialists in a number of areas, keyed in with statements like "If you have a problem with _____, call _____ at extension ____." Thus the customer with a complaint concerning, say, retrofit parts, knows immediately to call Bill Smith at extension 1234. This saves time for the customer, and time and money for the company by getting the complaint immediately to the right person without intermediate handling, or the possibility of the switchboard's misrouting the complaint to the wrong department.

In similar vein, several years ago Gulf Oil Company published a small booklet, "How to Complain to Gulf," which was included with credit card statements. The book identified three types of complaints, and provided a department and address for each: (1) a complaint about the credit card statement itself; (2) a complaint about a particular Gulf service station; or (3) a complaint about Gulf in terms of corporate policy, for example, its position in Third World countries. A variation on this is to provide customers a single "hotline" number where the individuals handling hotline calls perform the screening function, i.e., identify the calls by type and route to the appropriate individuals or departments according to predetermined guidelines. In some organizations, hotline operators may service some complaints themselves, and route others elsewhere using decision rules as illustrated in the chart in Figure 3.

Decision Rules in Complaint Handling

Decision rules are fundamental to business management in any situation involving delegation of decision making to lower levels, and indeed in any situation requiring repetitive decision making of almost any type. A good example of decision rules is found in inventory management, where each line item typically has a reorder point. The decision rule governing a reorder point of 100 units might be framed something like this:

Q. Is current inventory level at or below 100 units? If no, proceed to next inventory item. If yes, reorder immediately in indicated quantity.

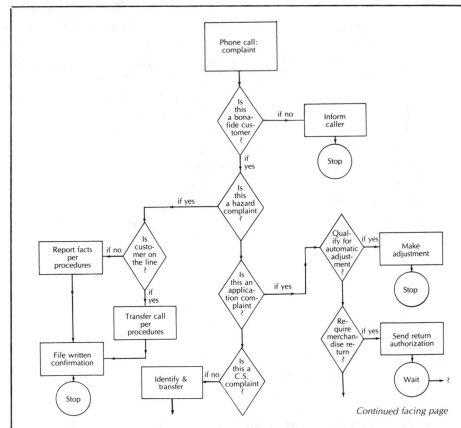

Continued facing page

Figure 24-3. Flow chart illustrating how decision rules can be applied to complaint handling in order to allow delegation of decision-making.

One of the most basic forms of inventory decision rules is found in the two-bin system, and would be phrased like this:

Q. Is the first bin empty? If yes, reorder (or refill) immediately. If no, do not reorder or refill.

As shown on the flow chart depicted in Figure 3, the decision rules start with identification of the caller as a bona fide customer and move from this point to decision rules to identify the type of complaint and the appropriate action to be taken. A common type

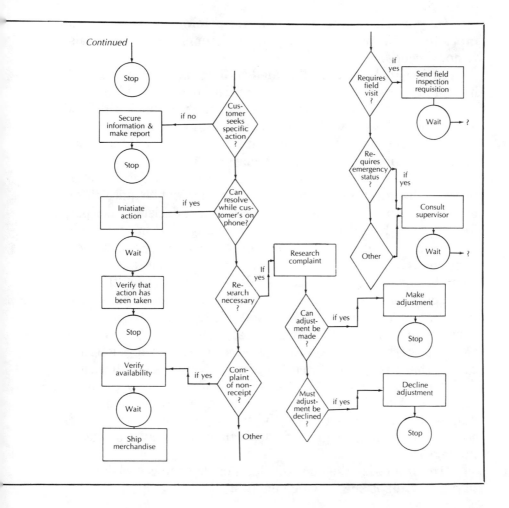

of complaint concerns returns of merchandise. Decision rules might read something like this:

Q. Is the caller a direct customer? If yes, proceed. If no, refer to local distributor with appropriate followup.

Q. What is the date of the invoice? If older than 90 days, inform customers that returns are ineligible. If within 90 days, proceed.

Q. Was the product custom-packaged or otherwise customized? If yes, inform customer of policy on custom work. If no, proceed.

Q. Was the purchase at special pricing, or special promotion conditions? If yes, inform customer of policy on specials. If no, proceed.

Q. Is the product still sealed in original cartons? If yes, inform customer that return authorization labels will be sent today. If no, inform customer of restocking/repack charges and ask whether he/she wishes to proceed with returns. If no, conclude transaction; if yes, inform that labels will be sent today and documents indicating restocking charges.

This is an oversimplified version, of course, and in actual practice the questions and policies involved might be quite different. However, it illustrates the basic role that decision rules play in complaint handling, and in virtually any kind of exceptions transaction between customers and the customer service department. It is absolutely essential that customer service personnel be provided with decision rules covering at least the most common situations; otherwise the company runs the risk of inconsistent (and sometimes expensive) decisions by customer service personnel making judgmental decisions that are beyond the scope of their jobs. Additionally, the absence of decision rules means that many reps faced with making judgmental decisions will not want to make them, and will bounce them back to the manager. And this, too, is costly, because repetitive decision making is a non-productive activity that prevents the manager from proactively managing the department the way it should be managed.

To summarize the need for decision rules in complaint handling, as well as the specific benefits:

1. Decision rules assure a uniform response. Regardless of location, department or rank of the individual complaint handler, all complaints that are basically the same will be handled the same way, i.e., all customers will be treated uniformly. Since decision rules reflect company policy, their use insures that policy is administered equally throughout the organization.

2. Decision rules assure the correct—and optimum—response. Since decision rules have been worked out in advance to deal with the most common types of complaints, they balance customer interests with those of the company and reflect management's considered judgment of the best course to take in complaints of a particular type.

3. Decision rules assist diagnosis. Because they follow basically the same lines as a troubleshooting guide as might be used in diagnosing automotive or equipment malfunctions, decision rules facilitate an early—and accurate—diagnosis of the complaint, and thus a more timely solution.

4. Decision rules assure correct routing. Among the most important decision rules are those which tell the customer service rep how and where to route specific complaints. For example, when a complaint contains certain "trigger" words (see Figure 4), the decision rules may instruct the customer service rep to route the complaint immediately to his or her supervisor for further handling. The implication of such words as "hurt," "sick," "dead," "fire," "fumes," etc. is that a major suit or claim may be in the offing, as well as the need to institute an immediate recall. Also, decision rules may refer to specific customers: "Complaints or claims from the following companies are to be referred immediately to _____," the implication here being that these are important or sensitive accounts that require exceptions handling. Indeed, decision rules may be formulated to cover both type of complaint as well as account and other circumstances in addition to actual severity of the complaint itself. This is explained in greater detail in the discussion of the Complaint Matrix, starting on page 500.

5. Decision rules avoid judgmental and repetitive decision making. As referred to earlier in this section, comprehensive decision rules assure that the right decision is made

hurt	die	sick	shock
cut	danger	burn	explosion
fumes	Senator	doctor	lawyer
Congressman	eyes	police	poison
children	shatter	hospital	emergency

Figure 24-4. Decision rules can be written instructing a customer service rep handling a complaint containing certain trigger words—such as those shown above—to refer the complaint immediately to his or her supervisor for further handling.

for the right situation and in so doing free personnel as well as managers for the more productive work that cannot be done on a programmed basis.

6. Decision rules can be applied to high-dollar or critical situations without requiring chain-of-command approval. For example, one manufacturer of farm equipment has a decision rule which says in effect: if a needed part is not available, and crops must be harvested without delay, the farmer will be provided with a complete combine or other equipment to complete the task. In a telephone equipment company there is a decision rule that if a hospital switchboard is down and cannot receive incoming calls, the customer service rep handling the account is automatically authorized to charter the company plane to fly in equipment to remedy the situation when it's not available locally.

Legal Aspects of Complaints

The complaint handling procedure should not overlook legal aspects of complaints. These may apply to the particular industry, or they may apply to all industries. For example, there are certain rules that apply to consumer mail order which are likely to be rather strenuously enforced by the Federal Trade Commission. There are other rules covering consumer products that are enforced by the Consumer Product Safety Commission. The

Department of Transportation enforces safety rules governing automobiles, trucks and other transport equipment. The Food and Drug Administration has far-reaching regulations, including a number which impact customer service policies on returned goods, lot identification, etc. Even the Departments of State and Agriculture may get involved. In many instances rules will be prescribed for product recall, and of course there are numerous rules controlling release, documentation, labeling and actual transport of controlled substances and hazardous materials.

It is beyond the scope of this book to go into detail in this area beyond emphasizing that the customer service manager should be aware of the rules and regulations applying to their particular industry. They should also be aware that companies with high public profiles may be more likely to be targeted for punitive action by regulatory agencies because of the publicity value.

Some government agencies use the "consent order" strategy, whereby a company charged with violations of law does not acknowledge that it has violated the law but is required to pay a fine and agree that it will not violate the law in the future, or that it will abide by certain conditions set forth by the government agency. Some companies agree to these consent orders and pay fines in excess of $500,000 or more even when they have not actually violated the law. In their estimation, it is less costly to do so than to undergo the expense and negative publicity of actually going to trial.

Poor handling of complaints may in some cases result in additional regulation and sometimes specific legislation. The customer service manager who establishes complaint handling procedures should be prepared to deal with inquiries from regulatory agencies as well as from Congressional or state and municipal offices that may have been originally triggered by an irate customer complaining to his or her Congressional office or other agency. Even when a company has excellent procedures and fair policies that favor the customer, there are still likely to be some customers who remain dissatisfied and want to "get back" at the company.

One company doing a high volume of consumer business

approached this problem by preparing a booklet specifically describing its complaint policies and procedures, which it sent to regulatory agencies and Congressional offices when they made inquiries as the result of customer complaints. It was very effective, and saved considerable correspondence. For although much of the regulation now on the books is the result of poor complaint handling practices by some companies in the past, the fact is that regulators and legislators in general are not likely to adopt punitive regulations and laws simply on a constituent's say-so. A brief description of complaint handling policies and procedures, either in booklet form or for quotation in correspondence can be very helpful in this respect.

Warranties and warranty interpretation represent another legal area of importance to many companies. It is also an area in which there have been many changes in recent years. Although the law does not require a manufacturer to provide a specific warranty covering products or services, the "implied warranty of fitness" in the Uniform Commercial Code and even common law itself may make the company more liable in the long run than if it had issued a written warranty which included specific time limits, for example, for claiming product defects or other breach of warranty. Warranties that place unreasonable requirements on the customer for verification or proof of loss may be interpreted as contrary to the public interest, and subject the firm to more expensive suits under common law.

It is also critical that warranty regulations be applied equally to all customers. If an exception is made for even one customer and a so-called "good will adjustment" offered after warranty expiration, it may create what the courts interpret as an "extension of warranty" and thus open the door to similar free adjustments to all other customers in the same condition. Clearly, warranties should be written and interpreted by legal staff, and any exceptions handled with due consideration of the possible consequences.

Note also that a disclaimer does not necessarily free the vendor from liability. The statement "this product is sold without warranty, express or implied," does not necessarily exempt the company from the Uniform Commercial Code requirement that a product be suitable for its intended use. Nor will a disclaimer exempt a company from liability for personal injury or death resulting from product defects. In short, disclaimers which can be interpreted as contrary to public policy may be set aside by the courts in the same way that unreasonable warranties may be set aside. Again, it should be emphasized that these matters should be handled in consultation with the legal staff. The information provided here is intended as a general guideline only, and not as a substitute for professional legal advice. (The previous sentence is itself a disclaimer which would probably be acceptable to most legal authorities!)

The final legal area of concern to the customer service manager is the contractual relationship with the customer. The value of a contract, from the point of view of both seller and buyer, is that it represents what a seller will provide, and under what conditions, and what the buyer will pay and the terms of payment. Additionally, a major contract will contain a clause enumerating "liquidated damages," i.e., the specific amount that will be paid, if the contract is broken, by the party breaking the contract to the other party.

Liquidated damages benefit the seller in the sense that they limit the seller's liability to a specific dollar amount; they also benefit the buyer by providing reasonable compensation for added costs that may be incurred as a result of the seller's failure to perform. One of the most common examples of this type of contract in customer service is the jobsite delivery agreement. In such cases, the customer is often a contractor who plans to have crews on hand for installation of materials or equipment at a specific time on a specific date. The agreement specifies the time and date and conditions, and a specific amount of liquidated damages should delivery not be made in accordance with the agreement. The liquidated damages represent an agreement between the seller and the buyer as to the extra costs that would be incurred in having crews and equipment on standby with no product or equipment to work on.

Of course, there are conditions the buyer must meet, too:

night and weekend telephone contacts in the event of en route delays, and an agreement that "x" hours advance notice of delay releases the vendor from liability for liquidated damages, etc. Most companies involved in jobsite deliveries have standard policies covering such matters; if not, the legal department should certainly be consulted.

The term "liquidated damages" simply means putting a dollar value on the injury or damage suffered by the injured party, before the fact rather than after. It can apply to the vendor as well as to the customer. The term "consequential damages" describes damages suffered by the injured party as a result of breach of contract by the other, and is generally used in court cases where there has been no prior agreement on liquidated damages.

Consequential damages are often far more difficult to collect because it is usually necessary to prove that both parties to the contract were fully aware of what the consequences would be if the contract were breached. For example, a business person checks luggage containing the one and only copy of a proposal he/she intends to deliver in person the following morning just ahead of the deadline for bids for a major Government contract. The airline loses the luggage and the proposal cannot be made, so the company has no chance at the contract. The business person sues the airline, but to no avail, because it cannot be established that the airline was aware or had any reason to be aware of the potential consequences of losing the luggage.

On the other hand, assume the proposal has been sent by special courier with specific instructions that it must be hand delivered by a certain time. The courier fails to make delivery by the specified time, and the company has no chance at the contract. It sues for $50,000 as representing the consequential damages of not having a chance to get the contract. It is more likely to recover, because the courier service had been made specifically aware of the importance of meeting a specific deadline, and the reason why. Again, it should be understood that these are general guidelines and not interpretations of the law per se.

Purchase orders, acknowledgments and statements of terms and conditions of sale also carry certain legal force. In general, a purchase offer may be considered a proposal to buy under certain specified conditions, and an acknowledgment acceptance of that proposal. Most sellers use their own acknowledgment forms and include a provision that their own terms and conditions printed on the acknowledgment form will govern the transaction. Although this is a general practice, it may have limited relevance to as many as three-quarters or more of a firm's transactions, simply because most sellers will make every attempt to accommodate a customer or reach agreement without going to court. Similarly, most customers will abide by terms of sale and policies when they are reasonable and represent accepted practice within the industry.

Perhaps the most important law that the customer service manager should be aware of is the Law of Common Sense. Many complaints can be avoided altogether simply by starting out with reasonable policies that are fair to and understood by customers, and by making it known to customers that convenient channels of complaint do exist for routine as well as unusual problems.

For example, many customers who experience minor customer service failures—a small shortage or a discrepancy of a few cents on an invoice—may decide not to burden the vendor with such a minor matter, particularly when the vendor has shown good faith in the matter of complaints generally. By contrast, a customer who doubts the vendor's good faith, or has been antagonized by its policies in the past, may go to great pains to register even the smallest complaint as a means of getting even, so to speak.

The good will and good faith that underlie effective complaint handling systems also make customers more receptive to reasonable settlements when complaints are actually registered, and more cooperative in providing the information, documentation and verification essential to quick resolution of such complaints.

Complaint Analysis and
The Complaint Handling Matrix

Two major stages in developing the complaint handling system are: (1) categorizing complaints by type, frequency and dollar cost; and (2) developing decision rules for identifying and handling the principal categories. The form shown in Figure 5 is used primarily for complaint analysis, i.e., categorizing complaints by type and cause and seriousness or dollar amount. This is essentially a research tool which the manager can use to seek out and correct the causes of complaints, wherever possible. It is also a tool for developing the actual decision rules to be used in day-to-day complaint handling—mainly in establishing priorities in terms of the most frequent complaints, as well as those lending themselves most readily to decision rules.

By way of contrast, the Complaint Handling Matrix shown in Figure 6 is a concise set of decision rules covering the most frequently heard complaints in a typical company. To clarify the difference further, one can visualize two doctors. The first is a pathologist performing post-mortems and seeking out the causes of death in the hopes of some day eradicating them. The second doctor is a toxicologist presented with a patient with extreme poisoning symptoms. The toxicologist must determine, not only the type of poison the patient is suffering from, but also the antidote and the treatment—and all in time to save the patient's life if possible.

The complaint analysis form is used comparably to the post-mortem work, whereas the Complaint Handling Matrix is for use in situations like the toxicologists where the customer service rep must work quickly and surely from diagnosis to discovery of the "antidote" suiting the particular customer and situation, and then the actual resolution of the complaint and follow-through with other departments where necessary.

The Complaint Handling Matrix depicted here is based mainly on applying two broad decision rules to identify each complaint that is received, and the further treatment that it should receive. The decision rules or identifiers are:

Identifying and Prioritizing Typical Complaints

Activity and Type of Problem	Dollar Amount	Percent Of Total
Clerical/Administrative:		
Incorrect customer billed	$ _____	_____ %
Incorrect product billed	$ _____	_____ %
Incorrect quantity billed	$ _____	_____ %
Incorrect price billed	$ _____	_____ %
Incorrect terms billed	$ _____	_____ %
Other _____	$ _____	_____ %
Warehouse/Service Building:		
Incorrect product delivered	$ _____	_____ %
Incorrect quantity delivered	$ _____	_____ %
Other _____	$ _____	_____ %
General Errors:		
Billed but not delivered	$ _____	_____ %
Computer errors	$ _____	_____ %
Unordered merchandise	$ _____	_____ %
Defective product	$ _____	_____ %
Short weight/fill	$ _____	_____ %
Tax error	$ _____	_____ %
Service Problems:		
Re-repair required	$ _____	_____ %
Serviceman-caused problems	$ _____	_____ %
Emergency parts shipments	$ _____	_____ %
Delivery:		
Product damaged during delivery	$ _____	_____ %
Product lost during delivery	$ _____	_____ %
Delivery delayed, consequential damages to customer	$ _____	_____ %
Other _____	$ _____	_____ %
Other _____:		
_____	$ _____	_____ %
_____	$ _____	_____ %
_____	$ _____	_____ %
_____	$ _____	_____ %

Figure 24-5. Form used to analyze complaints by type, cause, seriousness and/or dollar amount.

What the Customer Wants	Complaint About a Hazard	Complaint About an Application	Complaint About Customer Service
The customer wants to be soothed, placated or mollified	Usually (Note 1)	Sometimes (Note 2)	Frequently (Note 3)
The customer wants "it"—the product or service that was ordered but has not been provided			Usually
The customer wants compensation, refund, credit or other adjustment	Frequently	Frequently	Sometimes
Other (applicable to individual firms or industries)			

Note 1. Indicated Action: Notify designated company official immediately so that production may be frozen, lots segregated, recall initiated or other remedial steps taken as prescribed in standard procedures for personal injury and related incidents involving product or service.

Note 2. Indicated Action: Applying machine-down, line-down or other criteria of urgency and priority, inform designated technical and/or engineering personnel of problem and obtain response or action as necessary to resolve matter.

Note 3. Indicated Action: Handle within customer service department in accordance with usual priorities and standard department procedures.

Figure 24-6. Complaint matrix which can be used. Most complaints fall into one of three main categories, and represent varying requirements in terms of internal routing for action as well as speed and type of response in order to meet customer expectations. This matrix enables you to classify complaints both by type and by severity, as well as by source of response, and to write appropriate procedures and, where necessary, actual response scenarios or checklists.

A. **The actual subject of the complaint, falling into one of three major subgroups:**

1. A complaint of major seriousness involving: hazard, health or personal injury; potentially large dollar sums or consequential damages; unfavorable publicity for the company; or an important customer, even though the dollar amount may be relatively small.

2. A complaint about product quality, technical performance or failure in the intended or promised application.

3. A complaint about customer service operations: accuracy of order fulfillment, timeliness of delivery, errors in invoices, general complaints about policy, courtesy, etc.

B. **What the customer wants or expects as a result of registering the complaint, again falling to three major subgroups:**

1. "Soothing," i.e., empathy and understanding and appreciation of the importance of the complaint and the inconvenience to the complainer—all these on the part of the individual receiving the complaint (another reason why it is so important that complaint handlers have a positive attitude towards complaints).

2. The customer wants "it"—a specific service or product which was promised, or a specific quality or level of performance which was expected but has not yet been delivered or has not materialized. This would include fast replacement of defective products received and returned for replacement.

3. Money—the customer wants compensation for damages, refunds or credits for errors, overcharges, failure to perform and related occurrences. In some cases, this will include the customer's wish to return product for refunds. (Routine returns for credit under terms of sale would not be included, however, since they normally do not constitute complaints per se.)

Using these criteria, it is possible to develop a matrix along the lines shown in Figure 6, modifying it as necessary for individual company use. The matrix can then be used as a basis for identifying the nature of the complaint, determining what the customer wants or expects, and taking the appropriate action via management-approved decision rules. It should be noted that the matrix shown in Figure 6 contains one extra row of squares which have been purposely left blank to accommodate additional categories of complaints that might apply to individual companies. For example, a company receiving a significant number of policy-type complaints might wish to include these as a separate category, with appropriate decision rules keyed in.

The "Nothing-Wanted" Complaint

A major defect in some complaint handling systems is that they make no provision for the "nothing-wanted" type of complaint where the customer is not seeking a specific adjustment, compensation or refund, but simply wishes to express dissatisfaction with a policy or procedure. These complaints may concern policies or practices which directly inconvenience a particular customer, or they may be more general in nature: a customer who dislikes the new corporate logotype, for example.

It is a serious mistake to assume that because these complaints do not ask for something specific they should not be quickly and intelligently responded to. Apart from the relatively few lunatic fringe letters almost every company receives, most individuals who take the time and trouble to frame nothing-wanted complaints to a company do so because they are generally concerned and because they would like to continue doing business with that company. In many instances, the individual who writes a company about a policy matter does so in a genuine effort to be helpful and to present a customer's viewpoint which the company's management may not be aware of. Failure to respond to such communications quickly and courteously—and with some indication that the letter has been read and digested— can result in serious alienation of highly well-intentioned customers and prospective customers.

Two examples illustrate this point. In the first, a new charge customer wrote the manager of the local outlet of a major department store chain about a policy which inconvenienced customers and appeared to be losing the department store sales as well. When no acknowledgment was received within a reasonable period, the customer simply put her charge card away. Only the company knows how much business it lost simply through failure of the store's management to respond to a well-intentioned letter of complaint.

In the second example, the president of one firm wrote the president of a car rental firm complaining about that organization's policies on one-way rentals. In return, he received, not an acknowledgment of his complaint, but a form letter signed by a lower-level employee saying that he was not entitled to a refund. Since the complainant had not asked for a refund but had simply sought to share an opinion, from one company president to another, he concluded that the auto rental company was not concerned with his firm's business and decided to place it with a competitor. Again, only the car rental company knows the value of one corporate account that was lost simply because the car rental company's complaint handling system—as good as it was for routine complaints about tangible, refundable matters—had made no provision for responsive handling of nothing-wanted complaints.

The irony is that in both cases the cost of a response—perhaps as much as $10 if an individual letter was dictated and transcribed—would have been miniscule compared to the value of the measurable business that was lost for lack of responsive handling. The key word is of course "responsive"—reacting to a complaint in such a way that the complainer feels that his or her complaint has been received, is appreciated, and is being given consideration. Where the nature of the complaint may require some delay in order to research the issues raised, many companies acknowledge the complaint immediately with a Mailgram and promise a more detailed response within several weeks. If the original communication was directed to the president, the Mailgram may be sent out over somebody else's signature, along these lines: "Thank you for your letter of _____ addressed to Mr. _____, who is currently away from the office. Let me assure you that it will be called to his attention upon his return. In the meantime we will investigate the matters raised in your letter and report back to you shortly. Thank you again for sharing your concerns with us." Or, the Mailgram may simply say: "Mr. _____ has asked me to respond to your thoughtful letter of _____, and to thank you for sharing your concerns. A detailed letter will follow shortly. Thank you again for contacting us."

Clearly, letters containing threats should be turned over immediately to the firm's security department, regardless of how far-fetched they may seem. This would not, of course, include letters from customers threatening to take their business elsewhere, which would normally be treated as routine complaints. In fact, given almost any complaint from a customer, it can be assumed that one potential outcome if the complaint is not handled properly is the loss of that customer's business.

So far, two broad areas of complaint handling—first, policies and standards, and then procedures themselves—have been covered in detail. The final phase of complaint handling is implementation of the system via training of personnel. This is the subject of the next chapter.

25

TRAINING PERSONNEL IN EFFECTIVE COMPLAINT HANDLING

There is a tendency among many managers to feel that effective complaint handling requires: (a) individuals with exceptional human relations skills; (b) persons who can stand high levels of stress; and (3) persons with extensive training in interpersonal skills on the order of transactional analysis. This is generally a misperception. As indicated earlier, these qualifications are important in a few jobs such as airline ticket or gate agents who often must deal with a variety of complaints in rapid succession under extremely adverse conditions. But for the average complaint handler in a manufacturing environment, good, everyday skills in general customer service are usually quite ample. This assumes, of course, that the customer service representative is supported by sound and fair policies and an effective complaint handling system with standards of internal response that are enforced as a matter of course.

In short, the better the system, the less it is necessary to call on exceptional skills on the part of complaint handlers. Given this, the manager's first goal is to make customer service representatives aware that complaints are regarded *positively* throughout the firm, and that it is the rep's obligation to do the same. In this, the customer service manager is a role model for his or her employees; they will base their own attitudes and responses to complaints on what they perceive to be the manager's attitude.

The manager's next goal is to provide specific training in the firm's complaint handling system, including the use of logs, forms for recording complaints, followup and follow-through, and the specifics of dealing with other departments. Whenever possible, heads of other departments involved in customer complaints—traffic/distribution, warehousing and shipping, credit, production planning, etc.—should be invited to address the customer service group and explain their needs—for specific information,

---

Role Play Scenario 1-A
You are Charles Benton, purchasing manager for a Southwestern distributorship. You placed a significant order with your vendor, with a delivery date of March 25. It is now April 15, and no parts of your order have been received. You ask your buyer to call the vendor and find out what happened. She has done so, and was told that you personally had been notified that the order would be delayed. You have no recollection of this, and you think the vendor company is making the whole thing up to get off the hook. You begin to get worked up because you see it as an accusation on the vendor's part. You call the vendor and insist on knowing specifically what has happened, and in the process you accuse *them* of lying to *you*.

Role Play Scenario 1-B
You are Sue Gregory, customer service supervisor for the vendor company. Some time ago, your Southwestern distributor placed a large order with a delivery date of March 25. You were later notified by Production Planning that key elements of the order were behind schedule and it had been decided to repromise the order for May 15. You instructed one of your reps to contact the customer, and have a copy of your memo. You don't have any other documentation, and the rep is no longer with your firm or in the area. However, she was reliable and conscientious, and you are almost certain she told you verbally that she had contacted the purchasing agent himself. Thus when a buyer in the customer's purchasing department calls and asks about the order, claiming that it is already late, you have no hesitation in saying that it was repromised for May 15 in a

---

Figure 25-1. Sample role play scenarios that can be used in training customer service reps to handle complaints effectively.

advance notification, samples of material, etc.—in responding to complaints, and the approximate procedures employed in their own departments. This can be very helpful to customer service reps in explaining to a complaining customer the specific action that will be taken in investigating and resolving the complaint, and the time-frame that will normally be required to do so. The more the rep knows about other departments' internal functionings, the more credible a spokesman he or she will be in respond-

---

contact with the purchasing agent himself, and you expect to meet that date. You are considerably shaken when the purchasing agent himself calls you and accuses you of lying to his subordinate, claiming that no repromise was ever made, that he is in deep trouble as a result, and it's up to you to do something—fast.

Role Play Scenario 2-A
You're Sarah Simpson, a major customer of the vendor company. Your boss has been leaning on you about the service you've been getting from the company—you think they do a pretty good job, and you're friendly with the people there. They always treat you well. But the job you've just received from them is not up to their usual quality. You feel you have to reject it—in part to prove to your boss that you are doing your job. You're willing to compromise, if the company can come up with one that will allow you to make your point.

Role Play Scenario 2-B
You're John Carey, customer service rep at the vendor company. You get a call from Sarah Simpson, who is with a major customer of yours. You get along well with Sarah, and you've always been able to work out any problems you may have had in the past. Which is why you're surprised that Sarah comes on a little strong, and threatens to reject the job you just finished for them. Says it's not a quality job—and she can't accept it. If you have to have the job rerun, it will cost the company money—and time you can't afford to waste. You try to come up with a compromise that will keep you from having to have the job re-done.

ing to customer concerns where those departments are involved in both the problem and the solution.

Next there is formal training itself. Very often this can be provided by an in-house training resource. Role-playing can be a very effective means of training reps, casting one rep as the customer, another as the rep, and re-creating a typical complaint situation where the customer's role as well as the rep's is expected to be reenacted faithfully and realistically. Many companies have one or two (or more) extremely difficult customers, and it's often very enlightening to write one of these customers into the role-playing script . . . and ask the particular role-player to provide a sound reason why the particular customer acts in his or her peculiarly difficult manner. Some examples of role-playing scripts are reproduced as Figure 1. These can be adapted to fit the individual company's situation.

There are also a number of off-shelf training packages which are for the most part moderately priced. A sampling of these is listed at the end of this chapter. However, the manager should be aware that most training materials are oriented primarily to consumer or retail situations rather than to typical customer service functions in the manufacturing environment. In any event, any filmstrip, film or slide presentation should be reviewed by the manager from start to finish, and provision made to adapt or relate its contents during the actual presentation.

This can often be done by interrupting the show and observing: "This situation involves a retail transaction, but in many ways it's quite similar to what we encounter every day in the manufacturing business. Jack, what's a situation you've been in lately that's similar to what we've seen here? And how did you deal with it?"

Another possibility is to send personnel to outside seminars dealing with customer service skills including complaint handling. Most of these are too general in nature and reps from a manufacturing background are likely to find it difficult to relate program content to their own experience. It's a fact of life that the manager must face: most existing training programs in complaint handling are aimed at industries where there are large numbers of reps dealing with relatively few types of complaints: in public utilities, for example, banks, hotels and service industries in general. There are almost none dealing specifically with complaint handling in manufacturing industries.

A more practical solution may be to use outside trainers in complaint handling and customer service skills who have sufficient background in manufacturing to relate the training they offer to the individual company's situation. As a rule it is usually far less expensive to use such trainers than to send personnel to outside seminars. Also, the manager can control program format and content in an in-house seminar but cannot do so in the case of outside seminars open to all comers. Trainers with a manufacturing background quite often already have suitable scripts for role-playing and other exercises related to complaint handling, as well as the experience of hundreds of other reps to draw from.

The material that follows has been derived from training materials that have been widely used in training customer service representatives in the handling of complaints in the one-on-one situation while the customer—often an extremely irate one—is on the phone actually registering a complaint. The associated paperwork and information flows will vary from one company to another, but the principles for dealing with the complaint will usually apply across the board. The manager using these materials should adapt them to the individual company's situation, making sure that reps are fully aware of the specific procedural steps they are expected to take as followup after the complaint has been registered.

The ABCs of Complaint Handling—
A Guide for Customer Service Representatives

A. Defuse the Situation

1. *Accept and acknowledge the customer's feelings.* The customer's emotion may seem unreasonable or unjustified. But it's real. It has to be accepted. There is no harm in acknowledging

the customer's anger by saying: "I can see you're quite disturbed. What can I do to help?"

2. *Empathize.* When the customer has described the problem, reply: "No wonder you're upset! I would be, too!"

3. *Look for feelings or statements you can agree with.* Even if it's something as basic as the customer's anger. Customer: "I'm mad as hell!" CSR: "I see you are. How can I help?"

4. *Avoid counterarguments or defensive statements.* Questions like "Did you read the instructions?" or statements like "You must be mistaken, that order was double-checked!" only serve to antagonize the customer further.

5. *Stay on the subject.* The angry customer is apt to wander, and even to raise criticisms that have nothing to do with the immediate problem. Don't be tempted to get into a debate about these other matters which are irrelevant in any event. Even personalities and name-calling are irrelevant. The best thing to do is ignore them or say, simply, "I'm sorry you feel that way. Can you tell me what happened next?" That way you're acknowledging that a statement has been made, but at the same time firmly returning the customer to the subject of the complaint.

6. *Accept responsibility as appropriate.* In routine complaints where it's clear that the company has made a mistake, the rep should not hesitate to accept responsibility and at the same time tell the customer how the company will respond. The more costly mistakes, or those exposing the company to possible lawsuits, should be received courteously and empathetically, and passed on to the appropriate channels, but without any acknowledgment of liability. Where the company has a policy of automatic adjustment for claims or complaints below a certain dollar level, the issue of responsibility or liability should not be introduced. It is enough to respond to the effect of "I'm sorry to hear that you've had a problem with (that you're disappointed with) _____. We'll be glad to send you a refund (make an adjustment, etc.)." The same applies to automatic exchange policies: "If you'll return the product to us, we'll be glad to send a replacement at no charge, plus a check to cover your shipping

charges." Note that the actual content of the statement—e.g., the part on shipping charges—will depend on individual company practices.

7. *Avoid use of the word "complaint" whenever possible. Use the word "problem" instead.* The word "complaint" implies an adversary situation between the customer and the company, or the customer and the rep—an "us-against-you" type of situation. The word "problem" suggests that the company and the rep empathize with the customer, recognize that it *is* a problem, and that it's important to the customer that it be solved quickly. Which of course is true: customers who complain are almost always looking for a solution to a particular problem, not to try to hurt the seller or gratify their personal feelings of hostility.

B. Get the Facts: Identify the Problem

1. *Make sure you are talking to the right person.* It's not uncommon for a customer with a problem to delegate the job of complaining to a secretary or assistant. Often it's done very casually: "Call up so-and-so and give 'em the devil about _____." The subordinate doesn't really know what the problem is to begin with and—of even greater importance— often doesn't have the authority to accept a settlement on the spot. Thus it can be difficult and time-consuming, both to identify or define the problem and to work out an acceptable solution, if you are not talking to the person who is familiar with the problem and has the authority to accept your proposed solution right away. Remember that fast handling of complaints is a critical element, and the more people a complaint has to go through the more delay you encounter—and the more chances for a complaint to get blown up out of proportion or otherwise distorted.

- 2. *Make sure the customer is talking to the right person.* For virtually the same reasons, it's essential that the person taking the complaint have the appropriate skills and knowledge to handle the complaint. If it becomes clear that you are not the person to be handling a particular complaint, perform the empathetic, "soothing" functions to reassure the customer that the company *does* care, and then route the call to the appropriate person in your organization. Make sure that the person to whom you're transferring the call is in fact the right person and is available; provide him or her with a capsule version of the problem before putting the customer on the line. The point is to avoid making the customer tell the story to a number of different people, and to progress the call as quickly as possible. If you're not sure, get all the facts and set a time to call the customer back, or to have the appropriate person call back. And see that the appointment is kept!

3. *Don't be intimidated by the customer's status; get all the facts, and all the details necessary.* The key word is "necessary." Don't let a customer's blustering manner or strong language fluster you so that you forget to ask for key information. But at the same time don't aggravate the situation by asking for irrelevant information, or information you already have in your own records. Avoid any semblance of red tape and stonewalling. If you haven't done so already, find out beforehand how your manager prefers you to handle calls where an irate customer demands to speak to the manager.

4. *Don't take it for granted that the customer's information is correct, or that the customer has defined the problem accurately.* Perhaps one of the most common complaints is a customer's claim of non-delivery. In a surprising number of these cases the goods have been received, signed for and placed in storage. The receiving department simply didn't notify the end user. Or when a complaint is registered by the customer's purchasing department for wrong merchandise received; the end user verbally approved a substitution but didn't notify the purchasing department. There are many variations on these examples, sometimes resulting from communications breakdowns on the customer side, sometimes simply from misdefinition of the problem. Again, take the angry customer who insists on talking to the manager—his or her problem is not getting through to the manager, it's something else which the customer thinks only the manager can solve. If you say to the customer, "I'm sorry, the manager is out of her office right now, but if you could give me some information I'll pass it along to her the moment she re-

turns," you are likely to find out that the real problem is something you yourself can solve without having to go through the manager at all. This can also cement a good relationship with the customer which will make future incidents easier to handle.

5. *Don't let the severity of the problem affect your judgment: identify liability situations, those involving personal injury or hazard, those involving large dollar amounts, those involving important customers, and—especially—those situations which will become even worse if quick action isn't taken.* Think of the worst possible kind of complaint you might be called on to handle in each of these classes or categories. How would you handle it? If you don't know, now is the time to find out from your supervisor or manager. All of these represent the types of complaints where fast, *accurate* action is vital. Once you've learned the preferred course of action, keep your cool! When you hear a complaint in these categories, a certain amount of damage has already been done. Don't let it get worse through inaction, or the wrong action!

6. *Don't take it for granted that problems that look alike* are *alike.* Investigate each complaint to the extent necessary to determine the real problem. For example: 10 customers call in to complain about non-delivery of orders. Can it be assumed that the cause is the same in each case? Of course not—at least not until more facts have been developed. All complaints should be evaluated on the basis of facts, not appearances nor—as often happens—misdefinition of the problem by the customer as described above.

7. *Notify other departments as appropriate.* Here again, guidelines should be available telling you whom to notify and the kind of information to provide. Some of this may be actual documentation, some of it verbal discussion. Be particularly careful to avoid "confrontational" scenes with personnel in other departments. Don't "accuse" other departments of causing problems, even when you know it to be true. Don't call another department and say: "My customer says you screwed up his shipment for real!" That's almost guaranteed to get you a retort to the effect of "And I say the h---- with you and your customer. You're always blaming your problems on *us*!" Instead, try some-

thing milder, like: "Could you give me a hand with a *really* irate customer who's just put me through the wringer, and then some?" In short, stress the team approach to complaint handling—the objective is to solve the problem as quickly as possible, *not* to find somebody to blame for it.

8. *Keep a written record of key points and promises; use a tickler or followup file to stay on schedule.* Don't rely on your own memory (or anybody else's) as to what was promised, and when. Don't take it for granted that others will do what they said they would do, or that they'll do it *when* or *how* they said they would. Use your company's forms for recording key data on complaints, and for transmitting information to others. The more detail you can record, the easier it will be to reconstruct months later if you're called on to do so.

9. *When getting information from others, restate, rephrase and paraphrase—but without passing judgment.* It's critically important that the facts you record, or the information you use in resolving the complaint, are those that the customer intended to convey to you. When you restate what the customer has said, but in your own words, this gives the customer a chance to correct or amplify any points that might otherwise go into the record incorrectly. Use the same approach with others in your company, so that when you retransmit information from one of your departments to the customer you are sure it is as intended by the originator. But avoid any phrases, terms or questions that suggest you dispute the customer's version. *Correct:* "As I understand it, this is what happened—please correct me if I've missed something—. . ." *Incorrect:* "You allege that . . ."

10. *Follow your company's established procedures for fact-finding and recording information.* If this involves sending forms to the customer, do so right away. Make it part of the record that you did so. In particularly sensitive cases, you may want to follow up with the customer to make sure the forms were received and have been filled out. Somebody could have thrown them away thinking they were advertising . . . or just on general principles. When using forms to take information over the telephone, move fast and don't let the form get in the way of getting information.

Don't disparage your forms to the customer—"I've got to fill out these stupid forms, so please bear with me . . ." If the forms present problems, pass the information along to your manager . . . and suggest improvements that will make the job easier without sacrificing usefulness.

11. *Don't call back for additional information unless it's absolutely necessary.* If the customer furnished all information requested either on the phone or by filling in the form(s) you sent, it is very likely to rekindle the customer's ire if you ask for additional information. Get the information on the first go-round; when you go back a second time seeking additional information, it begins to appear that you're simply delaying. Of course, there are bona fide cases where you have to go back, and don't hesitate to do so in such cases. Also, if the additional information you secure may lead to a more favorable settlement for the customer, don't hesitate to say so.

C. **Keep the Customer**

1. *Make automatic adjustments as policies permit.* If your company has a policy of allowing automatic adjustment on all complaints or claims below a certain dollar limit, this was done to relieve you of the problem of deciding who's entitled and who isn't. To allow the adjustment to some and not to others solely on the basis of personal judgment and without having facts to support it might be construed as discriminatory treatment and could cause serious problems for your company. If you think some companies are taking unfair advantage of a liberal returns or refund policy, notify your manager, and cite the facts to support your suspicions. But don't let your personal likes and dislikes govern who gets the automatic refund and who doesn't.

2. *Take immediate action to mitigate when necessary.* Certain kinds of complaints concern problems that will get worse if immediate action isn't taken. For example, a product defect that can endanger human lives. Or a quality control problem that will result in a high rate of rejects by customers. Or a potential production line shutdown by a customer because of non-delivery of an order, or delivery of the wrong materials, etc. In such cases

it's important to do whatever you can to mitigate—to lessen or reduce—the damage to the customer or to your own company. In many instances your company will already have procedures indicating the action to take; in others, it may be up to your personal judgment. But the most important rule is common sense: when delay means damage, take action now . . . and worry about filling out the forms later on.

3. *For complaints not covered by an automatic adjustment policy, determine if there is another immediate solution that can be applied—and apply it.* A settlement that is acceptable to the customer and can be made right away is ideal. Even though it may mean giving the customer the benefit of the doubt, in the long run it will save the company money as well as considerable good will. For example, some companies will permit substitution of a higher-priced item, without additional charge, for the lower-priced item the customer ordered but can't get. A tire company, for example, offers 12-ply tires in place of 10-ply without additional charge in such instances. The reduced profit on the sale is more than offset by the potential loss of sales to a dissatisfied customer.

4. *Negotiate when possible.* If permissible in your company, you can sometimes negotiate settlements with customers using, as one example, the firm's automatic adjustment or substitution policy. "Under our firm's policy, I can authorize a $50 refund right away without any additional paperwork or documentation; would this be acceptable?" You may also want to negotiate quantities and delivery dates with customers complaining about lost orders, failure to allocate sufficient product to them, etc. In such cases, start with the very *least* you can concede, and then negotiate back to the *most* you can concede. For example, if product is currently not available but you know you can ship the complete order in ten days, you might want to start by telling the customer: "I can ship in 15 days," and negotiate back to the 10 days if necessary. Or, you may decide to say: "I can ship you four cartons by air today, and the balance by surface freight in 10 days." The purpose is not to mislead customers, but to not strain your resources beyond what you can

reasonably do. And it's important to recognize that, with some customers, if you offer your best solution first, they won't believe that it actually *is* your best solution.

5. *When you have to say "no," do so—but suggest alternatives.* The prime example is when the customer has misordered, and is dissatisfied with the performance of the product. "I'm sorry, Ms. Brown, but that material wasn't designed for thermal applications; it's printed on the outer carton and also on all the inner packages as well. What you need is our LX-2 sheet, which was designed specifically for the type of application you describe. It costs 11¢ a pound more, but it does the job. Can I write your order for a carton?" In general, the fact that the customer is at fault is definitely *not* a signal to terminate the complaint-handling process. On the contrary, extra effort may be required to help the customer out of his or her trouble. Some of the most lasting business friendships started with a customer who was at fault—and a customer service representative who went the extra mile to help the customer solve the problem.

6. *Leave the door open for possible new information, or referral to others in the firm.* There may be additional facts that neither you nor the customer are aware of at the time of the original problem or complaint. When saying "no" to the customer, it may be desirable to say "if you have any additional information which you feel might have a bearing on the problem, by all means let me have it." Remember that the customer has a basic right to complain, and a *legal* right to a fair resolution of a legitimate complaint. There is nothing to be gained by making it difficult for a customer to pursue a complaint, or by discouraging complaints in general. In fact there may be quite a bit to be lost. And bear in mind that some customers won't accept "no" from you in any event, and will go over your head to your supervisor or manager, or in some cases to the top echelons of the company. On occasion, your "no" will be changed to a "yes," not because you did anything wrong but simply because somebody further up the line decided it was in the best interests of the company to do so. Rather than resent such "reversals"—which they really aren't anyway—you should try to arrange things so that you yourself

are the one who brings the good news to the customer. In fact, when you yourself feel that a "no" should be changed to a "yes" in the interests of the company and the relationship with the particular customer, don't hesitate to say so to your manager. If he or she agrees, you will have won some important points with your customer.

7. *When you can't take immediate action, tell the customer what procedures will be followed in resolving the complaint, and the approximate time-frame.* In short, what you'll do and when you'll do it. And, as appropriate, who else will be involved in the resolution. Whatever you do, it's important that you convey *a sense of action* on the complaint. Setting up a realistic and descriptive timetable is usually the best way to do so.

8. *Report back to the customer—even when there's nothing to report.* An important element in conveying that all-important sense of action is reporting back to the customer periodically, even when there is nothing new to report. This serves a dual purpose: (1) It lets the customer know that you're on top of the situation, and that the complaint isn't just gathering dust some place; and (2) it lets the customer know that you care—a message that is often more important than the actual resolution of the complaint.

9. *Follow through with other departments.* This is a must. Regardless of what others *say* they will do, in the long run getting it done is *your* responsibility. And the only way to be 100% sure that complaint handling commitments to customers are actually met is to personally follow through with the other departments involved. Don't assume that a phone call or memo will do the job. Personnel in other departments have jobs to do, too, and they don't necessarily attach the same priorities to customer complaints that you do. So, it's up to you to keep complaints from getting sidetracked or buried when they have to be referred elsewhere for action. Be diplomatic, of course, but don't be afraid to needle—don't hesitate to put a little pressure even on others who outrank you in the company. Remember, the customer outranks you both!

10. *Use the complaint to correct deficiencies in your own*

system (and thank the customer for helping). Remember that complaints themselves are an excellent form of quality control. You get fast feedback, detailed information on what went wrong. The kind of information that only customers who use your products daily can provide—the kind of perspective on your customer service system that only your customers can provide. Take advantage of that feedback to improve the system and avoid repetitions. And above all, don't forget to thank customers for pointing up those shortcomings—you'd pay a consultant thousands of dollars for the same kind of information and advice your customers give you for free!

11. *Diplomatically show customers how to avoid recurrences of "contributory" problems resulting in complaints.* A contributory problem is one where the customer, if not directly responsible for the problem, at least had a hand in it—contributed to the problem, so to speak. A good example is the customer who calls you late on a Friday in a "crisis" situation and almost begs you to ship that same day. Trying to be helpful, you agree to do so. But something goes wrong and the shipment doesn't go out until the following Tuesday. The customer complains that you didn't keep your promise. It's no defense to say that the customer caused the problem, even though it's basically true in this case, because this particular customer seems to move from crisis to crisis. Or, you could decide never to make a promise to *that* customer again. Don't—there's a better way. Acknowledge *your* role: "If I could only get your orders on Wednesday, Mr. Erskine, I know I could get them out by Friday!"

12. *Set an example for your customers.* If you show restraint, concern, and an ability to get things done in your company, your customers will end up being far more cooperative and far less demanding. The irate, shouting customer who finds you responding in a calm, quiet tone will cool off a lot quicker than if you raised *your* voice and started replying in kind. Not that you should see yourself as a punching bag for customers, not at all. Complaint handling boils down to a relatively simple formula. Keeping customers by helping them; helping your company—and yourself—by helping your customers.

Selected Sources of Training Materials On Complaint Handling

Birsner, E. Patricia and Ronald D. Balsley. *How to Improve Customer Service.* (New York: AMACOM, 1980)

Blanding, Warren. *Customer Service Seminar.* (Washington, D.C.: Marketing Publications Inc., 1982)

Blanding, Warren, Leslie Hansen Harps and William R. Henry, Jr. *133 Ways to Handle Customer Complaints.* (Washington, D.C.: Marketing Publications Inc., 1979)

Improving Customer Relations. (Northbrook, Ill.: Universal Training Systems, 1979)

Telephone Dynamics. (Northbrook, Ill: Universal Training Systems, 1970)

(For more information on these references, contact Customer Service Institute, 8701 Georgia Avenue, Silver Spring, MD 20910).

Appendix A

PROFESSIONAL ORGANIZATIONS FOR DISTRIBUTION CUSTOMER SERVICE MANAGERS

International Customer Service Association, 111 East Wacker Drive, Suite 600, Chicago, IL 60601. 312/644-6610. ICSA was founded to provide a forum for the development and exchange of knowledge and information relevant to the profession of customer service. The organization's membership is made up primarily of customer service managers in manufacturing, distribution, mail order and service companies.

American Telemarketing Association, P.O. Box 532, Howell, NJ 07731. 201/577-0877. This trade association was organized to meet the need of telemarketers to keep informed about the high-speed changes in technology and marketing methodology in a fast growing field. The ATA's goals are to increase member firms' marketing potential, to influence positive legislation, and to endorse ethical standards of business conduct.

Association of Field Service Managers, 6237 Presidential Court, Suite B, Ft. Myers, FL 33907. 813/482-6418. This organization of field service managers in high-technology firms emphasizes the post-sales marketing environment where service operates as a business. Its stated goal is to increase the competency and fulfillment of members in this profession, which has expanded to encompass all aspects of providing service and support.

National Association of Service Managers, 6022 West Touhy Avenue, Chicago, IL 60648. 312/763-7350. NASM is an organization of executives whose concern is primarily "after sales service," i.e., field support of machinery, electronics and other equipment. While parts support is one ingredient of this service, a principal concern is the training and deployment of technical personnel so as to maximize response and minimize downtime on customer equipment—a major thrust in marketing both consumer hard goods and industrial/commercial machinery.

National Council of Physical Distribution Management, 2803 Butterfield Road, Suite 380, Oak Brook, IL 60521. 312/655-0985. This organization has devoted considerable resources to research and study in the customer service field, particularly as it relates to the large scale distribution of consumables and support materiel for machinery and equipment. NCPDM, as it is known, is a professional organization with primary appeal to individuals in manufacturing, transportation and warehousing industries.

Appendix B

TYPICAL JOB DESCRIPTIONS
FOR CUSTOMER SERVICE POSITIONS

Please note: These job descriptions were developed for actual positions. They are for illustrative purposes, and should be adapted to reflect individual company requirements.

Customer Service Manager: Is responsible for effectively managing the customer service functional responsibility area. This requires the ability to coordinate and administer a wide range of tasks in order to fulfill the significantly different needs of 1. the customer; and 2. internal company departments. Is responsible for ensuring that all company policies and procedures relating to all departments (Marketing, Sales, Credit, Accounting, Distribution, Traffic, as well as Customer Service) are represented accurately to the customer. Daily activities will involve establishing objectives which are specific, realistic and measurable; motivating and training personnel; controlling costs; measuring achievement; initiating changes in internal procedures or suggesting changes in external policies and procedures affecting the customer relationship.

This position includes total responsibility for the processing, distribution and filing of all invoices; total responsibility for ensuring that all customer inquiries are saisfactorily resolved within 30 days; total responsibility for the administration of the adjustment system; total responsibility for coordinating all regional warehouse billing activity; total responsibility for the design and ordering of forms for order entry, for customer inquiry/status reports, for request for credit forms; total responsibility for the formulation of detailed internal procedures used by Customer Service.

Customer Service Manager: Organizes, manages and controls the activities of the Customer Service Department to be responsive to the company's sales and operational objectives. These activities include inside sales, order entry, customer services, international account/distributor sales and servicing, corporate office services, and all assigned special projects.

Specific duties include:

1. Organize, manage and control an order entry function.

2. Organize, manage and control a customer services function that effectively accomplishes the handling of customer and salesperson inquiries/complaints; maintenance of customer files; the furnishing of sales/product literature; equipment repair/service; administration of return goods policy; and selected sales administration function.

3. Maintain an acceptable level of customer service in terms of prompt and

accuarate editing and entry of customer orders and harmonious customer relations.

4. Maintain necessary liaison with Data Processing to ensure that computer support is available and compatible with Customer Service requirements for both day-to-day operations and management reporting.

5. Coordinate with Sales/Marketing/Advertising in development of sales programs, special programs, promotions, sales literature, etc., to assure compatability with Customer Service and Data Processing policies and procedures.

6. Furnish feedback acquired through normal Customer Service operations to appropriate organizations to facilitate actions for operational improvements, e.g., problem notifications, requests for new products, complaints, identifiable trends, product performance/quality, etc.

7. Compile, analyze and distribute customer service/sales-related statistical data, periodically and on special assignment, to assist in optimizing company operations.

8. Prepare annual departmental operating budgets on a monthly basis, and take corrective actions when required.

9. Train and maintain an effective staff of personnel to accomplish assigned departmental operations within the framework of applicable company policies and procedures.

Customer Service Manager: Responsible for developing and maintaining favorable customer relationships through Customer Service activities for all products. Specific responsibilities include:

1. Direct and control with guidance from Sales the release of orders to Shipping that will enable customers to have their goods shipped on time while meeting management shipping goals each fiscal month.

2. Coordinate all production planning, production and shipping efforts to fill shortages of merchandise, and specify production rates needed to allow release of orders and preparation of shipment for on-time shipping.

3. Develop for approval policies governing commitments to customers in order to optimize service.

4. Maintain scoreboards that measure the on-time shipping results against plan by account.

5. Select, develop and train a customer service staff that treats customers courteously and provides them promptly with answers to their questions within 24 hours.

6. Maintain past and open order account information that guarantees quick and accurate response to customer inquiries.

7. Develop an organization that has a core of well-trained, key people year-round that can be enlarged during the heavy season with staff requiring only minimum training to be effective.

8. Maintain a daily control and audit on the correctness of information entered into the computer system by the Customer Service staff through input terminals.

9. Develop an annual budget for Customer Service.

Senior Customer Service Administrator: Supervises an assigned section of Customer Service and is responsible for the efficient, timely and profitable operation of his or her section; under the direction of the customer service manager. Maintains favorable customer relations; proper and timely processing of purchase orders; reviews contractural requirements on purchase orders; plans, lays out and regulates flow of work; selects, trains and supervises personnel; maintains department compliance with corporate procedures; responsible for timely reporting of department activities; determines and corrects errors in customer purchase orders; maintains timely and smooth flow of incoming and outgoing phone calls; resolves all customer complaints on a fair and timely basis; resolves all internal problems related to customer orders; ensures profitability of customer change orders; recommends changes in procedures which would enhance overall department operation.

Supervisor—Order Entry Group: Supervises personnel of the Order Entry Group in accomplishing all functions associated with the receipt, editing and entry of customer orders for products. Reports to Customer Service Manager. Specific duties include:

1. Supervise the editing and entry of orders received by phone, by mail and via salespeople.

2. Supervise the maintenance of computer files for customers, products, prices and salespeople.

3. Coordinate with Data Processing to assure availability and compatibility between computer equipment and systems, and order entry procedures and sales programs.

4. Coordinate to assure order entry and file maintenance availability and compatibility between divisions.

5. Review and approve, as to compatibility with order entry systems, all special programs, promotions, price lists, and sales literature.

6. Coordinate with Accounting, Sales, Shipping, and all other departments as necessary to assure effective order processing.

7. Maintain logs and prepare reports required for operational control and special programs.

8. Develop and/or assist in development of Order Entry Group and Customer Service Department procedures.

9. Administer all company personnel policies as they pertain to Order Entry Group employees.

10. Assign and control entry of all new product numbers.

11. Collect data for monthly sales activity report and other reports as requested.

12. Prepare all internal and external correspondence as required by the performance of the above duties.

Supervisor, Customer Services Group: Supervise personnel of the Customer Services Group in accomplishing all functions associated with handling customer/sales inquiries, maintenance of customer information files, providing product information. Coordinate with and accomplish selected sales administrative functions for the Sales Department. Specific duties include:

1. Supervise and assist customer service representatives in investigating and responding to customer and salespeople inquiries/complaints.

2. Supervise and assist customer service reps in administering company's return goods policy.

3. Coordinate the handling of merchandise returned for testing through Receiving and Quality Control including the notification of results to customers.

4. Supervise customer information files and distribution of Customer Service Department incoming mail.

5. Supervise the providing of product information and samples in compliance with existing programs and procedures.

6. Administer order cancellation procedures including maintenance of records/logs.

7. Coordinate as necessary with field sales personnel to furnish new product information, answer inquiries, and initiate sample requests.

8. Investigate refused or undelivered shipments and take required action and follow-up.

9. Coordinate with Accounting, Sales, Shipping and all other departments as necessary to assure effective customer service operations.

10. Provide telephone communications training as necessary.

11. Record sales literature/samples mailings information and prepare monthly and annual reports of materials furnished.

12. Develop and/or assist in development of group and department procedures.

13. Administer all company personnel policies as they pertain to Customer Services Group employees.

Senior Customer Service Representative: Under readily available supervision, carries out processing of all types of customer orders, complaints, emergencies. Each Customer Service Representative is a member of a group all of whom process orders plus additional duties for their particular assignment. Major duties and responsibilities include:

1. Process orders received by phone, mail, telex or in person. Type emergency orders on such orders that cannot meet our computer scheduling.

2. Handle problems involving orders still in-house.

3. Make arrangements for priority packages with air freight carrier, notify customer of flight and delivery time.

4. Authorize returns caused by a shipping or office error.

5. Explain various policies to customers.

6. Type express mail labels for shipments as necessary.

7. Issue credits due to incorrect pricing, wrong customer code (i.e., office-type clerical error).

8. Coordinate with Shipping.

9. Handle complaints ranging from invoice adjustments, misshipments, credits, backorder delivery dates.

10. Handle correspondence as necessary.

11. Carry out special assignments as directed.

Customer Service Representative: Receives, investigates and responds to all customer inquiries regarding shipments and product/service complaints. Administers company's return goods policies. Specific duties include:

1. Investigate and respond to all customer/salespeople inquiries (by phone or mail) concerning orders, shipments, products and related problems, e.g., order tracking, defective products, shipping/billing errors.

2. Initiate tracer and claims action with carriers.

3. Initiate changes to or cancellation of in-house orders/backorders.

4. Initiate orders for replacement parts, for correcting errors (shortages, wrong items shipped, etc.)

5. Initiate file maintenance for corrections to computer's customer file.

6. Coordinate with Accounts Receivable as necessary on incorrect billings and related matters including requests for issuance of credit memos.

7. Call customers when necessary to obtain approvals for product substitutions, advise of unavailability of stock, delay in shipment, etc.

8. Administer company's return goods policy, investigate claims, check warranties, issue return authorizations, follow-up outstanding R.A.'s.

9. Coordinate inspections and/or perform tests of returned defective products with Quality Control.

10. Take necessary action on unauthorized returns.

11. Review open order list regularly and initiate investigative action on aged open orders.

12. Maintain files of return authorizations, customer service inquiry forms, related documents.

13. Initiate and distribute Customer Service Problem Notification Forms with supporting documentation.

14. Collect data for monthly customer service activity report and other reports as requested.

15. Prepare all internal and external correspondence required by the performance of the above duties.

Order Entry Clerk: Receives, edits and enters orders placed with the company by phone and mail, including the upgrading of phone orders through provision of product and program descriptions. Specific duties include:

1. Enter order data directly into computer terminal during receipt of phoned-in orders from customers and field sales personnel.

2. Edit orders received via mail and Sales Department and prepare for computer terminal entry.

3. Enter edited mailed-in orders into computer terminals.

4. Process cash received with orders.

5. Furnish product/program information to customers placing orders by phone, upgrading orders whenever possible.

6. Correspond as necessary with customers and sales personnel to obtain order information necessary to process orders.

7. Initiate file maintenance as required to update customer file.

8. Initiate requests for product information mailings.

9. Review night phone recorder messages for orders and callbacks.

10. Maintain files (price lists, catalogs, letters, memos, sample transfers, etc.) necessary to accomplish the duties described above.

11. Obtain feedback information from customers to support Sales/Marketing projects.

Appendix C

HOW TO DETERMINE
THE NUMBER OF TELEPHONE LINES
NEEDED TO PROVIDE CUSTOMER SERVICE

*by Paul S. Bender**

Determining how many telephone lines to provide for customer service is a major decision. If too few lines are provided, customer access is difficult and this exacerbates their problems. If too many lines are provided, access is good but costs increase significantly. For that reason, it is necessary to evaluate the impact on customer access of different numbers of telephone lines available. With such information, it is possible to relate the cost of varying numbers of lines to quality of telephone service; thus, well-founded decisions can be made to provide good service, at an acceptable cost.

Determining how many telephone lines are needed is a queuing problem. It is similar to the problems of determining how many cashiers are needed at a supermarket, or how many tellers are needed at a bank, to ensure that the average customer does not wait more than a specified time, and that the average number of customers waiting in line is below some established level.

In a typical customer service system, all customers call the same telephone number, often an 800 number. The calls are then taken by several operators who receive the calls in the sequence they came in. When all operators are busy, incoming calls are staged in a single queue and fed into the system so as to ensure that customers are attended on a first-called, first-served basis.

Assuming that the quality of the service provided is good enough not to discourage any customers from waiting in the queue until attended, we can calculate the characteristics of a waiting queue given two types of data: the average call rate, and the average answer rate.

Average Call Rate (ACR)

The number of customer calls per hour can vary significantly during the day, from day to day during the week, and from week to week during the year. Thus, it is necessary to establish the most critical conditions to be served. This can be done keeping a log, showing for a critical period how many calls were received each hour during that period. In analyzing that data it is important to notice whether it is complete or not: if an important number of callers may have

*Mr. Bender is President, Bender Management Consultants, New York, N.Y.

hung up rather than wait, you must compensate for them by increasing the number of calls shown in the log.

Average Answer Rate (AAR)

In the same log it is necessary to record the length of each call received. Call length may also show seasonality, therefore, the same considerations discussed for ACR apply.

If call lengths are recorded, then all call lengths for the observation period can be added up, and the total divided by the number of calls. That quotient is the average length of a call.

Since the ACR is usually expressed in calls per hour, we need to express the AAR in the same units. This is done dividing the average length of a call into 60 minutes: that quotient is the average answer rate (AAR) in calls answered per hour.

With the two data elements calculated as explained above, we can use a set of queuing tables to determine the effect of varying numbers of telephone lines on the average number of customers waiting to be attended (L), and on the average waiting time they can expect (W). Typical queuing tables are presented in Exhibit 1.

To illustrate these ideas, let us consider an example.

A log indicates that during the most critical day of the year there were 62 calls in total, and during the most critical hour there were 12 calls. Adding up the duration of all calls we find that it was 249 minutes. Therefore,

$$\text{Average duration of a call } = \frac{249}{62} = 4.02$$

Therefore,

$$\text{Average Answer Rate } = \frac{60}{4.02} = 14.9 \text{ calls answered per hour.}$$

We can round that value to 15 calls per hour.

Looking at the queuing tables for 1 line, we find that for an average call rate of 12 and an average answer rate of 15, we obtain

$$L = 3$$
$$W = 16$$

Therefore, if we use 1 telephone line, we can expect to have an average of 3 customers waiting in line, and their average waiting time will be 16 minutes.

We then go to the table for 2 lines, with the same values for ACR and AAR, and we find

$$L = 0$$
$$W = 1$$

which look like acceptable values. To be sure, we check the table for 3 lines, and we find

$$L = 0$$
$$W = 0$$

The conclusion is that with 2 lines, the average number of customers waiting will be less than .5 and their average waiting time will be less than 1.5 minutes, since all table values are rounded. Those values are acceptable, and justify the cost of the additional line.

In using the tables, there are two other considerations: first, all values greater than 999 are shown as *** since they are not of practical interest. Second, if the values calculated for ACR and AAR fall between values shown in the tables, either they can be rounded if close enough, or their corresponding values of L and W can be calculated by interpolation.

Average Call Rate (Calls per Hour)
Number of Lines = One

AAR	Parameter	0.5	1.0	1.5	2.0	2.5	3.0	3.5	4.0	5.0	6.0	7.0	8.0	9.0	10.0	11.0	12.0	15.0	20.0	30.0	60.0
0.55	L	9	***	***	***	***	***	***	***	***	***	***	***	***	***	***	***	***	***	***	***
	W	***	***	***	***	***	***	***	***	***	***	***	***	***	***	***	***	***	***	***	***
0.60	L	4	***	***	***	***	***	***	***	***	***	***	***	***	***	***	***	***	***	***	***
	W	500	***	***	***	***	***	***	***	***	***	***	***	***	***	***	***	***	***	***	***
0.65	L	3	***	***	***	***	***	***	***	***	***	***	***	***	***	***	***	***	***	***	***
	W	308	***	***	***	***	***	***	***	***	***	***	***	***	***	***	***	***	***	***	***
0.70	L	2	***	***	***	***	***	***	***	***	***	***	***	***	***	***	***	***	***	***	***
	W	214	***	***	***	***	***	***	***	***	***	***	***	***	***	***	***	***	***	***	***
0.80	L	1	***	***	***	***	***	***	***	***	***	***	***	***	***	***	***	***	***	***	***
	W	125	***	***	***	***	***	***	***	***	***	***	***	***	***	***	***	***	***	***	***
0.90	L	1	***	***	***	***	***	***	***	***	***	***	***	***	***	***	***	***	***	***	***
	W	83	***	***	***	***	***	***	***	***	***	***	***	***	***	***	***	***	***	***	***
1.00	L	1	***	***	***	***	***	***	***	***	***	***	***	***	***	***	***	***	***	***	***
	W	60	***	***	***	***	***	***	***	***	***	***	***	***	***	***	***	***	***	***	***
1.25	L	0	3	***	***	***	***	***	***	***	***	***	***	***	***	***	***	***	***	***	***
	W	32	192	***	***	***	***	***	***	***	***	***	***	***	***	***	***	***	***	***	***
1.50	L	0	1	***	***	***	***	***	***	***	***	***	***	***	***	***	***	***	***	***	***
	W	20	80	***	***	***	***	***	***	***	***	***	***	***	***	***	***	***	***	***	***
1.75	L	0	1	5	***	***	***	***	***	***	***	***	***	***	***	***	***	***	***	***	***
	W	14	46	206	***	***	***	***	***	***	***	***	***	***	***	***	***	***	***	***	***

Figure 1. Example of Queuing Tables.

Period		W (bottom → top, i.e. increasing parameter)
2.00	L	0, 1, 2
	W	10, 30, 90
2.50	L	0, 0, 1, 3
	W	6, 16, 36, 96
3.00	L	0, 0, 1, 1, 4
	W	4, 10, 20, 40, 100
3.50	L	0, 0, 1, 1, 2, 5
	W	3, 7, 15, 23, 43, 103
4.00	L	0, 0, 0, 1, 2, 2, 6
	W	2, 5, 9, 15, 25, 45, 105
5.00	L	0, 0, 0, 0, 1, 1, 2, 3, 4
	W	1, 3, 5, 8, 12, 18, 28, 48, 50
6.00	L	0, 0, 0, 0, 0, 1, 1, 1, 2, 6
	W	1, 2, 3, 5, 7, 10, 14, 20, 23, 53
8.00	L	0, 0, 0, 0, 0, 0, 1, 1, 1, 2, 8
	W	1, 1, 2, 3, 5, 6, 8, 9, 10, 14, 54
10.00	L	0, 0, 0, 0, 0, 0, 1, 1, 2, 4, 10
	W	0, 1, 1, 2, 3, 4, 5, 7, 15, 25, 55
12.00	L	0, 0, 0, 0, 0, 0, 0, 1, 1, 2, 4
	W	0, 1, 1, 2, 2, 3, 4, 6, 8, 15, 25
15.00	L	0, 0, 0, 0, 0, 0, 0, 1, 1, 1, 2, 3
	W	1, 1, 1, 2, 3, 3, 5, 6, 8, 11, 16

Average Call Rate (Calls per Hour)
Number of Lines = Two

AAR	Parameter	0.5	1.0	1.5	2.0	2.5	3.0	3.5	4.0	5.0	6.0	7.0	8.0	9.0	10.0	11.0	12.0	15.0	20.0	30.0	60.0
0.55	L	0	9	***	***	***	***	***	***	***	***	***	***	***	***	***	***	***	***	***	***
	W	28	519	***	***	***	***	***	***	***	***	***	***	***	***	***	***	***	***	***	***
0.60	L	0	4	***	***	***	***	***	***	***	***	***	***	***	***	***	***	***	***	***	***
	W	21	227	***	***	***	***	***	***	***	***	***	***	***	***	***	***	***	***	***	***
0.65	L	0	2	***	***	***	***	***	***	***	***	***	***	***	***	***	***	***	***	***	***
	W	16	134	***	***	***	***	***	***	***	***	***	***	***	***	***	***	***	***	***	***
0.70	L	0	1	***	***	***	***	***	***	***	***	***	***	***	***	***	***	***	***	***	***
	W	13	89	***	***	***	***	***	***	***	***	***	***	***	***	***	***	***	***	***	***
0.80	L	0	1	14	***	***	***	***	***	***	***	***	***	***	***	***	***	***	***	***	***
	W	8	48	544	***	***	***	***	***	***	***	***	***	***	***	***	***	***	***	***	***
0.90	L	0	0	4	***	***	***	***	***	***	***	***	***	***	***	***	***	***	***	***	***
	W	6	30	152	***	***	***	***	***	***	***	***	***	***	***	***	***	***	***	***	***
1.00	L	0	0	2	***	***	***	***	***	***	***	***	***	***	***	***	***	***	***	***	***
	W	4	20	77	***	***	***	***	***	***	***	***	***	***	***	***	***	***	***	***	***
1.25	L	0	0	1	3	***	***	***	***	***	***	***	***	***	***	***	***	***	***	***	***
	W	2	9	27	85	***	***	***	***	***	***	***	***	***	***	***	***	***	***	***	***
1.50	L	0	0	0	1	4	***	***	***	***	***	***	***	***	***	***	***	***	***	***	***
	W	1	5	13	32	91	***	***	***	***	***	***	***	***	***	***	***	***	***	***	***
1.75	L	0	0	0	1	1	5	***	***	***	***	***	***	***	***	***	***	***	***	***	***
	W	1	3	8	17	36	95	***	***	***	***	***	***	***	***	***	***	***	***	***	***

2.00	L	0	0	0	0	1	2	6	***	***	***	***	***	***	***	***	***	***	***	***	***
	W	0	2	5	10	19	39	98	***	***	***	***	***	***	***	***	***	***	***	***	***
2.50	L	0	0	0	0	0	1	1	3	***	***	***	***	***	***	***	***	***	***	***	***
	W	0	1	2	5	8	13	23	43	***	***	***	***	***	***	***	***	***	***	***	***
3.00	L	0	0	0	0	0	0	1	1	4	***	***	***	***	***	***	***	***	***	***	***
	W	0	1	1	3	4	7	10	16	45	***	***	***	***	***	***	***	***	***	***	***
3.50	L	0	0	0	0	0	0	0	1	1	5	***	***	***	***	***	***	***	***	***	***
	W	0	0	1	2	3	4	6	8	18	47	***	***	***	***	***	***	***	***	***	***
4.00	L	0	0	0	0	0	0	0	0	1	2	6	***	***	***	***	***	***	***	***	***
	W	0	0	1	1	2	2	4	5	10	19	49	***	***	***	***	***	***	***	***	***
5.00	L	0	0	0	0	0	0	0	0	0	1	1	3	8	***	***	***	***	***	***	***
	W	0	0	0	1	1	1	2	2	4	7	12	21	51	***	***	***	***	***	***	***
6.00	L	0	0	0	0	0	0	0	0	0	0	1	1	2	4	10	***	***	***	***	***
	W	0	0	0	0	0	1	1	1	2	3	5	8	13	23	53	***	***	***	***	***
8.00	L	0	0	0	0	0	0	0	0	0	0	0	0	1	1	1	2	14	***	***	***
	W	0	0	0	0	0	0	0	1	1	1	2	3	3	5	7	10	54	***	***	***
10.00	L	0	0	0	0	0	0	0	0	0	0	0	0	0	0	0	1	2	***	***	***
	W	0	0	0	0	0	0	0	0	0	1	1	1	2	2	3	3	8	***	***	***
12.00	L	0	0	0	0	0	0	0	0	0	0	0	0	0	0	0	0	1	4	***	***
	W	0	0	0	0	0	0	0	0	0	0	0	1	1	1	1	2	3	11	***	***
15.00	L	0	0	0	0	0	0	0	0	0	0	0	0	0	0	0	0	0	1	***	***
	W	0	0	0	0	0	0	0	0	0	0	0	0	0	1	1	1	1	3	***	***

Average Call Rate (Calls per Hour)
Number of Lines = Three

AAR	Parameter	0.5	1.0	1.5	2.0	2.5	3.0	3.5	4.0	5.0	6.0	7.0	8.0	9.0	10.0	11.0	12.0	15.0	20.0	30.0	60.0
0.55	L	0	1	8	***	***	***	***	***	***	***	***	***	***	***	***	***	***	***	***	***
	W	4	33	333	***	***	***	***	***	***	***	***	***	***	***	***	***	***	***	***	***
0.60	L	0	0	4	***	***	***	***	***	***	***	***	***	***	***	***	***	***	***	***	***
	W	3	22	140	***	***	***	***	***	***	***	***	***	***	***	***	***	***	***	***	***
0.65	L	0	0	2	***	***	***	***	***	***	***	***	***	***	***	***	***	***	***	***	***
	W	2	16	80	***	***	***	***	***	***	***	***	***	***	***	***	***	***	***	***	***
0.70	L	0	0	1	18	***	***	***	***	***	***	***	***	***	***	***	***	***	***	***	***
	W	1	12	51	547	***	***	***	***	***	***	***	***	***	***	***	***	***	***	***	***
0.80	L	0	0	1	4	***	***	***	***	***	***	***	***	***	***	***	***	***	***	***	***
	W	1	7	26	105	***	***	***	***	***	***	***	***	***	***	***	***	***	***	***	***
0.90	L	0	0	0	2	11	***	***	***	***	***	***	***	***	***	***	***	***	***	***	***
	W	1	4	15	47	259	***	***	***	***	***	***	***	***	***	***	***	***	***	***	***
1.00	L	0	0	0	1	4	***	***	***	***	***	***	***	***	***	***	***	***	***	***	***
	W	0	3	9	27	84	***	***	***	***	***	***	***	***	***	***	***	***	***	***	***
1.25	L	0	0	0	0	1	3	12	***	***	***	***	***	***	***	***	***	***	***	***	***
	W	0	1	4	9	21	52	210	***	***	***	***	***	***	***	***	***	***	***	***	***
1.50	L	0	0	0	0	0	1	2	6	***	***	***	***	***	***	***	***	***	***	***	***
	W	0	1	2	4	9	18	37	96	***	***	***	***	***	***	***	***	***	***	***	***
1.75	L	0	0	0	0	0	0	1	2	18	***	***	***	***	***	***	***	***	***	***	***
	W	0	0	1	2	5	9	15	28	219	***	***	***	***	***	***	***	***	***	***	***

	2.00		2.50		3.00		3.50		4.00		5.00		6.00		8.00		10.00		12.00		15.00	
	L	W	L	W	L	W	L	W	L	W	L	W	L	W	L	W	L	W	L	W	L	W
	***	***	***	***	***	***	***	***	***	***	***	***	***	***	***	***	***	***	***	***	***	***
	***	***	***	***	***	***	***	***	***	***	***	***	***	***	***	***	***	***	4	7	1	2
	***	***	***	***	***	***	***	***	***	***	***	***	***	***	4	11	1	3	0	1	0	0
	***	***	***	***	***	***	***	***	***	***	***	***	4	14	1	3	0	1	0	0	0	0
	***	***	***	***	***	***	***	***	***	***	3	13	1	4	0	1	0	1	0	0	0	0
	***	***	***	***	***	***	***	***	***	***	9	51	1	8	1	3	0	1	0	0	0	0
	***	***	***	***	***	***	***	***	18	109	4	21	1	5	0	2	0	1	0	0	0	0
	***	***	***	***	***	***	***	***	4	30	2	11	1	4	0	2	0	0	0	0	0	0
	***	***	***	***	***	***	6	48	2	14	1	7	0	2	0	1	0	0	0	0	0	0
	***	***	12	105	3	26	2	18	1	8	0	4	0	2	0	1	0	0	0	0	0	0
	4	42	1	13	1	9	1	11	0	4	0	2	0	1	0	0	0	0	0	0	0	0
	1	13	0	5	0	4	0	8	0	2	0	1	0	1	0	0	0	0	0	0	0	0
	0	8	0	3	0	1	0	4	0	2	0	1	0	0	0	0	0	0	0	0	0	0
	0	5	0	2	0	1	0	2	0	1	0	0	0	0	0	0	0	0	0	0	0	0
	0	3	0	1	0	1	0	1	0	1	0	0	0	0	0	0	0	0	0	0	0	0
	0	1	0	1	0	0	0	0	0	0	0	0	0	0	0	0	0	0	0	0	0	0
	0	1	0	0	0	0	0	0	0	0	0	0	0	0	0	0	0	0	0	0	0	0
	0	0	0	0	0	0	0	0	0	0	0	0	0	0	0	0	0	0	0	0	0	0

Average Call Rate (Calls per Hour)
Number of Lines = Four

AAR	Parameter	0.5	1.0	1.5	2.0	2.5	3.0	3.5	4.0	5.0	6.0	7.0	8.0	9.0	10.0	11.0	12.0	15.0	20.0	30.0	60.0
0.55	L	0	0	1	8	***	***	***	***	***	***	***	***	***	***	***	***	***	***	***	***
	W	1	7	34	242	***	***	***	***	***	***	***	***	***	***	***	***	***	***	***	***
0.60	L	0	0	1	3	***	***	***	***	***	***	***	***	***	***	***	***	***	***	***	***
	W	0	4	21	99	***	***	***	***	***	***	***	***	***	***	***	***	***	***	***	***
0.65	L	0	0	0	2	23	***	***	***	***	***	***	***	***	***	***	***	***	***	***	***
	W	0	3	14	54	550	***	***	***	***	***	***	***	***	***	***	***	***	***	***	***
0.70	L	0	0	0	1	6	***	***	***	***	***	***	***	***	***	***	***	***	***	***	***
	W	0	2	10	34	155	***	***	***	***	***	***	***	***	***	***	***	***	***	***	***
0.80	L	0	0	0	1	2	13	***	***	***	***	***	***	***	***	***	***	***	***	***	***
	W	0	1	5	16	48	260	***	***	***	***	***	***	***	***	***	***	***	***	***	***
0.90	L	0	0	0	0	1	3	33	***	***	***	***	***	***	***	***	***	***	***	***	***
	W	0	1	3	9	23	66	563	***	***	***	***	***	***	***	***	***	***	***	***	***
1.00	L	0	0	0	0	1	2	5	***	***	***	***	***	***	***	***	***	***	***	***	***
	W	0	0	2	5	13	31	89	***	***	***	***	***	***	***	***	***	***	***	***	***
1.25	L	0	0	0	0	0	1	1	2	***	***	***	***	***	***	***	***	***	***	***	***
	W	0	0	1	2	4	9	17	36	***	***	***	***	***	***	***	***	***	***	***	***
1.50	L	0	0	0	0	0	0	0	1	3	***	***	***	***	***	***	***	***	***	***	***
	W	0	0	0	1	2	3	6	11	39	***	***	***	***	***	***	***	***	***	***	***
1.75	L	0	0	0	0	0	0	0	0	1	4	***	***	***	***	***	***	***	***	***	***
	W	0	0	0	0	1	2	3	5	14	42	***	***	***	***	***	***	***	***	***	***

Each rate column below is split into an L and a W value (shown as "L/W"). "***" denotes a value that falls off the chart.

Row	2.00	2.50	3.00	3.50	4.00	5.00	6.00	8.00	10.00	12.00	15.00
1	***/***	***/***	***/***	***/***	***/***	***/***	***/***	***/***	***/***	***/***	***/***
2	***/***	***/***	***/***	***/***	***/***	***/***	***/***	13/26	2/3	1/1	0/0
3	***/***	***/***	***/***	***/***	***/***	***/***	3/10	1/2	0/1	0/0	0/0
4	***/***	***/***	***/***	***/***	***/***	13/52	2/6	1/2	0/1	0/0	0/0
5	***/***	***/***	***/***	***/***	4/21	2/8	0/2	0/1	0/0	0/0	0/0
6	***/***	***/***	***/***	9/49	2/11	1/5	0/2	0/1	0/0	0/0	0/0
7	***/***	***/***	***/***	3/20	1/7	1/3	0/1	0/0	0/0	0/0	0/0
8	***/***	***/***	7/47	2/10	1/4	0/2	0/1	0/0	0/0	0/0	0/0
9	***/***	***/***	2/18	1/6	0/3	0/1	0/0	0/0	0/0	0/0	0/0
10	***/***	5/44	1/9	0/3	0/1	0/0	0/0	0/0	0/0	0/0	0/0
11	2/15	0/4	0/2	0/1	0/0	0/0	0/0	0/0	0/0	0/0	0/0
12	1/6	0/2	0/1	0/0	0/0	0/0	0/0	0/0	0/0	0/0	0/0
13	0/3	0/1	0/0	0/0	0/0	0/0	0/0	0/0	0/0	0/0	0/0
14	0/2	0/0	0/0	0/0	0/0	0/0	0/0	0/0	0/0	0/0	0/0
15	0/1	0/0	0/0	0/0	0/0	0/0	0/0	0/0	0/0	0/0	0/0
16	0/0	0/0	0/0	0/0	0/0	0/0	0/0	0/0	0/0	0/0	0/0
17	0/0	0/0	0/0	0/0	0/0	0/0	0/0	0/0	0/0	0/0	0/0
18	0/0	0/0	0/0	0/0	0/0	0/0	0/0	0/0	0/0	0/0	0/0

Average Call Rate (Calls per Hour)
Number of Lines = Five

AAR	Parameter	0.5	1.0	1.5	2.0	2.5	3.0	3.5	4.0	5.0	6.0	7.0	8.0	9.0	10.0	11.0	12.0	15.0	20.0	30.0	60.0
0.55	L	0	0	0	1	8	***	***	***	***	***	***	***	***	***	***	***	***	***	***	***
	W	0	1	8	34	188	***	***	***	***	***	***	***	***	***	***	***	***	***	***	***
0.60	L	0	0	0	1	3	***	***	***	***	***	***	***	***	***	***	***	***	***	***	***
	W	0	1	5	20	74	***	***	***	***	***	***	***	***	***	***	***	***	***	***	***
0.65	L	0	0	0	0	2	10	***	***	***	***	***	***	***	***	***	***	***	***	***	***
	W	0	1	3	12	40	196	***	***	***	***	***	***	***	***	***	***	***	***	***	***
0.70	L	0	0	0	0	1	4	***	***	***	***	***	***	***	***	***	***	***	***	***	***
	W	0	0	2	8	24	80	***	***	***	***	***	***	***	***	***	***	***	***	***	***
0.80	L	0	0	0	0	0	1	5	***	***	***	***	***	***	***	***	***	***	***	***	***
	W	0	0	1	4	11	28	85	***	***	***	***	***	***	***	***	***	***	***	***	***
0.90	L	0	0	0	0	0	1	2	6	***	***	***	***	***	***	***	***	***	***	***	***
	W	0	0	1	2	6	13	31	89	***	***	***	***	***	***	***	***	***	***	***	***
1.00	L	0	0	0	0	0	0	1	2	***	***	***	***	***	***	***	***	***	***	***	***
	W	0	0	0	1	3	7	15	33	***	***	***	***	***	***	***	***	***	***	***	***
1.25	L	0	0	0	0	0	0	0	1	2	22	***	***	***	***	***	***	***	***	***	***
	W	0	0	0	0	1	2	4	8	27	216	***	***	***	***	***	***	***	***	***	***
1.50	L	0	0	0	0	0	0	0	0	1	2	12	***	***	***	***	***	***	***	***	***
	W	0	0	0	0	0	1	2	3	8	22	101	***	***	***	***	***	***	***	***	***
1.75	L	0	0	0	0	0	0	0	0	0	1	2	8	***	***	***	***	***	***	***	***
	W	0	0	0	0	0	0	1	1	3	8	19	64	***	***	***	***	***	***	***	***

	2.00		2.50		3.00		3.50		4.00		5.00		6.00		8.00		10.00		12.00		15.00	
	L	W	L	W	L	W	L	W	L	W	L	W	L	W	L	W	L	W	L	W	L	W
	***	***	***	***	***	***	***	***	***	***	***	***	***	***	***	***	***	***	***	***	2	2
	***	***	***	***	***	***	***	***	***	***	***	***	***	***	1	3	0	1	0	0	0	0
	***	***	***	***	***	***	***	***	***	***	2	7	1	2	0	0	0	0	0	0	0	0
	***	***	***	***	***	***	4	16	1	6	0	1	0	1	0	0	0	0	0	0	0	0
	***	***	***	***	22	108	2	11	1	4	0	2	0	1	0	0	0	0	0	0	0	0
	***	***	5	29	1	6	0	3	0	1	0	0	0	0	0	0	0	0	0	0	0	0
	***	***	2	13	1	4	0	2	0	1	0	0	0	0	0	0	0	0	0	0	0	0
	7	46	1	7	0	2	0	1	0	0	0	0	0	0	0	0	0	0	0	0	0	0
	2	17	1	4	0	1	0	1	0	0	0	0	0	0	0	0	0	0	0	0	0	0
	1	8	0	2	0	1	0	0	0	0	0	0	0	0	0	0	0	0	0	0	0	0
	0	4	0	1	0	0	0	0	0	0	0	0	0	0	0	0	0	0	0	0	0	0
	0	2	0	0	0	0	0	0	0	0	0	0	0	0	0	0	0	0	0	0	0	0
	0	1	0	0	0	0	0	0	0	0	0	0	0	0	0	0	0	0	0	0	0	0
	0	0	0	0	0	0	0	0	0	0	0	0	0	0	0	0	0	0	0	0	0	0
	0	0	0	0	0	0	0	0	0	0	0	0	0	0	0	0	0	0	0	0	0	0
	0	0	0	0	0	0	0	0	0	0	0	0	0	0	0	0	0	0	0	0	0	0
	0	0	0	0	0	0	0	0	0	0	0	0	0	0	0	0	0	0	0	0	0	0
	0	0	0	0	0	0	0	0	0	0	0	0	0	0	0	0	0	0	0	0	0	0

Average Call Rate (Calls per Hour)
Number of Lines = Six

AAR	Parameter	0.5	1.0	1.5	2.0	2.5	3.0	3.5	4.0	5.0	6.0	7.0	8.0	9.0	10.0	11.0	12.0	15.0	20.0	30.0	60.0
0.55	L	0	0	0	0	1	8	***	***	***	***	***	***	***	***	***	***	***	***	***	***
	W	0	0	2	9	33	152	***	***	***	***	***	***	***	***	***	***	***	***	***	***
0.60	L	0	0	0	0	1	3	32	***	***	***	***	***	***	***	***	***	***	***	***	***
	W	0	0	1	6	18	59	555	***	***	***	***	***	***	***	***	***	***	***	***	***
0.65	L	0	0	0	0	0	2	6	***	***	***	***	***	***	***	***	***	***	***	***	***
	W	0	0	1	3	11	30	110	***	***	***	***	***	***	***	***	***	***	***	***	***
0.70	L	0	0	0	0	0	1	3	17	***	***	***	***	***	***	***	***	***	***	***	***
	W	0	0	1	2	7	18	50	262	***	***	***	***	***	***	***	***	***	***	***	***
0.80	L	0	0	0	0	0	0	1	3	***	***	***	***	***	***	***	***	***	***	***	***
	W	0	0	0	1	3	8	18	44	***	***	***	***	***	***	***	***	***	***	***	***
0.90	L	0	0	0	0	0	0	0	1	10	***	***	***	***	***	***	***	***	***	***	***
	W	0	0	0	1	2	4	8	17	121	***	***	***	***	***	***	***	***	***	***	***
1.00	L	0	0	0	0	0	0	0	1	3	***	***	***	***	***	***	***	***	***	***	***
	W	0	0	0	0	1	2	4	9	35	***	***	***	***	***	***	***	***	***	***	***
1.25	L	0	0	0	0	0	0	0	0	1	2	12	***	***	***	***	***	***	***	***	***
	W	0	0	0	0	0	1	1	2	7	21	99	***	***	***	***	***	***	***	***	***
1.50	L	0	0	0	0	0	0	0	0	0	1	2	6	***	***	***	***	***	***	***	***
	W	0	0	0	0	0	0	0	1	2	6	14	43	***	***	***	***	***	***	***	***
1.75	L	0	0	0	0	0	0	0	0	0	0	1	1	4	17	***	***	***	***	***	***
	W	0	0	0	0	0	0	0	0	1	2	5	11	26	105	***	***	***	***	***	***

	2.00		2.50		3.00		3.50		4.00		5.00		6.00		8.00		10.00		12.00		15.00	
	L	W	L	W	L	W	L	W	L	W	L	W	L	W	L	W	L	W	L	W	L	W
	***	***	***	***	***	***	***	***	***	***	***	***	***	***	***	***	***	***	3	3	1	1
	***	***	***	***	***	***	***	***	***	***	***	***	3	6	0	1	0	0	0	0	0	0
	***	***	***	***	***	***	17	52	3	9	1	2	0	1	0	0	0	0	0	0	0	0
	***	***	***	***	3	12	1	4	0	2	0	0	0	0	0	0	0	0	0	0	0	0
	***	***	2	10	1	3	0	1	0	0	0	0	0	0	0	0	0	0	0	0	0	0
	9	47	1	6	0	2	0	1	0	0	0	0	0	0	0	0	0	0	0	0	0	0
	3	18	1	3	0	1	0	0	0	0	0	0	0	0	0	0	0	0	0	0	0	0
	1	8	0	2	0	1	0	0	0	0	0	0	0	0	0	0	0	0	0	0	0	0
	1	4	0	1	0	0	0	0	0	0	0	0	0	0	0	0	0	0	0	0	0	0
	0	2	0	1	0	0	0	0	0	0	0	0	0	0	0	0	0	0	0	0	0	0
	0	1	0	0	0	0	0	0	0	0	0	0	0	0	0	0	0	0	0	0	0	0
	0	0	0	0	0	0	0	0	0	0	0	0	0	0	0	0	0	0	0	0	0	0
	0	0	0	0	0	0	0	0	0	0	0	0	0	0	0	0	0	0	0	0	0	0
	0	0	0	0	0	0	0	0	0	0	0	0	0	0	0	0	0	0	0	0	0	0
	0	0	0	0	0	0	0	0	0	0	0	0	0	0	0	0	0	0	0	0	0	0
	0	0	0	0	0	0	0	0	0	0	0	0	0	0	0	0	0	0	0	0	0	0
	0	0	0	0	0	0	0	0	0	0	0	0	0	0	0	0	0	0	0	0	0	0
	0	0	0	0	0	0	0	0	0	0	0	0	0	0	0	0	0	0	0	0	0	0

Appendix D

SPECIAL REPORT ON CLAIMS AND RETURNS PRACTICES IN U.S. FIRMS

by Leslie Hansen Harps
Reprinted from Customer Service Newsletter, Vol. 12 No. 12, December 15, 1984.

Customer service managers concerned with the shortcomings of their companies' policies and performance in handling claims and returns and the associated documentation will find some consolation in one universal truth in this winter of 1984-85: they are not alone. For example, from a representative sample of what most business experts would consider upscale manufacturing and distributive firms come the following dismal statistics on current practices:

    — 76% of companies do not have policies for automatic adjustment of claims for even the most minute amounts.

    — In 35% of companies, customers are frequently—and in some companies *always*—sent dunning notices for amounts that are being processed as credits.

    — Certainly a contributing factor to the dunning problem is the fact that it takes an average of 33 days—and sometimes a good deal longer—for a credit to appear on the customer's statement or for a refund check to be issued.

    — As another delaying factor, 83% of companies require customers to obtain authorization before returning merchandise, even when the vendor is clearly responsible for misshipment, errors, quality problems and the like.

    — Some companies—including a number of large and otherwise sophisticated firms—don't even have published policies on claims and returns.

    — Some 25% of companies don't even analyze their claims and credits by type, cause, potentials for avoidance, alternative measures for resolution, etc.

    — And, understandably, half of all customer service managers are unhappy with their companies' present policies and systems for handling claims and returns!

The Survey: Poor Numbers That Translate Into Rich Opportunities

    The survey that generated this frequently discouraging data was conducted over a period of several months during 1984, and the preliminary findings were reported at the annual conference of the International Customer Service Association by Lynn Dunston and Leslie Hansen Harps of Marketing Publications Incorporated. At cutoff, the survey had recorded a statistically reliable 28.2% response.

SPECIAL REPORT ON CLAIMS AND RETURNS PRACTICES

Not all of the respondents reported "bad news," of course, and indeed some companies reported practices which could well be termed state-of-the-art, not only in terms of actual methodology via computer and associated support systems, but also in terms of sound marketing practice, recognizing the value and contribution to profit of quick, effective resolution of these matters, in some cases even where the customer is clearly—or arguably—at fault.

An additional optimistic note appears in the *potential for improvement* that clearly exists for most companies in the claims/returns area. At a time when there is great concern among professional customer service managers with changing their image from reactive to proactive, their managements are equally concerned with practical means for capitalizing on the Peters-Waterman principle of getting—and staying—close to customers as a major key to corporate excellence and success.

Given this, the next logical step for customer service managers would appear to lie in the direction of researching their own customers to determine how well they are doing in this area as perceived by customers, how their performance is affecting customer relations and sales, how competitors are perceived—and what needs doing to improve the system. And then of course doing it.

Overall Policies

In most industries, a significant number of respondents accept returns only by the book, i.e., as per terms of sale, as shown in Table 1. However, some respondents do point out that, while this is published policy, they can be more flexible in practice.

For some industries, 50% or more of the respondents answered "other." These policies ranged from "as per our warranty" to "we allow customers to return a certain percentage of their annual purchases," to "we accept only returns as a result of our error." A few respondents stated flatly that they accept no returns of any sort.

But the vast majority of respondents who answered "other" reported that their policies required that customers obtain authorization from the company before making a return. Many respondents stated that each request for return—regardless of reason—is investigated and judged on an individual basis, rather than according to a pre-defined set of criteria. Some respondents even reported that requests for returns had to be authorized by the Vice President of Sales!

Overall, 83% of respondents do require customers to obtain authorization prior to returning product, as shown in Table 2. Note that there is some variation by industry, ranging from 100% of health and beauty aid firms (this segment of our sample was fairly small, so perhaps not statistically reliable) to only 33% of service organizations.

Restocking Charges Specific to Industry

Whether or not a firm levies restocking charges depends a great deal on the industry. For example, while the average for all industry groups is 68%, as shown in Table 3, 100% of automotive supply firms have a restocking charge, while 40% of apparel firms and only 16% of food companies do.

If you have a restocking charge, and your competitors don't, you might be at a competitive disadvantage as the economy slows and customers aggressively seek the best overall deals. This is certainly one area where research into competitors' practices could pay off.

One Month Required to Process Credits

The average length of time it takes to get a credit on a customer's statement—or to issue a refund check—from the time one is first requested is shown in Table 4. According to our respondents, it takes the average company more than a month to process this request! Again, this ranges significantly by industry, from a high of 41 days in the automotive supply industry to a two-week turnaround in the highly competitive food industry.

We also asked respondents to give their company or departmental standard for this period of time, so that we could track performance against standard—but only a tiny portion of our respondents reported even having such a standard. One who does has an interesting approach: claims under a certain dollar amount, relatively small, are to be processed within two days; over that amount, within 30 days.

As a result of the length of time required to process customers' requests for credits/refunds, overall only 14% of companies reported that they never dunned customers for an amount that was in the process of being credited or refunded; 35% reported that they frequently or always sent invoices or overdue account notices on such amounts. (See Table 5.) Half of those in the computer hardware industry frequently or always dun customers on these amounts, as do 42% of

	(a) Accept All	(b) Under $ Amount	(c) Per Terms of Sale	(d) Other
Average, all industry groups	15%	3%	38%	44%
Apparel	6%	6%	35%	53%
Automotive Supply	12%	6%	59%	24%
Chemicals	11%	--	23%	66%
Computer Hardware	--	8%	58%	33%
Consumer Durables	17%	3%	24%	55%
Consumer Non-Durables	20%	2%	27%	51%
Grocery Products	23%	3%	32%	42%
Health & Beauty Aids	18%	1%	45%	36%
Industrial Durables	10%	3%	38%	49%
Industrial Non-Durables	10%	3%	38%	49%
Medical/Hospital Supply	15%	6%	51%	28%
Office/Computer Supply	22%	6%	33%	39%
Publishing	38%	--	38%	24%
Services	6%	13%	31%	50%

Table 1. What guidelines most nearly describe your credits and returns policy? Options included (a) accept all returns without question; (b) accept all returns under a set dollar amount; (c) accept returns only per terms of sale; (d) other.

medical firms, 41% of industrial non-durables and 40% of industrial durables.

One respondent says, "This can be a source of irritation!" Another explains succinctly, "We're working on this."

Automatic Adjustments: Overlooked by Most

A whopping 76% of all respondents do not have a policy for automatic

	Yes	No
Total, all industry groups	83	17
Apparel	81	19
Automotive Supply	94	6
Chemicals	89	11
Computer Hardware	83	17
Consumer Durables	71	29
Consumer Non-Durables	77	23
Grocery Products	94	6
Health & Beauty Aids	100	--
Industrial Durables	86	14
Industrial Non-Durables	93	7
Medical/Hospital Supply	86	14
Office/Computer Supply	68	32
Publishing	37	63
Services	33	67

Table 2. Must customers obtain authorization before return of merchandise is accepted?

	Yes	No	Sometimes
Average, all industry groups	68	32	2
Apparel	40	60	--
Automotive Supply	100	--	--
Chemicals	71	20	9
Computer Hardware	64	36	--
Consumer Durables	69	21	10
Consumer Non-Durables	55	45	--
Grocery Products	16	84	--
Health & Beauty Aids	60	40	--
Industrial Durables	85	10	5
Industrial Non-Durables	78	19	3
Medical/Hospital Supply	80	20	--
Office/Computer Supply	56	44	--
Publishing	--	100	--
Services	NA	NA	NA

Table 3. Is there a restocking charge for returns?

credit/refunds—that is, criteria under which requests are automatically accepted. (See Table 6.) Again, this differs largely by industry. In the publishing industry, where returns are accepted as part of doing business, 47% of respondents report an automatic adjustment policy. Similarly, 43% of service organizations, 37% of apparel firms, and a third of office and computer supply companies have automatic adjustment policies, while only 8% of chemicals and plastics firms have such a policy.

	Number of Days
Average, all industry groups	33
Apparel	27
Automotive Supply	41
Chemicals	30
Computer Hardware	25
Consumer Durables	24
Consumer Non-Durables	30
Grocery Products	14
Health & Beauty Aids	36
Industrial Durables	32
Industrial Non-Durables	34
Medical/Hospital Supply	32
Office/Computer Supply	16
Publishing	25
Services	30

Table 4.   What is the average length of time from credit/return request to credit appearing on customer's statement (or refund check issued)?

	Never	Sometimes	Frequently	Always
Average, all industry groups	14	52	15	20
Apparel	7	71	14	7
Automotive Supply	23	46	15	15
Chemicals	23	43	26	9
Computer Hardware	10	40	40	10
Consumer Durables	17	53	17	13
Consumer Non-Durables	11	62	2	24
Grocery Products	15	56	11	19
Health & Beauty Aids	20	80	--	--
Industrial Durables	13	48	15	25
Industrial Non-Durables	13	50	17	24
Medical/Hospital Supply	10	48	13	29
Office/Computer Supply	12	65	18	6
Publishing	21	53	16	11
Services	15	70	15	--

Table 5.   While credits/refunds are being processed, are customers sent invoices/overdue account notices which include the amount in question?

The criteria for automatic adjustments were many, ranging from
  – *Within a certain dollar amount*— such as less than $25, less than $50, or less than $100
  – *Within a certain amount of time*— common timeframes were within five days, or 30 or 90
  – *A combination of time and money*—for example, under $3,000, within 150 days; or under $1,000, less than a year and a half old
  – *For certain classes of customers*—including top customers, or as part of a contractual agreement
  – *By type of claim*—One company automatically replaces any shortage; other firms accept all quality complaints, or, in the case of one company, any complaint where the customer is dissatisfied: "It's a customer relations tool for us."
  Advantages of an automatic adjustment policy, according to respondents, are
  – Less time required to process claims
  – Reduced manpower costs
  – Improved customer relations
  Disbenefits of an automatic adjustment policy are few, according to respondents, many of whom said "none." Those who felt there were disadvantages pointed out *the fear,* not the fact, that customers might take advantage. Virtually no respondents reported that customers indeed did take advantage of such a policy.
  Another danger in an automatic policy, where claims are processed without being investigated, is that it may hide a serious problem which would be uncovered if claims were investigated.

	Yes	No
Average, all industry groups	24%	76%
Apparel	37%	63%
Automotive Supply	31%	69%
Chemicals & Plastics	8%	92%
Computer Hardware	18%	82%
Consumer Durables	29%	71%
Consumer Non-Durables	32%	68%
Grocery Products	28%	72%
Health & Beauty Aids	14%	86%
Industrial Durables	18%	82%
Industrial Non-Durables	24%	76%
Medical/Hospital Supply	15%	85%
Office/Computer Supply	33%	67%
Publishing	47%	53%
Services	43%	57%

Table 6.   Do you have a policy for automatic credit/refunds?

Statistics Tracked/Analyzed

An amazing 48% of consumer durables and 41% of chemical companies do not analyze reasons for credits and returns, according to our respondents. Overall, 26% do not track these statistics, as shown in Table 7. Analyzing these figures proved in many companies to be well worth the effort, according to our survey respondents because, as a result, top management mandated changes ranging from improving the order entry system to training salespeople, from rewriting label directions to changing packaging to reduce damage.

Other changes included adding a restocking charge, training customer service personnel; checking orders before entering; checking for confirming orders before entering; centralizing returns in Customer Service under a specialist; emphasizing quality control; rewriting catalog description; improving product information; discontinuing certain products; and assigning trackable codes for claims/returns, charging them to the responsible department.

Still other charges included publicizing the results of the reasons for claims/returns to all departments; improving warehousing picking/packing; tracking distributor claims and returns, and counseling those with a high rate; teaching customers how to order; simplifying the procedure for returns authorization; and using good carriers and monitoring their service.

Many of these changes could only be accomplished with top management support, particularly those involving other departments. So capturing and analyzing causes for credits and returns can be important steps in convincing management to make a change.

Many Managers Are Unhappy

Just about half of our respondents reported that they were unhappy with their present credits and returns system. A few—very few—of our respondents.

	Yes	No
Average, all industry groups	74	26
Apparel	100	
Automotive Supply	69	31
Chemicals	59	41
Computer Hardware	82	18
Consumer Durables	52	48
Consumer Non-Durables	87	13
Grocery Products	68	32
Health & Beauty Aids	100	
Industrial Durables	72	28
Industrial Non-Durables	72	28
Medical/Hospital Supply	87	13
Office/Computer Supply	75	25
Publishing	71	29
Services	71	29

Table 7.   Are statistics on credits and returns tracked by your company?

felt that their present system was too lenient. One person said, "Our policy is too easy—it's riskless for the customer." Others said they wanted to change the policy so that they accepted no returns except those caused by their errors.

But most of these respondents wanted to significantly change their present system in order to, as one respondent said, "make it easier for the customer." Some of these changes included

- Have responsibility under Customer Service rather than Finance
- Increase the accountability of other departments
- Set and enforce standards for interdepartmental response. Said one customer service manager, "Accounting Department response is horrible!"
- In the words of another manager, "revamp the whole thing."
- Speed up credits
- Move influence from salespeople
- Reduce paperwork. As one respondent explains, "There's too much manual work required for small dollars. We have almost as many people handling credits and returns as we do pricing, editing and order entry."
- Compare policy with the competition
- Increase top management support

Most surprisingly, respondents from some very large companies indicated that they had not yet formulated a company-wide system that worked. For example, some managers said:

- "Our policy should be written down and distributed to each of our dealers."
- "A policy must be written and announced."
- "We have no formal procedures. . ."

A Good Starting Point

These results point up the fact that customer service managers who take the initiative and track and analyze credits and returns, then make recommendations to management based on sound facts and figures, can make some very real improvement in their credits and returns system.

These systems have been overlooked or taken for granted by a surprising number of companies, many of them household names known for sophisticated business practices. But some companies are making major changes in their policies, streamlining their systems, making it easier for both their customers and themselves, and making a significant contribution to the bottom line.

What about you?

Department	%	Department	%
Customer Service	39	Sales/Marketing	5
Billing, A/R, Accounting, Credit		Distribution	3
Controller, Finance	28	Data Processing	2
Returns Department	7	Operations	2
Quality Control	5	Warranty Administration	2
Administrative Manager	5	Other	2

Table 8.   Who tracks credits/returns statistics?

Appendix E

AN APPROACH TO MEASURING GROUP PERFORMANCE IN THE CUSTOMER SERVICE DEPARTMENT

by Jeffrey A. DeVries, Manger of Sales Administration, Becton-Dickinson, division of Becton Dickinson and Company.

The measurement system in place at Becton-Dickinson was converted in September 1982 from a micro (individual) to a macro (group) system. (See pages 147-150 for a discussion of the individual approach.) This was prompted by three factors:

1. A need to reduce the significant number of hours spent calculating, maintaining and analyzing standards;

2. Response to employees concerned about lengthy recordkeeping; and

3. The need to identify the workload of two divisions now sharing customer service support in preparation for a divisional and departmental split.

The macro program was developed by Robert D. Greenberg and James W. Kloiber of the B-D systems department, and provides productivity data as well as indices on quality, expense and backlog performance. These four statistics are blended into a *combined index* which gives staff management an overall picture of departmental performance. It also allows line management to focus on individual areas needing attention. The principles applied in this approach, can be adapted to apply to any customer service environment.

Input Is Simple, Easily Obtained

The statistical ingredients are few. Some you may already capture on a regular basis. Others are simple to collect:

● **Work counts of the task being measured.** Select a task that represents the main business mission of the group, i.e., inquiries, orders or credits processed. Limit the task (primary activity) to one per group whenever possible. You *can* measure more than one task within a group, but keep in mind that you must split the group's hours among the tasks when analyzing the data.

● **Man-hours expended.** Time cards, payroll records or flextime registers will provide this data with very little effort on your part. Should it not be readily available, you could photocopy time cards before submission or ask the people involved to keep track of their regular *and* overtime hours, summarizing them at month's end.

● **Actual direct expense.** A monthly departmental expense statement showing head count, salary and fringe expense and general administrative expense should be available to you. If possible, exclude "uncontrollable" costs such as telephone charges, depreciation, and administrative charges to or from other departments.

• **Carryover.** More commonly called "backlog," we classify carryover as work that would have been done had there been sufficient time. The term "backlog" more accurately describes work which is delayed pending action by others. In any event, people involved in the study should count the carryover of the primary activity at the end of each week (or, at the minimum, monthly) and submit this with their work counts.

Set up a matrix similar to Figure 1, Performance Summary Report, for each group you want to measure. If you like, you can develop statistics weekly, although monthly is more practical as it tends to smooth any non-standard occurrences and coincides with the expense reporting process.

Log the group's weekly task count for each week of the month and determine the monthly total. Also enter the group's carryover where noted. Next, enter the regular, overtime and total hours expended by the group

ITEM	W/E 3/5	W/E 3/12	W/E 3/19	W/E 3/26	W/E 4/2	TOTAL
Inquiries	1449	1385	1365	1213	770	6182
Errors						81
Carryover						
Regular Hours						
Overtime Hours						
Total Hours						848.0
Actual Direct Expense						$13,873
Productivity						
Man-hrs./Inquiry Actual						8.23 min.
Man-hrs./Inquiry Goal						9.0 min.
% Perf. Goal to Actual						109%
Inquiries/Man-hr. Actual						7.29
Inquiries/Man-hr. Goal						6.6
% Perf. Goal to Actual						109%
Quality						
Errors Corrected Actual						
Errors Corrected Goal						
% Perf. Goal of Actual						
Expenses						
Cost/Inquiry Actual						$2.24
Cost/Inquiry Goal						2.00
% Perf. Goal to Actual						89%
Carryover						
No. Workdays Actual						.36
No. Workdays Goal						1.00
% Perf. Goal to Actual						100%
Staffing						
Utilized						4.52
Actual						6.00
Required						5.80

Figure 1. Performance Summary Report

performing this particular task. Also enter the actual direct expense of the group for that month. If six out of ten people in the department are performing the task, use 60% of the actual direct cost. Should you wish to monitor multiple tasks by a person or group, distribute the total hours accordingly (50/50, 70/30, etc.).

To calculate productivity, divide total hours by total units processed and multiply this number by 60 (minutes). This will yield actual minutes spent per unit of work. Now, establish a goal (standard) against which to measure actual performance. This can be based on historical data, a predetermined standard, stopwatch measurement, work sampling, or "best guess." Regardless of what method is used, if it is used consistently, the standard will always be a consistent yardstick against which actual performance is measured. Divide standard minutes by actual minutes to determine percent performance.

You can check your work by calculating actual units of work per man-hour. Divide credits processed by total hours. Again, set a goal consistent with the standard time per unit above. For example, if your goal per unit of work was six minutes per unit, then your goal for units per hour would be 10. Divide actual units/hr. by standard units/hr. This performance figure should match the one above.

Calculate Quality, Expense and Carryover

Where possible, errors rejected by computer or manual checks can be used to calculate a quality index. After capturing the error volume, set an error goal based on a percentage of total units processed. If 6,000 units of work were processed, a goal of 1% would yield an acceptance rate of 60 errors. Let's say actual errors for the period are 70%. Divide goal by actual to determine an 86% performance rate for errors.

To determine cost per unit, divide actual direct expense for the group by total units processed. Again, set a goal and divide goal by actual to calculate performance. Remember, if you are tracking more than one task, to distribute the dollars accordingly, as you did with the hours when calculating productivity.

To calculate carryover, multiply total carryover by standard minutes per unit. Divide this number by 60 (minutes) to determine standard hours required to process the carryover. To complete this equation, first calculate the utilized staff, which is simply the hours worked expressed as people. For instance, based on a 37.5 hour week, 75 hours equals two people, 90 hours equals 2.4 people, etc.

To calculate your utilized staff, divide total man-hours expended by the number of regular man-hours on the month. Again based on a 37.5 hour week, a four-week month equals 150 man-hours; a five-week month, 187.5 manhours. When calculating carryover, multiply utilized staff by 7.5 (hours per day in a 37.5 hour week) to determine total utilized hours per day. Now divide standard hours required to process carryover by total utilized hours per day. The result: Number of days' carryover. Once again, set a goal for number of workdays' carryover and divide goal by actual to determine performance. If carryover is half a day or less, default to 100% performance instead of showing an unrealistic figure which is confusing and which will skew the data.

We already know, from previous calculations, our utilized staff and, of course, our actual staff. To calculate required staff, multiply total units processed by standard minutes (goal) per unit. Divide this figure by 60 (minutes) to determine standard hours required to process the work.

To calculate required staff, we must apply an allowance factor for holidays, vacations, absence, etc. The generally accepted rate is 15%, which leaves 85% of each week, or approximately 32 hours, available for productive work. Therefore, actual hours per month available for productive work would be 128 for a four-week month or 160 for a five-week month. Divide the standard hours noted above by 128 or 160 as appropriate to determine required staff. This figure represents the number of people required to process *this month's* workload. The figure will vary from month to month with the workload.

You now have the ingredients to establish a combined index of overall productivity. Add the four performance figures for productivity, quality (if calculated), expense and carryover and divide by four (or three if no quality percentage was calculated). This yields your overall productivity. Figure 2 shows how this data might be presented.

After performing this exercise for several months, you may notice performance trends, especially if you graph the data. Periodically evaluate your task standards (goals) to reaffirm their reasonableness and, if necessary, make adjustments.

Although no performance measurement system is perfect in all respects, this one offers a great deal in terms of easy administration by the layman, employee acceptance, and management orientation. Its principles are simple and sound, and you don't have to be an Industrial Engineer to develop, present and use the data to your company's advantage. You can do something about office productivity instead of just talking about it!

	(ACTUAL) NO. OF	PERFORMANCE				
FUNCTION	PEOPLE	PROD.	EXPSE.	BACK LOG	COMB. INDEX	REQ. STAFF
H/M Reps	6.0	109	89	100	99	5.80
Backorder	1.0	94	122	100	105	1.23
Order Desk	1.0	109	130	100	113	.74
Metpath, NHL	1.0	138	125	100	121	1.35
Proof of Delivery	.5	66	69	53	63	.37
Int'l. Inquiries	.8	138	127	82	116	1.22
Int'l. Orders	.2	157	164	100	140	.35
Transfer of Mdse.	.5	124	121	100	115	.70
R.A.'s/Gen'l Cr.	1.0	91	86	139	105	1.23
Sub-Total	12.0				108	12.99
File Section-Lookups	5.0	85	90	100	92	4.77
Total	17.0				107	17.76

Figure 2. Combined Index of Productivity

Appendix F

BIBLIOGRAPHY

Bender, Paul S., *Design & Operation of Customer Service Systems,* AM-ACOM, New York, 1976, 211 pp.

*Berry, Dick, *Managing Service for Results,* Instrument Society of America, Research Triangle Park, N.C., 1983, 265 pp.

*Birsner, E. Patricia and Ronald D. Balsley, *How to Improve Customer Service,* AMACOM, New York, 1980, audio program with workbook and cassettes.

*_____, *Practical Guide to Customer Service Management and Operations,* AMACOM, New York, 1982, 216 pp.

*Blanchard, Benjamin S. and E. Edward Lowery, *Maintainability,* McGraw-Hill Book Company, New York, 1969, 336 pp.

*Blanding, Warren, *Customer Service Seminar,* Marketing Publications Inc., Silver Spring, Md., 1982, 170 pp.

*Blanding, Warren and Leslie Hansen Harps, *101 Ways to Improve Customer Service,* Marketing Publications Inc., Silver Spring, Md., 1981, 78 pp.

*Blanding, Warren, Leslie Hansen Harps and William R. Henry, Jr., *133 Ways to Handle Customer Complaints,* Marketing Publications Inc., Silver Spring, Md., 1979, 99 pp.

*Bleuel, William H. and Joseph D. Patton, Jr., *Service Management: Principles and Practices,* Instrument Society of America, Research Triangle Park, N.C., 1978, 265 pp.

*Brown, Robert Goodell, *Advanced Service Parts Inventory Control,* Materials Management Systems Inc., Norwich, Vt., 1982, 434 pp.

*Clark, Barkley and Christopher Smith, *Warranties in the Sale of Business Equipment and Consumer Products,* Practising Law Institute, New York, 1982, 696 pp.

Cron, Rodney L., *Assuring Customer Satisfaction: A Guide for Business and Industry,* Van Nostrand Reinhold Company, New York, 1974, 364 pp.

Customer Communicator, The, Marketing Publications Inc., Silver Spring, Md., monthly newsletter for customer contact personnel.

Customer Service Newsletter, Marketing Publications Inc., Silver Spring, Md., monthly newsletter for customer service managers.

Dowdy, Lemuel, Jill Goodrich-Mahoney, Kerry Stoebner, *Handling Customer*

Complaints: In-House and Third-Party Strategies, Federal Trade Commission, 1980, 28 pp.

*Fear, Richard A., *The Evaluation Interview,* 3rd ed., McGraw-Hill Book Company, New York, 1984, 330 pp.

Fenvessy, Stanley J., *Keep Your Customers (and Keep Them Happy),* Dow Jones/Irwin, Homewood, Ill., 1976, 174 pp.

French, Benjamin I., Jr., *Customer Service Manual with Model Letters and Forms,* Prentice-Hall, Inc., Englewood Cliffs, N.J., 1976, 200 pp.

Gober, Mary and Bob Tannehill, *The Art of Giving Quality Service,* Tannehill-Gober Associates International, Williamsville, N.Y., 1984, 104 pp.

Gold, Carol Sapin, *Sold Gold Customer Relations: A Professional Resource Guide,* Prentice-Hall, Inc., Englewood Cliffs, N.J., 1983, 122 pp.

*Harps, Leslie Hansen, *Customer Service in Action,* Marketing Publications Inc., Silver Spring, Md., 1980, 90 pp.

Hise, Richard T., *Product/Service Strategy,* Mason/Charter Inc., New York, 1977, 305 pp.

* *How to Improve Your Listening Skills,* John Wiley & Sons, New York, 1983, audio program with cassettes and workbook.

* *Improving Customer Relations, Edition II,* Universal Training Systems, Northbrook, Ill., 1979, audio program with slides, cassettes, workbooks.

*Joseph, William, *Professional Service Management,* McGraw-Hill Book Company, New York, 1983, 229 pp.

Kissell, Irwin R. and Ann Kissel Grun, *How to Handle Claims and Returns,* McGraw-Hill Book Company, New York, 1973, 137 pp.

*Kordahl, Eugene B., *Telemarketing for Business: A Guide to Building Your Own Telemarketing Operation,* Prentice-Hall, Inc., Englewood Cliffs, N.J., 1984, 324 pp.

*LeBoeuf, Michael, *Working Smart: How to Accomplish More in Half the Time,* McGraw-Hill Book Company, New York, 1979, 232 pp.

LaLonde, Bernard J. and Paul H. Zinszer, *Customer Service: Meaning and Measurement,* National Council of Physical Distribution Management, Chicago, 1976, 492 pp.

*Matthies, Leslie H., *The New Playscript Procedure: Management Tool for Action,* 2nd ed., Office Publications, Inc., Stamford, Conn., 1977, 192 pp.

*McCafferty, Donald N., *Successful Field Service Management,* AMACOM, New York, 1980, 181 pp.

*Nance, H.W., *Office Work Measurement,* rev. ed., Robert E. Krieger Publishing Company, Inc., Malabar, Fla., 1983, 157 pp.

*Patton, Joseph D., Jr., *Service Parts Management,* Instrument Society of America, Research Triangle Park, N.C., 1984, 293 pp.

*Peters, Thomas J. and Robert H. Waterman, Jr., *In Search of Excellence:*

Lessons from America's Best-Run Companies, Warner Books, New York, 1982, 360 pp.

*Roman, Murray, *Telemarketing Campaigns that Work,* McGraw-Hill Book Company, New York, 1983, 282 pp.

*————, *Telephone Marketing: How to Build Your Business by Telephone,* McGraw-Hill Book Company, New York, 1976, 218 pp.

Tavernier, Gerard, *After Sales Service Systems and Records,* Gower Press, London, 1971, 115 pp.

**Telephone Dynamics,* Universal Training Systems, Northbrook, Ill., 1970, audio program with cassettes, workbooks and supervisor's guide.

**Understanding and Managing Stress,* American Management Associations, New York, 1984, audio program with cassettes and workbook.

---

*Information on these books is available from Customer Service Institute division of Marketing Publications Inc., 8701 Georgia Avenue, Silver Spring, MD 20910, 301/585-0730.

Index